Communication and Agreement Abstractions for Fault-Tolerant Asynchronous Distributed Systems

Synthesis Lectures on Distributed Computing Theory

Editor

Nancy Lynch, *Massachusetts Institute of Technology*

Synthesis Lectures on Distributed Computing Theory is edited by Nancy Lynch of the Massachusetts Institute of Technology. The series will publish 50- to 150 page publications on topics pertaining to distributed computing theory. The scope will largely follow the purview of premier information and computer science conferences, such as ACM PODC, DISC, SPAA, OPODIS, CONCUR, DialM-POMC, ICDCS, SODA, Sirocco, SSS, and related conferences. Potential topics include, but not are limited to: distributed algorithms and lower bounds, algorithm design methods, formal modeling and verification of distributed algorithms, and concurrent data structures.

Communication and Agreement Abstractions for Fault-Tolerant Asynchronous Distributed Systems
Michel Raynal
2010

The Mobile Agent Rendezvous Problem in the Ring
Evangelos Kranakis, Danny Krizanc, and Euripides Markou
2010

Communication and Agreement Abstractions for Fault-Tolerant Asynchronous Distributed Systems

Michel Raynal

ISBN: 978-3-031-00872-6   paperback
ISBN: 978-3-031-02000-1   ebook

DOI 10.1007/978-3-031-02000-1

A Publication in the Springer series
SYNTHESIS LECTURES ON DISTRIBUTED COMPUTING THEORY

Lecture #2
Series Editor: Nancy Lynch, *Massachusetts Institute of Technology*
Series ISSN
Synthesis Lectures on Distributed Computing Theory
ISSN pending.

Communication and Agreement Abstractions for Fault-Tolerant Asynchronous Distributed Systems

Michel Raynal

IRISA, Université de Rennes

SYNTHESIS LECTURES ON DISTRIBUTED COMPUTING THEORY #2

ABSTRACT

Understanding distributed computing is not an easy task. This is due to the many facets of uncertainty one has to cope with and master in order to produce correct distributed software.

Considering the uncertainty created by asynchrony and process crash failures in the context of message-passing systems, the book focuses on the main abstractions that one has to understand and master in order to be able to produce software with guaranteed properties. These fundamental abstractions are communication abstractions that allow the processes to communicate consistently (namely the register abstraction and the reliable broadcast abstraction), and the consensus agreement abstractions that allows them to cooperate despite failures. As they give a precise meaning to the words "communicate " and "agree" despite asynchrony and failures, these abstractions allow distributed programs to be designed with properties that can be stated and proved.

Impossibility results are associated with these abstractions. Hence, in order to circumvent these impossibilities, the book relies on the failure detector approach, and, consequently, that approach to fault-tolerance is central to the book.

KEYWORDS

asynchronous message-passing system, consensus abstraction, failure detectors, process crash, register abstraction, uniform reliable broadcast abstraction

Contents

Notations

n	number of processes
t	upper bound on the number of faulty processes
f	actual number of faulty processes
$t < n/2$	"majority of non-faulty (correct) processes" assumption
FIFO	first in first out
CO	causal order
TO	total order
CONS	consensus object
URB	uniform reliable broadcast
FIFO-URB	FIFO uniform reliable broadcast
CO-URB	causal order uniform reliable broadcast
TO-URB	total order uniform reliable broadcast
1WMR	single writer/multi-reader register
MWMR	multi-writer/multi-reader register
NBAC	non-blocking atomic commit problem
P	class of perfect failure detectors
AP	class of anonymous perfect failure detectors
$?P$	class of anonymously perfect failure detectors
$\diamond P$	class of eventually perfect failure detectors
Ω	class of eventual leader failure detectors
Σ	class of quorum failure detectors
Θ	class of theta failure detectors
HB	class of heartbeat failure detectors
R	class of binary random oracles
CC	class of common coin random oracles
$\diamond Syn$	eventual synchrony assumption
$\diamond T$	eventual timely channel assumption
$\mathcal{AS}_{n,t}[\emptyset]$	asynchronous system of n processes with reliable channels and up to t process crashes
$\mathcal{AAS}_{n,t}[\emptyset]$	$\mathcal{AS}_{n,t}[\emptyset]$ where the processes are anonymous
$\mathcal{AS}\_\mathcal{F}_{n,t}[\emptyset]$	asynchronous system of n processes with fair channels and up to t process crashes
$\mathcal{AS}\_\mathcal{W}_{n,t}[\emptyset]$	$\mathcal{AS}\_\mathcal{F}_{n,t}[\emptyset]$ with weak connectivity
$\mathcal{XYZ}_{n,t}[X, Y]$	$\mathcal{XYZ}_{n,t}[\emptyset]$ enriched with (assumption, failure detector, object) X and Y

List of Figures

Preface

> *The significant problems we have cannot be solved at*
> *the same level of thinking with which we created them.*
> Albert Einstein.

What distributed computing is   Distributed computing was born in the late seventies when people started taking into account the intrinsic characteristics of physically distributed systems. The field then emerged as a specialized research area distinct from networks, operating systems and parallelism. Its birth certificate is usually considered as the publication in 1978 of Lamport's most celebrated paper "Time, clocks and the ordering of events in a distributed system" (Communications of the ACM, 21(7):558-564). Since then, several high level journals and conferences have been devoted to distributed computing.

Distributed computing arises when one has to solve a problem in terms of entities (usually called processes, agents, sensors, peers, actors, processors, nodes, etc.) such that each entity has only partial knowledge of the many parameters involved in the problem that has to be solved. While parallelism and real-time can be characterized by the words *efficiency* and *on time computing*, respectively, distributed computing can be characterized by the word *uncertainty*. This uncertainty is created by asynchrony, failures, unstable behaviors, non-monotonicity, system dynamism, mobility, low computing capability, scalability requirements, etc. Mastering one form or another of uncertainty is pervasive in all distributed computing problems. Finally, as the aim of a theory is to codify knowledge in order it can be transmitted (to students, engineers, practitioners, etc.), research in distributed computing theory is fundamental. When something works, we must know why it works, and when something does not work ... we must know why it does not work.

Why this book?   Understanding distributed computing is not an easy task. As just indicated, this is due to the many facets of uncertainty one has to cope with and master in order to produce provably correct distributed software.

Considering the uncertainty created by asynchrony and process crashes in message-passing systems, this book focuses on the main abstractions that one has to understand and master in order to be able to produce software with guaranteed properties. These abstractions are communication abstractions that allow the processes to communicate consistently and agreement abstractions that allow them to cooperate in a consistent way. These abstractions are fundamental. One has to give a precise meaning to the word "communicate " and "agree" in order that distributed programs have a precise meaning and that their properties can be precisely stated and proved.

The communication abstractions that are presented in this book are the register abstraction and the uniform reliable broadcast abstraction. The agreement abstraction that is presented is the consensus abstraction.

Impossibility results are associated with these abstractions. Hence, in order to circumvent these impossibilities, the book relies on the failure detector-based approach (a failure detector is a device that gives hints on failures to each process). Since the introduction of this concept in 1991 by Chandra and Toueg, numerous papers involving failure detectors have been published, but only very few surveys have addressed this topic in a comprehensive way. Hence, the failure detector-based approach to fault-tolerance is a topic that is central to this book.

As the reader can see, the key-words that characterize the book are consequently the following: message-passing system prone to process crash, register abstraction, uniform reliable broadcast abstraction, consensus problem, and failure detector.

Content, approach, and features   The main feature of this book on fault-tolerant distributed computing, which makes it unique, is the fact it presents basic principles that underlie the design of fundamental distributed abstractions from the failure detector perspective. It presents impossibility results and numerous failure detector-based algorithms. It is made up of three parts.

- The first part, composed of two chapters, focuses on the *register* abstraction. Such an abstraction captures one of the most basic communication objects, namely an object that provides processes with only read and write operations. A register object abstracts physical base objects such as shared memory words, shared disks, etc.

  Chapter 1 presents this abstraction and its main properties. Then, Chapter 2 presents algorithms that implement it in asynchronous systems prone to process crashes. It also shows that a register cannot be constructed as soon as half or more processes that compose the system may crash. Failure detectors are then introduced, and it is shown how an appropriate class of failure detectors can be used to circumvent this impossibility. It is also shown that this class is the weakest class that allows implementing a register despite any number of process crashes.

- The second part, also composed of two chapters, is devoted to the *uniform reliable broadcast* abstraction. Such an abstraction allows processes to reliably disseminate data inside a system. Chapter 3 defines this communication abstraction and variants that offer additional quality of service (first in first out and causal order message delivery).

  Then, Chapter 4 presents a family of algorithms that implement it in asynchronous systems prone to crash and where channels may lose messages but are fair. It is shown that, without additional assumption, the uniform reliable broadcast abstraction is impossible to build if half or more processes can crash. The weakest failure detector class to circumvent this impossibility is then introduced.

Then, the notion of *quiescent* implementation of a communication abstraction is introduced and quiescent algorithms are presented. These are based on an appropriate failure detector class. Finally, the case where only a subset of the communication channels is deemed fair is investigated.

- The third (and last) part, composed of three chapters, is devoted to *agreement* abstraction.

  Chapter 5 presents one of the most fundamental agreement abstractions, namely the *consensus* problem. To motivate it, it is shown that consensus is a universal object when one has to implement any object defined by a sequential specification. This is the well-known *state machine replication* paradigm introduced by Lamport.

  Then, this chapter shows that consensus is impossible to solve in asynchronous message-passing systems where even a single process may crash. This is the famous impossibility result due to Fischer, Lynch and Paterson.

  Chapter 6 focuses on algorithms that solve the consensus problem in crash-prone asynchronous systems that are appropriately enriched. Consensus algorithms for systems equipped with various types of failure detectors are first studied, namely, perfect failure detectors, and eventual leader failure detectors. Then, consensus algorithms for systems equipped with a random oracle are presented. Transformation algorithms that solve the multivalued consensus problem from underlying binary consensus objects are also presented.

  Basically, a consensus object captures and allows to solve the non-determinism inherent to the net effect of asynchrony and failures. This chapter shows that there are particular deterministic cases, where consensus can be solved efficiently in one communication step. This chapter then considers consensus in an anonymous, asynchronous crash-prone system.

  Finally, after having presented the two facets of failure detectors, Chapter 7 (the last chapter) is devoted to their construction. Three classes are examined and algorithms constructing failure detectors of these classes are presented. The two first are the classes of perfect failure detectors and the class of eventually perfect failure detectors. The third one is the class of eventual leader failure detectors. For that class, different behavioral assumptions that allow implementing an eventual leader failure detector are investigated. Then, this chapter considers systems where no process initially knows the system membership and systems where a process can recover after having crashed.

An important feature of the book is that nearly all the algorithms that are presented are proved.

Readership   This book has been written first for people who are not familiar with the topic and the concepts that are exposed. This includes mainly the following:

- Graduate students and senior level undergraduate students in computer science, computer engineering, and graduate students in mathematics who are interested in the foundations of fault-tolerant distributed computing.

- Practitioners and engineers who want to be aware of state-of-the-art fault-tolerant distributed algorithms and basic principles that underlie their design.

Prerequisites for this book includes undergraduate courses on algorithms and synchronization. Knowledge of distributed systems can be helpful but is not necessary.

Acknowledgments This book originates from lecture notes for graduate courses on distributed computing that I give at the University of Rennes (France) and, as an invited professor, in several other universities all over the world. I would like to thank all the graduate students for their questions that, in one way or another, have contributed to this book.

I would also thank all the researchers whose results are exposed in this book. Without their work, this book would not exist. I thank my colleagues of the Distributed Computing area with whom I had numerous discussions on the fascinating topics addressed in this book. Special thanks to my "local colleagues" François Bonnet, Achour Mostéfaoui and Matthieu Roy who read and commented early drafts. Special thanks also to Jennifer Welch (and her graduate students Zakia Asad, Hyun-Chul Chung, Srikanth Sastry, Saira Viqar, and Jiaqi Wang, and her colleague Hyunyoung Lee) for their constructive comments on all chapters. I want also to thank Mikel Larrea and David Powell for comments on specific chapters.

Finally, I would like to thank Nancy Lynch for her kind invitation to write a book for the *Synthesis Lectures on Distributed Computing Theory* series she is editing for Morgan & Claypool Publishers.

Michel Raynal

June 25 – September 30, 2009
Rennes, Montréal (ICDCS'09), Estoril (DSN'09), Saint-Philibert,
Bento Gonçalves (COLIBRI'09), Lake Louise, Calgary (PODC'09),
Puebla, Saint-Grégoire, Elche/Elx (DISC'09)

PART I

The Register Abstraction

C H A P T E R   1

The Atomic Register Abstraction

This chapter introduces the concepts of a regular register and of an atomic register. An informal presentation is first given in Section 1.1. Then, Section 1.2 provides the reader with a formal approach of the atomicity notion. It also discusses a fundamental property provided by the atomicity consistency criterion, namely locality.

1.1   THE REGISTER ABSTRACTION

1.1.1   CONCURRENT OBJECTS AND REGISTERS

Concurrent object   A *concurrent object* is an object that can be accessed concurrently by two or more sequential processes. As it is sequential, a process that has invoked an operation on an object has to wait for a corresponding response before invoking another operation on the same or another object. When this occurs, we say that the operation is *pending*.

   While each process can access at most one object at a time, an object can be simultaneously accessed by several processes. This occurs when two or more processes have pending invocations on the same object, hence the name "concurrent object".

Register object   One of the most fundamental concurrent objects is the shared register object (in short, *register*). Such an object abstracts physical objects such as a word (or a set of words) of a shared memory, a shared disk, etc. A register R provides the processes with an interface made up of two operations denoted R.read() and R.write(). The first allows the invoking process to obtain the value of the register R, while the second allows it to associate a new value with the register.

Type of register   According to the value that can be returned by a read operation, several types of registers can be defined. We consider here two types of registers: the *regular* register and the *atomic* register. In both cases, the value returned by a read operation is a value that has been written by a write operation. The actual value returned depends on the concurrency pattern in which is involved the corresponding read operation. Regularity and atomicity differ in the way each addresses (and captures) concurrency.

   A register type defines which are the correct behaviors of a register of that type. Hence, the regular (resp. atomic) type defines *regularity* (resp. *atomicity*) consistency condition.

Underlying time notion   The definitions that follow refer to a notion of *time*. This time notion can be seen as given by an imaginary clock that models the progress of a computation as perceived by an external omniscient observer. It is accessible neither to the processes, nor to the register objects. Its aim is to capture the fact that, from the point of view of an omniscient external observer, the flow of operations is such that (1) some operation invocations have terminated while others have not yet started, and (2) some operation invocations overlap in time (they are concurrent). (These notions will be formally defined in Section 1.2.)

1.1.2   REGULAR REGISTER

Definition   A *regular register* is a one-writer/multi-reader (1WMR) register, i.e., a read/write object that can be written by a single process and read by any number of processes. The definition of a regular register assumes a single writer in order to prevent write conflicts. More precisely, as the writer is sequential, the write operations are totally ordered (the corresponding sequence of write operations is called the *write sequence*). The value returned by a read is defined as follows:

- If no write is concurrent with the read, the read returns the current value of the register (i.e., the value written by the last write in the current write sequence).

- If writes are concurrent with the read, the read returns the value written by one of these writes or the last value of the register before these writes.

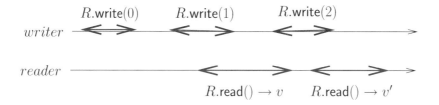

Figure 1.1: Possible behaviors of a regular register

Examples   The definition of the regularity consistency condition is illustrated in Figure 1.1 where a writer process and a single reader process are considered. The notation "R.read() $\rightarrow v$" is used to indicate that the read operation returns the value v. As far as concurrency patterns are concerned, the durations of each operation are indicated on the figure with double-arrow segments.

The writer issues three write operations that sequentially write into the register R the values 0, 1 and 2. On its side, the reader issues two read operations; the first obtains the value v, while the second obtains the value v'. The first read is concurrent with the writes of the values 1 and 2 (their executions overlap in time). According to the definition of regularity, it can return for v any of the values 0, 1 or 2. The second read is concurrent only with the write of the value 2. It can, consequently, return for v' the value 1 or the value 2.

So, in this example, the regular type allows the second read to return 1 (which has been written before the value 2), while the first read (that precedes it) is allowed to return the value 2 (which has been written after the value 1). This is called a *new/old inversion*: in presence of read/write concurrency, a sequence of read operations is not required to return a sequence of values that complies with the sequence of write operations. It is interesting to notice that, if we suppress R.write(2) from the figure, v is restricted to be 0 or 1, while v' can only be the value 1 (and, as we are about to see, the register then behaves as if it was atomic).

Observation   An object is defined by a *sequential specification* when its correct behaviors can be defined by sequences (traces) on its operations. As an example, let us consider an infinite queue object Q defined by the classical operations Q.enqueue() and Q.dequeue(). Its sequential specification includes all the sequences (involving only these two operations) such that, for any prefix of any sequence, the number of Q.dequeue() operations is never more than the number of Q.enqueue() operations.

It is easy to see that, due to the possibility of new/old inversions, a regular register cannot have a sequential specification.

1.1.3   ATOMIC REGISTERS

Definition   There are two main differences between regularity and atomicity, namely, an atomic register (1) can be a multi-writer/multi-reader (MWMR) register and (2) does not allow for new/old inversions (i.e., it has a sequential specification). Let us notice that a 1WMR atomic register is also regular. More precisely, an atomic register is defined by the following properties.

- All the read and write operations appear as if they have been executed sequentially,

- This sequence respects the time order of the operations (i.e., if op_1 has terminated before op_2 has started, then op_1 appears in the sequence before op_2),

- Each read returns the value written by the closest preceding write in this sequence (or the initial value if there is no preceding write operation).

The corresponding sequence of operations is called a *witness* sequence. Let us notice that the concurrent operations can be ordered arbitrarily as long as the sequence obtained is a witness sequence. Basically, this definition states that everything has to appear as if each operation has been executed instantaneously at some point of the time line (of the omniscient external observer) between its invocation (start event) and its termination (end event).

Examples   An example of an execution of a MWMR atomic register accessed by three processes is described in Figure 1.2. (Two dotted arrows are associated with each operation invocation. They meet at a point of the "real time" line at which the corresponding operation could have instantaneously occurred. These points of the time lime defines a sequence on the operation invocations that belongs to the specification of the object.) In that example, everything appears as if the operations have been

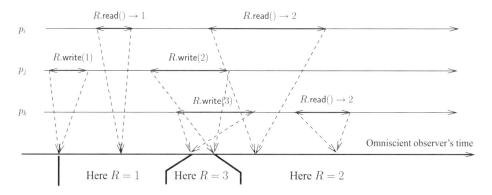

Figure 1.2: Behavior of an atomic register

executed according to the following witness sequence:

$$R.\text{write}(1),\ \ R.\text{read}() \to 1,\ \ R.\text{write}(3),\ \ R.\text{write}(2),\ \ R.\text{read}() \to 2,\ \ R.\text{read}() \to 2.$$

The concurrent operations $R.\text{write}(3)$ and $R.\text{write}(2)$ could have been ordered the other way. In that case, the last two read operations would have to return the value 3 in order that the register R behaves atomically.

When we consider the example described in Figure 1.1 with $v = 2$ and $v' = 1$, there is a new/old inversion, and, consequently, the register R does not behave atomically. Differently, if (1) either $v = 0$ or 1 and $v' = 1$ or 2, (2) or $v = v' = 2$, there is no new/old inversion, and, consequently, the behavior of the register is atomic.

Why atomicity is important   The atomicity consistency condition is fundamental. This is because atomicity allows the composition of atomic objects without losing the benefit of atomicity. That is why atomicity is called a *local* consistency condition. A consistency condition C is local if, when considering several concurrent objects (here the registers) as a single object O, the concurrent object O satisfies the condition C when each object taken alone satisfies C (see section 1.2.4).

This is very important both when one has to reason about multiprocess programs that access shared registers, and when one has to implement shared registers.

- From a theoretical point of view, locality means that we can keep *reasoning sequentially* whatever the number of atomic registers involved in the computation. Locality allows us to reason on a set of atomic registers as if they were a single atomic object. We can reason in terms of witness sequences, not only for each register separately, but also on all the registers as if they were a single atomic object.

As an example, let us consider an application composed of processes that share two atomic registers $R1$ and $R2$. Then, the composite object $[R1, R2]$, that provides the processes with the four operations: $R1.\text{write}()$, $R1.\text{read}()$, $R2.\text{write}()$, and $R2.\text{read}()$, behaves atomically (everything appears as if one operation at a time was executed, and the projection of this global sequence on the operations of $R1$ -resp. $R2$- is a witness sequence for $R1$ -resp. $R2$-).

- From a practical point of view, locality means *modularity*. This has several advantages. On the one side, each atomic register can be implemented in its own way: the implementation of one atomic register is not required to interfere with the implementation of the other registers.

  On the other side, as soon as we have an algorithm that implements an atomic register (e.g., in a message-passing system as we will see in the next chapter), we can use multiple independent instantiations of it, one for each register, and the system will behave correctly without any additional control or synchronization.

To summarize, locality means that atomic registers compose for free (i.e., their composition is at no additional cost).

1.2   A FORMAL APPROACH TO ATOMICITY

1.2.1   PROCESSES, OPERATIONS AND EVENTS

Processes and operations   A multiprocess program consists of a finite set of n (application) processes, denoted $p_1, \ldots, p_n$ that cooperate through a set of registers. As already indicated, each register R provides the processes with two operations R.write() and R.read(). The notation R.op(arg)(res) is used denote any operation on a register R, where arg is the input parameter (empty for a read, and the value v to be written for a write), and res is the response returned by the operation (*ok* for a write, and the value v obtained from R for a read operation).

Events   The execution of an operation op() on a register R by a process p_i is modeled by two events, namely, the events denoted $inv[R.\text{op}(arg)$ by $p_i]$ that occurs when p_i invokes the operation (invocation event), and the event denoted $resp[R.\text{op}(res)$ by $p_i]$ that occurs when the operation terminates. (When there is no ambiguity, we talk about operations where we should be talking about operation executions.) We say that these events are generated by process p_i and associated with register R. Given an operation R.op(arg)(res), the event $resp[R.\text{op}(res)$ by $p_i]$ is called the *reply event* matching the *invocation event* $inv[R.\text{op}(arg)$ by $p_i]$.

1.2.2   HISTORIES

Representing an execution as a history of events   This paragraph formalizes what we usually intend when we use the word *execution* or *run*.

As simultaneous (invocation and reply) register events generated by sequential processes are independent, it is always possible to order simultaneous events in an arbitrary way without altering the behavior of an execution. This makes it possible to consider a total order relation (denoted $<_H$ in the following) on the events that abstracts the time order in which the events do actually occur (i.e., the time of the omniscient external observer). This is precisely how executions are formally captured.

Hence, the interaction between a set of sequential processes and a set of shared registers is modeled by a sequence of invocation and reply events, called a *history* (sometimes also called a *trace*), and denoted $\widehat{H} = (H, <_H)$ where H is the set of events generated by the processes and $<_H$ a total order on these events.

The notation $\widehat{H}|p_i$ ($\widehat{H}$ at p_i) denotes the subsequence of $\widehat{H}$ made up of all the events generated by process p_i. It is called the *local* history at p_i.

As a simple example, Figure 1.3 describes the history (the sequence of 12 events $e_1 \ldots, e_{12}$) associated with the execution depicted in Figure 1.2. (Only the first four events are described explicitly.)

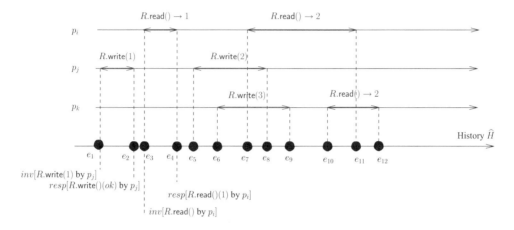

Figure 1.3: Example of a history

Equivalent histories   Two histories $\widehat{H}$ and $\widehat{H'}$ are said to be *equivalent* if they have the same local histories, i.e., for each p_i, $\widehat{H}|p_i = \widehat{H'}|p_i$. That is, equivalent histories are built from the same set of events (remember that an event includes the name of an object, the name of a process, the name of an operation and its input or output parameter).

Well-formed histories   As we consider histories generated by sequential processes, we restrict our attention to the histories $\widehat{H}$ such that, for each process p_i, $\widehat{H}|p_i$ (local history at p_i) is sequential: it starts with an invocation, followed by its matching reply, followed by another invocation, etc. We say in this case that $\widehat{H}$ is *well-formed*.

Partial order on operations   A history $\widehat{H}$ induces an irreflexive partial order on its operations as follows. Let op= X.op1 () by p_i and op' = Y.op2() by p_j be two operations. Operation op precedes operation op' (denoted op$\rightarrow_H$op') if op terminates before op' starts, where "terminates" and "starts" refer to the time line abstracted by the $<_H$ total order relation. More formally:

$$\left(\text{op} \rightarrow_H \text{op'} \right) \stackrel{\text{def}}{=} \left(resp[\text{op}] <_H inv[\text{op'}] \right).$$

Two operations op and op' are said to *overlap* (as already seen, we also say they are *concurrent*) in a history $\widehat{H}$ if neither $resp[\text{op}] <_H inv[\text{op'}]$, nor $resp[\text{op'}] <_H inv[\text{op}]$. Notice that two overlapping operations are such that $\neg(\text{op} \rightarrow_H \text{op'})$ and $\neg(op' \rightarrow_H \text{op})$.

The partial order generated by the execution described in Figure 1.2 is given in Figure 1.4.

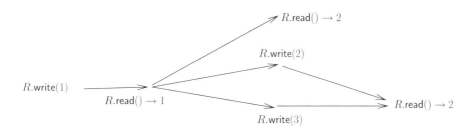

Figure 1.4: Partial order on the operations

Sequential history   A history $\widehat{H}$ is *sequential* if its first event is an invocation, and then (1) each invocation event is immediately followed by the matching reply event, and (2) each reply event (except possibly the last if the execution is infinite) is immediately followed by an invocation event. If $\widehat{H}$ is a sequential history, it has no overlapping operations, and, consequently, the order $\rightarrow_H$ on its operations is a total order. A history $\widehat{H}$ that is not sequential is *concurrent*.

A sequential history models a sequential multiprocess computation (there are no overlapping operations in such a computation), while a concurrent history models a concurrent multiprocess computation (there are at least two overlapping operations in such a computation). The very important point is that, with a sequential history, one can thus reason about executions at the granularity of operations invoked by processes, instead of the granularity of underlying events.

1.2.3   ATOMICITY

The motivation that underlies the definition of atomicity is pretty simple, namely, its aim is (1) to permit one to consider an execution of a set of processes accessing a set of shared objects as if only one operation at a time occurs, (2) while being independent of the number of atomic objects (this point addresses "object composition"): several atomic objects have to behave as if they were a single "big" atomic object. Point (1) is addressed in this section, while point (2) is addressed in the following one.

Legal history   Given a sequential history $\widehat{S}$ and a register R, let $\widehat{S}|R$ ($\widehat{S}$ at R) denote the subsequence of $\widehat{S}$ made up of all events involving only register R. (Notation $\widehat{S}|R$ is -voluntarily- similar to $\widehat{S}|p_i$: in both cases, it denotes the subsequence of $\widehat{S}$ made up of all events involving only register R or process p_i.) Let us notice that, as $\widehat{S}$ is a sequential history, each $\widehat{S}|R$ is also a sequential history.

We say that a sequential history $\widehat{S}$ is *legal* if, for each register R, the sequence $\widehat{S}|R$ is such that each of its read operations returns the value written by the closest preceding write in $\widehat{S}|R$ (or the initial value of R if there is no preceding write).

Atomic history   We define here atomicity for histories without pending operations, i.e., each invocation event of $\widehat{H}$ has a matching reply event in $\widehat{H}$. (Extending the definition to histories with pending operations is left as an exercise.)

Definition   A history $\widehat{H}$ is *atomic* if there is a "witness" history $\widehat{S}$ such that:

1. $\widehat{H}$ and $\widehat{S}$ are equivalent,

2. $\widehat{S}$ is sequential and legal, and

3. $\rightarrow_H \subseteq \rightarrow_S$.

The definition above states that for a history $\widehat{H}$ to be atomic, there must exist a permutation $\widehat{S}$ (witness history) of $\widehat{H}$, which satisfies the following requirements. First, $\widehat{S}$ has to be composed of the same set of events as $\widehat{H}$ [item 1]. Second, $\widehat{S}$ has to be sequential (i.e., an interleaving of the process histories at the granularity of complete operations) and legal (i.e., it has to respect the sequential specification of each register) [item 2]. Notice that, as $\widehat{S}$ is sequential, $\rightarrow_S$ is a total order. Finally, $\widehat{S}$ has also to respect the occurrence order of the operations as defined by $\rightarrow_H$ [item 3]. $\widehat{S}$ represents a history that could have been obtained by executing all the operations, one after the other, while respecting the occurrence order of all the non-overlapping operations. Such a sequential history $\widehat{S}$ is sometimes called a *linearization* of $\widehat{H}$.

Remark on non-determinism   It is important to notice that the notion of atomicity includes inherently a form of non-determinism in the sense that, given a history $\widehat{H}$, several linearizations of $\widehat{H}$ might exist.

Linearization point   The very existence of a linearization of an (atomic) history $\widehat{H}$ means that each operation of $\widehat{H}$ could have been instantaneously executed at a point of the time line (as defined by the total order $<_H$) that lies between its invocation and reply time events. Such a point is called the *linearization point* of the corresponding operation.

Let us notice that one way to prove that all the histories generated by an algorithm are atomic, consists in identifying a linearization point for each of its operations. These points have to (1) respect the time occurrence order of the non-overlapping operations and (2) be consistent with the sequential specification of the object.

1.2.4   ATOMICITY IS A LOCAL PROPERTY

Let P be any property defined on a set of objects. As already indicated, P is *local* if the set of objects as a whole satisfies P whenever each object taken alone satisfies P. As already discussed, locality is an important concept that states that objects can be composed for free.

This section proves that the atomicity consistency criterion is a local property. Intuitively, the fact that atomicity is local comes from the fact that it involves the time occurrence order on non-concurrent operations whatever the objects and the processes concerned by these operations are. We will rely on this aspect in the proof of the following theorem. As the following theorem is correct not only for the atomic registers, but more generally for any object that has a sequential specification, it is formulated and proved on an object basis (as we have previously seen, an atomic register is a particular object that provides the processes with a read and a write operations and is defined by a sequential specification).

Theorem 1.1   *A history $\widehat{H}$ is atomic if, and only if, for each object X involved in $\widehat{H}$, $\widehat{H}|X$ is atomic.*

Proof The "$\Rightarrow$" direction (only if) is an immediate consequence of the definition of atomicity: if $\widehat{H}$ is atomic then, for each object X involved in $\widehat{H}$, $\widehat{H}|X$ is atomic. So, the rest of the proof is restricted to the "$\Leftarrow$" direction.

Given an object X, let $\widehat{S_X}$ be a linearization of $\widehat{H}|X$. It follows from the definition of atomicity that $\widehat{S_X}$ defines a total order on the operations involving X. Let $\rightarrow_X$ denote this total order. We construct an order relation $\rightarrow$ defined on the whole set of operations of $\widehat{H}$ as follows:

1. For each object X: $\rightarrow_X \subseteq \rightarrow$,

2. $\rightarrow_H \subseteq \rightarrow$.

Basically, "$\rightarrow$" totally orders all operations on the same object X, according to $\rightarrow_X$ (item 1), while preserving $\rightarrow_H$, i.e., the real-time occurrence order on operations (item 2).
Claim C. "$\rightarrow$ is acyclic". This means that $\rightarrow$ indeed defines a partial order on the set of all the operations of $\widehat{H}$. Assuming this claim, it is thus possible to construct a sequential history $\widehat{S}$ including all events of $\widehat{H}$ and respecting $\rightarrow$. We trivially have $\rightarrow \subseteq \rightarrow_S$ where $\rightarrow_S$ is the total order on the operations defined from $\widehat{S}$. We have the three following conditions: (1) $\widehat{H}$ and $\widehat{S}$ are equivalent (they contain the same events); (2) $\widehat{S}$ is sequential (by construction) and legal (due to item 1 above); and (3) $\rightarrow_H \subseteq \rightarrow_S$ (due to item 2 above and $\rightarrow \subseteq \rightarrow_S$). It follows that $\widehat{H}$ is linearizable.

Proof of   claim C. We show (by contradiction) that $\rightarrow$ is acyclic. Assume first that $\rightarrow$ induces a cycle involving the operations on a single object X. Indeed, as $\rightarrow_X$ is a total order, in particular transitive, there exist two operations op_i and op_j on X such that $op_i \rightarrow_X op_j$ and $op_j \rightarrow_H op_i$. We have the following.

- $op_i \rightarrow_X op_j \Rightarrow inv[op_i] <_H resp[op_j]$ because X is atomic, and
- $op_j \rightarrow_H op_i \Rightarrow resp[op_j] <_H inv[op_i]$,

which shows a contradiction, as $<_H$ is a total order on the whole set of events.
It follows that any cycle must involve at least two objects. To obtain a contradiction, we show that, in that case, a cycle in $\rightarrow$ implies a cycle in $\rightarrow_H$ (which is acyclic). Let us examine the way the cycle could be obtained. If two consecutive edges of the cycle are due to either some $\rightarrow_X$ (because

of an object X), or $\rightarrow_H$ (due the total order $<_H$), then the cycle can be shortened as any of these relations is transitive. Moreover, $op_i \rightarrow_X op_j \rightarrow_Y op_k$ is not possible for $X \neq Y$, as each operation is on one object only ($op_i \rightarrow_X op_j \rightarrow_Y op_k$ would imply that op_j is on both X and Y).

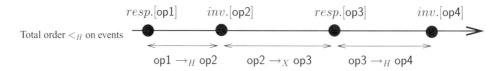

Figure 1.5: Developing $op1 \rightarrow_H op2 \rightarrow_X op3 \rightarrow_H op4$

So, let us consider any sequence of edges of the cycle such that: $op1 \rightarrow_H op2 \rightarrow_X op3 \rightarrow_H op4$. We have (see Figure 1.5):

1. $op1 \rightarrow_H op2 \Rightarrow resp[op1] <_H inv[op2]$ (definition of $op1 \rightarrow_H op2$),
2. $op2 \rightarrow_X op3 \Rightarrow inv[op2] <_H resp[op3]$ (as X is atomic),
3. $op3 \rightarrow_H op4 \Rightarrow resp[op3] <_H inv[op4]$ (definition of $op3 \rightarrow_H op4$).

Combining these statements, we obtain $resp[op1] <_H inv[op4]$ from which we can conclude that $op1 \rightarrow_H op4$. It follows that all the edges due to the relations $\rightarrow_X$ (associated with every object X) can be suppressed, and, consequently, any cycle in $\rightarrow$ can be reduced to a cycle in $\rightarrow_H$, which is a contradiction as $\rightarrow_H$ is an irreflexive partial order. End of proof of claim C. $\square_{Theorem\ 1.1}$

As already indicated, atomicity allows the programmer to reason as if the operations issued by processes on the objects were executed one at a time. The previous theorem is fundamental. It states that to reason about sequential processes that access atomic registers, one can reason on a per object basis without losing the atomicity property of the whole computation.

1.3   BIBLIOGRAPHIC NOTES

- The notion of a regular register has been introduced by Lamport [110]. The notion of an atomic read/write object (register), as studied here, has been investigated and formalized by Lamport in the same paper. (Lamport has also introduced the notion of a *safe* register that is a notion weaker than a regular register. This notion has not been addressed and developed here because its interest is very limited in the context of message passing systems.)

  A more hardware-oriented investigation of atomic registers has been given by Misra [123]. An extension of the regularity condition to MWMR registers is described in [155].

- The generalization of the atomicity consistency condition to any object defined by a sequential specification (set of traces) has been developed by Herlihy and Wing under the name linearizability [98].

- The notion of local property (composition) and the theorem stating that atomicity is a local property are due to Herlihy and Wing [98].

• It is important to notice that, differently from atomicity, sequential consistency [109] and the major part of the consistency conditions encountered in database concurrency control [23, 141] are consistency conditions that do not satisfy the locality property.

CHAPTER 2

Implementing an Atomic Register in a Crash-Prone Asynchronous System

This chapter is on the implementation (we also say construction) of an atomic register in a message-passing system prone to process crashes. It first presents, in an incremental way, the construction of a multi-writer/multi-reader (MWMR) atomic register. This construction assumes a majority of non-faulty processes. Then, after having shown that this assumption is a necessary requirement for such a construction, the chapter considers a failure detector approach in order to circumvent this necessity.

2.1 THE UNDERLYING SYSTEM MODEL

Processes   The system on top of which we want to build an atomic register is made up of a set of n sequential processes denoted $\Pi = \{p_1, \ldots, p_n\}$ (we also sometimes use Π to denote the set of identities $\{1, \ldots, n\}$). Each process p_i is an automaton. It has an initial state and executes a sequence of steps defined by a transition function called the *local algorithm* assigned to that process. A step is atomic (i.e., executed entirely or not at all). A step corresponds to the execution of an internal statement (i.e., a statement involving only the local state automaton), the sending of a message or the reception of a message. The set of these local algorithms is called a *distributed algorithm*.

Failure model   A process can crash. After it has crashed, a process executes no more steps. There is no recovery. A process that crashes in a run is *faulty* in that run; otherwise, it is *non-faulty*.

   The model parameter t $(0 \leq t < n)$ denotes the maximum number of processes that may crash during an execution. We are interested in *t-resilient* algorithms, i.e., in algorithms that have to always behave correctly when at most t processes crash. Conversely, when more than t processes crash, there is no guarantee on their behavior.

Communication medium   Each pair of processes is connected by a bidirectional *link* (sometimes also called *channel*). In order to simplify the description of the algorithms, we sometimes consider that a process can also send a message to itself.

   To send a message m to a process p_j, a process p_i invokes the operation "send m to p_j". To receive a message from p_j, it invokes " receive () from p_j" (or " receive m from p_j" where m will contain the received message); p_i can invoke " receive ()" where the sender of the message can be any process. When a process invokes a receive operation, it is blocked until a message arrives.

Each communication channel is assumed to be reliable: there are neither creation, modification, nor loss of messages. The notation " broadcast m" is used as a shortcut for

for each $j \in \{1, \ldots, n\}$ **do** send m to p_j **end for**

where $j \in \{1, \ldots, n\}$ means that the order in which the message m is sent to every process is arbitrary. It is important to see that " broadcast m" is not an all-or-nothing operation: if p_i crashes while executing it, an arbitrary subset of the processes receive message m. Moreover, when it executes " broadcast m", a process p_i sends a message to itself. This allows us to write more concise algorithms. (Of course, simple modifications of these algorithms allow the sending of such messages to be suppressed in practical implementations.)

Timing model   The processes are asynchronous. This means that each process proceeds at its own speed. There is no assumption on the relative speed of one process with respect to another. The only assumption is that, until it crashes -if it ever crashes-, the speed of a process is always positive: a non-faulty process eventually executes the next step of its algorithm.

At the communication level, there is no bound on message transfer delays. The only guarantee is that, if a process returns from the send of a message and the destination process is non-faulty, then the destination process eventually receives the message (because communication channels are assumed to be reliable) if it executes " receive ()"operation infinitely often.

This message-passing system model is called the *asynchronous* model. It is also sometimes called *time-free* model. It is important to notice that the processes are not provided with a notion of global time. If a process uses a local physical clock, the dates and durations measured by its clock are meaningful only for itself, which means that they have no meaning for the other processes.

Notation   In the following, we use the notation $\mathcal{AS}_{n,t}[\emptyset]$ to denote the previous message-passing crash-prone asynchronous system model.

Let P be a predicate on the model parameters n and t, e.g., $P \equiv (t < n/2)$. $\mathcal{AS}_{n,t}[P]$ denotes the system model that is the restriction of $\mathcal{AS}_{n,t}[\emptyset]$ to the runs where P is always satisfied. As an example, $\mathcal{AS}_{n,t}[t < n/2]$ denotes any system where, in each run (history), a majority of processes do not crash.

Finally, $\mathcal{AS}_{n,t}[T]$, where T is the type of a distributed object, denotes the system model $\mathcal{AS}_{n,t}[\emptyset]$, where the processes can additionally access objects of the type T to cooperate. An example (that will be studied in Section 2.4), $\mathcal{AS}_{n,t}[\Sigma]$ denotes a system model where the processes have access to a failure detector object of the class (type) Σ.

More generally, $\mathcal{AS}_{n,t}[P, T]$, where T is an object type and P a predicate (e.g., $t < n/2$), denotes the system model $\mathcal{AS}_{n,t}[\emptyset]$ where the processes can access objects of type T, and all the executions (histories) satisfy predicate P.

2.2   BUILDING AN MWMR ATOMIC REGISTER IN $\mathcal{AS}_{n,t}[t < n/2]$

2.2.1   PROBLEM SPECIFICATION

Specification   The MWMR atomic register R is implemented collectively by the n processes. To that end, each process executes an appropriate algorithm such that the safety and liveness properties of R.read() and R.write() operations associated with R are satisfied. These properties are the following:

- Safety. This property is nothing else than the atomicity consistency condition: any execution of R.read() and R.write() operations is such that these operations (except possibly the last operation issued by faulty processes) appear as if they have been executed sequentially. This total order complies with the operations' real time order (see the previous chapter for a formal statement of atomicity).

- Liveness. This property states that, whatever the operation (R.read() or R.write()), if the invoking process is non-faulty, then that operation terminates (the invoking process obtains a response).

An incremental construction   The algorithm building an atomic MWMR register is presented incrementally. An algorithm building a 1WMR regular register is first introduced. It is then enriched to prevent new/old inversions in order to obtain a 1WMR atomic register. Finally, a simple modification extends it to go from a 1WMR atomic register to an MWMR atomic register. All these constructions require a majority of processes to be non-faulty, so they assume that the underlying system model is $\mathcal{AS}_{n,t}[t < n/2]$.

2.2.2   IMPLEMENTING A 1WMR REGULAR REGISTER IN $\mathcal{AS}_{n,t}[t < n/2]$

Underlying principle   The idea that underlies the construction is quite simple. Let p_w denote the writer process. On the one hand, p_w associates a sequence number with each of its write operations and broadcasts the pair (new value, sequence number). On the other hand, every process p_i keeps in its local memory the pair with the highest sequence number it has ever seen.

Both the safety property (regularity) and the liveness property associated with a regular register are obtained from the "majority of correct processes" assumption ($t < n/2$). This is because this assumption allows a process to always communicate with a majority of processes (i.e., with at least one non-faulty process) before terminating its current read or write operation.

Local variables   Each process p_i manages the following local variables.

- cur_val_i is a data variable that contains the current value of the register R (as known by p_i).

- w_sn_i is a control variable that keeps the sequence number associated with the value currently kept in cur_val_i. As far as p_w is concerned, w_sn_w is also used to generate the increasing sequence numbers associated with the values written into R.

- req_sn_i is a control variable containing the sequence number that p_i has associated with its last read of R. (These sequence numbers allow every ACK () to be correctly associated with the request that gives rise to its sending.)

All the local variables used to generate a sequence number are initialized to 0. The register R is assumed to be initialized to some value (say v_init). Consequently, all the local variables cur_val_i are initialized to v_init.

The construction   The algorithm that builds a regular 1WMR register R is described in Figure 2.1. The statement "**wait until** (TAG(sn) received)" means that the invoking process is blocked until its input buffer contains a message whose type is TAG and that carries the value sn. When the wait statement terminates the message is consumed and suppressed from the input buffer.

When p_w invokes R.write (v), it computes the next sequence number w_sn_w, broadcasts the message WRITE(v, w_sn_w), and waits for corresponding acknowledgments from a majority of processes before terminating the write operation. When a process p_i receives such a message, it updates its current pair (cur_val_i, w_sn_i) if $w\_sn_w \geq w\_sn_i$, and sends back to p_w an acknowledgment ACK_WRITE_REQ(w_sn) to p_w. Otherwise, the message WRITE(v, w_sn_w) is an old message and p_i discards it.

When a process p_i invokes R.read (), it broadcasts an inquiry message READ_REQ (req_sn_i) where req_sn_i is a sequence number used to identify each read request of p_i. When a process p_k receives such a message it sends back its current value of the register. Then, when p_i has received ACK_READ_REQ ($req\_sn_i, -, -$) messages from a majority of processes, it returns the value v it has received that is associated with the greatest sequence number.

Remarks   When it receives a WRITE (val, w_sn) message from the writer p_w, a process p_i evaluates the predicate $w\_sn \geq w\_sn_i$. Actually this predicate could be strengthened in $w\_sn > w\_sn_i$ for a process $p_i \neq p_w$. Using the predicate $w\_sn \geq w\_sn_i$ allows us not to distinguish p_w from the other processes.

The code of the algorithm can be easily modified to save a few messages. When p_w executes R.write (), it is not necessary to send a message to itself. It can instead write directly v into cur_val_w. Moreover, when p_w wants to read R, it can directly return the current value of cur_val_w. In the same vein, when a process p_i ($i \neq w$) invokes R.read (), it can save the sending of a message to itself as long as, in addition to the acknowledgment messages it receives, it also considers its own pair (w_sn_i, cur_val_i) when it determines the value to be returned. Finally, when it waits for acknowledgments, a process has now to wait for messages from a majority of processes minus one.

Cost   It is easy to see that the cost of a read or a write operation is $2n$ messages. As far as the time complexity is concerned, let us assume that (a) local computation durations are negligible when compared to message transit delays, and (b) every message takes one time unit. The number of "time units" that are needed by an operation is actually counts the number of sequential communication steps this operation gives rise to.

---

operation R.write (v): % This code is only for the single writer p_w %
    $w\_sn_w \leftarrow w\_sn_w + 1$;
    broadcast WRITE (v, w_sn_w);
    wait until (ACK_WRITE (w_sn_w) received from a majority of processes);
    return (ok).

% The code snippets that follow are for every process p_i $(i \in \{1, \ldots, n\})$ %

operation R.read (): % This code is for any process p_i %
    $req\_sn_i \leftarrow req\_sn_i + 1$;
    broadcast READ_REQ (req_sn_i);
    wait until (ACK_READ_REQ $(req\_sn_i, -, -)$ received from a majority of processes);
    let max_sn **be** the greatest sequence number (w_sn) received in
                an ACK_READ_REQ $(req\_sn_i, w\_sn, -)$ message;
    let v **be** such that ACK_READ_REQ (req_sn_i, max_sn, v) has been received;
    return (v).

when WRITE (val, w_sn) **is received from** p_w:
    if $(w\_sn \geq w\_sn_i)$ **then** $cur\_val_i \leftarrow val$; $w\_sn_i \leftarrow w\_sn$ **end if**;
    send ACK_WRITE (w_sn) to p_w.

when READ_REQ (r_sn) **is received from** p_j $(j \in \{1, \ldots, n\})$:
    send ACK_READ_REQ $(r\_sn, w\_sn_i, cur\_val_i)$ to p_j.

Figure 2.1: An algorithm that constructs a regular 1WMR register in $\mathcal{AS}_{n,t}[t < n/2]$

An operation thus takes 2 time units (let us remember that the communication graph is complete, i.e., each pair of processes is connected by an independent bidirectional channel). Hence, the time complexity (number of sequential communication steps) does not depend on n.

When the communication graph is not complete   The algorithm described in Figure 2.1 is based on the assumption that the underlying communication graph is completely connected: any pair of processes is connected by a reliable channel.

So, an interesting question is "What does happen when this is not the case?" It is easy to see that the algorithm can be easily modified in order to work in all the runs for which the communication graph connecting the non-faulty processes remains strongly connected (i.e., any pair of non-faulty processes is connected by a path of non-faulty processes). The only modification of the algorithm consists in adding an appropriate routing for the messages. In that case, both the message complexity and the time complexity depend on the communication graph.

Theorem 2.1   *The algorithm described in Figure 2.1 constructs a 1WMR regular register in $\mathcal{AS}_{n,t}[t < n/2]$ (asynchronous message-passing system prone to up to t crashes with $t < n/2$).*

Proof
Proof of the liveness property. We have to prove here that any operation invoked by a non-faulty

process terminates. Let us notice that the only statement where a process can block forever is a **wait until** statement. The fact that no process blocks forever in such a statement follows directly from the four following observations: (1) a process broadcasts an inquiry message (identified with a sequence number) before waiting for acknowledgments from a majority of processes, (2) every inquiry message is systematically answered by every non-faulty process, (3) there is a majority of non-faulty processes, and (4) the channels are reliable.

Proof of the safety property. Let us first observe that, as there is a single writer, write operations are totally ordered. Moreover, every write operation is identified with a sequence number.

To prove the safety property that defines a regular register, we have to prove that, when a process p_i invokes R.read (), it obtains either the last value written before the read operation was invoked, or a value that is written by a concurrent write operation.

Let rsn be the sequence number associated with the value returned by p_i. Let $x \geq 0$ be the sequence number of the last value written before the operation R.read () is invoked, and $x + 1$, ..., $x + y$ be the sequence numbers of the write operations, if any, that are concurrent with R.read (). ($y = 0$ corresponds to the case where there is no write concurrent with the read.) The proof consists in showing that $rsn \in \{x, \ldots, x + y\}$.

As the write of the value associated with x is terminated, it follows from the algorithm that (at least) a majority of processes p_k are such that $w\_sn_k \geq x$. As the R.read () obtains sequence numbers from a majority of processes, it obtains at least one sequence number $\geq x$, and we consequently have $rsn \geq x$.

On the other hand, due to its definition, the read operation is not concurrent with write operations whose sequence numbers are greater than $x + y$, which means that the read operation has terminated when the write numbered $x + y + 1$ is issued by the writer (if such a write is ever issued). Consequently, we have $rsn \leq x + y$, which concludes the proof of the safety property.

$$\square_{Theorem\ 2.1}$$

When the writer crashes   If the writer crashes outside the write operation, the processes will obtain the last value it has written. The case where it crashed while executing the write operation is more "interesting". It is possible that it crashes after sending its new value to less than a majority of processes. In that case, depending on asynchrony and the actual crash pattern, it is possible that, when some processes read, they will always obtain the new value, while others always obtain the previous value. This is not in contradiction with the definition of a regular register. Actually, if the writer process crashes during a write operation, that operation may never terminate (it is then concurrent with all the future read operations).

It is easy to see that the crash of a process during a read operation has no effect on the behavior of other processes. This is because a read operation does not entail modifications on local variables of other processes.

2.2.3   FROM REGULARITY TO ATOMICITY

The previous algorithm does not ensure atomicity   Let us consider the scenario described in Figure 2.2. There are 5 processes, and none of them has crashed. The numbers on a process axis are sequence numbers. The bold line (cutting the axes of all the processes) is the "write line" associated with the write of the value with sequence number 15. As an example, let us consider the process p_i: before the cut by the write line, cur_val_i contains the value whose sequence number is 14, and contains the value whose sequence number is 15 just after. As far as p_j is concerned, this process receives the message WRITE$(-, 15)$ before the ones carrying the sequence numbers 11 to 14. Due to asynchrony these messages are late (they have been bypassed by the message WRITE$(-, 15)$) and will be discarded by p_j when they arrive. Let us remember that the channels are reliable but are not required to be "first in, first out".

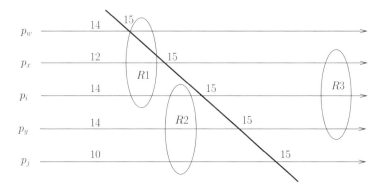

Figure 2.2: Regular is not atomic

An ellipsis corresponds to a read operation, so there are three reads denoted $R1$, $R2$ and $R3$. Let us assume that the read $R1$ is issued by p_i. It obtains the values and the sequence numbers of the set of the three processes p_w, p_x and itself, that constitutes a majority. It follows that $R1$ returns the value whose associated sequence number is 15. If we consider $R3$, it is easy to see that it returns the value whose sequence number is 15. Let us now consider $R2$. It obtains the sequence numbers 14, 14 and 10, and consequently returns the value associated with the sequence number 14.

When we look at Figure 2.2 from an operation duration point of view, we see that, while $R1$ terminates before $R2$ starts, it obtains the new value while $R2$ obtains the old value. There is a new/old inversion. Consequently, the algorithm described in Figure 2.1 does not ensure the atomicity consistency criterion.

The key to obtain atomicity: force a read to write   An easy way to enrich the previous algorithm to obtain an algorithm that guarantees atomicity consists in preventing new/old inversions. This can be easily realized by forcing a read operation to write the value v it is about to return. This ensures that, when the read terminates, a majority of the processes have a value as recent as v in their local memory. The parts of the algorithm described in Figure 2.1 that are modified to go from regularity to atomicity are described in Figure 2.3.

Thanks to this embedded write of the read value, if the invoking process p_i does not crash while executing the read, a majority of the processes will have a value with a sequence number greater than or equal to sn, where sn is the sequence number of the value it is about to return. It is easy to see that this prevents new/old inversions from occurring. If p_i crashes before returning from the read operation, the WRITE() message it has sent to p_j (if any) is taken into account by p_j only if it carries a value not older than the one kept in cur_val_j. It follows that a process that crashes during a read cannot create inconsistency. Its only possible effect is to refresh the content of local variables with more up to date values.

Finally, as now not only the writer but any process can send WRITE() messages, the processing of these messages has to be slightly modified: the ACK_WRITE_REQ() message has to be sent back to the sender of the WRITE() message.

---

operation R.read ():
    $req\_sn_i \leftarrow req\_sn_i + 1$;
    broadcast READ_REQ (req_sn_i);
    wait until (ACK_READ_REQ $(req\_sn_i, -, -)$ received from a majority of processes);
    let max_sn be the greatest sequence number (w_sn) received in
                     an ACK_READ_REQ $(req\_sn_i, w\_sn, -)$ message;
    let v **be** such that ACK_READ_REQ (max_sn, v) has been received;
    broadcast WRITE(v, max_sn);
    wait until (ACK_WRITE (max_sn) received from a majority of processes);
    return (v).

when WRITE (val, w_sn) **is received from** p_j $(j \in \{1, \ldots, n\})$:
    if $(w\_sn \geq w\_sn_i)$ **then** $cur\_val_i \leftarrow val$; $w\_sn_i \leftarrow w\_sn$ **end if**;
    send ACK_WRITE (w_sn) to p_j.

Figure 2.3: Modifying the R.read () operation to obtain atomicity

2.2.4   FROM A 1WMR ATOMIC REGISTER TO AN MWMR ATOMIC REGISTER

Replacing sequence numbers by timestamps   To go from a 1WMR atomic register to an MWMR atomic register, the new problem to solve is to allow the processes to share a single sequence number generator for the values they write into R. A simple way to do it is to use the set of local variables $\{w\_sn_i\}_{1 \leq i \leq n}$ as follows.

When a process p_i wants to write, it broadcasts a message WRITE_REQ(req_sn_i) in order to obtain the current sequence numbers w_sn_j from a majority of processes. It then adds 1 to the maximal value it has received and associates this new sequence number with the value v it wants to write. Let us observe that the same local variable req_sn_i is used now to associate an identity to both its write requests and its read requests.

Of course, this does not prevent several processes from associating the same sequence number with their writes. (Let us notice that, when this occurs, the corresponding writes are concurrent.) This can easily be solved, by associating a timestamp (instead of a "unidimensional" sequence number) with each write operation.

A *timestamp* is a pair (sequence number, process identity). The two fundamental properties of timestamps are that they evolve with the progress of the processes and define a total order consistent with this progress. Let $(sn1, i)$ and $(sn2, j)$ be two timestamps. The timestamp total order is defined as follows (lexicographical ordering):

$$(sn1, i) < (sn2, j) \equiv \big((sn1 < sn2) \vee (sn1 = sn2 \wedge i < j)\big).$$

The final construction   The algorithm building an MWMR atomic register in $\mathcal{AS}_{n,t}[t < n/2]$ is described in Figure 2.4. Each process manages a new local variable $last\_writer_i$ that contains the identity of the process that issued the write of the value currently kept in cur_val_i ($last\_writer_i$ can be initialized to any process identity, e.g., 1).

The timestamp of the value in cur_val_i is consequently the pair $(w\_sn_i, last\_writer_i)$. The code associated with the reception of a WRITE(val, w_sn) message takes now into account the timestamp of the value that is about to be written, instead of only its sequence number.

Let us also notice that now, not only the read/write request messages and their acknowledgments are tagged with a request sequence number defined by the requesting process, but the write messages also are tagged the same way. This allows for an unambiguous identification of the write acknowledgments sent to a writer.

On two-phase algorithms   The algorithms implementing the R.write () and R.read () operations have exactly the same structure: they first broadcast a request to obtain the more recent control information, do local computation, and finally issue a second broadcast to write a value.

This structure is encountered in a lot of distributed algorithms called *distributed two-phase algorithms*. These phases refer to communication. The first phase consists in acquiring information on the system state, while (according to the information obtained and some local computation) the second phase consists in updating the system state.

2.2.5   CORRECTNESS PROOF OF THE MWMR ATOMIC REGISTER CONSTRUCTION

Lemma 2.2   *The execution of an R.write () or R.read () operation by a non-faulty process always terminates.*

Proof The reasoning is exactly the same as the one stated in the proof of Theorem 2.1 where only the case of the 1WMR regular register was considered. We repeat it here only to make the reading

```
operation R.write (v):
    req_sn_i ← req_sn_i + 1;
    % Phase 1: acquire information on the system state %
    broadcast WRITE_REQ (req_sn_i);
    wait until ( ACK_WRITE_REQ (req_sn_i, −) received from a majority of processes );
    let max_sn be the greatest sequence number (w_sn) received in
                    an ACK_WRITE_REQ (req_sn_i, w_sn) message;
    % Phase 2 : update system state %
    broadcast WRITE (req_sn_i, v, max_sn + 1, i);
    wait until ( ACK_WRITE (req_sn_i) received from a majority of processes );
    return (ok).

operation R.read ():
    req_sn_i ← req_sn_i + 1;
    % Phase 1: acquire information on the system state %
    broadcast READ_REQ (req_sn_i);
    wait until ( ACK_READ_REQ (req_sn_i, −, −, −) received from a majority of processes );
    let (max_wsn, max_lw) be the greatest timestamp (w_sn, last_writer) received in
                    an ACK_READ_REQ (req_sn_i, w_sn, last_writer, −) message;
    let v be such that ACK_READ_REQ (req_sn_i, max_wsn, max_lw, v) has been received;
    % Phase 2 : update system state %
    broadcast WRITE (req_sn_i, v, max_wsn, max_lw);
    wait until ( ACK_WRITE (req_sn_i) received from a majority of processes );
    return (v).

when WRITE (r_sn, val, w_sn, last_writer) is received from p_j (j ∈ {1, . . . , n}):
    if(w_sn, last_writer) ≥ (w_sn_i, last_writer_i)
        then cur_val_i ← val; w_sn_i ← w_sn; last_writer_i ← last_writer end if;
    send ACK_WRITE(r_sn) to p_j.

when READ_REQ (r_sn) is received from p_j (j ∈ {1, . . . , n}):
    send ACK_READ_REQ (r_sn, w_sn_i, last_writer_i, cur_val_i) to p_j.

when WRITE_REQ (r_sn) is received from p_j (j ∈ {1, . . . , n}):
    send ACK_WRITE_REQ(r_sn, w_sn_i) to p_j.
```

Figure 2.4: An algorithm that constructs an atomic MWMR register in $\mathcal{AS}_{n,t}[t < n/2]$ (code for any p_i)

easier. The fact that no process blocks forever in a **wait until** statement follows directly from the four following observations: (1) a process broadcasts an inquiry message (identified with a proper sequence number) before waiting for acknowledgments from a majority of processes, (2) every inquiry message is systematically answered by every non-faulty process, (3) there is a majority of non-faulty processes, and (4) the channels are reliable. $\square_{Lemma\ 2.2}$

Definition 2.3   An *effective write* operation is such that at least one process has received its WRITE () message. An *effective read* operation is such that the invoking process does not crash while executing it.

The timestamp of an effective R.write () operation is the timestamp it associates with the value it writes. The timestamp of an effective R.read () operation is the timestamp associated with the value it returns.

An effective write is a write whose value is taken into account by at least one process. Let us observe that all write operations issued by non-faulty processes are effective. On the other hand, some of write operations whose invoking process crashes during the invocation are effective, while others are not.

Lemma 2.4   *Let* w1 *and* w2 *be two effective write operations time stamped* $(sn1, id1)$ *and* $(sn2, id2)$, *respectively.* w1 $\neq$ w2 $\Rightarrow$ $(sn1, id1) \neq (sn2, id2)$,

Proof Let us first observe that if w1 and w2 are issued by different processes, the second field of their timestamps are different, and the lemma follows. So, let us consider the case where w1 and w2 are issued by the same process p_i. Let $(sn1, i)$ the timestamp of w1 and $(sn2, i)$ the timestamp of w2.

Without loss of generality, let us assume that w1 is executed first. As p_i is sequential, it follows that w1 was terminated when p_i issues w2, from which we conclude that a majority of processes p_j are such that $(w\_sn_j, last\_writer_j) \geq (sn1, i)$ when w1 terminates.

Let us now consider the first phase of w2. During this phase, p_i collect sequence numbers from a majority of processes. As any two majorities intersect, it follows that at least one of these sequence numbers is greater than or equal to $sn1$. Finally, the lemma follows from the fact that $sn2$ is set to a value greater than the greatest sequence number received. $\square_{Lemma\ 2.4}$

Lemma 2.5   *Let* op1 *and* op2 *be two effective operations time stamped* $(sn1, id1)$ *and* $(sn2, id2)$, *respectively, such that* op1 *terminates before* op2 *starts. We have the following:*
If op1 *is a read or a write operation and* op2 *is a read operation, then* $(sn1, id1) \leq (sn2, id2)$.
If op1 *is a read or a write operation and* op2 *is a write operation, then* $(sn1, id1) < (sn2, id2)$.

Proof The proof of this lemma uses Lemma 2.4 and is similar to it. The only difference is that, while a write operation increases a timestamp value, a read operation does not. A development of a complete proof is left to the reader as an exercise. $\square_{Lemma\ 2.5}$

Lemma 2.6   *There is a total order* $\widehat{S}$ *on all the effective operations* (i) *that respects their real time occurrence order, and* (ii) *is such that any read operation obtains the value written by the last write operation that precedes it in* $\widehat{S}$.

Let us remember that the notion of "time occurrence order" has been defined in the previous chapter. An operation op1 precedes an operation op2 if the response event of op1 appears before the invocation event of op2 in the event history $\widehat{H} = (H, <_H)$ that models the execution.

Proof Let us consider the total order $\widehat{S}$ on all the effective operations defined as follows. The operations are first ordered in $\widehat{S}$ according to their timestamps. As all the write operations are totally ordered by their timestamps (Lemma 2.4), it follows that, if two operations have the same timestamps, one of them is necessarily a read operation. If a read and a write have the same timestamps, the write is ordered in $\widehat{S}$ before the read. If two reads have the same timestamp, the one that starts first, is ordered in $\widehat{S}$ before the other one. (The first is the one whose invocation event appears first in the associated history $\widehat{H}$).

The total order $\widehat{S}$ being defined, we are now able to show that it is a witness sequence (or linearization) of the execution.

- Proof of property (i). Let op1 (time stamped $(sn1, id1)$) and op2 (time stamped $(sn2, id2)$) be effective read or write operations such that op1 terminates before op2 starts. Due to Lemma 2.5, we have $(sn1, id1) \leq (sn2, id2)$ if op2 is a read operation, and $(sn1, id1) < (sn2, id2)$ if op2 is a write operation. We conclude from the way $\widehat{S}$ is built (from both the order on the operations defined by their timestamps and the order on the response/invocation events), that op1 is ordered before op2 in $\widehat{S}$.

- Proof of property (ii). Let read be a read operation that returns a value v time stamped (sn, j). We conclude that v has been written by p_j after it has computed the write sequence sn. The fact that read obtains the value of the last preceding write in $\widehat{S}$ follows directly from the way $\widehat{S}$ is built and the fact that no two written values have the same timestamp (Lemma 2.4).

$\square_{Lemma\ 2.6}$

Theorem 2.7 *The algorithm described in Figure 2.4 constructs an atomic MWMR register in $\mathcal{AS}_{n,t}[t < n/2]$.*

Proof The proof follows from Lemma 2.2 (liveness) and Lemma 2.6 (safety). $\square_{Theorem\ 2.7}$

2.3   AN IMPOSSIBILITY THEOREM

The previous constructions of a 1WMR and a MWMR atomic registers are t-resilient (i.e., they cope with up to t process crashes) where $t < n/2$. So, a natural question that comes immediately to mind is the following one: "Is it possible to design atomic register algorithms for any value of t, or is $t < n/2$ a fundamental barrier that cannot be bypassed when one has to cope with the net effect of asynchrony and process failures?"

This section answers the previous fundamental question by showing that it is impossible to design a distributed algorithm that builds a register in $\mathcal{AS}_{n,t}[\emptyset]$. Interestingly, this proof is based on an *indistinguishability argument* that is common to several impossibility results, namely the fact that some processes cannot distinguish one execution from another one. In that sense, although it is very simple, this proof depicts an essential feature that lies at the core of fault-tolerant distributed computing.

Theorem 2.8   *There is no algorithm that constructs an atomic register in $\mathcal{AS}_{n,t}[t \geq n/2]$.*

Proof Given $t \geq n/2$, let us partition the processes in two subsets $P1$ and $P2$ (i.e., $P1 \cap P2 = \emptyset$ and $P1 \cup P2 = \{p_1, \ldots, p_n\}$) such that $|P1| = \lceil n/2 \rceil$ and $|P2| = \lfloor n/2 \rfloor$. Let us observe that $|P1| \leq t$ and $|P2| \leq t$, which means that the system model accepts executions in which all the processes of $P1$ crash, and executions in which all the processes of $P2$ crash.

The proof is by contradiction. Let us assume that there is an algorithm A that builds an atomic register R for $t \geq n/2$. Let 0 be the initial value of R. Let us define the following executions (depicted in Figure 2.5 where $n = 5$ and $t = 3$). Let us repeat that, according to the system model and the previous assumptions, these executions can happen.

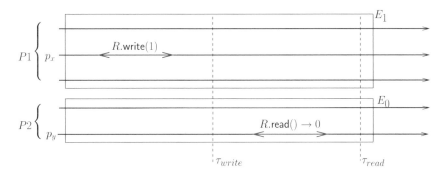

Figure 2.5: There is no register algorithm in $\mathcal{AS}_{n,t}[\emptyset]$

- Execution E_1. In this execution, all the processes of $P2$ crash initially (so no process of $P2$ ever executes a step in E_1), and all the processes in $P1$ are non-faulty. Moreover, a process $p_x \in P1$ issues R.write (1), and no other process of $P1$ invokes an operation. As the algorithm A is correct (assumption), it satisfies the liveness property and, consequently, this write operation does terminate. Let τ_{write} be a (finite) time after it has terminated.

- Execution E_0. In this execution, all the processes of $P1$ crash initially, the processes of $P2$ are non-faulty and do nothing until τ_{write}. Let us observe that, due to asynchrony, this is possible. After τ_{write}, a process $p_y \in P2$ issues R.read (), and no other process of $P2$ invokes an operation. As the algorithm A is correct, this read operation terminates and returns the initial value 0 to p_y. Let τ_{read} be a (finite) time after which this read operation has terminated. (In the following "the same as" means that in both executions, the processes issues the same operations (and receive the same results) at the very same time.)

- Execution E_{10}. That execution is defined as follows.

- No process crashes.

- E_{10} is the same as E_1 until τ_{write}.

- E_{10} is the same as E_0 until the time τ_{read}.

- If any, the messages that the processes of $P1$ send to the processes of $P2$ are delayed to be received after time τ_{read}. Similarly, if any, the messages that the processes of $P2$ send to the processes of $P1$ are delayed to be received after time τ_{read}. (Let us remember that, due the system asynchrony, messages can be delayed in that way.)

Let us consider the process $p_y \in P2$. This process cannot distinguish between E_0 and E_{10} until τ_{read}. Hence, as it reads 0 in E_0, it has to read the same value in E_{10}. But, as the algorithm A ensures atomicity, p_y should read 1 in E_{10} (the last write that precedes the read operation has written the value 1). We obtain a contradiction, from which we conclude that there is no algorithm A with the required properties. $\square_{Theorem\ 2.8}$

2.4   THE FAILURE DETECTOR APPROACH TO CIRCUMVENT IMPOSSIBILITIES

2.4.1   WHAT A FAILURE DETECTOR IS

The concept of *failure detector* is one of the main approaches that has been proposed to circumvent impossibility results in fault-tolerant asynchronous distributed computing (i.e., in the system model $\mathcal{AS}_{n,t}[\emptyset]$). From an operational point of view, a failure detector can be seen as an oracle made up of several modules, each associated with a process. The module attached to process p_i provides it with hints concerning which processes have failed. Failure detectors are divided into classes, based on the particular type of information they provide on failures. Different problems may require different classes of failure detectors in order to be solved in an otherwise fault-prone asynchronous distributed system. One can identify two main characteristics of the failure detector approach, namely, one associated with its software engineering feature, the other associated with its computability dimension.

The software engineering dimension of failure detectors   A failure detector class is defined by a set of abstract properties. This way, a failure detector-based distributed algorithm relies only on the properties that define the failure detector class, regardless of the way they are implemented in a given system. This *software engineering dimension* of the failure detector approach favors algorithm design, algorithm proof, modularity, and portability.

Similarly to a stack and a queue that are defined by their specification, and can have many different implementations, a failure detector of a given class can have many different implementations each taking into account appropriate features of a particular underlying system (such as its topology, local clocks, distribution of message delays, timers, etc.). Due to the fact that a failure detector is defined by abstract properties and not in terms of a particular implementation, an algorithm that uses it does not have to be rewritten when the underlying system is modified.

It is important to notice that, in order for a non-trivial failure detector to be implementable, the underlying system has to satisfy additional behavioral properties (that in some sense restrict its asynchrony). (If not, the impossibility result -that the considered failure detector allows to circumvent- would no longer be impossible.)

Let Pb be a problem that can be solved with the help of a failure detector class FD. (With the previous notation, this means that P can be solved in $\mathcal{AS}_{n,t}[FD]$.) The failure detector concept favors separation of concerns as follows.

- Design and prove correct an FD-based distributed algorithm that solves Pb.

- Independently of the previous item, investigate the system behavioral properties that have to be satisfied for FD to be implementable, and provide an implementation of FD for these systems.

The computability dimension of failure detectors   Given a problem Pb that cannot be solved in an asynchronous system prone to failures (e.g., the construction of an atomic register in $\mathcal{AS}_{n,t}[\emptyset]$), the failure detector approach allows us to investigate and state the minimal assumptions on failures the processes have to be provided with, in order for the problem Pb to be solved. This is the *computability dimension* of the failure detector approach.

An interesting side of this computability dimension lies in the ranking of problems it allows. This ranking is based on the weakest failure detectors these problems require to be solved. (The notion of "weakest" failure detector for the register problem will be discussed in Section 2.5, and addressed in a general way in the last chapter). This provides us with a failure detector-based method to establish a hierarchy among distributed computing problems.

2.4.2   FORMAL DEFINITIONS

Failure pattern   A failure pattern defines a possible set of failures, with their occurrence times, that can occur during an execution. Formally, a failure pattern is a function $F : \mathbb{N} \rightarrow 2^{\Pi}$, where $\mathbb{N}$ is the set of natural numbers (time domain), and 2^{Π} is the power-set of Π (the set of all sets of process identities). $F(\tau)$ denotes the set of processes that have crashed up to time τ. As a crashed process does not recover, we have $F(\tau) \subseteq F(\tau + 1)$. Let $Faulty(F)$ be set of processes that crash in an execution with failure pattern F. Let τ_{max} denote the end of that execution. We have $Faulty(F) = F(\tau_{max})$. As τ_{max} is not known and depends on the execution, and we want to be as general as possible (and not tied to a time-specific class of executions), we (conceptually) consider that an execution never ends, i.e., we consider that $\tau_{max} = +\infty$. We have accordingly $Faulty(F) = \cup_{1 \leq \tau < +\infty} F(\tau) = \lim_{\tau \rightarrow +\infty} F(\tau)$. Let $Non\text{-}faulty(F) = \Pi - Faulty(F)$ (the set of processes that do not crash in F). $Correct(F)$ is used as a synonym of $Non\text{-}faulty(F)$.

It is important to notice that the notion of faulty and correct are defined with respect to a failure pattern, i.e., to the failure pattern that occurs in a given execution.

Failure detector history with range $\mathcal{R}$ A *failure detector history with range* $\mathcal{R}$ describes the behavior of a failure detector during an execution. $\mathcal{R}$ defines the type of information on failures provided to the processes. We consider here failure detectors whose range $\mathcal{R}$ is 2^{Π} (i.e., a value of $\mathcal{R}$ is a set of process identities). This means that the information a process obtains from its failure detector module is always a set of processes.

Formally, a failure detector history is a function $H : \Pi \times \mathbb{N} \to \mathcal{R}$, where $H(p_i, \tau)$ is the value of the failure detector module of process p_i at time τ.

Failure detector class FD *with range* $\mathcal{R}$ A *failure detector class* FD *with range* $\mathcal{R}$ is a function that maps each failure pattern F to a set of failure detector histories with range $\mathcal{R}$. This means that $FD(F)$ represents the whole set of possible behaviors that the failure detector FD can exhibit when the actual failure pattern is F.

In the following, we sometimes say "a failure detector FD" as a shortcut for "a failure detector of the class FD".

Remark   It is important to notice that the output of a failure detector does not depend on the computation, it depends only on the actual failure pattern. On another hand, a given failure detector might associate several histories with each failure pattern. Each history represents a possible sequence of outputs for the same failure pattern. This feature captures the inherent non-determinism of a failure detector.

Remark   The failure detector classes presented in this book do not appear in their "historical order" (the order in which they have been chronologically introduced in research articles). They are introduced according to the order in which this book presents problems they allows us to solve. Hence, as it allows for an optimal implementation of a register whatever the number of process that may crash, the first class of failure detector that is presented is the class Σ. (The optimality notion cited above is with respect to the information on failure that is needed to solve a given problem.)

2.4.3   THE CLASS Σ OF QUORUM FAILURE DETECTORS

Definition   A quorum is a non-empty set of processes. The class of *quorum failure detectors*, that is denoted Σ, contains all the failure detectors that provide each process p_i with a quorum local variable, denoted $sigma_i$, that p_i can only read, and such that the set of local variables $\{sigma_i\}_{1 \leq n}$ collectively satisfy the intersection and liveness properties stated below.

Let us denote $sigma_i^{\tau}$ the output of Σ at process p_i at time τ (using the formalism introduced in the previous section we have $sigma_i^{\tau} = H(p_i, \tau)$).

- Intersection. $\forall i, j \in \{1, \ldots, n\}: \forall \tau, \tau' \in \mathbb{N}: sigma_i^{\tau} \cap sigma_j^{\tau'} \neq \emptyset$.
- Liveness. $\exists \tau \in \mathbb{N}: \forall \tau' \geq \tau: \forall i \in Correct(F): sigma_i^{\tau'} \subseteq Correct(F)$.

The intersection property states that any two quorum values do intersect, whatever the times at which they are output. As it has to be always satisfied, this property in called a *perpetual* property: it is an invariant provided by Σ. A Σ-based algorithm that aims to construct an atomic register can rely on this invariant to prevent partitioning (and consequently prevents occurrence of the bad scenario described in the proof of Theorem 2.8), and thereby guarantee the required atomicity (safety) property of a register.

The second property states that, after some finite time, the quorum values output at any non-faulty process contain only non-faulty processes. These processes are not required to be the same forever. They can change as long as the intersection property remains satisfied. This property is called an *eventual* property: it states that, after some finite time, "something" has to be forever satisfied. Its aim is to allow a Σ-based algorithm to guarantee that the read and write operations issued by the non-faulty processes always terminate.

Implementing Σ when $t < n/2$ There is a very simple algorithm that builds a failure detector of the class Σ in $\mathcal{AS}_{n,t}[t < n/2]$ (Figure 2.6). Each process p_i manages a queue (denoted $queue_i$) that contains the n process identities. The initial value is any permutation of these identities. Each process broadcasts forever (i.e., until it crashes if it ever crashes) ALIVE () messages to indicate it has not crashed. When a process p_i receives such a message from a process p_j, it moves j in $queue_i$ from its current position to the head of $queue_i$. Finally, it defines the current value of $sigma_i$ as the majority of the processes that are at the head of $queue_i$.

---

background task: repeat forever broadcast ALIVE () **end repeat.**

when ALIVE () **is received from** p_j ($j \in \{1, \ldots, n\}$:
    suppress j from $queue_i$; add j at the head of $queue_i$;
    $sigma_i \leftarrow$ the $\lceil \frac{n+1}{2} \rceil$ processes at the head of $queue_i$.

Figure 2.6: Building a failure detector of the class Σ in $\mathcal{AS}_{n,t}[t < n/2]$

The intersection property trivially follows from the fact that any two majorities do intersect. As far as the liveness property is concerned, let c be the number of correct processes. We have $c > n/2$, i.e., $c \geq \lceil \frac{n+1}{2} \rceil$. Let us observe that, after some time, only the c non-faulty processes send messages, and consequently, only these processes will appear in the first c positions of the queue of any non-faulty process. The liveness follows immediately from $c \geq \lceil \frac{n+1}{2} \rceil$.

Remark   As we have seen, it is possible to build an atomic register in $\mathcal{AS}_{n,t}[t < n/2]$, and as we are about to see, it is also possible to build an atomic register in $\mathcal{AS}_{n,t}[\Sigma]$. Hence, it is not counter-intuitive that a failure detector of the class Σ can be built in $\mathcal{AS}_{n,t}[t < n/2]$.

On another hand, thanks to Theorem 2.8, and the fact that Σ allows the construction of an atomic register, we can conclude that it is not possible to build a failure detector of the class Σ in $\mathcal{AS}_{n,t}[\emptyset]$. Such a construction requires additional assumptions that the underlying system has to satisfy.

The fundamental added value supplied by a failure detector   The fundamental added value, when considering Σ with respect to the assumption $t < n/2$, is that we *do know* which is the weakest information on failures the processes have to be provided with in order to build an atomic register. "$t < n/2$" is a model assumption, it is not the weakest information on failures that allows the construction of an atomic register.

2.4.4   A Σ-BASED ALGORITHM THAT BUILDS A 1W1R ATOMIC REGISTER

This section presents a Σ-based algorithm that builds a 1W1R atomic register R (i.e., it builds a register in the system model $\mathcal{AS}_{n,t}[\Sigma]$). The algorithm appears in Figure 2.7. Extending this algorithm to build an MWMR atomic register is straightforward. It can be easily done using an incremental construction similar to the one described in Section 2.2.

One writer, one reader, but the other processes have to participate   The writer is denoted p_w, while the reader is denoted p_r. It is important to notice that all the processes have to participate in the algorithm. If only p_w and p_r were used to implement the register R, the operation R.write() could block forever if p_r crashes while p_w does not (p_w waiting forever for a message from p_r). And similarly, R.read() could block forever if p_w crashes while p_r does not. This would violate the liveness property of the write (or the read) operation. Each process p_i has consequently to manage a local copy cur_val_i of R, as in the previous algorithms.

The algorithm   The code of the algorithm is very close to the previous ones. The local variables have the same meaning as in previous algorithms, and the basic structure is also the same. There are only two differences.

- The first is the use of a quorum failure detector of the class Σ instead of the majority of non-faulty processes assumption. As the value of the quorum failure detector module $sigma_i$ can change forever, its use is encapsulated in a **repeat** statement to express the fact that a process has to wait for messages until it has received a message from each process of a quorum output by Σ. The messages a process is waiting for can be received in any order, and at different time instants.

- The second difference is not related to the use of Σ, but to the fact that there is a single reader. As p_r is the only reader, when it issues a R.read() invocation, it is not necessary for it to execute the second phase of the R.read() operation (write phase), whose aim is to ensure that the value kept in the local memories of the other processes is at least as recent as the value it is about to return (this was required in Figure 2.3 and Figure 2.4 to obtain a 1WMR atomic register and a MWMR atomic register, respectively). As no other process is allowed to read, it is sufficient that p_r keeps a local copy of the value it is about to return, in order to prevent new/old inversions. So, the second phase of a read operation required to guarantee atomicity is now simply a local write (that actually depends on the sequence number of the returned value).

```
% This code is only for the single writer p_w %
operation R.write (v):
    w_sn_w ← w_sn_w + 1;
    broadcast WRITE (v, w_sn_w);
    repeat quorum_i ← sigma_i
        until ( ∀j ∈ quorum_i: ACK_WRITE (w_sn_w) received from p_j ) end repeat;
    return (ok).
```

```
% This code is only for the single reader p_r %
operation R.read ():
    req_sn_i ← req_sn_i + 1;
    broadcast READ_REQ (req_sn_i);
    repeat quorum_i ← sigma_i
        until ( ∀j ∈ quorum_i: ACK_READ_REQ (req_sn_i, −, −) received from p_j ) end repeat;
    let max_sn be the greatest sequence number (w_sn) received in
                    an ACK_READ_REQ (req_sn_i, w_sn, −) message;
    if (max_sn > w_sn_i) then
        cur_val_i ← v such that ACK_READ_REQ (req_sn_i, max_sn, v) has been received;
        w_sn_i ← max_sn
    end if;
    return (cur_val_i).
```

```
% The code snippets that follow are for every process p_i, i ∈ {1, . . . , n}.

when WRITE (val, w_sn) is received from p_w:
    if (w_sn ≥ w_sn_i) then cur_val_i ← val; w_sn_i ← w_sn end if;
    send ACK_WRITE (w_sn) to p_w.

when READ_REQ (r_sn) is received from p_r:
    send ACK_READ_REQ (r_sn, w_sn_i, cur_val_i) to p_r.
```

Figure 2.7: An algorithm that constructs an atomic 1W1R atomic register in $\mathcal{AS}_{n,t}[\Sigma]$

The proof is a simplified version of the proof of the algorithm described in Figure 2.4 where the majority of correct processes assumption is replaced by the properties of Σ. It is consequently left to the reader as an exercise.

2.5   Σ IS THE WEAKEST FAILURE DETECTOR CLASS TO BUILD AN ATOMIC REGISTER

2.5.1   WHAT DOES "WEAKEST FAILURE DETECTOR CLASS" MEAN?

Notion of extraction algorithm   The previous section has shown that it is possible to build an atomic register in $\mathcal{AS}_{n,t}[\Sigma]$. Said another way, Σ is sufficient to implement an atomic register in an asynchronous system prone to any number of process crashes. This section shows that, as soon as we rely on information on failures when we want to build a register, Σ is also necessary.

Let D be a failure detector class such that it is possible to build a register in $\mathcal{AS}_{n,t}[D]$. Intuitively, "necessary" means that the information on failures provided by D "includes" information on failures provided by Σ. More precisely, let D be any failure detector class such that it is possible to build an atomic register in $\mathcal{AS}_{n,t}[D]$, and A be any algorithm that builds a register in $\mathcal{AS}_{n,t}[D]$. Proving the necessity of Σ to build an atomic register consists in designing an algorithm that, given the previous D-based algorithm A as an input, builds a failure detector of the class Σ. We say that this algorithm *extracts* Σ from the D-based algorithm A (see Figure 2.8).

Figure 2.8: Extracting Σ from a register D-based algorithm A

Remark   It is important to notice that the notion of "weakest" used here is related to information on failures only. Nothing prevents us from designing an oracle that does not provide processes with hints on failures but with another type of information (e.g., about the synchrony of the system) that would allow the construction of an atomic register despite any number of process crashes. "Weakest" means that any oracle that (1) provides processes only with information on failures (i.e., any failure detector class), and (2) allows processes to build an atomic register, allows the construction of a failure detector of class Σ.

2.5.2   THE EXTRACTION ALGORITHM

Aim   As just indicated, the aim is to design an algorithm that emulates the output of Σ at each process p_i. This algorithm uses as a subroutine any algorithm A and failure detector D such that A is a n-process D-based algorithm that implements an atomic register in an n-process asynchronous message-passing system prone to any number of crashes.

An array of atomic registers   Let Q be a non-empty set of processes, and $REG_Q[1..n]$ an array of n atomic registers (initialized to $[\perp, \dots, \perp]$) such that each atomic register $REG_Q[x]$ is implemented by the n-process algorithm A executed only by $|Q|$ threads, each associated with a process of Q.

A simple register-based algorithm (task)   Let WR_Q be the following register-based algorithm (also called a task) where each process p_i such that $i \in Q$ executes the following algorithm (where $reg_i[1..n]$ is an array local to p_i):

    algorithm WR_Q:
      $REG_Q[i].\text{write}(\top)$; **for each** $x \in \{1, ..., n\}$ **do** $reg_i[x] \leftarrow REG_Q[x].\text{read}()$ **end for**.

The process p_i first writes the value $\top$ in its entry of the array REG_Q, and then reads asynchronously all its entries. The $REG_Q[i].\text{write}(\top)$ and $REG_Q[x].\text{read}()$ operations are provided to the processes by the previous algorithm A. (Let us notice that the value obtained by a read is irrelevant. As we will see, what is important is the fact that $REG_Q[x]$ has been written or not.) A corresponding run (history) of WR_Q is denoted E_Q. In that run, no process outside Q sends or receives messages related to the task WR_Q. When we consider the underlying failure detector-based algorithm A that implements the registers $REG_Q[1..n]$, as the processes that are not in Q do not participate in WR_Q, the messages sent by the processes of Q to these processes are never received, or are delayed for an arbitrarily long period. (Alternatively, we could say that, in WR_Q, the processes of Q "omit" sending messages to the processes that are not in Q.)

Let $\mathcal{C}$ denote the set of non-faulty processes in the run we consider. Let us observe that, as the underlying failure detector-based algorithm A that builds a register is correct, if the set Q contains all the correct processes (i.e., $\mathcal{C} \subseteq Q$), E_Q is such that every correct process terminates the task WR_Q. In the other cases, i.e., for the tasks WR_Q such that $\neg(\mathcal{C} \subseteq Q)$, E_Q is such that a process of Q either terminates WR_Q, or blocks forever, or crashes (this depends on the actual failure pattern, the outputs of the underlying failure detector D used by the algorithm A, and the code of A).

Running concurrently $2^n - 1$ *tasks*   The extraction algorithm considers the $2^n - 1$ distinct tasks WR_Q where Q is a non-empty set such that $Q \in 2^\Pi$. To that end, each process p_i manages 2^{n-1} threads, one for each subset Q such that $i \in Q$. Let us notice that the crash of a process p_i entails the crash of all its threads.

The extraction algorithm   The algorithm that extracts Σ is described in Figure 2.9. Let us recall that its aim is to provide each process p_i with a local variable $sigma_i$ such that the $(sigma_x)_{1 \leq x \leq n}$ variables satisfy the intersection and liveness properties defined in Section 2.4.3.

To that end, each process p_i manages two local variables: a set of sets of process identities, denoted $quorum\_sets_i$, and a queue denoted $queue_i$. The aim of $quorum\_sets_i$ is to contain all the sets Q such that p_i has terminated WR_Q (task $T1$), while $queue_i$ is managed in such a way that eventually any correct process appears in it before any faulty process (tasks $T2$ and $T3$).

The idea is to select an element of $quorum\_sets_i$ as the current output of $sigma_i$. As we will see in the proof, given any pair of processes p_i and p_j, any quorum in $quorum\_sets_i$ has a non-empty intersection with any quorum in $quorum\_sets_j$, thereby supplying the required intersection property.

The main issue is to ensure the liveness property of $sigma_i$ (eventually $sigma_i$ has to contain only correct processes) while preserving the intersection property. This is realized with the help of the local variable $queue_i$ as follows: the current output of $sigma_i$ is the set (quorum) of $quorum\_sets_i$ that appears as being the "first" in $queue_i$. The formal definition of "first element of $quorum\_sets_i$ with respect to $queue_i$" is stated in the task $T4$. To make it easy to understand, let us consider the following example. Let $quorum\_sets_i = \{\{3, 4, 9\}, \{2, 3, 8\}, \{1, 2, 4, 7\}\}$, and $queue_i = < 4, 8, 3, 2, 7, 5, 9, 1, \cdots >$. The set $S = \{2, 3, 8\}$ is the first set of $quorum\_sets_i$ with respect to $queue_i$ because each of the other sets $\{3, 4, 9\}$ and $\{1, 2, 4, 7\}$ includes an element (e.g., 9 and 7, respectively) that appears in $queue_i$ after the elements of S. (In case several sets are "first", any of them can be selected). The notion of "first quorum in $queue_i$" is used to ensure that Σ_i eventually includes only correct processes.

Init: $quorum\_sets_i \leftarrow \{\{1 \ldots, n\}\}$; $queue_i \leftarrow < 1, \ldots, n >$;
    for each $Q \in (2^\Pi \setminus \{\emptyset, \{1, \ldots, n\}\})$ **do**
      if $(i \in Q)$ **then** launch a thread associated with the task WR_Q **end if end for**.
    % Each process p_i participates concurrently in all the tasks WR_Q such that $i \in Q$ %

Task $T1$: **when** p_i terminates task WR_Q: $quorum\_sets_i \leftarrow quorum\_sets_i \cup \{Q\}$.

Task $T2$: **repeat periodically** broadcast ALIVE(i) **end_repeat**.

Task $T3$: **when** ALIVE (j) **is received**: suppress j from $queue_i$; enqueue j at the head of $queue_i$.

Task $T4$: **when** p_i reads $sigma_i$:
    let $m = \min_{Q \in quorum\_sets_i} (\max_{x \in Q} (rank[x]))$ where $rank[x]$ denotes the rank of x in $queue_i$;
    return (a set Q such that $\max_{x \in Q} (rank[x]) = m$).

Figure 2.9: Extracting Σ from a failure detector-based algorithm A that implements a register (code for p_i)

Remark   Initially $quorum\_sets_i$ contains the set $\{1, \ldots, n\}$. As no set of processes is ever withdrawn from $quorum\_sets_i$ (task $T1$), $quorum\_sets_i$ is never empty. Moreover, it is not necessary to launch the task $WR_{\{1,\ldots,n\}}$ in which all processes participate. This is because, as the underlying failure detector-based algorithm A (that implements a register) is correct, it follows that each correct process decides in task $WR_{\{1,\ldots,n\}}$. This case is directly taken into account in the initialization of $quorum\_sets_i$ (thereby saving the execution of the task $WR_{\{1,\ldots,n\}}$).

2.5.3   PROOF OF CORRECTNESS

Theorem 2.9   *Let A be any failure detector-based algorithm that implements an atomic register in an asynchronous message-passing system prone to any number of process crashes. Given A, the algorithm described in Figure 2.9 is a bounded construction of a failure detector of the class Σ.*

Let us recall that a *bounded* construction is an algorithm whose all variables and messages have a bounded size.

Proof Proof of the intersection property. The proof is by contradiction. Let us first observe that the set $sigma_i$ returned to a process p_i is a set of $quorum\_set_i$ (that contains the set $\{1, \ldots, n\}$ -initial value- plus all the sets Q such that p_i has terminated WR_Q). Let us assume that there are two sets Q_1 and Q_2 such that (1) $Q_1, Q_2 \in \bigcup_{1 \leq j \leq n} (quorum\_set_j)$, and (2) $Q_1 \cap Q_2 = \emptyset$. The first item means that Q_1 and Q_2 can be returned to some processes as their local value for Σ.

Let p_i be a process that terminates WR_{Q_1} and p_j a process that terminates WR_{Q_2} (due to the "contradiction" assumption, such processes do exist). Using the fact that the message-passing system is asynchronous, let us construct the runs E_{Q_1} and E_{Q_2} associated with WR_{Q_1} and WR_{Q_2} as follows. If any, every message sent by any process in Q_1 to any process in Q_2 (when these processes execute A to implement a register of the array REG_{Q_1}) is delayed until p_i has added Q_1 to $quorum\_set_i$ and p_j has added Q_2 to $quorum\_set_j$. Let us delay similarly messages sent by processes in Q_2 to processes in Q_1 when they execute A for each register of the array REG_{Q_2}.

Let us observe that, in concurrent runs E_{Q_1} and E_{Q_2}, algorithm A, which is executed only by (1) processes of Q_1 in E_{Q_1} to build registers $REG_{Q_1}[1..n]$, and (2) processes of Q_2 in E_{Q_2} to build registers $REG_{Q_2}[1..n]$, is fed with the same outputs of the underlying failure detector D. Due to the fact that (if any) messages from Q_1 to Q_2 and from Q_2 to Q_1 are delayed, we have that p_i reads $\bot$ from $REG_{Q_1}[j]$ in E_{Q_1}, and p_j reads $\bot$ from $REG_{Q_2}[i]$ in E_{Q_2}.

Let us construct a run $E_{Q_{12}}$, where $Q_{12} = Q_1 \cup Q_2$, that is a simple merge of E_{Q_1} and E_{Q_2} defined as follows. In this run, algorithm A (that involves only the processes in Q_{12} and implements the array of registers $REG_{Q_{12}}[1..n]$) is fed with the same failure detector outputs as the ones supplied to the concurrent runs E_{Q_1} and E_{Q_2}. Moreover, messages from Q_1 to Q_2 and from Q_2 to Q_1 are delayed as in E_{Q_1} and E_{Q_2}. So, p_i (resp., p_j) receives the same messages and the same outputs from the underlying failure detector in $E_{Q_{12}}$ and E_{Q_1} (resp., E_{Q_2}).

- On the one hand, we have the following. As process p_i receives the same messages and the same failure detector outputs in $E_{Q_{12}}$ as in E_{Q_1}, arrays $REG_{Q_1}[1..n]$ and $REG_{Q_{12}}[1..n]$ contain the same values. Consequently, p_i reads $\bot$ from $REG_{Q_{12}}[j]$. Similarly, p_j reads $\bot$ from $REG_{Q_{12}}[i]$.

- On the other hand, we have the following. In $E_{Q_{12}}$, process p_i writes $\top$ into $REG_{Q_{12}}[i]$ and the process p_j writes $\top$ into $REG_{Q_{12}}[j]$. Moreover, one of these operations terminates before the other. Without loss of generality, let us assume that the write by p_i terminates before the write by p_j. Consequently, p_j reads $REG_{Q_{12}}[i]$ after it has been written. Due to the atomicity of that register, it follows that p_j obtains the value $\top$ when it reads $REG_{Q_{12}}[i]$.

The second item contradicts the first one. It follows that the initial assumption (namely, the existence of a failure detector-based algorithm A that builds a register, $Q_1, Q_2 \in \bigcup_{1 \leq j \leq n}(quorum\_set_j)$ and $Q_1 \cap Q_2 = \emptyset$) is false, from which we conclude that at least one of the assertions $Q_1, Q_2 \in \bigcup_{1 \leq j \leq n}(quorum\_set_j)$ and $Q_1 \cap Q_2 = \emptyset$ is false, which completes the proof of the intersection property (Corollary 2.10 -stated below- is an immediate consequence of that property).

Proof of the liveness property. As far as the liveness property is concerned, let us consider the task $WR_{\mathcal{C}}$ (recall that $\mathcal{C}$ is the set of correct processes). As the underlying failure detector-based algorithm A that implements the registers $REG_{\mathcal{C}}[1..n]$ is correct by assumption, each correct process p_i terminates its $REG_{\mathcal{C}}[i].write(\top)$ and $REG_{\mathcal{C}}[x].read()$ operations in $E_{\mathcal{C}}$. Consequently, in the extraction algorithm, the variable $quorum\_set_i$ of each correct process p_i eventually contains the set $\mathcal{C}$.

Moreover, after some finite time, each correct process p_i receives ALIVE(j) messages only from correct processes. This means that, at each correct process p_i, every correct process eventually precedes every faulty process in $queue_i$. Due to the definition of "first set of $quorum\_set_i$ with respect to $queue_i$" stated in task $T4$, it follows that, from the time at which $\mathcal{C}$ has been added to $quorum\_set_i$, the quorum Q selected by the task $T4$ is always such that $Q \subseteq \mathcal{C}$, which proves the liveness property of $sigma_i$.

The construction is bounded. A simple examination of the extraction algorithm shows that (1) both the variables $queue_i$ and $quorum\_sets_i$ are bounded, and (2) messages carry bounded values, from which it follows that the construction is bounded.
$\square_{Theorem\ 2.9}$

An additional property   The proof of intersection property shows that it is not possible to have two sets Q_1 and Q_2 such that $Q_1 \cap Q_2 = \emptyset$ and at least one process of Q_1 terminates WR_{Q_1} and at least one process of Q_2 terminates WR_{Q_2}. Hence the following corollary.

Property 2.10   Let two sets Q_1 and Q_2 be such that $Q_1 \cap Q_2 = \emptyset$. Then, no process of Q_1 terminates WR_{Q_1} or no process of Q_2 terminates WR_{Q_2} (or both).

2.6   BIBLIOGRAPHIC NOTES

- As indicated in the previous chapter, the notions of regular and atomic registers were introduced by Lamport [110].
- The construction of an atomic register on top of an asynchronous message-passing system prone to process crashes has first been investigated by Attiya, Bar-Noy and Dolev in [15]. Other constructions are described in [14, 16, 117].
- Algorithms that build an atomic register in dynamic systems (i.e., systems where processes can enter and leave) are described in [2, 9, 40, 53, 74, 118]. The case of a regular register is addressed in [17, 153]. The case where registers are network attached disks is analyzed in [8].
- The notion of failure detectors was introduced by Chandra and Toueg in [34].

  Weakest failure detectors to solve several fundamental problems in distributed computing (such as consensus, non-blocking atomic commitment, quittable consensus) are presented in [48].

  It is shown in [103] that any non-trivial distributed computing problem has a weakest failure detector.

  Pedagogic presentations of this concept can be found in [85, 127, 148].
- The notion of quorum has been introduced by Gifford in [79] in the context of duplicated data management. General methods to define quorums can be found in [124, 142]. Quorums

suited to Byzantine failures (that are more severe than crash failures) have been studied by Malkhi and Reiter [120].

The class Σ of quorum failure detectors was introduced by Delporte-Gallet, Fauconnier and Guerraoui [47].

• The first proof that shows that Σ is the weakest class of failure detectors to build a register despite asynchrony and any number of process crashes was given by Delporte-Gallet, Fauconnier and Guerraoui [47, 48].

The proof presented here is due to Bonnet and Raynal [30]. An extension of the class Σ, where the intersection property is no longer required to be perpetual, is presented in [71].

A general method to extract quorum failure detectors is presented in [24].

• Lots of advanced algorithms that implement an atomic register in asynchronous message-passing systems prone to crash failures are presented in the literature. Those algorithms investigate mainly lower bounds and efficiency of the read and write operations. Examples of such distributed algorithms can be found in [40, 55, 58, 91].

PART II

The Uniform Reliable Broadcast Abstraction

CHAPTER 3

The Uniform Reliable Broadcast Abstraction

This chapter focuses on the *uniform reliable broadcast* (URB) abstraction and its implementation in an asynchronous message-passing system prone to process crashes. Such a communication abstraction is central in the design and the implementation of fault-tolerant distributed systems, as many non-trivial fault-tolerant distributed applications require communication with provable guarantees on message deliveries.

After having defined the URB abstraction, the chapter presents a construction of it in an asynchronous message passing system prone to process crashes but with reliable channels (i.e., in the system model $\mathcal{AS}_{n,t}[\emptyset]$). The chapter considers then two properties (related to the quality of service) that can be added to URB without requiring to enrich the system model with additional assumptions. These properties are on the message delivery order and are "first in first out" (FIFO) message delivery, and "causal order" (CO) message delivery.

3.1 THE UNIFORM RELIABLE BROADCAST PROBLEM

3.1.1 FROM BEST EFFORT TO GUARANTEED RELIABILITY

The broadcast operation "broadcast (m)", introduced in the previous chapter, was a simple abbreviation used to replace the statement

for each $j \in \{1, \ldots, n\}$ **do** send m to p_j **end for**.

In the system model $\mathcal{AS}_{n,t}[\emptyset]$, this operation has a *best effort* semantics in the following sense. If the sender p_i is correct, a copy of the message m is sent to every process, and as the channels are reliable, every process (that has not crashed) receives a copy of the message. As the channels are asynchronous, these copies can be received at distinct independent time instants. Differently, if the sender crashes while executing broadcast m, an arbitrary subset of the processes receives the message m. Hence, in presence of failures, the specification of " broadcast m" provides no indication on which processes will receive the message m and which will not receive it. The aim of this section is to introduce a broadcast operation that provides the processes with stronger message delivery guarantees.

3.1.2   UNIFORM RELIABLE BROADCAST (URB)

URB provides the processes with two communication operations which are denoted "URB_broadcast (m)" and "URB_deliver ()". The first allows a process p_i to send a message m to all the processes (including the sender), while the second one allows a process to deliver a message that has been broadcast. In order to prevent ambiguities, when a process invokes "URB_broadcast m" we say that it "URB-broadcasts the message m", and when it returns from "URB_deliver ()," we say that it "URB-delivers a message" (sometimes, we also suppress the prefix "URB", when clear from the context). Differently, the primitives "send() to" and "receive()" are used for the messages sent and received at the underlying network level.

The specification of these operations assumes that every message that is broadcast is unique. This is easy to implement by associating a unique identity with each message m. Such an identity is made up of a pair $(m.sender, m.seq\_nb)$ where $m.sender$ is the identity of the sender process, and $m.seq\_nb$ is a sequence number locally generated by $p_{m.sender}$. The sequence numbers associated with the messages broadcast by a process are the natural integers 1, 2, etc.

Definition   The specification consists of the three following properties (this means that, to be correct, any implementation of "URB_broadcast (m)" and "URB_deliver ()" has to satisfy these properties):

- Validity. If a process URB-delivers a message m, then m has been previously URB-broadcast (by $p_{m.sender}$).
- Integrity. A process URB-delivers a message m at most once.
- Termination. (1) If a non-faulty process URB-broadcasts a message m, or (2) if a process URB-delivers a message m, then each non-faulty process URB-delivers the message m.

The validity property relates an output (here a message that is delivered) with an input (a message that has been broadcast). Said differently, there is no creation or alteration of messages. The integrity property states that there is no message duplication. Taken together, these two properties define the safety property of the URB problem. Let us observe that they are satisfied even if no message is ever delivered, whatever the messages that have been sent. So, for the specification to be complete, a liveness property is needed, namely, not all the messages can be lost. This is the aim of the termination property: if the process that URB-broadcasts a message is non-faulty, or if at least one process (be it faulty or non-faulty, this is why the abstraction is called *uniform*) URB-delivers a message, then that message has to be URB-delivered (at least) by the non-faulty processes. (Hence, this termination property belongs to the family of "all or none/nothing" properties.)

Remark   It is easy to see from the previous specification that, during each execution, (1) the non-faulty processes deliver the same set of messages, (2) set includes all messages broadcast by non-faulty processes, and (3) each faulty process delivers a subset of the messages delivered by non-faulty processes. (Let us observe that two distinct faulty processes may deliver different subsets of messages.)

It is important to see that a message URB-broadcast by a faulty process might be or not delivered. It is not possible to place a requirement on such a message as the sender can crash before the message has been sent to a non-faulty process. The delivery of such messages depends on the execution.

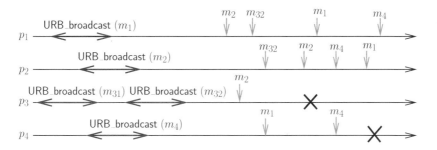

Figure 3.1: An example of the uniform reliable broadcast delivery guarantees

A simple example appears in Figure 3.1. There are four processes that URB-broadcast 5 messages. Processes p_1 and p_2 are non-faulty while p_3 and p_4 crash (crosses in the figure). The message deliveries are indicated with vertical top to bottom arrows on the process axes. Both p_1 and p_2 deliver the same set M of messages, while each faulty process delivers a subset of M. Moreover, not only the message m_{31}, that is sent by a faulty process, is never delivered, but the faulty process p_3 delivers none of the messages m_{31} and m_{32} that it has broadcast. More, the message m_{32} that has been sent by p_3 after m_{31} is delivered by the non-faulty processes, while m_{31} is not. This is due to the net effect of asynchrony and process crashes. It is easy to see that the message deliveries in Figure 3.1 respect the specification of the uniform reliable broadcast.

URB is a paradigm   The uniform reliable broadcast problem is a paradigm that captures a family of distributed coordination problems. As an example, "URB_broadcast (m)" and " URB_deliver ()" can be given the meaning "this is an order" and "I execute it", respectively. It follows that non-faulty processes will execute the same set of actions, this set including all the orders issued by the non-faulty processes, plus a subset of orders issued by faulty processes.

Let us notice that URB is a *one-shot* problem. The specification applies to each message that is URB-broadcast separately from the other messages that are URB-broadcast.

Reliable broadcast   The *reliable broadcast* communication abstraction is a weakened form of URB. It is defined by the same validity and integrity properties (no message loss, corruption or duplication) and the following weaker termination property:

- Termination. If a non-faulty process (1) URB-broadcasts a message m, or (2) URB-delivers a message m, then each non-faulty process URB-delivers the message m.

This means that a process that is faulty can deliver messages not delivered by the non-faulty processes. This termination property is the URB termination property without its *uniformity* requirement.

Let us observe that the termination property of the reliable broadcast abstraction does not state that the messages delivered by a faulty process have to be a subset of the messages delivered by the non-faulty processes. Hence, reliable broadcast is much less constraining (and consequently less powerful) than uniform reliable broadcast.

In the following, we do not consider this simple reliable broadcast abstraction because it is not useful for practical applications. As it is not known in advance whether a process will crash or not, it is sensible to require a process to behave as if it was non-faulty until it possibly crashes.

3.1.3   BUILDING URB IN $\mathcal{AS}_{n,t}[\emptyset]$

There is a very simple construction of the URB abstraction in the system model $\mathcal{AS}_{n,t}[\emptyset]$. This is due to the fact that the point-to-point channels are reliable. The structure of the construction is given in Figure 3.2.

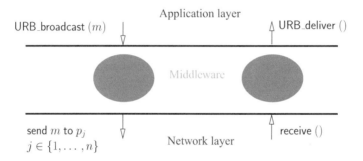

Figure 3.2: URB: architecture view

A simple construction   The algorithms implementing URB_broadcast (m) and URB_deliver () are described in Figure 3.3. To broadcast a message m, a process p_i sends m to itself. When a process p_i receives a message, it discards it if it has already received a copy. Thanks to the unique identity $(m.sender, m.seq\_nb)$ carried by each message m, it is easy for p_i to check if m has already been received. If it is the first time it receives m, p_i forwards it to the other processes (but itself and the message sender), and only then delivers m to itself (at the application layer).

It is important to notice that the statement associated with the reception of MSG (m) is not required to be atomic. A process p_i can interleave the execution of several such statements.

Notation   Let us notice that a tag MSG is added to each message (this tag will be used in the next sections). A message m is called an *application message*, while a message MSG (m) is called a *protocol message*.

Theorem 3.1   *The algorithm described in Figure 3.3 constructs a uniform reliable broadcast communication abstraction in $\mathcal{AS}_{n,t}[\emptyset]$.*

```
operation URB_broadcast (m):
    send MSG(m) to p_i.

when MSG (m) is received from p_k:
    if (first reception of m) then
        for each j ∈ {1, . . . , n} \ {i, k} do send MSG (m) to p_j end for;
        URB_deliver (m) % deliver m to the upper layer application %
    end if.
```

Figure 3.3: Uniform reliable broadcast in $\mathcal{AS}_{n,t}[\emptyset]$ (code for p_i)

Proof The proof of the validity property follows directly from the text of the algorithm that forwards only messages that have been received. The proof of the integrity property follows directly from the fact that a message m is delivered only when it is received for the first time.

The termination property is a direct consequence of the "forward first and then deliver" strategy. Let us first consider a message m broadcast by a non-faulty process p_i. As p_i is non-faulty, it forwards the protocol message MSG (m) to every other process and delivers it to itself. As channels are reliable, each process will eventually receive a copy of MSG (m) and URB-delivers m (the first time it receives MSG (m)).

Let us now consider the case of a (faulty or non-faulty) process p_j that delivers a message m. Before delivering m, p_j has forwarded MSG (m) to all, and the same reasoning as before applies, which completes the proof of the termination property. $\square_{Theorem}$ 3.1

3.2   IMPROVING THE QUALITY OF SERVICE

Uniform reliable broadcast provides guarantees on which messages are delivered to processes. As we have seen, non-faulty processes deliver the same set S of messages, and each faulty process p_i delivers a subset $S_i \subseteq S$.

FIFO and CO message delivery   Some applications are easier to design when processes are provided with stronger guarantees on message delivery. These guarantees are on the order in which messages are delivered to the upper layer application. We consider here two types of such guarantees: the *First In, First Out* (FIFO) property, and the *Causal Order* (CO) property. (A third delivery property, called *Total Order* (TO) will be studied in another chapter.)

A modular view of the FIFO and CO uniform reliable constructions presented in this section is given in Figure 3.4. Each arrow corresponds to a construction. It is important to see that these constructions can be built in any system where the URB abstraction can be built. When compared to URB, neither FIFO-URB nor CO-URB requires additional computability-related assumptions (such as restrictions on the model on top of which URB is built or failure detector-like additional objects).

Figure 3.4: From URB to CO-URB in $\mathcal{AS}_{n,t}[\emptyset]$

One-shot vs multi-shot problems   As we have seen, URB is a one-shot problem. It considers each message separately from the other messages. Differently, the FIFO-URB problem and the CO-URB problem are not one-shot problems. This is because (as we are about to see) their specifications involve all the messages that are broadcast.

3.2.1 "FIRST IN, FIRST OUT" (FIFO) MESSAGE DELIVERY

Definition   The FIFO-URB abstraction is made up of two operations denoted "FIFO_broadcast m" and "FIFO_deliver ()". It is the URB abstraction (defined by the validity, integrity and termination properties stated in Section 3.1.2) enriched with the following additional property.

- FIFO message delivery. If a process FIFO-broadcasts a message m and then FIFO-broadcasts a message m', then no process FIFO-delivers m' unless it has FIFO-delivered m before.

This property states that the messages broadcast by each source (taken separately) are delivered according to their sending order. There is no delivery constraint placed on messages broadcast by different sources. It is important to notice that the FIFO property prevents a faulty process from delivering m' while never delivering m. Given any process p_i, a faulty process delivers a prefix of the messages broadcast by p_i.

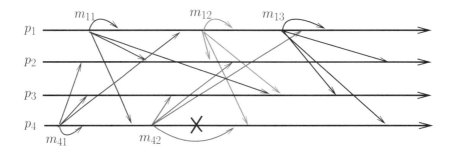

Figure 3.5: An example of FIFO message delivery

An example   A simple example is depicted in Figure 3.5 where the transfer of each message is explicitly indicated. Process p_1 FIFO-broadcasts m_{11}, then m_{12}, and finally m_{13}. Process p_4 FIFO-broadcasts m_{41} and then m_{42}. The FIFO message delivery property states that m_{11} has to be delivered before m_{12}, which in turn has to be delivered before m_{13}. Similarly, with respect to the source p_4, no process is allowed to deliver m_{42} before m_{41}. In this example, p_4 crashes before delivering its own message m_{42}.

As the FIFO specification imposes no constraint on the messages broadcast by distinct processes, we can easily see that the delivery of the messages from p_1 and the ones from p_4 can be interleaved differently at distinct receivers.

A simple construction   The construction assumes that the underlying communication layer provides processes with a uniform reliable broadcast abstraction as depicted in Figure 3.6.

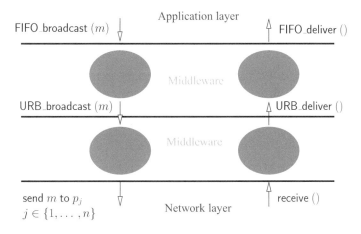

Figure 3.6: FIFO uniform reliable broadcast: architecture view

An easy way to ensure the FIFO message delivery property consists in associating an appropriate predicate with message delivery. While the predicate remains false, the message remains in the input buffer of the corresponding process, and is delivered as soon as the predicate becomes true. The construction for FIFO URB is described in Figure 3.7.

Each process p_i manages two local variables. The set msg_set_i (initialized to $\emptyset$) is used to keep the messages that have been URB-delivered but not yet FIFO-delivered by p_i. The array $next_i[1..n]$ (initialized to $[1, \ldots, 1]$) is such that $next_i[j]$ denotes the sequence number of the next message that p_i will FIFO-deliver from p_j (the sequence number of the first message broadcast by a process p_i is 1, the sequence number of the second message is 2, etc.).

The operation "FIFO_broadcast (m)" consists of a simple invocation of "URB_broadcast (m)". When a message m is URB-delivered by the underlying communication layer, p_i deposits it in the set msg_set_i if m arrives too early with respect to its FIFO-delivery order. Otherwise, p_i FIFO-delivers

```
operation FIFO_broadcast (m):
    m.sender ← i; m.seq_nb ← p_i's next seq. number (starting from 1);
    URB_broadcast MSG(m).

when MSG(m) is URB-delivered: % m carries its identity (m.sender, m.seq_nb) %
    let j = m.sender;
    if (next_i[j] = m.seq_nb)
      then FIFO_deliver (m);
            next_i[j] ← next_i[j] + 1;
            while ( ∃m' ∈ msg_set_i : (m'.sender = j) ∧ (next_i[j] = m'.seq_nb) )
                do FIFO_deliver (m');
                    next_i[j] ← next_i[j] + 1;
                    msg_set_i ← msg_set_i \ {m'}
            end while
      else  msg_set_i ← msg_set_i ∪ {m}
    end if.
```

Figure 3.7: FIFO message delivery in $\mathcal{AS}_{n,t}[\emptyset]$ (code for p_i)

m. After having delivered m, p_i FIFO-delivers the messages from the same sender (if any) whose sequence numbers agree with the delivery order. The processing associated with the URB-delivery of a message m is assumed to be atomic, i.e., a process p_i executes one URB-delivery code at a time.

Theorem 3.2   *The algorithm described in Figure 3.7 constructs a FIFO uniform reliable broadcast communication abstraction in any system in which URB can be built.*

Proof The proof is an immediate consequence of the properties of the underlying URB abstraction (Theorem 3.1) and the use of sequence numbers. $\square_{Theorem\ 3.2}$

3.2.2   "CAUSAL ORDER" (CO) MESSAGE DELIVERY

A partial order on messages   Let M be the set of messages that are URB-broadcast during an execution, and $\widehat{M} = (M, \rightarrow_M)$ be the relation where $\rightarrow_M$ is defined on M as follows. Given $m, m' \in M$, $m \rightarrow_M m'$ (and we say that "m causally precedes m'"):

- m and m' have been broadcast by the same process and m has been broadcast before m', or
- m has been delivered by a process p_i before p_i broadcasts m', or
- There is message $m'' \in M$ such that $m \rightarrow_M m''$ and $m'' \rightarrow_M m'$.

Let us notice that, as a message cannot be delivered before being broadcast, $\widehat{M}$ is a partial order.

Causal message delivery   The causal order URB abstraction (CO) is made up of two operations denoted "CO_broadcast m" and "CO_deliver ()". It is the URB abstraction (defined by the validity, integrity and termination properties stated in Section 3.1.2) enriched with the following additional property.

- CO message delivery. If $m \rightarrow_M m'$, then no process CO-delivers m' unless it has previously CO-delivered m.

The FIFO delivery order is a restriction of the causal delivery order on a process basis. This means that the causal delivery order generalizes the FIFO delivery order to all the messages whose broadcasts are related by the "message happened before" relation ($\rightarrow_M$), whatever their senders are.

An example An example of CO message delivery is depicted in Figure 3.8. We have $m_{11} \rightarrow_M m_{42}$ and $m_{41} \rightarrow_M m_{42}$. As the messages m_{11} and m_{41} are not "$\rightarrow_M$"-related, it follows that every process can deliver them in any order. Differently, m_{42} has to be delivered at any process after m_{41} (FIFO order is included in CO order), and m_{42} has to be delivered at any process after m_{11} (because p_4 delivers m_{11} before broadcasting m_{42}). So, despite the fact that p_1 and p_2 deliver m_{11} and m_{41} in different order, these messages delivery orders are correct. The message delivery order is also correct at p_3 if m_{42} is delivered according to the plain arrow, and it is not correct if m_{42} is delivered according to the dotted arrow (i.e., before m_{11}).

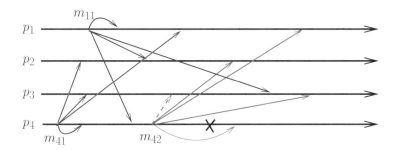

Figure 3.8: An example of CO message delivery

The local order property The definition of this property is motivated by Theorem 3.3 that follows, which gives a characterization of causal order, namely, CO is FIFO + local order.

- Local order. If a process delivers a message m before broadcasting a message m', no process delivers m' unless it has previously delivered m.

Theorem 3.3 *Causal order is equivalent to the combination of FIFO order and local order.*

Proof It follows from its very definition that the causal order property implies the FIFO property and the local order property. Let us show the other direction.

Assuming the FIFO order property and the local order property are satisfied, let m and m' be two messages such that $m \rightarrow_M m'$, and p be a process that delivers m'. The proof consists in showing that p delivers m before m'.

As $m \to_M m'$, there is a finite sequence of messages $m = m_1, m_2, \ldots, m_{k-1}, m_k = m'$, with $k \geq 2$, that have been broadcast by the processes $q_1, q_2, \ldots, q_k$, respectively, and are such that, $\forall x : 1 \leq x < k$, we have $m_x \to_M m_{x+1}$ due to the first or the second item of the CO delivery definition (i.e., not taking into account the third item on transitivity). For any x such that $1 \leq x < k$, we have one of the following cases.

- If $q_x = q_{x+1}$: m_x and m_{x+1} are broadcast by the same process. It follows from the FIFO order property that p delivers m_x before m_{x+1}.
- If $q_x \neq q_{x+1}$: m_x and m_{x+1} are broadcast by different processes, and q_{x+1} delivers m_x before broadcasting m_{x+1}. It follows from the local order property that p delivers m_x before m_{x+1}.

It follows that when p delivers $m_k = m'$, it has previously delivered m_{k-1}. Similarly, when it delivers m_{k-1}, it has previously delivered m_{k-2}, etc. until $m_1 = m$. It follows that if p delivers m', it has previously delivered m.
$\square_{Theorem\ 3.3}$

Remark   Theorem 3.3 is important, from a proof modularity point of view, when one has to prove that an algorithm satisfies CO delivery property. Namely, one has only to show that the algorithm satisfies both the FIFO property and the local order property. It then follows from Theorem 3.3 that the algorithm satisfies to CO delivery property. We will proceed that way in the proof of Theorem 3.4. (A direct proof of the CO delivery property would require a long and tedious induction on the length of "message causality chains" defined by the relation "$\to_M$".)

3.2.3   FROM FIFO-BROADCAST TO CO-BROADCAST

A simple CO-broadcast construction from URB-broadcast   Before presenting a CO-broadcast construction based on the FIFO-broadcast abstraction, this paragraph presents a very simple (but very inefficient) construction of the CO broadcast abstraction on top of the URB abstraction (Figure 3.9). This construction consists in associating with every message all the messages that causally precede it.

To that end, each process p_i manages a local variable, denoted $causal\_pred_i$, that contains the sequence of all the messages m' such that $m' \to_M m$, where m is the next message that p_i will CO-broadcast. The variable $causal\_pred_i$ is initialized to the empty sequence (denoted ϵ). The operator $\oplus$ denotes the concatenation of a message at the end of $causal\_pred_i$.

When it CO-broadcasts m, p_i URB-broadcasts the protocol message MSG ($causal\_pred_i \oplus m$), and then updates $causal\_pred_i$ to $causal\_pred_i \oplus m$ as, from now on, the application message m belongs to the causal past of the next application messages that p_i will broadcast.

When it URB-delivers MSG ($\langle m_1, \ldots, m_\ell \rangle$), p_i considers, one after the other, each application message m_x of the received sequence. If it has already CO-delivered m_x, it discards it. Otherwise, it CO-delivers it and adds it at the end of $causal\_pred_i$.

Both the code associated with the URB-delivery of a message and the code associated with the CO-broadcast operation are assumed to be executed atomically. This construction is highly inefficient as the size of protocol messages increases forever.

```
operation CO_broadcast (m):
    URB_broadcast MSG (causal_pred_i ⊕ m);
    causal_pred_i ← causal_pred_i ⊕ m.

when MSG (⟨m_1, . . . , m_ℓ⟩) is URB-delivered:
    for x from 1 to ℓ do
        if (m_x not yet CO-delivered) then
            CO_deliver (m_x);
            causal_pred_i ← causal_pred_i ⊕ m_x
        end if
    end for.
```

Figure 3.9: A simple URB-based CO-broadcast construction in $\mathcal{AS}_{n,t}[\emptyset]$ (code for p_i)

From FIFO-broadcast to CO-broadcast: the construction A FIFO broadcast-based construction of the CO broadcast abstraction is described in Figure 3.11. Its underlying principle is as follows. It uses the FIFO property provided by the underlying FIFO broadcast in order to replace the sequence $causal\_past_i$ used in Figure 3.9 by a suffix of it, denoted $im\_causal\_past_i$. More precisely, while $causal\_past_i$ increases without bound, the FIFO delivery property allows a resetting of $causal\_past_i$ to the empty sequence each time p_i CO-broadcast a new message. This sequence is consequently renamed $im\_causal\_past_i$ and contains only messages that p_i has CO-delivered since its previous CO-broadcast.

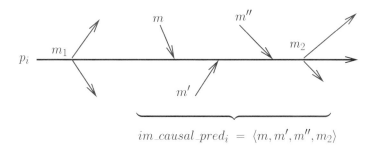

Figure 3.10: How is built the sequence of messages $im\_causal\_pred_i$

As an example illustrating this idea, let us consider Figure 3.10 where the process p_i CO-broadcasts two messages, first m_1 and then m_2. Between these two broadcasts, p_i has CO-delivered the messages m, m' and m'', in that order. Hence, when p_i CO-broadcasts m_2, it actually FIFO-broadcasts the sequence $\langle m, m', m'', m_2 \rangle$, thereby indicating that, if not yet CO-delivered, messages m, m' and m'' have to be CO-delivered before m_2. Hence, we have $im\_causal\_pred_i = \langle m, m', m'' \rangle$ when p_i is about to CO-broadcast m_2.

As before, both the code associated with the FIFO-delivery of a message and the code associated with the CO-broadcast operation are assumed to be executed atomically.

```
operation CO_broadcast (m):
    FIFO_broadcast MSG (im_causal_pred_i ⊕ m);
    im_causal_pred_i ← ε.

when MSG (⟨m_1, ..., m_ℓ⟩) is FIFO-delivered:
    for x from 1 to ℓ do
        if (m_x not yet CO-delivered) then
            CO_deliver (m_x);
            im_causal_pred_i ← im_causal_pred_i ⊕ m_x
        end if
    end for.
```

Figure 3.11: From FIFO URB to CO message delivery in $\mathcal{AS}_{n,t}[\emptyset]$ (code for p_i)

Let us remember that, due to Theorem 3.2, it is possible to build a FIFO reliable broadcast abstraction in any system in which URB can be built. So, the construction of the CO reliable broadcast abstraction on top of the URB abstraction does not require additional assumptions.

Remark   The processing associated with a FIFO-delivery is "fast" in the sense that, when a sequence of messages is FIFO-delivered, each message contained in that sequence is CO-delivered (if not yet done). The price that has to be paid to obtain this delivery efficiency property is that the FIFO communication abstraction has to handle "big" protocol messages that are sequences of application messages. Moreover, the underlying FIFO broadcast abstraction cannot enjoy this "fast delivery" property (each process has to manage a local "waiting room" msg_set_i in which messages can be momentarily delayed).

Theorem 3.4   *The algorithm described in Figure 3.11 constructs a CO uniform reliable broadcast communication abstraction in any system in which URB can be built.*

Proof   Proof of the validity and integrity properties. Let us first observe that, as "CO_broadcast (m)" is implemented on top of FIFO-broadcast, it directly inherits its validity property (neither creation nor alteration of protocol messages), and integrity property (a protocol message is FIFO-delivered at most once). It follows that no application message m can be loss or modified. It is also clear from the test done before CO-delivering an application message that such a message can be CO-delivered at most once.

Proof of the termination property. As far as termination is concerned, we have the following. When a process CO-broadcasts an application message m, it FIFO-broadcasts a protocol message MSG($seq ⊕ m$). Moreover, when a sequence of application messages MSG($⟨m_1, ..., m_ℓ⟩$) is

FIFO-delivered, if not yet CO-delivered, each application message m_x, $1 \leq x \leq \ell$, is CO-delivered without being delayed. Consequently, the CO-broadcast algorithm inherits also the termination property of the underlying FIFO broadcast, from which it follows that each application message that has been CO-broadcast is CO-delivered.

Proof of the CO delivery property. We have to prove that, for any two messages m and m' such that $m \rightarrow_M m'$ (as defined in the previous paragraph), no process CO-delivers m' unless it has previously CO-delivered m_x. This proof is based on three claims.

Claim C1. Let us suppose that a process p_i FIFO-broadcasts $\text{MSG}(seq' \oplus m')$ (where seq' is a sequence of application messages), and either p_i has previously FIFO-broadcast $\text{MSG}(seq \oplus m)$ or $m \in seq'$. Then, no process CO-delivers m' unless it has previously CO-delivered m.

Proof of claim C1. The proof is by contradiction. Let us assume that, while the assumption of the claim is satisfied, some process CO-delivers m' before m. Let τ be the first time instant at which a process CO-delivers m' without having previously CO-delivered m, and let p_j be such a process. We consider two cases, according to what caused p_j to CO-deliver m'.

- Case 1. p_j has FIFO-delivered $\text{MSG}(seq' \oplus m')$. There are two sub-cases (due to the assumption in the claim).

    - Sub-case 1: $m \in seq'$.
    - Sub-case 2: p_i has FIFO-broadcast $\text{MSG}(seq \oplus m)$ before $\text{MSG}(seq' \oplus m')$. It then follows from the FIFO delivery property that p_j has FIFO-delivered $\text{MSG}(seq \oplus m)$ before $\text{MSG}(seq' \oplus m')$.

    It is easy to conclude from the text of the algorithm that, whatever the sub-case, p_j CO-delivers m before m', which contradicts the assumption that p_j CO-delivers m' before m.

- Case 2. p_j has FIFO-delivered a message $\text{MSG}(seq'' \oplus m'')$ such that $m' \in seq''$ and m is not before m' in seq'' (proof hypothesis). Let p_k be the sender of that message. Since $m' \in seq''$, process p_k has CO-delivered m' before FIFO-broadcasting $\text{MSG}(seq'' \oplus m'')$.

    Due to the FIFO order property, p_j has FIFO-delivered all the previous protocol messages FIFO-broadcast by p_k. Since, by assumption, p_j does not CO-deliver m before m', the application message m was not included in any of these FIFO-broadcasts, and m does not appear before m' in seq''. Hence, when p_k CO-delivered m', it has not previously CO-delivered m. Moreover, p_k CO-delivered m' before p_j CO-delivered it. We consequently have $\tau' < \tau$, where τ' is the time instant at which p_k has CO-delivered m'. But this contradicts the definition of τ that states that τ is the first time instant at which a process CO-delivers m' without having previously CO-delivered m.

As both cases lead to a contradiction, the claim follows. End of proof of claim C1.

The proof of the CO delivery property follows from the claims C2 and C3 that follow. C2 establishes that the algorithm satisfies the FIFO message delivery property, while C3 establishes that it satisfies the local order property. Once these claims are proved, the CO delivery property is obtained as an immediate consequence of Theorem 3.3 that states the following: FIFO message delivery + local order $\Rightarrow$ CO message delivery.

Claim C2. The algorithm satisfies the FIFO (application) message delivery property.
Proof   of   claim C2. Let us suppose that p_i CO-broadcasts m before m'. It follows that p_i FIFO-broadcasts MSG($seq \oplus m$) before MSG($seq' \oplus m'$). Let us consider the channel from p_i to p_j. It follows from Claim C1 that p_j cannot CO-delivers m' unless it has CO-delivered m, which proves the claim. End of proof of claim C2.

Claim C3. The algorithm satisfies the local order property (for application messages).
Proof   of claim C3. Let p_i be a process that CO-delivers m before CO-broadcasting a message m', and p_j a process that CO-delivers m'. We must show that p_j CO-delivers m before m'.

Let m'' be the first message that p_i CO-broadcasts after it has CO-delivered m (notice that m'' could be m'). When it CO-broadcasts m'', p_i FIFO-broadcasts MSG($seq'' \oplus m''$) (for some seq''). Due to the text of the algorithm and the definition of m'', it follows that $m \in seq''$. Due to claim C1, p_i CO-delivers m before m''. If $m'' = m'$, the claim follows. Otherwise, p_i CO-broadcasts m'' before m'. Then due to claim C2, p_j CO-delivers m'' before m'. Consequently, as $m \in seq''$, it follows that p_j CO-delivers m before m', as requested. End of proof of claim C3.

$\square_{Theorem\ 3.4}$

3.2.4   FROM URB TO CO-BROADCAST: CAPTURING MESSAGE CAUSAL PAST IN A VECTOR

The delivery condition   Differently from the previous one, this construction of the CO broadcast abstraction is built directly on top of the uniform reliable broadcast abstraction (so the layer structure is the same as the one of Figure 3.6 where FIFO is replaced by CO).

Each process p_i manages a vector (vector clock), denoted $last\_sn_i[1..n]$ and initialized to $[0, \ldots, 0]$, such that $last\_sn_i[k]$ contains the sequence number of the last message CO-broadcast by p_k that has been CO-delivered by p_i. Thanks to this control data, each application message m can piggyback a vector of integers denoted $m.last\_sn[1..n]$ such that

$$m.last\_sn[k] = \text{ number of messages } m' \text{ CO-Broadcast by } p_k \text{ such that } m' \rightarrow_M m.$$

Let m be a message that is URB-delivered to p_i. Its CO-delivery condition can be easily stated: m can be CO-delivered if all the messages m' such that $m' \rightarrow_M m$ have already been locally CO-delivered by p_i. Operationally, this is locally captured by the following delivery condition:

$$DC_i(m) \equiv \big(\forall k : \ last\_sn_i[k] \geq m.last\_sn[k]\big).$$

Let us notice that, when a process CO-broadcasts a message m, it can immediately CO-deliver it. This is because, due to the very definition of the causal precedence relation "$\rightarrow_M$", all the messages m' such that $m' \rightarrow m$ have already been CO-delivered, and, consequently, $DC_i(m)$ is then satisfied.

```
operation CO_broadcast (m):
    done_i ← false;
    m.last_sn[1..n] ← last_sn_i[1..n];
    m.sender ← i; m.seq_nb ← p_i's next seq. number;
    URB_broadcast MSG (m);
    wait (done_i).

when MSG (m) is URB-delivered:
    if DC_i(m)
        then CO_deliver (m);
            let j = m.sender;
            last_sn_i[j] ← m.seq_nb;
            done_i ← (m.sender = i);
            while ( ∃m' ∈ msg_set_i : DC_i(m') )
                do CO_deliver (m');
                    let j = m'.sender;
                    last_sn_i[j] ← m'.seq_nb;
                    msg_set_i ← msg_set_i \ {m'}
            end while
        else msg_set_i ← msg_set_i ∪ {m}
    end if.
```

Figure 3.12: From URB to CO message delivery in $\mathcal{AS}_{n,t}[\emptyset]$ (code for p_i)

The construction   The construction is described in Figure 3.12. In addition to its sequence number, each message m CO-broadcast by a process p_i, carries in its field $m.last\_sn$ a copy of the local array $last\_sn_i$ (which encodes the causal past of m from the CO-broadcast point of view). The value of $m.last\_sn[k]$ represents the number of messages m' such that $m' \rightarrow_M m$.

To CO-broadcast a message m, first updates the control fields of m, and then URB-broadcasts m and waits until it locally URB-delivers m. The boolean $done_i$ is used to ensure that if m is CO-broadcast by p_i before m', the broadcast of m is correctly encoded in $m'.last\_sn[1..n]$.

As far as the sender p_i of m is concerned, the CO-delivery of m is not done directly within the operation CO_broadcast (m). This is in order to benefit from the properties of the underlying URB broadcast abstraction, namely, if p_i URB-delivers m, we know from the termination property of the URB abstraction that all the non-faulty processes eventually URB-deliver m.

When a message m is URB-delivered by a process p_i, that process tests the delivery condition $DC_i(m)$. If it is false, there are messages m' such that $m' \rightarrow_M m$ that have not yet been CO-delivered. Consequently, m is deposited in the set msg_set_i. If $DC_i(m)$ is true (this is always the case when $m.sender = i$), p_i updates accordingly $last\_sn_i[m.sender]$ to $m.seq\_nb$ (this is where the array

$last\_sn_i$ is updated with the sequence number of the message that is CO-delivered), and sets $done_i$ to *true* if $m.sender = i$.

After it has CO-delivered a message m, process p_i checks if messages in the waiting room msg_set_i can be CO-delivered. If there are such messages, it CO-delivers them, suppresses them from msg_set_i, and updates accordingly $last\_sn_i$.

Except for the wait statement at the end of the operation "CO_broadcast (m)", the first three lines of "CO_broadcast (m)", on one side, and all the statements associated with the URB-delivery of a message are executed atomically.

Example   A simple example of the vector-based CO broadcast construction is described in Figure 3.13. Messages m_1, m_2 and m_3 are such that $m_1.sender = 1$, $m_1.seq\_nb = 1$, $m_2.sender = 2$, $m_2.seq\_nb = 1$, $m_3.sender = 3$, and $m_3.seq\_nb = 1$. Messages m_1 and m_2 have no messages in their causal past (i.e., there is no message m' such that $m' \rightarrow_M m_1$ or $m' \rightarrow_M m_2$, respectively), so we have $m_1.last\_sn = m_2.last\_sn = [0, 0, 0]$. As their broadcasts are not CO-related, these messages can be CO-delivered in different order at different processes. Differently, message m_3 is such that $m_1 \rightarrow_M m_3$. So, $m_3.last\_sn = [1, 0, 0]$ that encodes the fact that the first message CO-broadcast by p_1 (namely m_1) has been CO-delivered by p_3 before p_3 CO-broadcasts m_3.

Consequently, as show in the figure, while m_3 is URB-delivered at p_2 before m_1, its CO-delivery condition forces it to remain in p_2's input buffer msg_set_2 until m_1 has been CO-delivered at p_2 (this is indicated by a dotted arrow in the figure).

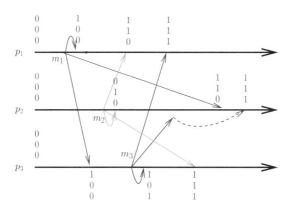

Figure 3.13: How the vectors are used to construct the CO broadcast abstraction

Lemma   3.5   *Let   m   and   m′   be   two   messages.* $(m \rightarrow_M m') \Rightarrow \big(\forall k \ (m.last\_sn[k] \leq m'.last\_sn[k])\big) \land (\exists k : m.last\_sn[k] < m'.last\_sn[k])\big)$.

Proof Let us remember that, when a process p_i CO-broadcasts a message m, the sequence number associated with m is the rank of m in the sequence of messages CO-broadcast by p_i.

Let us first consider the case where the messages m and m' are CO-broadcast by the same process p_i. Due to the fact the sequence numbers are strictly increasing, it follows from the text of the algorithm that we have $m.last\_sn[i] \leq m.seq\_nb - 1$ when m is CO-broadcast, and $m.seq\_nb \leq m'.last\_sn[i]$ when m' is CO-broadcast, from which we conclude $m.last\_sn[i] < m'.last\_sn[i]$. As far the entries $k \neq i$ are concerned, let us observe that the successive sequence numbers contained in $last\_sn_i[k]$ are increasing, from which we conclude $\forall k : m.last\_sn[k] \leq m'.last\_sn[k])$, which completes the proof for this case.

Let us now consider the case where m and m' are CO-broadcast by different processes. As $m \rightarrow_M m'$, there is a finite chain of messages such that $m = m_0 \rightarrow_M m_1 \rightarrow_M \cdots \rightarrow_M m_z = m'$, such that, for each message m_x, $1 \leq x \leq z$, the process that the process that CO-broadcasts m_x has previously CO-delivered m_{x-1}. (if m_1 is m', the length of the chain is 1.) We claim that $(\forall k \ (m.last\_sn[k] \leq m_1.last\_sn[k])) \ \wedge \ (\exists k : m.last\_sn[k] < m_1.last\_sn[k])$. Then the proof of the lemma follows directly by a simple induction on the length of the message chain.

Proof of the claim. Let p_i be the process that CO-broadcast m, and p_j ($i \neq j$) the process that CO-delivered m before CO-broadcasting m_1. It follows from the definition of $m \rightarrow_M m_1$, the fact that m is CO-delivered by p_j, and the delivery condition $DC_j(m)$ that $\forall k \ (m.last\_sn[k] \leq last\_sn_j[k])$ just after m is CO-delivered by p_j. On another side, when p_j CO-delivered m, it executed the statement $last\_sn_j[i] \leftarrow m.seq\_nb$. Hence, we have $m.last\_sn[i] < m.last\_sn[i] + 1 = last\_sn_j[i] = m.seq\_nb$, and, consequently, $(\forall k \ (m.last\_sn[k] \leq last\_sn_i[k])) \ \wedge \ (\exists k : m.last\_sn[k] < last\_sn[k]_i)$.

As, due to the algorithm we have $(\forall k \ (m_1.last\_sn[k] \geq last\_sn_i[k])$ when p_j CO-broadcasts m_1, the claim follows. End of proof of the claim. $\square_{Lemma\ 3.5}$

Theorem 3.6   *The algorithm described in Figure 3.11 constructs a CO uniform reliable broadcast communication abstraction in any system in which URB can be built.*

Proof Proof of the validity and integrity properties. The validity property follows directly from the validity of the underlying URB broadcast abstraction, and the text of the algorithm (that does not create applications messages).

The integrity property of the underlying URB abstraction guarantees that, for every application message m that is CO-broadcast, a process p_i URB-delivers at most one protocol message MSG (m). If $DC_i(m)$ is satisfied, the message m is immediately CO-delivered. Otherwise, it deposited in msg_set_i, and is suppressed from this set when it is CO-delivered. It follows that no message m can be CO-delivered more than once by each process p_i. Hence the integrity property of the CO abstraction.

Proof of the termination property. The termination property of the underlying URB abstraction guarantees that (1) if a non-faulty process CO-broadcasts a message m (as in that case it URB-broadcasts MSG (m)), or (2) if any process URB-delivers MSG (m), then each non-faulty process URB-delivers MSG (m). It follows that if (1) or (2) occurs, then every non-faulty process p_i either CO-delivers m or deposits m in msg_set_i. Hence, to prove the termination property of the CO broadcast abstraction, we have to show that any non-faulty process p_i eventually CO-delivers all the messages that are deposited in its set msg_set_i. Let us observe that, as no two messages sent by the same process have the same sequence number, for any two messages m and m', we have $m.last\_sn \neq m'.last\_sn$.

Let us assume by contradiction that some messages remain forever in msg_set_i. Let us denote $blocked_i$ this set of messages, and let us totally order the messages $m \in blocked_i$, according to the lexicographic order $<_{lex}$ defined by their vectors $m.last\_sn$. (Let $v = [a, b, c]$ and $v' = [a', b', c']$ be two vectors. Let us remember that $v <_{lex} v'$ if $(a < a') \lor (a = a' \land b < b') \lor (a = a' \land b = b' \land c < c')$.) Finally, let m be the first message of msg_set_i according to lexicographical order. Let p_x be the process that has issued CO_broadcast (m).

As m remains forever in msg_set_i, $DC_i(m)$ remains forever false, and, consequently, there is at least one process identity k such that $last\_sn_i[k] < m.last\_sn[k]$. Let β be the last value taken by $last\_sn_i[k]$, and let $\alpha = m.last\_sn[k]$. Hence, $\beta < \alpha$. Let m' be the last message CO-broadcast by p_k and CO-delivered by p_x, just before it issues CO_broadcast (m). Hence, we have $m.last\_sn[k] = last\_sn_x[k] = \alpha$. This is depicted in Figure 3.14.

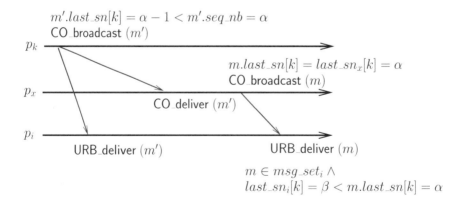

Figure 3.14: Proof of the CO-delivery property (second construction)

As p_x has CO-delivered m', it has previously URB-delivered MSG (m'). It then follows from the termination property of the URB abstraction, that any non-faulty process (hence p_i) eventually URB-delivers MSG (m'). When p_i URB-delivers MSG (m'), there are two cases.

- $DC_i(m')$ is false and remains false forever. In that case, as we have $m'.last\_sn <_{lex} m.last\_sn$ (consequence of Lemma 3.5), it follows that m is not the first message of msg_set_i according to lexicographical order. A contradiction.

- m' is eventually CO-delivered by p_i. In that case, $last\_sn_i[k]$ becomes equal to α, which contradicts the fact that the last value taken by $last\_sn_i[k]$ is $\beta < \alpha$.

In both cases, we obtain a contradiction, which completes the proof of the termination property.

Proof of the CO delivery property. Let us first consider the case where p_i is not the process that issued CO_broadcast (m). The CO delivery property follows directly from the associated delivery condition $DC_i(m)$: $m.last\_sn[1...n]$ encodes all the messages m' such that $m' \to_M m$ (Lemma 3.5), while $last\_sn_i[1..n]$ encodes all the messages already CO-delivered by p_i.

Let us now consider the CO-delivery at p_i of a message m that has been CO-broadcast by the same process p_i. The messages m' such that $m' \to m$ are encoded in the value $last\_sn_i$ at the time at which p_i issues CO_broadcast (m), which means that we then have $m.last\_sn = last\_sn_i$. It follows that the delivery condition $DC_i(m)$ is always satisfied when p_i URB-delivers its own message MSG (m), which completes the proof of the CO delivery property. $\square_{Theorem\ 3.6}$

3.2.5   THE TOTAL ORDER BROADCAST ABSTRACTION REQUIRES MORE

From FIFO/CO to the total order broadcast abstraction   It is very important to notice that the message delivery constraints imposed by the previous FIFO and CO communication abstractions do not require the addition of control messages. The delivery constraints are on local variables and control values piggybacked by the messages. Among other features, a message that has been broadcast can be delivered by its sender immediately after it has been broadcast.

This is because the constraints on the delivery order on the messages are defined only from their causal past (which messages have been broadcast before it by the same process for FIFO order, and by any process for CO order). As we will see, this is no longer the case when one has to implement the Total Order (TO) delivery property. In that case, any pair of messages has to be delivered in the same order at any process, even if the broadcast of these messages are neither FIFO-related, nor CO-related.

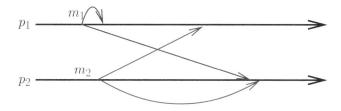

Figure 3.15: Total order message delivery requires cooperation

Let us consider the messages m_1 and m_2 broadcast in Figure 3.15. None of these broadcasts are related to the other (i.e., there is neither a FIFO nor a CO relation linking them). Hence, ensuring the Total Order message delivery property cannot rely only on control information piggybacked by the messages that are broadcast by the application. The processes have to cooperate (exchange additional control messages) to establish a common delivery order. Such an order has to be defined by both p_1 and p_2, and if m_1 is delivered first at p_1, p_2 cannot deliver m_2 just after it has been broadcast.

Actually, as we will see in Chapter 5, it is impossible to construct a total order broadcast abstraction in $\mathcal{AS}_{n,t}[\emptyset]$. This is a fundamental result of fault-tolerant distributed computing. Such a communication abstraction requires a system model strictly stronger than $\mathcal{AS}_{n,t}[\emptyset]$. From a computability point of view, the FIFO and CO broadcast abstractions are weaker than the TO broadcast abstraction: they can be implemented in a weaker system model than the one needed to implement the TO broadcast abstraction.

The FIFO and CO constructions are very general   As the previous FIFO and CO reliable broadcast constructions do not use additional control messages, it follows that they work in any system where the URB communication abstraction can be built. They can consequently be used on top of the URB constructions described in the next chapter that addresses the case where, in addition to process crashes, the channels are not reliable, i.e., in systems weaker than $\mathcal{AS}_{n,t}[\emptyset]$.

3.3   BIBLIOGRAPHIC NOTES

- The problem of broadcasting messages in a reliable way in asynchronous systems prone to process failures has given rise to a large literature. Early seminal works can be found in [28, 36, 42, 77, 143]. Recent surveys can be found in [18, 44].

  A nice and very comprehensive presentation of fault-tolerant broadcast problems, their specifications and algorithms that solve them has been given by Hadzilacos and Toueg in [93].

- The causal message delivery property has been introduced by Birman and Joseph [28].

  The construction from FIFO to CO broadcast is due to Hadzilacos and Toueg [93]. The presentation we have followed is theirs.

  The second CO construction is a variant of an algorithm proposed by Raynal, Schiper and Toueg that was designed for asynchronous failure-free systems [149].

  The notion of causal message delivery has been extended to messages that carry data whose delivery is constrained by real-time requirements in [19] and to mobile environment [145].

- The total order broadcast is strongly related to the state machine replication paradigm [107, 154]. Its impossibility in asynchronous systems prone to process crashes is related to the consensus impossibility in these systems [68].

- Different types of broadcast operations are studied in [27, 59]. The books [26, 90] present distributed programming approaches based on reliable broadcast.

- The word "know" has sometimes been used in this chapter (and will be used in the next chapters) with an anthropomorphic meaning where a process "learns" facts and thereafter "knows" them. The interested reader will find formal knowledge-based approaches in [35, 94, 125]. The book [61] is entirely devoted to reasoning about knowledge.

CHAPTER 4

Uniform Reliable Broadcast Abstraction Despite Unreliable Channels

The previous chapter has presented several constructions for the uniform reliable broadcast (URB) abstraction. These constructions consider the underlying system model $\mathcal{AS}_{n,t}[\emptyset]$. They differ in the quality of service they provide to the application processes, this quality being defined with respect to the order in which the messages are delivered (namely, FIFO or CO order). This order restricts message asynchrony.

This chapter presents constructions of the URB abstraction suited to asynchronous systems prone to process crashes and unreliable channels, i.e., asynchronous system models weaker than $\mathcal{AS}_{n,t}[\emptyset]$.

4.1   A SYSTEM MODEL WITH UNRELIABLE CHANNELS

4.1.1   FAIRNESS NOTION FOR CHANNELS

Restrict the type of failures   Trivially, if a channel can lose all the messages, it has to transmit from a sender to a receiver, no communication abstraction with provable guarantees can be defined and implemented. So, in order to be able to do useful computation, we need to restrict the type of failures a channel is allowed to exhibit. This is exactly what is addressed by the concept of channel *fairness*.

All the messages transmitted over a channel are *protocol messages* (let us remember that the transmission of an application message gives rise to protocol messages that are sent at the underlying abstraction layer). Several types of protocol messages can co-exist at this underlying layer, e.g., protocol messages that carry application messages and protocol messages that carry acknowledgments. In the following, we consider that each protocol message has a type, and μ is used to denote such a type. Moreover, when there is no ambiguity, the word "message" is used as a shortcut for "protocol message", and "μ-message" is used as a shortcut for "protocol message of type μ".

Fairness with respect to μ-messages   Considering a uni-directional channel that allows a process p_i to send message to a process p_j, let us remark that, at the network level, process p_i can send the same message several times to p_j (for example, message retransmission is needed to overcome message losses). This channel is *fair with respect to the message type μ* if it satisfies the three following properties. All the messages that appear in these properties are messages carried by the channel from p_i to p_j.

- Validity. If the process p_j receives a μ-message (on this channel), then this message has been previously sent by p_i to p_j.

- Integrity. If p_j receives an infinite number of μ-messages from p_i, then p_i has sent an infinite number of μ-messages to p_j.

- Termination. If p_i sends an infinite number of μ-messages to p_j, and p_j is non-faulty and executes "receive () from p_i" infinitely often, it receives an infinite number of μ-messages from p_i.

As they capture similar meanings, these properties have been given the same names as in the URB specification stated in the previous chapter. The validity property means that there is neither message creation nor message alteration. The integrity property states that, if a finite number of messages of type μ are sent, the channel is not allowed to duplicate them an infinite number of times (it can nevertheless duplicate them an unknown but finite number of times). Intuitively, this means that the network performs only the retransmissions issued by the sender.

Finally, the termination property states the condition under which the channel from p_i to p_j has eventually to transmit messages of type μ, i.e., the condition under which a μ-message msg cannot be lost. This is the liveness property of the channel. From an intuitive point of view, this property states that if the sender sends "enough" μ-messages, some of these messages will be received. In order to be as less restrictive as possible, "enough" is formally stated as "an infinite number". This is much weaker than a specification such as "every 10 sendings of μ-messages, at least one is received", as this kind of specification would restrict unnecessarily the bad behavior that a channel is allowed to exhibit.

4.1.2   FAIR CHANNEL AND FAIR LOSSY CHANNEL

Fair channel   The notion of "*fair* channel" encountered in the literature corresponds to the case where (1) each protocol message defines a specific message type μ, and (2) the channel is fair with respect to all the message types. Hence, the specification of a fair channel is defined by the following properties.

- Validity. If p_j receives a message msg from p_i, then msg has been previously sent by p_i to p_j.

- Integrity. For any message msg, if p_j receives msg from p_i an infinite number of times, then p_i has sent msg to p_j an infinite number of times.

- Termination. For any message msg, if p_i sends an infinite number of times msg to p_j, if p_j is non-faulty and executes "receive () from p_i" infinitely often, it receives msg from p_i an infinite number of times.

As described by the termination property, the only reception guarantee is that each message msg that is sent infinitely often cannot be lost. This means that if a message msg is sent an arbitrary but finite number of times, there is no guarantee on its reception. Let us observe that the requirement "msg sent an infinite number of times" for a message to be received, does not prevent any number of copies of msg to be lost, even an infinite number of copies to be lost (as an example, this is the case when all the even sendings of msg are lost and all the odd sendings are received).

Fair lossy channel   The notion of "*fair lossy* channel" encountered in the literature corresponds to the case where all the protocol messages belongs to the same message type. Hence, there is a single message type. Hence, the specification of a fair lossy channel is defined by the following properties.

- Validity. If p_j receives a message from p_i, this message has been previously sent by p_i to p_j.
- Integrity. If p_j receives an infinite number of messages from p_i, then p_i has sent an infinite number of times to p_j.
- Termination. If p_i sends an infinite number of messages to p_j, if p_j is non-faulty and executes "receive () from p_i" infinitely often, it receives an infinite number of messages from p_i.

While the termination property states that the channel transmits messages, it gives no information on which are the messages that are received.

Comparing fair channel and fair lossy channel   As we are about to see, given an infinite sequence of protocol messages, the notions of fair channel and fair lossy channel are different, and none of them includes the other one.

To that end, let us consider that the given infinite sequence of protocol messages is the infinite sequence of positive integers 1,2,etc. (each integer being a distinct message). Hence, no two messages sent by p_i are the same. If the channel from p_i to p_j is fair lossy, the termination property guarantees that p_j will receive an infinite sequence of integers (while maybe an infinite number of different integers will never be received). Differently, if the channel is fair, it is possible that no integer is ever received (this is because no integer is sent an infinite number of times).

Let us now consider that the sequence of protocol messages that is sent by p_i is the alternating sequence of 1, 2, 1, 2, 1, etc. If the channel from p_i to p_j is fair, both 1 and 2 are received infinitely often (this is because both integers are sent an infinite number of times). Differently, if the channel is fair lossy, it is possible that p_j receives the integer 1 an infinite number of times and never receives the integer 2 (or receives 2 and never receives 1).

This means that when one has to prove a construction based on unreliable channels, one has to be very careful on the type of these unreliable channels, namely, fair or fair lossy.

From a fair lossy channel to fair channel   Given an infinite sequence of protocol messages msg_1, msg_2, msg_3, etc., that p_i wants to send to p_j, it is possible to construct new protocol messages (the ones that are really sent over the channel) such that each message msg_x is eventually received by p_j (if it is non-faulty) under the assumption that the channel is fair lossy.

Let msg_1 be the first protocol message that p_i wants to send to p_j. It actually sends instead the "real" protocol message $\langle msg_1 \rangle$. When it wants to sends the second protocol message msg_2, it actually sends the "real" protocol message made up of the sequence $\langle msg_1, msg_2 \rangle$. Similarly, p_i

sends the sequence $\langle msg_1, msg_2, msg_3 \rangle$ when it wants to send its third protocol message msg_3, etc. Hence, the sequence of protocol messages successively sent by p_i to p_j is the sequence $\langle msg_1 \rangle$, $\langle msg_1, msg_2 \rangle$, $\langle msg_1, msg_2, msg_3 \rangle$, etc. It follows that, in the infinite sequence of "real" protocol messages sent by p_i, all "real" protocol messages sent by p_i are different (each being a sequence that is a suffix of the sequence that constitutes the previous message). If p_j is non-faulty and the channel is fair lossy, this simple construction ensures that every msg_x is received infinitely often by p_j. Hence, assuming that p_i sends an infinite number of messages msg_x, this construction simulates a fair channel on top of a fair lossy channel. The price of this construction is the size of protocol messages that increases without bound.

4.1.3   RELIABLE CHANNEL IN PRESENCE OF PROCESS CRASHES

An abstraction for the application layer   A *reliable* channel is a communication abstraction stronger than the fair channel abstraction or the fair lossy channel abstraction. Intuitively, a reliable channel neither creates, nor duplicates nor loses messages. Its definition is at the same abstraction level as the definition of the URB abstraction. It is an abstraction offered to the application layer. Consequently, it considers that the messages are application messages and that each message m is unique.

   The formal definition of the reliable channel from p_i to p_j is given by the following three properties.

- Validity. If p_j receives a message m from p_i, then m has been previously sent by p_i to p_j.
- Integrity. The process p_j receives a message m at most once.
- Termination. If p_i completes the sending to p_j of k messages, then, if p_j is non-faulty and executes k times "receive () from p_i", p_j receives k messages from p_i.

   This definition captures the fact that each message m sent by p_i to p_j is received exactly once by p_j. The words "p_i completes the sending of m" means that, if p_i does not crash before returning from the invocation of that send operation, the "underlying network" (i.e., the implementation of the reliable channel abstraction) guarantees that m will attain p_j. Differently, if p_i crashes during the sending of its kth message to p_j, p_j eventually receives the previous $(k-1)$ messages sent by p_i while there is no guarantee on the reception of the kth message sent by p_i to p_j (this message can be or not received by p_j).

Remark   Let us notice that the termination property considers that p_j is non-faulty. This is because, if p_j crashes, due to process and message asynchrony, it is not possible to state a property on which messages can be received by p_j.

   Let us also notice that it is not possible to conclude from the previous specification that a reliable channel ensures that the messages are received in their sending order ($^{®}$FO reception order). This is because, once messages have been given to the "underlying network", nothing prevents it from reordering messages sent by p_i.

Reliable channel vs uniform reliable broadcast   As we have seen in the previous chapter, the URB abstraction is defined with respect to the broadcast of a single application message. This means that the broadcast of the message m_1 and the broadcast of the message m_2 constitute two distinct instances of the URB problem. Said in one word, URB is a *one-shot* problem.

Differently, the reliable channel abstraction is not a one-shot problem. Its specification involves all the messages sent by a process p_i to a process p_j. The difference in the specification of both communication abstractions appears clearly in their termination properties.

4.1.4   SYSTEM MODEL

In the rest of this chapter, we consider an asynchronous system made up of n processes prone to process crashes and where each pair of processes is connected by two unreliable but fair channels (one in each direction). This system model is denoted $AS\_\mathcal{F}_{n,t}[\emptyset]$. As in the previous chapters, $AS\_\mathcal{F}_{n,t}[Prop]$ and $AS\_\mathcal{F}_{n,t}[D]$ denote the system model $AS\_\mathcal{F}_{n,t}[\emptyset]$ enriched with the property *Prop* or a failure detector of the class D, respectively.

4.2   URB IN $AS\_\mathcal{F}_{n,t}[\emptyset]$

This section first presents an URB construction in $AS\_\mathcal{F}_{n,t}[t < n/2]$. It then shows that the property $t < n/2$ is a necessary requirement for such a construction when processes are not provided with information on the actual failure pattern.

4.2.1   A CONSTRUCTION FOR $t < n/2$

Principle   Constructing the URB abstraction in $AS\_\mathcal{F}_{n,t}[t < n/2]$ is pretty simple. The construction relies on two simple base techniques.

- First, use the classical retransmission technique in order to simulate a reliable channel on top of a fair channel.

- Second, to ensure the URB termination property, locally URB-deliver an application message m to the upper application layer only when this message has been received by at least one non-faulty process. As $n > 2t$, this means that, without risking to be blocked forever, a process may URB-deliver m as soon as it knows that at least $t + 1$ processes have received a copy of m.

As a message that is URB-delivered by a process is in the hands of at least one correct process, that correct process can transmit it safely to the other processes (by repeated sendings) thanks to the fair channels that connect it to the other processes.

The construction   The construction is described in Figure 4.1. When a process p_i wants to URB-broadcast a message m, it sends to itself the protocol message MSG (m) (we assume that the channel of a process to itself is reliable).

The central data structure used in the construction is an array of sets, denoted rec_by_i, where the set $rec\_by_i[m]$ is associated with the application message m. This set contains the identities of all the processes that, to p_i's knowledge, have received a copy of MSG (m).

```
operation URB_broadcast (m): send MSG (m) to p_i.

when MSG (m) is received from p_k:
    if (first reception of m)
        then allocate  rec_by_i[m]; rec_by_i[m] ← {i, k};
            activate  task Diffuse(m)
        else  rec_by_i[m] ← rec_by_i[m] ∪ {k}
    end if.

when (|rec_by_i[m]| ≥ t + 1) ∧ (p_i has not yet URB-delivered m): URB_deliver (m).

task Diffuse(m):
    repeat forever
        for each j ∈ {1, . . . , n} \ rec_by_i[m] do send MSG (m) to  p_j end for
    end repeat.
```

Figure 4.1: Uniform reliable broadcast in $\mathcal{AS}\_\mathcal{F}_{n,t}[t < n/2]$ (code for p_i)

When it receives MSG (m) for the first time, p_i creates the set $rec\_by_i[m]$ and updates it to $\{i, k\}$ where p_k is the process that sent MSG (m). Then p_i activates a task, denoted $Diffuse(m)$. If it is not the first time that MSG (m) is received, p_i only adds k to $rec\_by_i[m]$. $Diffuse(m)$ is the local task that is in charge of retransmitting the protocol message MSG (m) to the other processes in order to ensure the eventual URB-delivery of m.

Finally, when it has received MSG (m) from at least one non-faulty process (this is operationally controlled by the predicate $|rec\_by_i[m]| \geq t + 1$), p_i URB-delivers m, if not yet done.

Let us remember that, as in the previous chapter, the processing associated with the reception of a protocol message is atomic, which means here that the processing of any two messages MSG $(m1)$ and MSG $(m2)$ are never interleaved, they are executed one after the other. This atomicity assumption, that is on any protocol message reception (i.e., whatever its MSG or ACK type) is valid in all this chapter (ACK protocol messages will be used in Section 4.4). Differently, several tasks $Diffuse(m1)$, $Diffuse(m2)$, etc., are allowed to run concurrently.

Remark It is important to see that the task $Diffuse(m)$ sends forever protocol messages (and consequently, never terminates). The only use of acknowledgments cannot prevent this infinite sending of messages, as shown by the following scenario. Let p_j be a process that has crashed before another process p_i issues URB_broadcast (m). In that case p_j will never acknowledge MSG (m), and, consequently, p_i will retransmit forever MSG (m) to p_j. Preventing these infinite retransmissions requires to provide the processes with appropriate information on failures. This is the topic addressed in Section 4.4 of this chapter.

Theorem 4.1 *The algorithm described in Figure 4.1 constructs an URB abstraction in $\mathcal{AS}\_\mathcal{F}_{n,t}[t < n/2]$.*

Proof (The proof of this construction is a simplified version of the construction given in Section 4.4.) The validity property (no creation or alteration of application messages) and the integrity property (an application message is received at most once) of the URB abstraction follow directly from the text of the construction. So, we focus here on the proof of the termination property of the URB abstraction.

Let us first consider a non-faulty process p_i that URB-broadcasts a message m. We have to show that all the non-faulty processes URB-deliver m. (Let * denote this point in the proof, see below.) As p_i is non-faulty, it activates the task $Diffuse(m)$ and sends MSG (m) to every other process p_j an infinite number of times. As the channels are fair, it follows that each non-faulty process receives MSG (m) and activates the task $Diffuse(m)$ the first time it receives MSG (m). Hence, each non-faulty process infinitely often sends MSG (m) to every process. As there is a majority of non-faulty processes and the channels are fair, it follows that the set $rec\_by_i[m]$ eventually contains $(t+1)$ process identities. Hence, the URB-delivery condition of m becomes eventually true at every non-faulty process, which proves the theorem for the case of a non-faulty process that URB-broadcasts a message.

We have now to prove the second case of the termination property, namely, if a (non-faulty or faulty) process p_x URB-delivers a message m, then every non-faulty process URB-delivers m. If p_x URB-delivers a message m, we have $|rec\_by_x[m]| \geq t+1$, which means that at least one non-faulty process p_i has received the protocol message MSG (m). When that non-faulty process p_i has received MSG (m) for the first time, it has activated the task $Diffuse(m)$. The proof is then the same as in the part of the previous case that starts at (*). $\square_{Theorem\ 4.1}$

4.2.2   AN IMPOSSIBILITY RESULT

This section shows that the assumption $t < n/2$ is a necessary requirement when one wants to construct URB in $AS\_\mathcal{F}_{n,t}[\emptyset]$. The proof of this impossibility is based on an "indistinguishability" argument. (It is close to the proof of Theorem 3 of Chapter 2.)

Theorem 4.2   *There is no algorithm that constructs an URB abstraction in $AS\_\mathcal{F}_{n,t}[t \geq n/2]$.*

Proof   The proof is by contradiction. Let us assume that there is an algorithm A that constructs the URB abstraction in $AS\_\mathcal{F}_{n,t}[t \geq n/2]$. Given $t \geq n/2$, let us partition the processes into two subsets $P1$ and $P2$ (i.e., $P1 \cap P2 = \emptyset$ and $P1 \cup P2 = \{p_1, \ldots, p_n\}$) such that $|P1| = \lceil n/2 \rceil$ and $|P2| = \lfloor n/2 \rfloor$. Let us consider the following executions E_1 and E_2.

- Execution E_1. In that execution, all the processes of $P2$ crash initially, and all the processes in $P1$ are non-faulty. Moreover, a process $p_x \in P1$ issues URB_broadcast (m). Due to the very existence of the algorithm A, every process of $P1$ URB-delivers m.

- Execution E_2. In that execution, the processes of $P2$ are non-faulty, and no process of $P2$ ever issues URB_broadcast (). The processes of $P1$ behave as in $E1$: p_x issues URB_broadcast (m), and they all URB-deliver m. Moreover, after it has URB-delivered m, each process of $P1$

crashes, and all protocol messages ever sent by a process of $P1$ are lost (and consequently are never received by a process of $P2$). It is easy to see that this is possible as no process of $P1$ can distinguish this run from E_1.

Let us observe that the fact that no message sent by a process of $P1$ is ever received by any process of $P2$ is possible because the termination property associated with the fair channels that connect the processes of $P1$ to the processes of $P2$ requires that the sender of a protocol message be non-faulty to have the certainty that this message is ever received. (There is no reception guarantee for a message that is sent an arbitrary but finite number of times.)

In that execution, as no process of $P2$ ever receives a message from a process of $P1$, none of these processes can ever URB-deliver m, which completes the proof of the theorem.

$$\square_{Theorem\ 4.2}$$

Remark   Let us observe that the previous impossibility result is due to the *uniformity* requirement stated in the termination property of the URB abstraction. More precisely, this property states that, if a process p_i URB-delivers a message m, then every non-faulty process has to URB-deliver m. The fact that the process p_i can be a faulty or a non-faulty process defines the uniformity requirement.

If this property is weakened into "if a non-faulty process p_i URB-delivers a message m, then all the non-faulty processes URB-deliver m", then we have the simple reliable broadcast, and the impossibility result does no longer hold. When we look at the construction of Figure 4.1, the predicate $|rec\_by_i[m]| \geq t + 1$ is used to ensure the uniformity requirement. It ensures that, when a message is URB-delivered, at least one non-faulty process has a copy of it.

4.3   THE FAILURE DETECTOR CLASS Θ

The previous impossibility result gives rise to the following natural question is the following: Which information on failures do the processes have to be provided with in order for the URB abstraction to be built whatever the value of t? This section presents the failure detector class, denoted Θ, which is the weakest failure detector class among all the failure detector classes that answer the previous question. This means that any failure detector of a class D, such that the URB abstraction can be built in $\mathcal{AS}\_\mathcal{F}_{n,t}[D]$, can be used to build a failure detector of the class Θ. Said in another way, the information on failures provided by D "contains" the information on failures provided by Θ (as seen at the end of Chapter 2, an algorithm -usually pretty sophisticated- can be needed to extract this information).

4.3.1   DEFINITION OF Θ

A failure detector of the class Θ provides each process p_i with a read-only local variable, a set denoted $trusted_i$, that satisfies the following properties. Let $trusted_i^\tau$ denote the value of $trusted_i$ at time τ. Let us remember that this notion of time is with respect to an external observer: no process has access to it. Let us also remember that $Correct(F)$ denotes the set of processes that are non-faulty in that run. Given a run with the failure pattern F, Θ is defined by the following properties (using the notation introduced in the section devoted to a formal definition of failure detectors in Chapter 2, we have $trusted_i^{\tau} = H(i, \tau)$):

- Accuracy. $\forall i \in \Pi : \forall \tau \in \mathbb{N}: \left(trusted_i^{\tau} \cap Correct(F)\right) \neq \emptyset$.

- Liveness. $\exists \tau \in \mathbb{N}: \forall \tau' \geq \tau : \forall i \in Correct(F) : trusted_i^{\tau'} \subseteq Correct(F)$.

The accuracy property is a perpetual property that states that, at any time, any set $trusted_i$ contains at least one non-faulty process. Let us notice that this process is not required to be always the same, it can change with time. The liveness property states that, after some time, the set $trusted_i$ of any non-faulty process p_i contains only non-faulty processes.

4.3.2   URB IN $\mathcal{AS\_F}_{n,t}[\Theta]$

A construction   Constructing an URB abstraction in the system model $\mathcal{AS\_F}_{n,t}[\emptyset]$ enriched with a failure detector of the class Θ is particularly easy. The only modification to do to the construction described in Figure 4.1 consists in replacing the "$t < n/2$" assumption by the use of the Θ failure detector. From an operational point of view, this amounts to replacing the condition to URB-deliver a message m used in Figure 4.1, namely,

$$(\|rec\_by_i[m]\| \geq t + 1) \wedge (p_i \text{ has not yet URB-delivered } m),$$

by

$$(trusted_i \subseteq rec\_by_i[m]) \wedge (p_i \text{ has not yet URB-delivered } m).$$

The accuracy property of Θ guarantees that, when p_i URB-delivers m, at least one non-faulty process has a copy of m. As we have seen in the construction of Figure 4.1, this guarantees that the application message m that is URB-delivered can no longer be lost). The liveness property of Θ guarantees that eventually m can be locally URB-delivered (if a faulty process could remain forever in $trusted_i$, it could prevent the predicate $trusted_i \subseteq rec\_by_i[m]$) from ever becoming true).

4.3.3   COMPARING Θ AND Σ

Θ *when* $t < n/2$ The URB communication abstraction can be implemented in $\mathcal{AS\_F}_{n,t}[t < n/2]$ without the additional power of a failure detector, and (as we have just seen) can be implemented in $\mathcal{AS\_F}_{n,t}[\Theta]$, whatever the value of t. So, a natural question is the following: Can Θ be implemented in $\mathcal{AS\_F}_{n,t}[t < n/2]$?

Actually, the same algorithm as the one that is described in Figure 6 of Chapter 2 (that builds Σ in $\mathcal{AS}_{n,t}[t < n/2]$) builds a failure detector of the class Θ in $\mathcal{AS\_F}_{n,t}[t < n/2]$. This follows from the fact that, when $t < n/2$, any majority of processes contains always a non-faulty process, and as every non-faulty process sends forever ALIVE () messages, the fair channels connecting each pair of non-faulty processes simulate reliable channels.

Θ *with respect to* Σ The class of quorum failure detectors (Σ) has been introduced in Chapter 2, where it has been shown to be the weakest failure detector class that allows circumventing the impossibility to construct an atomic register in $\mathcal{AS}_{n,t}[\emptyset]$. Let us remember that Σ provides each process p_i with a set $sigma_i$ such that, after some finite time, $sigma_i$ contains only non-faulty processes, and any two quorums $sigma_i$ and $sigma_j$, each taken at any time, do intersect.

Let us consider any system where neither Σ nor Θ can be built. The following theorem shows that Θ can be built in any such system enriched with Σ, while the converse is not true (Σ cannot be built in any such system enriched with Θ).

Theorem 4.3   *In any system where $t \geq n/2$, Σ is strictly stronger than Θ (i.e., Θ can be built from Σ, but Σ cannot be built from Θ).*

Proof Let us first observe that it follows from their definitions that Σ is at least as strong as Θ. This follows from the following two observations. First, their liveness properties are the same. Second, the combination of the intersection and liveness properties of Σ implies that any set $sigma_i$ contains a correct process, which is the accuracy property of Θ. (Let us observe that this is independent of the value of t.)

The rest of the proof shows that, when $t \geq n/2$, the converse is not true, from which follows that Σ is strictly stronger than Θ in systems where $t \geq n/2$.

The proof is by contradiction. Let us assume that there is an algorithm A that, accessing any failure detector of the class Θ, builds a failure detector of the class Σ. Let us partition the processes into two subsets $P1$ and $P2$ (i.e., $P1 \cap P2 = \emptyset$ and $P1 \cup P2 = \{p_1, \ldots, p_n\}$) such that $|P1| = \lceil n/2 \rceil$ and $|P2| = \lfloor n/2 \rfloor$.

Let FD be a failure detector such that, in any failure pattern in which at least one process $p_x \in P1$ (resp., $p_y \in P2$) is non-faulty, outputs p_x (resp. p_y) at all the processes of $P1$ (resp., $P2$). Moreover, in the failure patterns in which all the processes of $P1$ (resp., $P2$) are faulty, FD outputs at all the processes the same non-faulty process $\in P2$ (resp., $P1$).

It is easy to see that FD belongs to the class Θ: no faulty process is ever output (hence we have the liveness property), and at least one non-faulty process is always output at any non-faulty process (hence we have the accuracy property).

Let us consider a failure pattern F where some process $p_x \in P1$ is non-faulty, and FD outputs $trusted_x = \{x\}$, and some process $p_y \in P2$ is non-faulty, and FD outputs $trusted_y = \{y\}$. The process p_x cannot distinguish the failure pattern F from the failure pattern in which all the processes of $P2$ are faulty. Similarly, p_y cannot distinguish the failure pattern F from the failure pattern in which all the processes of $P1$ are faulty. It follows from these observations and the fact that $trusted_x \cap trusted_y = \emptyset$, that the intersection of Σ cannot be ensured, which concludes the proof of the theorem.

$\square_{Theorem\ 4.3}$

The previous theorem actually shows that Σ is Θ + the non-empty intersection of any two sets that are output by Θ.

4.3.4   THE ATOMIC REGISTER ABSTRACTION VS THE URB ABSTRACTION

The atomic register abstraction is strictly stronger than the URB abstraction   An immediate consequence of Theorem 4.3 is that, whatever the value of $t \geq n/2$, Θ can be built in $\mathcal{AS}_{n,t}[\Sigma]$ and $\mathcal{AS}\_\mathcal{F}_{n,t}[\Sigma]$ while Σ can be built neither in $\mathcal{AS}_{n,t}[\Theta]$ nor in $\mathcal{AS}\_\mathcal{F}_{n,t}[\Theta]$.

On another side, as we have seen in Chapter 2, when $t \geq n/2$, Σ is the weakest failure detector class that needs to be added to $\mathcal{AS}_{n,t}[\emptyset]$ in order to be able to build an atomic register. On its side, Θ is the weakest failure detector class that allows the construction of the URB communication abstraction in this type of systems.

This means that, when looking from a *failure detector class point of view*, as the atomic register abstraction requires a stronger failure detector class than the one required by URB, it is a problem strictly stronger than the URB abstraction. This is depicted in Figure 4.2 where an arrow from X to Y means that Y can be built on top of X.

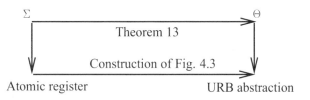

Figure 4.2: From the failure detector class Σ to the URB abstraction ($1 \leq t < n$)

A direct construction   We now present a direct construction of the URB abstraction in any system where the atomic register abstraction can be built. This construction corresponds to the bottom left-to-right arrow of Figure 4.2. This shows that, in crash-prone systems, the atomic register is a strictly stronger abstraction than the URB abstraction.

```
operation URB_broadcast (m):
    sent_i ← sent_i ⊕ m; REG[i].write(sent_i).

background task T:
    repeat forever
        for each j ∈ {1, . . . , n} do
            reg_i[j] ← REG[j].read();
            for each m ∈ reg_i[j] not yet URB-delivered do URB_deliver (m) end for
        end for
    end repeat.
```

Figure 4.3: From atomic registers to URB (code for p_i)

The construction uses an array of 1WMR atomic registers $REG[1..n]$ such that $REG[i]$ can be read by any process but written only by p_i. Moreover, each process p_i manages a local variable denoted $sent_i$ and an array $reg_i[1..n]$. Each atomic register $REG[x]$, and each local variable $sent_x$ or $reg_i[x]$ contains a sequence of messages. Each is initialized to the empty sequence; $\oplus$ denotes message concatenation.

To URB-broadcast a message m a process p_i appends m to the local sequence $sent_i$ and writes its new value into $REG[i]$. The URB-deliveries occur in a background task T. This task is an infinite loop that reads all the atomic registers $REG[j]$ and URB-delivers once all the messages that they contain.

Theorem 4.4   *The algorithm described in Figure 4.3 constructs a URB communication abstraction in any system in which atomic registers can be built.*

Proof   As the algorithm does not forge new messages, the validity property of URB is trivial. Similarly, it follows directly from the text of the algorithm that a message is URB-delivered at most once, hence the integrity property.

For the termination property, let us observe that a non-faulty process p_i that URB-broadcasts a message m adds this message to the sequence of messages contained in $REG[i]$. Then, when p_i executes the background task T, it reads $REG[i]$, and, consequently, $reg_i[i]$ contains m. According to the text of the algorithm, p_i eventually URB-delivers m.

The previous observation has shown that, if a non-faulty process URB-broadcasts a message m, it eventually URB-delivers it. It remains to show that, if any process URB-delivers a message m, then every non-faulty process URB-delivers m.

So, let us assume that a (faulty or non-faulty) process p_x URB-delivers a message m. It follows that p_x has read m from an atomic register $REG[j]$. Due to the atomicity property of $REG[j]$, (1) the process p_j has executed a $REG[j].\mathsf{write}(sent_j)$ operation such that $sent_j$ contains m, and (2) each $REG[j].\mathsf{read}()$ operation issued after this write operation obtains a sequence that contains m. As any non-faulty process p_y reads the atomic registers infinitely often, it will obtain infinitely often m from $REG[j].\mathsf{read}()$ and will URB-deliver it, which concludes the proof of the theorem. $\Box_{Theorem\ 4.4}$

4.4   QUIESCENT UNIFORM RELIABLE BROADCAST

After having introduced the quiescence property, this section introduces three failure detector classes that can be used to obtain quiescent uniform reliable broadcast algorithms. The first one is the class of *perfect* failure detectors (denoted P), the second one is the class of *eventually perfect* failure detectors (denoted $\Diamond P$), and the third one is the class of *heartbeat* failure detectors (denoted HB).

It is shown that P ensures more than the quiescence property (namely, it also ensures termination, which means that there is a time after which a process knows it will never have to send more messages). The class $\Diamond P$ is the weakest class of failure detectors (with bounded outputs) that allows for the construction of quiescent uniform reliable broadcast. Unfortunately, no failure detector of the classes P and $\diamond P$ can be implemented in a pure asynchronous system (see Chapter 7). Finally, the class HB allows quiescent uniform reliable broadcast to be implemented. The failure detectors of that class have unbounded outputs, but they can be implemented in pure asynchronous systems.

4.4.1   THE QUIESCENCE PROPERTY

An infinity of protocol messages   In the previous URB constructions, a correct process is required to send protocol messages forever. This is highly undesirable. This problem can easily be solved by using acknowledgments, in asynchronous systems where every channel is fair and no process ever crashes. Each time a process p_k receives a protocol message MSG (m) from a process p_i, it sends back ACK (m) to p_i, and when p_i receives this acknowledgment message it adds k to $rec\_by_i[m]$. Moreover, a process p_i keeps on sending MSG (m) only to the processes that are not in $rec\_by_i[m]$. Due to the fairness of the channels and the fact that no process crashes; eventually, $rec\_by_i[m]$ contains all the process identities, and, consequently, p_i will stop sending MSG (m).

Unfortunately, (as indicated in Section 4.2) this classical "retransmission + acknowledgment" technique does not work when processes may crash. This is due to the trivial observation that a crashed process cannot send acknowledgments, and (due to asynchrony) a process p_i cannot distinguish a crashed process from a very slow process or a process with which the communication is very slow.

The previous problem has been given the name *quiescence problem*, and solving it requires appropriate failure detectors.

Quiescent construction   An algorithm that implements a communication abstraction is *quiescent* (or "satisfies the quiescence property") if each application message it has to transfer to its destination process(es) gives rise to a finite number of protocol messages.

It is important to see that the quiescence property is not a property of a communication abstraction (it does not belong to its definition). It is a property of its construction. Hence, among all the constructions that correctly implement a communication abstraction, some are quiescent while others are not.

4.4.2   QUIESCENT URB BASED ON A PERFECT FAILURE DETECTOR

This section introduces the class of perfect failure detectors, denoted P, and shows how it can be used to design a quiescent URB construction.

The class P of perfect failure detectors   This failure detector class provides each process p_i with a set variable $suspected_i$ that p_i can only read. The range of this failure detector class is the set of process identities. Intuitively, at any time, $suspected_i$ contains the identities of the processes that p_i considers as having crashed.

More formally (as defined in Section 4.2 of Chapter 2), a failure detector of the class P satisfies the following properties. Let us remember that, given a failure pattern F, $F(\tau)$ denotes the set of processes that have crashed at time τ, $Correct(F)$ the set of processes that are non-faulty in the failure pattern F and $Faulty(F)$ the set of processes that are faulty in F. ($Correct(F)$ and

$Faulty(F)$ define a partition of $\Pi = \{1, \ldots, n\}$.) Moreover, let $Alive(\tau) = \Pi \setminus F(\tau)$ (the set of processes not crashed at time τ). Finally, $suspected_i^\tau$ denotes the value of $suspected_i$ at time τ.

- Completeness. $\exists \tau \in \mathbb{N}: \forall \tau' \geq \tau: \forall i \in Correct(F), \forall j \in Faulty(F): j \in suspected_i^{\tau'}$.
- Strong accuracy. $\forall \tau \in \mathbb{N}: \forall i, j \in Alive(\tau): j \notin suspected_i^\tau$.

The completeness property is an eventual property that states that there is a finite but unknown time (τ) after which any faulty process is definitely suspected by any non-faulty process. The strong accuracy property is a perpetual property that states that no process is suspected before it crashes.

It is trivial to implement a failure detector satisfying either the completeness or the strong accuracy property. Defining permanently $suspected_i = \{1, \ldots, n\}$ satisfies completeness, while always defining $suspected_i = \emptyset$ satisfies strong accuracy. The fact that, due to the asynchrony of processes and messages, a process cannot distinguish if another process has crashed or is very slow, makes it impossible to implement a failure detector of the class P without enriching the underlying unreliable asynchronous system with synchrony-related assumptions (this issue will be addressed in a deeper way Chapter 7).

P with respect to Θ A failure detector of the class Θ can easily be built in $\mathcal{AS}\_\mathcal{F}_{n,t}[P]$. This can be done by defining $trusted_i$ as being always equal to the current value of $\{1, \ldots, n\} \setminus suspected_i$.

Differently, a failure detector of the class P cannot be built in $\mathcal{AS}\_\mathcal{F}_{n,t}[\Theta]$, from which it follows that P is a failure detector class strictly stronger than Θ. This means that $\mathcal{AS}\_\mathcal{F}_{n,t}[\Theta, P]$ and $\mathcal{AS}\_\mathcal{F}_{n,t}[P]$ have the same computability power.

A quiescent URB construction in $\mathcal{AS}\_\mathcal{F}_{n,t}[\Theta, P]$ In this model, each process p_i has a read access to $trusted_i$ and $suspected_i$. Despite the fact that P is stronger than Θ, the construction that follows uses both. This is for a modularity and separation of concerns purpose.

- As we have already seen, Θ is used to ensure the second part of the termination property, namely, if a process URB-delivers a message m, any non-faulty process URB-delivers it. Hence, the "uniformity" of the reliable broadcast is obtained thanks to Θ.
- P is used to obtain the quiescence property. In later sections, P will be replaced by a weaker failure detector class.

The quiescent URB construction for $\mathcal{AS}\_\mathcal{F}_{n,t}[\Theta, P]$ is described in Figure 4.4. It is the same as the one described in Figure 4.1 (where the predicate $|rec\_by_i[m]| \geq t + 1$ is replaced by $trusted_i \subseteq rec\_by_i[m]$ to benefit from Θ) enriched with the following additional statements.

- Each time a process p_i receives a protocol message MSG (m), it systematically sends back an acknowledgment to its sender. This acknowledgment message is denoted ACK (m). Moreover, when a process p_i receives ACK (m) from a process p_k, it knows that p_k has a copy of the application message m and it consequently adds k to $rec\_by_i[m]$. (Let us observe that this would be sufficient to obtain a quiescent URB construction if no process ever crashes.)
- In order to prevent a process p_i from sending forever protocol messages to a crashed process p_j, the task $Diffuse(m)$ is appropriately modified. A process p_i repeatedly sends the protocol message MSG (m) to a process p_j only if $j \notin (rec\_by_i[m] \cup suspected_i)$.

---

operation URB_broadcast (m): send MSG (m) to p_i.

when MSG (m) **is received from** p_k:
    if (first reception of m)
        then allocate $rec\_by_i[m]$; $rec\_by_i[m] \leftarrow \{i, k\}$;
            activate task $Diffuse(m)$
        else $rec\_by_i[m] \leftarrow rec\_by_i[m] \cup \{k\}$
    end if;
    send ACK (m) to p_k.

when ACK (m) **is received from** p_k: $rec\_by_i[m] \leftarrow rec\_by_i[m] \cup \{k\}$.

when $(trusted_i \subseteq rec\_by_i[m]) \wedge (p_i$ has not yet URB-delivered $m)$: URB_deliver (m).

task $Diffuse(m)$:
    repeat
      for each $j \in \{1, \ldots, n\} \setminus rec\_by_i[m]$ **do**
      if $(j \notin suspected_i)$ **then** send MSG (m) to p_j **end if**
      end for
    until $(rec\_by_i[m] \cup suspected_i) = \{1, \ldots, n\}$ **end repeat**.

Figure 4.4: Quiescent uniform reliable broadcast in $\mathcal{AS\_F}_{n,t}[\Theta, P]$ (code for p_i)

Due to the completeness property of the failure detector class P, j will eventually appear in $suspected_i$ if p_j crashes. Moreover, due to the strong accuracy property of the failure detector class P, j will not appear in $suspected_i$ before p_j crashes (if it ever crashes).

The proof that this algorithm is a quiescent construction of the URB abstraction is similar to the proof (given below) of the construction given in Figure 4.5 for the system model $\mathcal{AS\_F}_{n,t}[\Theta, HB]$. It is consequently left to the reader.

Terminating construction   Let us observe that the construction of Figure 4.4 is not only quiescent but also *terminating*. Termination is a property stronger than quiescence.

    More precisely, for each application message m, task $Diffuse(m)$ not only stops sending messages, but eventually terminates. This means that there is a finite time after which the predicate $(rec\_by_i[m] \cup suspected_i) = \{1, \ldots, n\}$ that control the exit of the repeat loop becomes satisfied. When this occurs, the task $Diffuse(m)$ has no longer to send protocol messages and can consequently terminate.

    This is due to the properties of the failure detector class P from which we can conclude that (1) the predicate $rec\_by_i[m] \cup suspected_i = \{1, \ldots, n\}$ becomes eventually true, and (2), when it becomes true, the set $suspected_i$ contains only crashed processes (no non-faulty process is mistakenly considered as crashed by the failure detector).

As we are about to see below, the termination property can no longer be guaranteed when a failure detector of the class $\Diamond P$ or HB (defined below) is used instead of a failure detector of the class P.

The class $\Diamond P$ of eventually perfect failure detectors   This class is the class of eventually perfect failure detectors. As the class P, that class provides each process p_i with a set $suspected_i$ that satisfies the following property: the sets $suspected_i$ can output arbitrarily values during a finite but unknown period of time, after which their outputs are the same as the ones of a perfect failure detector. More formally, $\Diamond P$ includes all the failure detectors that satisfy the following properties.

- Completeness. $\exists \tau \in \mathbb{N}: \forall \tau' \geq \tau: \forall i \in Correct(F), \forall j \in Faulty(F): j \in suspected_i^{\tau'}$.
- Eventual strong accuracy. $\exists \tau \in \mathbb{N}: \forall \tau' \geq \tau: \forall i, j \in Alive(\tau'): j \notin suspected_i^{\tau'}$.

The completeness property is the same as for P: every process that crashes is eventually suspected by every non-faulty process. The accuracy property is weaker than the accuracy property of P. It requires only that there is a time after which only the faulty processes are suspected. Hence, the set $suspected_i$ of each non-faulty process eventually contains all the crashed processes (completeness) and only them (eventual strong accuracy).

As we can see, both properties are eventual properties. There is a finite anarchy period during which the values read from the sets $\{suspected_i\}_{1 \leq i \leq n}$ can be arbitrary (e.g., a non-faulty process can be mistakenly suspected, in a permanent or intermittent manner, during that arbitrarily long period of time). The class P is strictly stronger than the class $\Diamond P$. It is easy to see that the classes $\Diamond P$ and Θ cannot be compared, and $\Diamond P$ and Σ cannot be compared either. This is because, on the one side, the definition of both Θ and Σ involves a perpetual property -a property that has to be always satisfied while the definition of $\Diamond P$ involves only eventual properties, and on the other side, some correct processes can never appear in a set $trusted_i$ or $sigma_i$.

$\Diamond P$-based quiescent URB   A quiescent URB construction that works in $\mathcal{AS\_F}_{n,t}[\Theta, \Diamond P]$ is obtained by replacing the predicate that controls the termination of the task $Diffuse(m)$ in Figure 4.4, by the following weaker predicate $rec\_by_i[m] = \{1, \ldots, n\}$. This modification is due to the fact that a set $suspected_i$ no longer guarantees permanently that all the process it contains have crashed. During the finite but unknown anarchy period, these sets can contain arbitrary values. But, interestingly, despite the possible bad behavior of the sets $suspected_i$, the test $j \notin suspected_i$ (that controls the sending of a protocol message to p_j in the task $Diffuse(m)$) is still meaningful. This is due to the fact that we know that, after some finite time, $suspected_i$ will contain only crashed processes and will eventually contain all the crashed processes. It follows from the previous observation that the construction for $\mathcal{AS\_F}_{n,t}[\Theta, \Diamond P]$ cannot be terminating (according to the failure pattern, it is possible that the termination predicate $rec\_by_i[m] = \{1, \ldots, n\}$ be never satisfied).

4.4.3   THE CLASS HB OF HEARTBEAT FAILURE DETECTORS

The weakest class of failure detectors for quiescent communication   The range of the failure detector classes P and $\Diamond P$ is 2^{Π} (the value of $suspected_i$ is a set of process identities). So, their outputs are bounded. It has been shown that $\Diamond P$ is the weakest class of failure detectors (with bounded outputs) that can be used to implement quiescent reliable communication in asynchronous systems prone to process crashes and the channels of which are unreliable but fair. Unfortunately, it is impossible to implement a failure detector of the class $\Diamond P$ in $\mathcal{AS}_{n,t}[\emptyset]$ and, consequently, in $\mathcal{AS}\_\mathcal{F}_{n,t}[\emptyset]$ either. To be possible, such an implementation requires that the underlying system satisfies additional synchrony assumptions.

The class HB of heartbeat failure detectors   In fact, the uniformity and quiescence properties can be obtained in $\mathcal{AS}\_\mathcal{F}_{n,t}[\emptyset]$ as soon as this system is enriched with the following:

1. Either the assumption $t < n/2$ or a failure detector of the class Θ. This is used to ensure the uniformity property of message delivery (if a message is delivered by a process, it will be delivered by every non-faulty process).

2. A failure detector (of a class denoted HB) that provides each process p_i with an array of counters $HB_i[1..n]$ such that $HB_i[j]$ stops increasing only if p_j crashes. This failure detector is used to ensure the quiescence property.

Formally, a failure detector of the class HB (heartbeat) is defined by the following two properties where $HB_i^\tau[j]$ is the value of $HB_i[j]$ at time τ.

- Completeness. $\forall i \in Correct(F), \forall j \in Faulty(F): \exists K: \forall \tau \in \mathbb{N}: HB_i^\tau[j] < K$.
- Liveness.
    1. $\forall i, j \in \Pi: \forall \tau \in \mathbb{N}: HB_i^\tau[j] \leq HB_i^{\tau+1}[j]$,
    2. $\forall i, j \in Correct(F): \forall K: \exists \tau \in \mathbb{N}: HB_i^\tau[j] > K$.

The range of each entry of the array HB is the set of positive integers. Differently from $\Diamond P$, this range is not bounded. The completeness property states that the heartbeat counter at p_i of a crashed process p_j (i.e., $HB_i[j]$) stops increasing, while the liveness property states that such a heartbeat counter $HB_i[j]$ (1) never decreases and (2) increases without bound if both p_i and p_j are non-faulty.

Let us observe that the counter of a faulty process increases during a finite but unknown period, while the speed at which the counter of a non-faulty process increases is arbitrary (this speed is "asynchronous"). Moreover, the values of two local counters $HB_i[j]$ and $HB_k[j]$ are not related.

Implementing HB   There is a trivial implementation of a failure detector of the class HB in $\mathcal{AS}\_\mathcal{F}_{n,t}[\emptyset]$. Each process p_i manages its array $HB_i[1..n]$ (initialized to $[0,\dots,0]$) as follows. On the one side, p_i repeatedly sends the message HEARTBEAT (i) to each other process. On the other side, when it receives HEARTBEAT (j), p_i increases $HB_i[j]$. This very simple implementation is not quiescent. It requires the alive processes to send messages forever.

This means that HB has to be considered as a "black box" (i.e., we do not look at the way it is implemented) when we say that quiescent communication can be realized in $\mathcal{AS}\_\mathcal{F}_{n,t}[HB]$. In fact, a failure detector of a class such as P, $\Diamond P$, Θ or Σ, provides a system with additional computational power. Differently, a failure detector of a class *HB* constitutes an abstraction that "hides" implementation details (all the non-quiescent part is pieced together in a separate module, namely, the heartbeat failure detector).

A remark on oracles   The notion of *oracle* has first been introduced as a language whose words can be recognized in one step from a particular state of a Turing machine. The main feature of such oracles is to *hide* a sequence of computation steps in a single step, or to *guess* the result of a non-computable function. They have been used to define (a) equivalence classes of problems and (b) hierarchies of problems when these problems are considered with respect to the assumptions they require to be solved.

In our case, failure detectors are oracles that provide the processes with information that depends only on the failure pattern that affects the execution in which they are used. It is important to remember that the outputs of a failure detector never depend on the computation. According to the previous terminology, we can say that the classes such as P, $\Diamond P$, Θ, or Σ are classes of "guessing" failure detectors, while *HB* is a class of "hiding" failure detectors.

A URB construction in $\mathcal{AS}\_\mathcal{F}_{n,t}[\Theta, HB]$ A quiescent URB construction for $\mathcal{AS}\_\mathcal{F}_{n,t}[\Theta, HB]$ is described in Figure 4.5. It is nearly the same as the one for $\mathcal{AS}\_\mathcal{F}_{n,t}[\Theta, P]$ described in Figure 4.4. It differs only in the task *Diffuse*(m). Basically, a process p_i sends the protocol message MSG (m) to a process p_j only if $j \notin rec\_by_i[m]$ (from p_i's point of view, p_j has not yet received that message), and $HB_i[j]$ has increased since the last test (from p_i'point of view, p_j is alive). The local variables $prev\_hb_i[m][j]$ and $cur\_hb_i[m][j]$ are used to keep the two last values read from $HB_i[j]$.

Theorem 4.5   *The algorithm described in Figure 4.5 is a quiescent construction of the URB communication abstraction in* $\mathcal{AS}\_\mathcal{F}_{n,t}[\Theta, HB]$.

Proof   The proof of the URB validity property (no creation of application messages) and URB integrity property (an application message is delivered at most once) follow directly from the text of the construction. Hence, the rest of the proof addresses the URB termination property and the quiescence property. It is based on two preliminary claims. Let us first observe that, once added, an identity j is never withdrawn from $rec\_by_i[m]$.

Claim C1. If a non-faulty process activates *Diffuse*(m), all the non-faulty processes activate *Diffuse*(m).
Proof of claim C1. Let us consider a non-faulty process p_i that activates *Diffuse*(m). It does it when it receives MSG (m) for the first time. Let p_j be a non-faulty process. There are two cases.

- There is a time after which $j \in rec\_by_i[m]$. The process p_i has added j to $rec\_by_i[m]$ because it has received MSG (m) or ACK (m) from p_j. It follows that p_j has received MSG (m). The first time it has received this protocol message, it has activated *Diffuse*(m), which proves the claim for that case.

```
operation URB_broadcast (m): send MSG (m) to p_i.

when MSG (m) is received from p_k:
    if (first reception of m)
        then allocate  rec_by_i[m], prev_hb_i[m], cur_hb_i[m];
            rec_by_i[m] ← {i, k};
            activate task Diffuse(m)
        else rec_by_i[m] ← rec_by_i[m] ∪ {k}
    end if;
    send ACK (m) to p_k.

when ACK (m) is received from p_k: rec_by_i[m] ← rec_by_i[m] ∪ {k}.

when (trusted_i ⊆ rec_by_i[m]) ∧ (p_i has not yet URB-delivered m): URB_deliver (m).

task Diffuse(m):
    prev_hb_i[m] ← [−1, ..., −1];
    repeat
        cur_hb_i[m] ← HB_i;
        for each j ∈ {1, ..., n} \ rec_by_i[m] do
            if (prev_hb_i[m][j] < cur_hb_i[m][j]) then send MSG (m) to p_j end if
        end for;
        prev_hb_i[m] ← cur_hb_i[m]
    until rec_by_i[m] = {1, ..., n} end repeat.
```

Figure 4.5: Quiescent uniform reliable broadcast in $\mathcal{AS}\_\mathcal{F}_{n,t}[\Theta, HB]$ (code for p_i)

- The identity j is never added to $rec\_by_i[m]$. As p_j is non-faulty, it follows from the liveness of HB that $HB_i[j]$ increases forever, from which follows that the predicate $(prev\_hb_i[m][j] < cur\_hb_i[m][j])$ is true infinitely often. It then follows that p_i sends infinitely often MSG (m) to p_j. Due to the termination property of the fair channel connecting p_i to p_j, p_j receives MSG (m) infinitely often from p_i. The first time it receives it, it activates the task $Diffuse(m)$, which concludes the proof of the claim. End of the proof of claim C1.

Claim C2. If all the non-faulty processes activate $Diffuse(m)$, they all eventually execute URB_deliver (m).

Proof of the claim C2. Let p_i and p_j be any pair of non-faulty processes. As p_i executes $Diffuse(m)$ and p_j is non-faulty, p_i sends MSG (m) to p_j until $j \in rec\_by_i[m]$. Let us observe that, due to the systematic sending of acknowledgments and the termination property of the channels, we eventually have $j \in rec\_by_i[m]$. It follows that $rec\_by_i[m]$ eventually contains all the non-faulty processes.

On another side, it follows from the liveness property of Θ that there is a finite time from which $trusted_i$ contains only non-faulty processes.

It follows from the two previous observations that, for any non-faulty process p_i, there is a finite time from which the predicate $(trusted_i \subseteq rec\_by_i[m])$ becomes true forever, and, consequently, p_i can URB-delivers m. End of the proof of claim C2.

Proof of the termination property. Let us first show that, all the non-faulty processes URB-deliver the application message m when a non-faulty process p_i invokes URB_broadcast (m). As p_i is non-faulty, it sends the protocol message MSG (m) to itself and (by assumption) receives it. It then activates the task $Diffuse(m)$. It then follows from the Claim C1 that all the non-faulty processes activate $Diffuse(m)$, and from the Claim C2 that they all URB-deliver m.

Let us now show that if a (faulty or non-faulty) process p_i URB-delivers the application m, then all the non-faulty processes URB-deliver m. As p_i URB-delivers m, we have $trusted_i \subseteq rec\_by_i[m]$. Due to the accuracy property of the underlying failure detector of the class Θ, $trusted_i$ contains always a non-faulty process. Let p_j be a non-faulty process such that $j \in trusted_i$ when the delivery predicate $trusted_i \subseteq rec\_by_i[m]$ becomes true. As $j \in rec\_by_i[m]$, it follows that p_j has received MSG (m) (see the first item of the proof of Claim C1). The first time it has received such a message, p_j has activated $Diffuse(m)$. It then follows from Claim C1 that all the non-faulty processes activate $Diffuse(m)$, and from Claim C2 that they all URB-deliver m.

Proof of the quiescence property. We have to prove here that any application message m give rise to a finite number of protocol messages. This proof relies only on the underlying heartbeat failure detector and the termination property of the underlying fair channels.

Let us first observe that the reception of a protocol message ACK (m) never entails the sending of protocol messages. So, the proof amounts to show that the number of protocol messages of the type MSG (m) is finite. Moreover, a faulty process sends a finite number of protocol messages MSG (m), so we have only to show that the number of MSG (m) messages sent by each non-faulty process p_i is finite. Such messages are sent only inside the task $Diffuse(m)$. Let p_j be a process to which the non-faulty process p_i sends MSG (m). If there is a time from which $j \in rec\_by_i[m]$ holds, p_i stops sending MSG (m) to p_j. So, let us consider that $j \in rec\_by_i[m]$ remains forever false. There are two cases.

- Case p_j is faulty. In that case, there is a finite time after which, due to the completeness property of HB, $HB_i[j]$ no longer increases. It follows that there is a finite time from which the predicate $(prev\_hb_i[m][j] < cur\_hb_i[m][j])$ remains false forever. When this occurs, p_i stops sending messages MSG (m) to p_j, which proves the case.

- Case p_j is non-faulty. We show a contradiction. In that case, the predicate $(prev\_hb_i[m][j] > cur\_hb_i[m][j])$ is true infinitely often. It follows that p_i sends infinitely often MSG (m) to p_j. Due to the termination property of the fair channel from p_i to p_j, the process p_j receives MSG (m) from p_i an infinite number of times. Consequently, it sends back ACK (m) to p_i an infinite number of times, and due to the termination property of the channel from p_j to p_i, p_i receives this protocol message an infinite number of times. At the first reception of ACK (m), p_i adds j to $rec\_by_i[m]$. As no process identity is ever withdrawn from $rec\_by_i[m]$, the predicate $j \in rec\_by_i[m]$ remains true forever, contradicting the initial assumption, which concludes the proof of the quiescence property.

$$\square_{Theorem\ 4.5}$$

Quiescence vs termination   Differently from the quiescent URB construction for $\mathcal{AS\_F}_{n,t}[\Theta, P]$ (given in Figure 4.4), but similarly to the quiescent construction for $\mathcal{AS\_F}_{n,t}[\Theta, \Diamond P]$, the construction described in Figure 4.5 for $\mathcal{AS\_F}_{n,t}[\Theta, HB]$ is not terminating. It is easy to see that it is possible that the task $Diffuse(m)$ never terminates. In fact, while quiescence concerns only the activity of the underlying network activity (due to message transfers), termination is a more general property that is concerned by the activity of both message transfers and processes.

This is due to the fact that the properties of both $\Diamond P$ and HB are eventual. When $HB_i[j]$ does not change, we do not know if it is because p_j has crashed or because its next increase is arbitrarily delayed. This uncertainty is due to the net effect of asynchrony and failures. When the failure detector is perfect (class P), the "due to failures" part of this uncertainty disappears (as when a process is suspected we know for sure that it has crashed), and, consequently, a P-based construction has to cope only with asynchrony.

4.5   URB IN A SYSTEM WITH VERY WEAK CONNECTIVITY

4.5.1   THE SYSTEM MODEL $\mathcal{AS\_W}_{n,t}[\emptyset]$

This section investigates a quiescent construction of the URB abstraction in a system with very weak connectivity. Basically, from the channel assumption point of view, this type of network connectivity is the weakest in the sense that it prevents the system from partitioning while allowing channels to behave unreliably.

Fair channels and unreliable channels   The processes are asynchronous and may crash (as before). On the network side, we have the following. Each directed pair of processes is connected by a channel that is either fair or unreliable. An unreliable channel is similar to a fair channel as far as the validity and integrity properties are concerned, but it has no termination property. Whatever the number of times a message is sent (even an infinite number of times), the channel can lose all its messages. So, if an unreliable channel connects p_i to p_j, it is possible that no message sent by p_i is ever received by p_j on this channel, exactly as if this channel was missing.

An example of such a network is represented in Figure 4.6. A black or white big dot represents a process. A simple arrow from a process to another process represents a fair unidirectional channel. A double arrow indicates that both unidirectional channels connecting the two processes are fair. All the other channels are unreliable (in order not to overload the figure they are not represented).

Channel failure pattern   Given a run, the notion of a *channel failure pattern* (denoted F_c) associated with that run is defined as follows. F_c is the set of the channels that are not fair in that run. When considering Figure 4.6, the channel failure pattern includes all the unidirectional channels that are not explicitly represented.

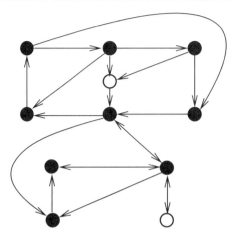

Figure 4.6: An example of a network with fair paths

Notion of fair path   In order to be able to construct a communication abstraction that, in any run, allows any pair of processes that are non-faulty (in that run) to communicate, basic assumptions on the connectivity of the non-faulty processes are required. Such an assumption is based on the notion of fair path.

More precisely, we assume that, in any run characterized by the process failure pattern F and channel failure pattern F_c, every directed pair of non-faulty processes is connected by a directed path made up of non-faulty processes and fair channels. Such a path is called a *fair path*.

When considering Figure 4.6, let the black dots denote the non-faulty processes, and the white dots denote the faulty ones. One can check that every directed pair of non-faulty processes is connected by a fair path.

Notation   The previous system model made up of asynchronous crash-prone processes, fair or unreliable unidirectional channel connecting any directed pair of processes, and the fair path assumption for any run, is denoted $\mathcal{AS\_W}_{n,t}[\emptyset]$.

4.5.2   IMPLEMENTING *HB* IN $\mathcal{AS\_W}_{n,t}[\emptyset]$

This section presents and proves correct a construction of a heartbeat failure detector *HB* in $\mathcal{AS\_W}_{n,t}[\emptyset]$. It is presented before a quiescent URB construction in $\mathcal{AS\_W}_{n,t}[\Theta, HB]$ because it is much simpler and is based on techniques that are re-used in the quiescent URB construction.

A forwarding technique   Each process p_i periodically sends a HEARTBEAT (i) message to all processes (but itself). The fair path assumption is used to cope with the unreliability of some channels in the following way. Whenever a process receives a message HEARTBEAT (i), it forwards it to all processes (but itself and p_i). While this will ensure that, for any pair of correct processes p_i and p_j, $HB_i[j]$ will increase forever, this technique suffers a redhibitory drawback. The processes can forward forever the very same HEARTBEAT (i) message, while p_i sent HEARTBEAT (i) only a finite number of times before crashing.

One could think that the previous problem can be solved by associating a sequence number sn with every HEARTBEAT (i) message sent by p_i. A process p_j forwards HEARTBEAT (i, sn) only if it has not yet received a heartbeat message that originated at p_i with a greater or equal sequence number. Unfortunately, this tentative solution is not satisfactory because the size of the heartbeat messages sent by the correct processes increases without bound. Even worst, it does not work in the fair channel model because a non-faulty process will not send an infinite number of times the very same message HEARTBEAT (i), but an infinite sequence of *different* messages, namely HEARTBEAT ($i, 1$), HEARTBEAT ($i, 2$), etc. As the reader can see, the channels should then be "fair lossy" instead of "fair" in order for the technique based on sequence numbers to work.

Hence, in order to have a construction based on fair channels, we are interested here in a construction in which the size of all messages sent by processes is bounded. This has a very interesting advantage: the message size is independent on the duration of runs (as we are about to see, this size depends only on the number of processes).

The construction   A bounded construction is described in Figure 4.7. The processes send messages of the form HEARTBEAT ($path$) whose content $path$ is a sequence of process identities. The operator $\oplus$ is used to add a process identity to the end of a sequence $path$. To ease the presentation, such a sequence $path$ is sometimes used as a set.

```
background task T:
    repeat forever
        for each j ∈ {1, . . . , n} \ {i} do send HEARTBEAT (⟨i⟩)  to  p_j end for
    end repeat.

when HEARTBEAT (path) is received:
    for each j ∈ path do HB_i[j] ← HB_i[j] + 1 end for;
    for each j ∈ {1, . . . , n} \ (path ∪ {i}) do send HEARTBEAT (path ⊕ i)  to  p_j end for.
```

Figure 4.7: A bounded construction of HB in $\mathcal{AS\_W}_{n,t}[\emptyset]$ (code for p_i)

Each process p_i periodically sends to all the other processes a message HEARTBEAT ($path$), where $path$ contains only its identity i. When a process p_i receives a message HEARTBEAT ($path$), it first increases $HB_i[j]$ for each process p_j such that $j \in path$. Let $path = \langle a, b, \dots, x \rangle$. As we can see from the text of the construction, we deduce from the message content $path = \langle a, b, \dots, x \rangle$, that a message HEARTBEAT ($\langle a \rangle$) originated at p_a, was then received by p_b that expanded it to HEARTBEAT ($\langle a, b \rangle$), that was then received by p_c, etc. Hence, the previous increases of the appropriate entries of HB_i encode the fact that every process in the sequence $path$ was not crashed when it expanded and forwarded the heartbeat message.

After it has increased the appropriate entries of HB_i, p_i forwards the updated heartbeat message HEARTBEAT ($path \oplus i$) to all the processes except itself and the processes already present in $path$ (these processes have been visited by prefixes of the message HEARTBEAT ($path \oplus i$) that originated at p_a where $path = \langle a, b, \ldots, x \rangle$).

Notation   The directed channel from p_i to p_j is denoted $\langle i, j \rangle$. A fair path of process identities $\langle a, b, \ldots, x \rangle$ is *simple* if no identity appears more than once in the path. For every fair path, there is a simple path with same source and same destination.

Theorem 4.6   *The algorithm described in Figure 4.7 is a correct construction of a failure detector of the class HB in $\mathcal{AS\_W}_{n,t}[\emptyset]$. Moreover, this construction uses bounded messages.*

Proof   Proof of the liveness property. The proof that, $\forall i, j$, $HB_i[j]$ never decreases, follows immediately from the text of the algorithm: the only statement where $HB_i[j]$ is updated increases its value.

To prove that, $\forall a, x \in Correct(F)$, $HB_x[a]$ is unbounded, let us first observe that, while the channel $\langle a, x \rangle$ can be unreliable, there is (by assumption) a simple fair path $\langle a, b, \ldots, w, x \rangle$. The process p_a sends infinitely often the heartbeat message HEARTBEAT ($\langle a \rangle$) to each other process. As the channel $\langle a, b \rangle$ is fair and process p_b is non-faulty, it receives the heartbeat message HEARTBEAT ($\langle a \rangle$) an infinite number of times. The process p_b expands each of them into HEARTBEAT ($\langle a, b \rangle$) and forwards this heartbeat message an infinite number of times to p_c, etc., until p_x that receives an infinite number of times the message HEARTBEAT $\langle a, b, \ldots, w \rangle$. It follows that p_x increases $HB_x[a]$ an infinite number of times.

Proof of the completeness   property. In order to prove this property, we first state three claims whose proofs are obvious from the text of the algorithm and, for C3, the channel integrity property.
Claim C1. If a process p_i sends HEARTBEAT ($path$), i is the last identity in the sequence $path$.
Claim C2. Given any HEARTBEAT ($path$) message, no process identity appears twice in $path$.
Claim C3. Let p_i and p_j be two processes and $path$ a non-empty sequence of process identities. If p_i receives the message HEARTBEAT ($path \oplus j$) an infinite number of times, then p_j receives the message HEARTBEAT ($path$) an infinite number of times.

We have to prove that, if p_i is a non-faulty-process and p_j is a faulty process, eventually $HB_i[j]$ stops increasing. The proof is by contradiction. Let us assume that $HB_i[j]$ increases unboundedly. This means that p_i receives an infinite sequence of messages HEARTBEAT ($path_1$), HEARTBEAT ($path_2$), etc., such that $\forall x$: $j \in path_x$. It follows from the claim C2 that the whole set of paths sent in all the heartbeat messages is finite, from which we conclude that there exists $path$ such that $j \in path$ and p_i receives HEARTBEAT ($path$) an infinite number of times. Let $path = \langle i_1, i_2, \ldots, i_x \rangle$. Then, for some $k \leq x$, we have $i_k = j$. There are two cases.

- $k = x$ (j is the last process identity in $path$). It then follows from the claim C1 that p_j sent HEARTBEAT ($path$), and from the integrity property of the channel $\langle j, i \rangle$ that p_j sent infinitely often this message. This contradicts the fact that p_j is faulty (i.e., it eventually crashes).

- $k < x$ (j is not the last process identity in $path$). In that case, by repeatedly applying the claim C3 to the pairs of processes (p_{i_x}, p_i), $(p_{i_{x-1}}, p_{i_x})$, etc., until $(p_{i_k}, p_{i_{k+1}})$, we conclude that $p_{i_{k+1}}$ receives infinitely often the message HEARTBEAT ($\langle i_1, i_2, \ldots, i_k \rangle$).

  As in the previous item, it then follows from the claim C1 that p_{i_k} (i.e., p_j) is the sender of this message HEARTBEAT ($\langle i_1, i_2, \ldots, i_k \rangle$), and from the integrity property of the channel $\langle i_k, i_{k+1} \rangle$, that it sent it infinitely often to $p_{i_{k+1}}$. This contradicts the fact that p_j is faulty (i.e., it eventually crashes).

Proof of the message boundedness property. Finally, the fact that the size of the messages used in the construction is bounded follows from the claim C2. $\square_{Theorem\ 4.6}$

4.5.3   URB IN $\mathcal{AS}\_\mathcal{W}_{n,t}[\Theta, HB]$

This section presents a quiescent URB construction suited to $\mathcal{AS}\_\mathcal{W}_{n,t}[\Theta, HB]$. This construction, described in Figure 4.10, uses the same local variables as the previous constructions. The part related to Θ is exactly the same as the construction presented in Figures 4.4 and 4.5; namely, $trusted_i$ is used to ensure that an application message can be URB-delivered only when a non-faulty process has a copy of it. As we have already seen, the simple replacement of the delivery predicate $trusted_i \subseteq rec\_by_i[m]$ by $|rec\_by_i[m]| \geq t + 1$ gives a construction that works in $\mathcal{AS}\_\mathcal{W}_{n,t}[t < n/2, HB]$.

How to achieve quiescence?   When compared to the previous constructions that rely on fair channels, the main issue of the construction that relies on fair paths is the following. As some channels are not fair, we have to ensure that each message m URB-broadcast by a non-faulty process p_i is appropriately conveyed to every non-faulty process. To that end, taking into account the fact that there is a (unknown) fair path connecting every directed pair of non-faulty processes, p_i can repeatedly send MSG (m) to all processes (but itself), and each time a process receives MSG (m) it forwards it, etc. This flooding technique will guarantee that all the non-faulty processes will receive a copy of the message.

In order to obtain a quiescent construction, this repeated send (along the unknown fair paths) has to eventually stop. One way might be to use acknowledgment messages (as done in Figures 4.4 and 4.5). The acknowledgments sent by p_j have to be transmitted along the (unknown) fair path that connects p_j to p_i using a flooding technique similar to the one use for the messages MSG (m). The question is then: How to stop the repeated sending of these acknowledgment messages in order to obtain the quiescence property? More precisely, how to stop the permanent forwarding of ACK (j, m) messages between two processes p_x to p_y that are on the fair path connecting process p_j, that initiates the sending of the ACK (j, m) messages, and process p_i that are their final destination? A corresponding scenario is depicted in Figure 4.8 (where only fair channels between

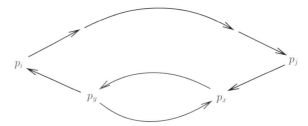

Figure 4.8: Permanent forwarding of ACK (j, m) messages between p_x and y

p_i and p_j are depicted).

The solution to this problem is based on an enrichment of the protocol messages MSG () that makes useless the explicit use of acknowledgment messages. This enrichment is done as follows. Each message MSG () carries now three values. The first one is the message m itself (as in figures 4.4 and 4.5), the second one (denoted rec_by) is a set of processes that have received a copy of m, and its third field is the sequence of process identities (denoted $path$) followed by that copy of m (this is the same as the $path$ field of the heartbeat messages of Figure 4.7).

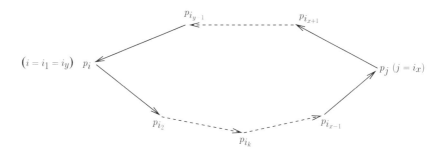

Figure 4.9: An example of fair paths connecting p_i and p_j

Let us consider Figure 4.9 to illustrate the previous items. This figure considers that the channels from p_i to p_j are not fair. Two simple fair paths are represented. Let $i_1 = i_y = i$ and $i_x = j$. A simple fair path from p_i to p_j is the sequence $\langle i_1, i_2, \ldots, i_k, \ldots, i_{x-1}, i_x \rangle$, while a simple fair from p_j to p_i is the sequence $\langle i_x, i_{x+1}, \ldots, i_{y-1}, i_y \rangle$. Let us notice that, as each fair path is simple, a process identity appears no more than once in each of them. Let us also notice that the fair path joining $p_{i_{x+1}}$ to $p_{i_{y-1}}$ can go through a process p_{i_k} that belongs to the simple fair path joining p_i to p_j. It follows that any process identity is contained at most twice in the fair path from p_i to itself $\langle i_1, \ldots, i_{x-1}, i_x, i_{x+1}, \ldots, i_y \rangle$ (that is the concatenation of the two previous simple fair paths).

The idea is that copies of m are forwarded from p_i to p_j through the simple fair path $\langle i_1, \ldots, i_x \rangle$, and their acknowledgments are forwarded from p_j to p_i through the simple fair path $\langle i_x, \ldots, i_y \rangle$. As both the copies of m and their acknowledgments are carried by MSG () messages, these messages are launched at p_i, have their rec_by and $path$ fields enriched while they progress on the concatenation of the fair paths, and return to p_i, thereby acknowledging the receipt of m by p_j.

---

operation URB_broadcast (m): send MSG $(m, \emptyset, \epsilon)$ to p_i.

when MSG $(m, rec\_by, path)$ **is received from** p_k:
  if (first reception of m)
    then allocate $rec\_by_i[m]$, $prev\_hb_i[m]$, $cur\_hb_i[m]$;
        $rec\_by_i[m] \leftarrow \{i\}$;
        activate task $Diffuse(m)$
  end if;
  $rec\_by_i[m] \leftarrow rec\_by_i[m] \cup rec\_by$;
  $dest_i \leftarrow \{x \mid x \in (\Pi \setminus \{i\}) \wedge x$ appears at most once in $path\}$;
  for each $j \in dest_i$ **do** send MSG $(m, rec\_by_i[m], path \oplus i)$ to p_j **end for**.

when $(trusted_i \subseteq rec\_by_i[m]) \wedge (p_i$ has not yet URB-delivered $m)$: URB_deliver (m).

task $Diffuse(m)$:
  $prev\_hb_i[m] \leftarrow [-1, \ldots, -1]$;
  repeat
    $cur\_hb_i[m] \leftarrow HB_i$;
    if $(\exists k : k \notin rec\_by_i[m]) \wedge (prev\_hb_i[m][k] < cur\_hb_i[m][k])$ **then**
      for each j such that $(prev\_hb_i[m][j] < cur\_hb_i[m][j])$
           do send MSG $(m, rec\_by_i[m], \langle i \rangle)$ to p_j
      end for;
      $prev\_hb_i[m] \leftarrow cur\_hb_i[m]$
    end if
  until $rec\_by_i[m] = \{1, \ldots, n\}$ **end repeat**.

Figure 4.10: Quiescent uniform reliable broadcast in $\mathcal{AS\_W}_{n,t}[\Theta, HB]$ (code for p_i)

The construction As already indicated, the construction is described in Figure 4.10. Its skeleton is the same as the one of the previous constructions. As before, $\oplus$ denotes concatenation of a new process identity at the end of a sequence (path), and ϵ denotes the empty sequence. We explain here only the behavior of a process p_i when it receives a protocol message MSG $(m, rec\_by, path)$, and the behavior of the task $Diffuse(m)$.

In the task $Diffuse(m)$, p_i periodically checks if there is a process p_k that, from its local point of view, has not yet received a copy of m (predicate $k \notin rec\_by_i[m]$) and is not crashed (predicate $prev\_hb_i[m][k] < cur\_hb_i[m][k]$). If there is a such a process, p_i sends MSG $(m, rec\_by_i[m], \langle i \rangle)$ to each process p_j that it considers as not crashed. Let us notice that the $path$ field of this message is the sequence $\langle i \rangle$, expressing the fact that this message originated at p_i. It is important to notice that p_i sends MSG $(m, rec\_by_i[m], \langle i \rangle)$ to all the processes that it considers alive and not only to the processes p_k such that $k \notin rec\_by_i[m]$. As we will see in the proof, this is done in order to benefit from the termination property of fair channels (that requires a sender to send an infinite number of times the very same message in order that the destination process receives it).

When p_i receives MSG $(m, rec\_by, path)$ for the first time, it initializes $rec\_by_i[m]$ to $\{i\}$ and activates the task $Diffuse(m)$. In all cases, p_i updates $rec\_by_i[m]$ with what it learns from the message field rec_by. Then, after it has computed the set $dest_i$ of the processes to which it has to forward MSG $(m, rec\_by_i[m], path \oplus i)$, p_i forwards that enriched message. The set $dest_i$ is made up of all the processes but p_i itself and the processes that appear twice or more times in $path$ (let us remember that a process identity can appear at most twice in the concatenation of two simple fair paths that connect two processes, one path in each direction; see our previous discussion concerning Figure 4.9).

4.5.4   PROOF OF THE CONSTRUCTION FOR $AS\_W_{n,t}[\Theta, HB]$

This section proves that the algorithm given in Figure 4.10 constructs a quiescent URB abstraction in the system model $AS\_W_{n,t}[\Theta, HB]$. The structure of the proof is similar to the structure of the proof of Theorem 4.5. The new technical issue consists in replacing the "fair channel" assumption by the "fair path" assumption. Lemmas that capture fundamental properties of the construction are first given.

Lemma 4.7 $\forall (m, path)$: *there is a finite number of distinct messages* MSG $(m, -, path)$.

Proof The field rb in MSG $(m, rb, path)$ is a set of process identities. As there are n processes, the number of possible sets rb is bounded. $\qquad \square_{Lemma\ 4.7}$

Lemma 4.8   *If* p_i *sends* MSG $(m, -, path)$, *no process identity appears more than twice in* $path$.

Proof The lemma follows from the following observations: (a) a process forwards a message only to processes whose identity appears at most once in the field $path$ and (b) a process that sends a message adds it identity to the end of the field $path$ of the message it sends. $\qquad \square_{Lemma\ 4.8}$

Lemma 4.9 $\forall i, j, m$: *(1) the first value of* $rec\_by_i[m]$ *is* $\{i\}$; *(2) if* j *is ever added to* $rec\_by_i[m]$, *it is never withdrawn thereafter; (3) if* $j \in rec\_by_i[m]$, *then* p_j *has received a copy of* m.

Proof The lemma follows directly from the text of the algorithm. $\qquad \square_{Lemma\ 4.9}$

Lemma 4.10   *If a non-faulty process* p_i *activates* $Diffuse(m)$, *every non-faulty process* p_j *activates* $Diffuse(m)$.

Proof We consider two cases according to the fact that there is a fair channel from p_i to p_j or not.

Case 1: There is a fair channel from p_i to p_j. Let us assume by contradiction that p_j never activates $Diffuse(m)$. As p_j adds (for the first time) j into $rec\_by_j[m]$ only when it receives MSG $(m, -, -)$, and as p_j does not invoke $Diffuse(m)$, it follows that we cannot have $j \in rec\_by_j[m]$. Hence, no message MSG $(m, rec\_by, -)$ can then be such that $j \in rec\_by$. It follows that we can never have $j \in rec\_by_i[m]$. As both p_i and p_j are non-faulty, it follows from the liveness property of the underlying heartbeat failure detector that the predicate $prev\_hb_i[m][j] < cur\_hb_i[m][j]$ is true infinitely often. Consequently, p_i sends to p_j messages MSG $(m, -, \langle i \rangle)$ an infinite number of times. As, due to Lemma 4.7, there is a finite number of such messages, it follows that there is a set rb such that p_i sends the message MSG $(m, rb, \langle i \rangle)$ to p_j an infinite number of times. By the termination property of the fair channel $\langle i, j \rangle$, p_j eventually receives such a message and activates the task $Diffuse(m)$, which shows a contradiction.

Case 2: There is no fair channel from p_i to p_j. Let $\langle i_1, i_2, \ldots, i_{x-1}, i_x \rangle$ (with $i_1 = i$ and $i_x = j$) be a fair path from p_i to p_j. It follows from the previous case, that p_{i_2} activates $Diffuse(m)$. Considering the fair channel $\langle i_2, i_3 \rangle$, it follows that p_{i_3} activates $Diffuse(m)$, etc., until p_j that activates $Diffuse(m)$. $\hfill \square_{Lemma\ 4.10}$

Lemma 4.11   *Let p_i and p_j be two non-faulty processes. If p_i invokes $Diffuse(m)$, then eventually the predicate $j \in rec\_by_i[m]$ holds forever.*

Proof Let p_i and p_j be two non-faulty processes. Let us first notice that, due to part (2) of Lemma 4.9, if j is added to $rec\_by_i[m]$, the predicate $j \in rec\_by_i[m]$ holds forever. Hence, the proof consists in showing that j is eventually added to $rec\_by_i[m]$.

The proof is by contradiction. Let us suppose that j is never added to $rec\_by_i[m]$. The notations are exactly the same as in Figure 4.9, namely: $i = i_1 = i_y$ and $i_x = j$; $\langle i_1, \ldots, i_x \rangle$ is a simple fair path from p_i to p_j, and $\langle i_x, \ldots, i_y \rangle$ is a simple fair path from p_j to p_i. Moreover, for $1 \leq \alpha < y$, let $P_\alpha = \langle i_1, \ldots, i_\alpha \rangle$. Let us notice that, as both paths $\langle i_1, \ldots, i_x \rangle$ and $\langle i_x, \ldots, i_y \rangle$ are simple, no process identity can appear more than twice in P_α. This allows us to conclude that the process identity $i_{\alpha+1}$ appears at most once in P_α.

Claim C. For each $\alpha \in \{1, \ldots, y - 1\}$, there is a set rb_{i_α}, containing $\langle i_1, \ldots, i_\alpha \rangle$, such that p_{i_α} sends MSG $(m, rb_{i_\alpha}, P_\alpha)$ to $p_{i_{\alpha+1}}$ an infinite number of times.

Assuming the claim C is true, let us consider $\alpha = y - 1$. It follows from the claim and the termination property of the fair channel from p_{i_α} ($= p_{i_{y-1}}$) to p_{i_y} ($= p_i$) that p_i eventually receives a message MSG $(m, rb_{i_{y-1}}, P_{y-1})$. When p_i receives such a message, it adds $rb_{i_{y-1}}$ to $rec\_by_i[m]$. As $rb_{i_{y-1}}$ contains $\{i_1, \ldots, i_{y-1}\}$, and $i_x \in \{i_1, \ldots, i_{y-1}\}$ (see Figure 4.9), we have $i_x \in rec\_by_i[m]$, i.e., $j \in rec\_by_i[m]$, which contradicts the assumption that j never belongs to $rec\_by_i[m]$ and proves the lemma.

Proof of the claim C. The claim is proved by induction on α. The base case involves p_{i_1} $(= p_i)$ and p_{i_2}. Let us remember that both p_{i_2} and p_j are non-faulty. We consequently have the following:
(1) the predicate $(j \notin rec\_by_i[m]) \land (prev\_hb_i[m][j] < cur\_hb_i[m][j])$ is true infinitely often ($j \notin rec\_by_i[m]$ comes from the contradiction assumption, while $prev\_hb_i[m][j] < cur\_hb_i[m][j]$ comes from the accuracy of the underlying heartbeat failure detector),
(2) the predicate $prev\_hb_i[m][i_2] < cur\_hb_i[m][i_2]$ is true infinitely often (this comes from the accuracy of the underlying heartbeat failure detector; let us observe that i_2 can be such that $i_2 \in rec\_by_i[m]$),
(3) the channel from p_{i_1} $(= p_i)$ to p_{i_2} is fair.
It follows from these observations that p_{i_1} $(= p_i)$ sends messages of the form MSG $(m, -, p_{i_1})$ to p_{i_2} an infinite number of times. Hence, due to Lemma 4.7, there is a set rb_{i_1} such that p_i sends MSG (m, rb_{i_1}, i_1) to p_{i_2} an infinite number of times. Finally, due to the parts (1) and (2) of Lemma 4.9, we have $i_1 \in rb_{i_1}$, which concludes the proof of the base case.

For the induction step, let us consider that for $1 \leq \alpha < x - 1$, p_{i_α} sends MSG $(m, rb_{i_\alpha}, P_\alpha)$ to $p_{i_{\alpha+1}}$ an infinite number of times, where rb_{i_α} contains $\{i_1, i_2 \ldots, i_\alpha\}$. As the channel from p_{i_α} to $p_{i_{\alpha+1}}$ is fair, $p_{i_{\alpha+1}}$ receives MSG $(m, rb_{i_\alpha}, P_\alpha)$ from p_{i_α} an infinite number of times. As $p_{i_{\alpha+2}}$ is non-faulty and appears at most once in $P_{\alpha+1}$, it follows that each time $p_{i_{\alpha+1}}$ receives MSG $(m, rb_{i_\alpha}, P_\alpha)$, it sends a message of the form MSG $(m, -, P_{\alpha+1})$ to $p_{i_{\alpha+2}}$. It is easy to see from the text of the algorithm that each message MSG $(m, rb, P_{\alpha+1})$ is such that rb contains rb_{i_α} and $i_{\alpha+1}$. It then follows from Lemma 4.7 that there is a set $rb_{i_{\alpha+1}}$ such that this set contains $\{i_1, \ldots, i_{\alpha+1}\}$, and $p_{i_{\alpha+1}}$ sends MSG $(m, rb_{i_{\alpha+1}}, P_{\alpha+1})$ to $p_{i_{\alpha+2}}$ an infinite number of times, which concludes the proof of the claim.   □$_{Lemma\ 4.11}$

Lemma 4.12   *If all the non-faulty processes activate Diffuse(m), they all eventually execute* URB_deliver *(m).*

Proof Let p_i and p_j be two non-faulty processes. It follows from Lemma 4.11 that we eventually have $j \in rec\_by_i[m]$, from which we conclude that $rec\_by_i[m]$ eventually contains all non-faulty processes. Moreover, it follows from part (2) of Lemma 4.9 that no identity is ever withdrawn from $rec\_by_i[m]$.

On another side, the liveness property of Θ states that there is a finite time from which $trusted_i$ contains only non-faulty processes. It follows that, after some unknown but finite time instant, the delivery predicate $trusted_i \subseteq rec\_by_i[m]$ remains true forever, which entails the URB-delivery of m by p_i.   □$_{Lemma\ 4.12}$

Theorem 4.13   *The algorithm described in Figure 4.10 is a construction of the URB abstraction.*

Proof The proof of the validity property and the integrity property of the URB abstraction (no creation or alteration of application messages for validity, and an application message is URB-delivered at most once for integrity) are obvious. The rest of the proof of the termination property of the URB abstraction is the same as the proof done in Theorem 4.5. It is repeated here for completeness.

Let us first consider the case of a non-faulty process p_i that URB-broadcasts an application message m. As p_i is non-faulty, it invokes $Diffuse(m)$. By Lemma 4.10, all the non-faulty processes eventually invoke $Diffuse(m)$, and by Lemma 4.12, they all URB-deliver m.

Let us now show that if a (faulty or non-faulty) process p_i URB-delivers m, then all the non-faulty processes URB-deliver m. As p_i URB-delivers m, we have $trusted_i \subseteq rec\_by_i[m]$. It follows from the accuracy property of Θ (namely, $trusted_i$ always contains a -possibly changing- non-faulty process), that there is non-faulty process p_j such that $j \in rec\_by_i[m]$. It then follows from part (3) of Lemma 4.9 that p_j has a copy of m. The first time it received a message MSG $(m, -, -)$, p_j has activated the task $Diffuse(m)$. Then, due to Lemmas 4.10 and 4.12, all the non-faulty processes URB-deliver m, which concludes the proof of the theorem. $\square_{Theorem\ 4.13}$

Theorem 4.14   *The algorithm described in Figure 4.10 is a quiescent construction.*

Proof Let us first show that if a non-faulty process p_i activates the task $Diffuse(m)$, it eventually stops sending messages in that task. Let p_j be another process. There are two cases.

- If p_j is non-faulty, due to Lemma 4.11, there is a finite time after which $j \in rec\_by_i[m]$ holds forever.

- If p_j is faulty, due to the completeness property of the underlying heartbeat failure detector, there is a finite time after which the predicate $(prev\_hb_i[m][j] < cur\_hb_i[m][j])$ remains forever false.

Therefore, there is a finite time after which the predicate $(j \notin rec\_by_i[m]) \wedge (prev\_hb_i[m][j] < cur\_hb_i[m][j])$ is always false, which proves that eventually p_i stops sending messages in the task $Diffuse(m)$.

We have now to prove that any process eventually stops sending messages of the form MSG $(m, -, -)$. The proof is by contradiction. Let us suppose that there is a process p_i that never stops sending messages of the form MSG $(m, -, -)$. Due to Lemma 4.8 and the fact that the number of processes is bounded, the third component of a message of the form MSG $(m, -, -)$ ranges over a finite set of values. Therefore, there is some fixed $path$ such that p_i sends an infinite number of times the same message MSG $(m, -, path)$. Finally, due to Lemma 4.7, there is a fixed value rb, such that p_i sends an infinite number of times the same message MSG $(m, rb, path)$.

Among all the messages that are sent infinitely often, let $path_0$ be a shortest one (there can be several that have the shortest length), and let p_i be the corresponding sending process. Let us notice that p_i is non-faulty. Due the first part of the proof, there is a time after which p_i stops sending messages in its task $Diffuse(m)$. It follows that p_i sends messages of the form MSG $(m, -, path_0)$ only when it receives a message. Let MSG $(m, -, path_1)$ be such a message. Due to the text of the algorithm, we have $path_0 = path_1 \oplus i$. Let $path_1 = \langle \ldots, j \rangle$. As p_i sends an infinity of messages of the form MSG $(m, -, path_0)$, it has received an infinity of messages of the form MSG $(m, -, path_1)$ from p_j. Due to the integrity property of the channel from p_j to p_i, p_j has sent messages of the form MSG $(m, -, path_1)$ to p_i. But $path_1$ is strictly shorter than $path_0$, which contradicts the minimality of $path_0$ and concludes the proof of the quiescence property. $\square_{Theorem\ 4.14}$

4.6   BIBLIOGRAPHIC NOTES

- The concept of failure detectors has been introduced by Chandra and Toueg in [34] where they have defined, among other failure detector classes, the classes P and $\diamond P$. The class P has been shown to be the weakest class of failure detectors to solve some distributed computing problems in [46, 95].

- The oracle notion in sequential computing is presented in numerous textbooks. Among other books, the reader can consult [78, 100].

- The weakest failure detector class Θ that allows to construct an URB abstraction despite asynchrony, the fact that any number of processes can crash and the channels are only fair, has been proposed by Aguilera, Toueg and Deianov [12].

  The relation between Θ and Σ has been established in [47].

- The notion of quiescent communication and the heartbeat failure detector class have been introduced by Aguilera, Chen and Toueg in [3, 5]. These notions have been investigated in [4] in the context of partitionable networks.

  The very weak communication model and the corresponding quiescent URB construction, that has been presented in the last section, have been introduced in [5].

- When we consider a system as simple as the one made up of two processes connected by a bidirectional channel, there are impossibility results related to the effects of process crashes, channel unreliability, or the constraint to use only bounded sequence numbers. Chapter 22 of Lynch's book [117] presents an in-depth study of the power and limit of unreliable channels.

- The effects of lossy channels on problems in general, in asynchronous systems that are not enriched with failure detectors, is addressed in [20].

- Given two processes that (a) can crash and recover, (b) have access to volatile memory only, and (c) are connected by a (physical) *reliable* channel, let us consider the problem that consists in building a (virtual) reliable channel connecting these two (possibly faulty) processes. Maybe surprisingly, this problem is impossible to solve [62]. This is mainly due to the absence of stable storage.

  It is also impossible to build a reliable channel when the processes are reliable (they never crash) and the underlying channel can duplicate and reorder messages (but cannot create or lose messages), and only bounded sequence numbers can be used [157].

  Differently, if processes do not crash and the underlying channel can lose and reorder messages but cannot create or duplicate messages, it is possible to build a reliable channel, but this construction is highly inefficient [1].

PART III

Agreement Abstractions

CHAPTER 5

The Consensus Abstraction

Consensus is one of the most fundamental problems in fault-tolerant distributed computing. It states that the processes that do not fail have to agree in a non-trivial way. This agreement takes the form of a value (called *decision value*) that has to be one of the values proposed by the processes to the consensus instance.

After having defined the consensus problem, this chapter investigates its use to build a total order uniform reliable broadcast abstraction, and shows that both problems are in fact equivalent. It also shows how, in an appropriate distributed system, it can also help solving the non-blocking atomic commit problem. This problem considers a global computation decomposed into a set of local computations, each associated with a process. After having executed their local computations, the processes have to collectively commit or abort their local computations. To that end, according to its local execution, each process issues a "yes/no" vote. If there is a "no" vote, all local computations have to be aborted. If all processes vote "yes" and there is no failure, each of them has to commit its local computation.

Finally, the chapter shows that consensus cannot be solved in pure asynchronous distributed systems prone to process crashes (i.e., in $\mathcal{AS}_{n,t}[\emptyset]$). This is the famous FLP impossibility result (named after Fischer, Lynch and Paterson who proved it). This impossibility is remarkable in the sense that it holds (1) even if the processes want to agree on a single bit, and (2) for a very benign type of failures (at most one process may fail and the failure consists in a premature stopping; moreover the channels are reliable). Hence, this impossibility exhibits a fundamental limitation of asynchronous message-passing systems in presence of process crash failures. An immediate consequence is that harder problems such as leader election and mutual exclusion cannot be solved either in $\mathcal{AS}_{n,t}[\emptyset]$. The next chapter will address how $\mathcal{AS}_{n,t}[\emptyset]$ has to be enriched in order for consensus to become solvable.

5.1 THE CONSENSUS ABSTRACTION

5.1.1 THE NEED FOR AGREEMENT

A simple agreement problem is the following coordination problem (called *unique action* problem). Each process proposes an action to execute, and they all have to execute once the very same action that has to be one of the actions that has been proposed.

Another example of agreement problem consists in enriching the uniform reliable broadcast (URB) abstraction investigated in the previous chapters with the following additional delivery property: the messages have to be delivered in the same order at all the non-faulty processes (this defines a message delivery sequence S), and the sequence of messages delivered by a faulty process has to be a prefix of S. (This is the *total order* URB abstraction informally discussed at the end of Chapter 3).

To attain this goal, the processes have to agree (in one way or another) on a common delivery order. One solution could be to ask one process to act as a server that would establish the common delivery order. But what to do when this process crashes? Elect another process? The processes will then have to execute a leader election protocol to agree on the same new server process, that has to be a non-faulty process. This approach only "moves" the problem of agreeing on a common delivery order to the problem of agreeing on a new server. In both cases, an agreement problem has to solved.

It appears that the unique action problem, the construction of a common message delivery order (and several other coordination problems) are particular instances of a more generic problem, called *consensus* problem. As we are about to see, consensus is one of the most fundamental problems of distributed computing in presence of failures.

5.1.2   THE CONSENSUS PROBLEM

Definition   In the consensus problem, each process p_i proposes a value v_i and all processes have to agree (we also say "decide") on the same value that has to be one of the proposed values. In a more precise way, this problem is defined by the following properties.

- Validity. If a process decides a value v, then v has been proposed by some process.
- Integrity. A process decides at most once.
- Agreement. No two processes decide different values.
- Termination. Each correct process decides.

Let A be an algorithm that is assumed to solve the consensus problem. This algorithm is correct if all its runs satisfy the previous properties. Validity, integrity and agreement define the consensus safety properties, while termination defines its liveness property.

Binary vs multivalued consensus   Let V be the (finite or infinite) set of values that can be proposed by the processes. If $|V| = 2$, only two values (usually denoted 0 and 1) can be proposed, and the consensus is *binary*. When $|V| > 2$, the consensus is *multivalued*.

Consensus object   Each instance of the consensus problem defines a concurrent object CS that provides processes with a single operation denoted $CS.\mathbf{propose}(v)$, where v is the value proposed by the invoking process. That operation returns to the invoking process the value decided by the consensus object. In that sense, a consensus object can be seen as a type of write-once object where the $\mathbf{propose}(v)$ operation atomically tries to write v and always returns the value of the object. Only one write succeeds. As a process can invoke $C.\mathbf{propose}(v)$ only once, the consensus problem is a *one-shot* agreement problem.

When considering, the "object terminology", the interface of a consensus object is the method `propose()`. That method returns a value (namely the same value) to every process that involves it.

Remark   While consensus can be solved in a trivial way in failure-free asynchronous systems (e.g., deciding the value proposed by the process with the smallest identity), this is no longer the case in failure-prone systems. The uncertainty created by the combined effect of asynchrony, concurrency, and failures makes the design of consensus algorithms in pure asynchronous systems such as $\mathcal{AS}_{n,t}[\emptyset]$ not only very difficult but (as we will see later) impossible.

5.1.3   WHY CONSENSUS IS FUNDAMENTAL

In a lot of distributed computing applications, the processes have to agree on the state of the application (or an appropriate part of it). Consensus can be used to help the processes solve easily this problem as follows.

Each process p_i first computes its local view of the system state. This view can be obtained from messages exchanged with other processes (as an example, in $\mathcal{AS}_{n,t}[\emptyset]$ a process can wait for messages from $n - t$ processes without being permanently blocked). Once computed, its local view of the system state becomes the value it proposes to a consensus instance. Then, thanks to the consensus properties, the very same view is adopted by all the processes that are alive. In that way, all these processes can continue from the same consistent view of the computation. This view is consistent in the sense that (1) it is not arbitrary (it has been computed by a process and is related to the past computation), and (2) no two processes can continue with different views. (If they apply the same deterministic function to that view, they will obtain the same result.)

5.1.4   CONSENSUS AND NON-DETERMINISM

While the specification of the consensus problem states that no two processes can decide different values, it does not state which value is decided. It only states that the decided value is one of the proposed values. Due to the uncertainty created by asynchrony and failures, that value cannot always be computed from a deterministic function on the proposed values. In that sense, a consensus object solves some form of non-determinism.

Actually, due to net effect of asynchrony and failures, the value decided depends on the run. (Differently, $\mathsf{fact}(n) = n!$ is deterministic. Given n, whatever the way $\mathsf{fact}()$ is implemented and whatever the run, the value of $\mathsf{fact}(n)$ is unique.)

5.2   THE TOTAL ORDER URB COMMUNICATION ABSTRACTION

5.2.1   THE TO-URB ABSTRACTION: DEFINITION

Similarly to the FIFO (first in, first out) and CO (causal order) URB communication abstractions, the TO-URB abstraction is the uniform reliable broadcast enriched with a delivery property stating that the processes deliver the messages in the same order (TO stands for "total order").

Definition   "TO_broadcast ()" and " TO_deliver ()" being its two communication operations, the TO-URB abstraction is defined by the following properties. Let us remember that, in the family of the URB abstractions, each application message m is unique, and $m.sender$ denotes the identity of the process that has issued the broadcast of m.

- Validity. If a process TO-delivers a message m, then m has been TO-broadcast by some process.
- Integrity. A process TO-delivers a message m at most once.
- Total order message delivery. If a process TO-delivers a message m and then TO-delivers a message m', then no process TO-delivers m' unless it has previously TO-delivered m.
- Termination. (1) If a non-faulty process TO-broadcasts a message m, or (2) if a process TO-delivers a message m, then each non-faulty process TO-delivers the message m.

Hence, TO-URB = URB + TO message delivery. It follows that, as FIFO-URB and CO-URB, TO-URB is not a one-shot problem. Its specification involves all the messages that are TO-broadcast.

Adding FIFO or CO to the TO message delivery property   While the URB abstraction requires that any two non-faulty processes deliver the same set S of messages, and that a faulty process delivers a subset of S, the TO-URB abstraction requires that the non-faulty processes deliver the same sequence of messages, and that a faulty process delivers a prefix of that sequence.

As URB can been enriched with FIFO (or CO) message delivery, it is possible to require that (1) the messages be delivered in the same order, (2) this total delivery order respecting the local FIFO order for each sender process, or the global CO order, whose definitions are recalled below.

- FIFO message delivery. If a process FIFO-broadcasts a message m and then FIFO-broadcasts a message m', no process FIFO-delivers m' unless it has FIFO-delivered m before.
- CO message delivery. (Let us remember that "$\rightarrow_M$" denotes the causality precedence relation defined on the messages.) If $m \rightarrow_M m'$, no process CO-delivers m' unless it has previously CO-delivered m.

We then obtain a TO+FIFO-URB communication abstraction or the stronger TO+CO-URB communication abstraction. Algorithms similar to the ones described in Section 2 of Chapter 3 can be designed to build a TO+FIFO-URB abstraction and a TO+CO-URB abstraction from a TO-URB abstraction. These algorithms correspond to the horizontal dotted arrows at the bottom of Figure 5.1. It is also possible to design "direct" constructions for the two dotted vertical arrows.

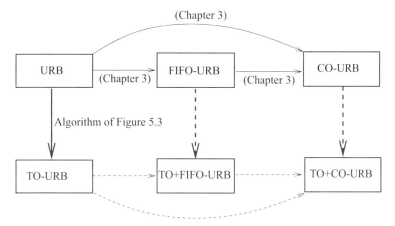

Figure 5.1: Adding total order message delivery to various URB abstractions

The fundamental missing link   The important point here is that, unfortunately, going from URB to TO-URB (and more generally designing constructions corresponding to the three top-down arrows of Figure 5.1) cannot be done within $\mathcal{AS}_{n,t}[\emptyset]$. The net effect of asynchrony and crashes makes it impossible. This impossibility will be formally addressed in Section 5.6.

Delivering the messages according to causal order is possible in $\mathcal{AS}_{n,t}[\emptyset]$ because (a coding of) the causal past of each message can be attached to it. This is no longer possible when one wants to deliver the messages according to a total order. Intuitively, this is because ordering in the same way, at each process, the delivery of messages whose broadcast are unrelated requires synchronization that cannot be implemented in presence of asynchrony and failures. Additional computing power from the underlying system is needed, which means that $\mathcal{AS}_{n,t}[\emptyset]$ has to be enriched in order TO-URB can be built. As we are about to see, this enrichment consists in consensus objects.

5.2.2   FROM CONSENSUS TO THE TO-URB ABSTRACTION

This section describes a TO-URB construction that works in $\mathcal{AS}_{n,t}[CONS]$, i.e., $\mathcal{AS}_{n,t}[\emptyset]$ enriched with consensus objects. This is not counter-intuitive as TO-URB pieces together a communication problem (URB abstraction) and an agreement problem (the definition of a common delivery order).

Structure of the construction   The structure of the construction is described in Figure 5.2. The middleware layer implementing the construction is defined by the algorithm described in Figure 5.3 that assumes an underlying URB-broadcast abstraction (that, as we have seen in Chapter 3) can be built in $\mathcal{AS}_{n,t}[\emptyset]$ and an unbounded number of consensus objects $CS[1..]$ shared by the processes.

Description of the construction   Each process p_i manages three local variables: a set $URB\_delivered_i$ (initially $\emptyset$) containing the messages that have been locally URB-delivered; a fifo queue $TO\_deliverable_i$ (initially the empty sequence denoted ϵ) that contains the sequence of messages

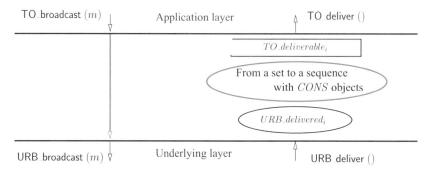

Figure 5.2: Adding total order message delivery to the URB abstraction

that, from the beginning, have been ordered the same way at all the processes; and a sequence number sn_i (initialized to 0) used to address a particular consensus object.

To make the presentation easier, the sequence $TO\_deliverable_i$ is sometimes considered as a set. As all the messages that are TO-broadcast are different, this does not create problems. The operator $\oplus$ denotes sequence concatenation.

---

init: $sn_i \leftarrow 0$; $TO\_deliverable_i \leftarrow \epsilon$; $URB\_delivered_i \leftarrow \emptyset$.

operation TO_broadcast (m): URB_broadcast (m).

when ($TO\_deliverable_i$ contains messages not yet TO-delivered):
    let m be the first message of $TO\_deliverable_i$ not yet TO-delivered;
    TO_deliver (m).

when m **is URB-delivered**: $URB\_delivered_i \leftarrow URB\_delivered_i \cup \{m\}$.

background task T:
    repeat forever
        wait $((URB\_delivered_i \setminus TO\_deliverable_i) \neq \emptyset)$;
        let $seq_i = (URB\_delivered_i \setminus TO\_deliverable_i)$;
        order (arbitrarily) messages in seq_i;
        $sn_i \leftarrow sn_i + 1$;
        $res_i \leftarrow CS[sn_i].propose (seq_i)$;
        $TO\_deliverable_i \leftarrow TO\_deliverable_i \oplus res_i$
    end repeat.

Figure 5.3: Building a TO-URB abstraction in $\mathcal{AS}_{n,t}[CONS]$ (code for p_i)

When it issues TO_broadcast (m), a process p_i simply URB-broadcasts m. When it URB-delivers a message m, it adds it to its local set $URB\_delivered_i$. To facilitate the presentation, the messages added to $URB\_delivered_i$ and $TO\_deliverable_i$ are never withdrawn. (In a practical setting, a garbage collection mechanism should be added.)

The core of the algorithm is the way messages from $URB\_delivered_i$ are ordered and placed at the tail of the sequence $TO\_deliverable_i$. This is the work of the background task T. Messages are TO-delivered in the order they have been deposited in $TO\_deliverable_i$.

The principle that underlies the task T is the following. This task T is an endless asynchronous distributed iteration. The first iteration determines a first sequence of messages that the processes append at the tail of their variables $TO\_deliverable_i$. The second iteration determines a second sequence of messages that the processes append at the tail of their variables $TO\_deliverable_i$, etc. Hence, all the processes p_i append the same sequence of messages at the tail their variables $TO\_deliverable_i$, and, consequently, they all will be able to TO-deliver the messages in the same order. A consensus object is associated with each loop iteration in order the processes agree on the same sequence of messages to add to their variables $TO\_deliverable_i$.

From an operational point of view, a process p_i first waits for messages that have been URB-delivered but not yet added to the sequence $TO\_deliverable_i$. Then p_i orders these messages (sequence seq_i) that it proposes to the next consensus object, namely, $CS[sn_i]$. The way messages are ordered in seq_i is arbitrary, the important point is here that seq_i is a sequence. Finally, let res_i be the sequence of messages decided by this consensus object, i.e., the value returned by $CS[sn_i]$.propose (seq_i). The sequence res_i (that has been proposed by some process) is the sequence of messages that the processes have agreed upon during their sn-th iteration, and each process p_i appends it to its variable $TO\_deliverable_i$.

The loop is asynchronous, which means that some seq_i proposed by p_i can contain few messages, while other can contain many messages. Moreover, several consensus instances can be concurrent, but distinct consensus instances are totally independent. An important point is here that a non-faulty process never stops executing the task T.

Remark: propose messages or propose message identities to a consensus object?   The previous algorithm considers that a consensus proposal is a sequence of messages. It could instead be the sequence of their identities, and the size of proposals would be consequently shorter. The algorithm can easily be modified to take into account this improvement. Then, $TO\_deliverable_i$ would be a sequence of message identities, and the full messages (content plus identity) would be kept in $URB\_delivered_i$. If we adopt this improvement, it becomes possible that a message identity belongs to $TO\_deliverable_i$ while the corresponding message has not yet been URB-delivered (and consequently is not presently in $URB\_delivered_i$). The TO-delivery of a message is now constrained by an additional **wait** statement. More precisely, when m has to be TO-delivered (its identity is the identity of the next message to be TO-delivered), while its content has not yet been URB-delivered, the process has to wait for the URB-delivery of that message in order to TO-deliver it.

Let us observe that (as done in Figure 5.3) when sequences of messages are proposed, it is possible that res_i contains a message m not yet URB-delivered p_i. But the previous problem cannot occur because, in that case, res_i contains the full message m and not only its identity.

Remark: on the number of consensus instances   It is easy to see that, if processes URB-broadcast a finite number (k) of messages, $k' \leq k$ consensus instances will be used. This means that this construction is "quiescent with respect to consensus instances".

Theorem 5.1   *The algorithm described in Figure 5.3 constructs a TO-URB abstraction in* $\mathcal{AS}_{n,t}[CONS]$.

Proof Notations. For any i and any $sn \geq 1$, let $seq_i[sn]$, $res_i[sn]$, and $TO\_deliverable_i[sn]$ denote the values of seq_i, res_i, and $TO\_deliverable_i$, respectively, in the last two lines of the sn-th iteration of the task T executed by p_i. Let also $res[sn]$ denote the sequence of messages decided by the consensus object $CS[sn]$ (due to the consensus agreement property, $res[sn]$ is unique). Finally, let $TO\_deliverable_i[0]$ denote the initial value of $TO\_deliverable_i$ (i.e., the empty sequence).

Claim C1. For any two processes p_i and p_j such that p_j is correct, and any $sn \geq 1$: (1) if p_i invokes $CS[sn]$.propose () then p_j invokes $CS[sn]$.propose (), (2) if p_i returns from its invocation, we have $TO\_deliverable_i[sn] = TO\_deliverable_j[sn] = res[1] \oplus \cdots \oplus res[sn]$.
Proof of the   claim C1. The proof is by simultaneous induction on (1) and (2).

- Base case: $sn = 1$. If p_i invokes $CS[1]$.propose (), then $URB\_delivered_i$ contains at least one message m. Due to the termination property of the underlying URB abstraction and the fact that p_j is non-faulty, eventually $m \in URB\_delivered_j$. Hence, there is a time after which the predicate $(URB\_delivered_j \setminus TO\_deliverable_j[0]) \neq \emptyset$ is true. When this occurs, p_j invokes $CS[1]$.propose ().

  Due to the termination property of the underlying consensus object $CS[1]$ and the fact that p_j is non-faulty, it returns from its invocation. Assuming that p_i also returns from its invocation, it follows from the agreement property of $CS[1]$ that $res_i[1] = res_j[1] = res[1]$, and as $TO\_deliverable_j[0]$ is the empty sequence, we have $TO\_deliverable_i[1] = TO\_deliverable_j[1] = res[1]$.

- Let us assume that the claim holds for all sn such that $1 \leq sn < k$. Let us first show that, if p_i (that is faulty or non-faulty) invokes $CS[k]$.propose () then the non-faulty process p_j invokes $CS[k]$.propose (). As p_i invokes $CS[k]$.propose (), $URB\_delivered_i$ must contain a message m such that $m \in URB\_delivered_i \setminus TO\_deliverable_i[k - 1]$. As $TO\_deliverable_i[k - 1] = TO\_deliverable_j[k - 1] = res[1] \oplus \cdots \oplus res[k - 1]$ (induction assumption), it follows that $m \notin TO\_deliverable_j[k - 1]$. Moreover, due to the termination property of the URB abstraction and the fact that p_j is non-faulty, m eventually belongs to $URB\_delivered_j$. When this occurs, if not yet done due to another message m', p_j invokes $CS[k]$.propose (), which proves the first item of the claim.

  The proof of the second item is the same as in the base case (after having replaced the consensus object $CS[1]$ by $CS[k]$), and we then have $TO\_deliverable_i[k] = TO\_deliverable_j[k] =$

$TO\_deliverable_j[k-1] \oplus res[k] = res[1] \oplus \cdots \oplus res[k]$.

End of the proof of the claim C1.

Proof of the validity property. This property follows from a simple examination of the text of the algorithm that shows that the algorithm does not create messages.

Proof of the total order message delivery property. This property follows from the Claim C1. Any two non-faulty processes p_i and p_j execute the same sequence of iterations (Item 1), and for each iteration sn, we have $TO\_deliverable_i[sn] = TO\_deliverable_j[sn] = res[1] \oplus \cdots \oplus res[sn]$ (Item 2).

Let us now consider a faulty process p_k. That process executes a finite number sn_k of iterations. During these iterations, it obtains from the consensus objects $CS[1]$, ..., $CS[sn_k]$, the same outputs $res[1]$, ..., $res[sn_k]$ as the non-faulty processes. Hence, $TO\_deliverable_k[sn\_k] = res[1] \oplus \cdots \oplus res[sn\_k]$, and, consequently, p_k TO-delivers a prefix of the sequence $res[1] \oplus \cdots \oplus res[sn\_k] \oplus \cdots$ of the messages TO-delivered by the non-faulty processes.

Proof of the termination property. Let us first consider the case of a non-faulty process that TO-broadcasts a message m. Suppose by contradiction that m is never TO-delivered by a non-faulty process. Eventually, (due to the termination property of URB) all the non-faulty processes URB-deliver m. Moreover, there is a time after which all the faulty processes have crashed and there are only non-faulty processes in the system. It follows that, there is an iteration k such that each process p_i proposes a sequence $seq_i[k]$ such that $m \in seq_i[k]$. Whatever, the sequence of messages $res[k]$ decided by the consensus object $CS[k]$, we necessarily have $m \in res[k]$. Hence, m is added to $TO\_deliverable_i$ and it is eventually TO-delivered, contradicting the initial assumption.

Let us now consider the case of a process p_x that TO-delivers a message m. In that case, there is an iteration k such that the consensus object $CS[k]$ returns $res[k]$ to p_x with $m \in res[k]$ (which has entailed the addition of m to $TO\_deliverable_x[k]$). It follows from the first item of the claim C1, that all non-faulty processes invoke $CS[k].\text{propose}()$. Hence, each non-faulty process p_i decides $res[k]$ from that consensus object, and consequently adds m to $TO\_deliverable_i$ which concludes the proof of the termination property.

Proof of the integrity property. We have to prove here that no message is TO-delivered twice. This property follows directly from the text of the algorithm. $\qquad \Box_{Theorem\ 5.1}$

Remark The reader can check that the construction described in Figure 5.3 is incorrect if, in addition to the validity, integrity and termination properties stated in Section 5.1.2, the underlying consensus objects satisfy only the following weaker agreement property: no two non-faulty processes decide different values. As we can see, this agreement property is only on the non-faulty processes and consequently is not *uniform* (uniformity states that a property is on all the processes, not only the non-faulty ones).

The algorithm is no longer correct because nothing prevent a faulty process to decide, before crashing, a value different from the value decided by the non-faulty processes. The construction of the TO-URB abstraction on top of non-uniform base consensus objects is possible, but it requires to appropriately modify the construction of Figure 5.3.

5.2.3   CONSENSUS AND TO-URB ARE EQUIVALENT

The previous section has shown that a TO-URB construction suited to the system model $\mathcal{AS}_{n,t}[CONS]$ is possible. This construction requires an unbounded number of consensus objects. (This number is actually upper bounded by the total number of messages that are TO-broadcast.) This is in agreement with the fact that consensus is a one-shot problem while TO-URB is not.

In a very interesting way, it is possible to construct a consensus object in any system that provides processes with a built-in TO-URB abstraction (e.g., in hardware). This consensus object construction, that is independent of the number of process crashes, is described in Figure 5.4.

Let CS be the consensus object that is being built. When a process p_i invokes CS.propose (v_i), where v_i is the value it proposes, it first TO-broadcasts a message containing that value. Then, it returns the value carried by the first message that it TO-delivers.

```
operation CS.propose (v_i):
    TO_broadcast (v_i);
    wait (the first value v that is TO-delivered);
    return (v).
```

Figure 5.4: Building a consensus object from the TO-URB abstraction (code for p_i)

Theorem 5.2   *The algorithm described in Figure 5.4 constructs a consensus object in any system that provides processes with a built-in TO-URB abstraction.*

Proof   The validity, integrity, and termination follow directly from their TO-URB counterparts. The consensus agreement property follows from the following simple observation: there is a single first message (value) received by a process, and due to the total order message delivery property, this message is the same for all the processes. $\square_{Theorem\ 5.2}$

The next theorem follows directly from the previous theorems 5.1 and 5.2.

Theorem 5.3   *Consensus and total order uniform reliable broadcast are equivalent in $\mathcal{AS}_{n,t}[\emptyset]$.*

5.3 THE CASE OF ASYNCHRONOUS SYSTEMS WITH FAIR CHANNELS ($\mathcal{AS\_F}_{n,t}[\emptyset]$)

5.3.1 ASYNCHRONOUS SYSTEM WITH FAIR CHANNELS

The previous section has considered message passing systems prone to process crashes, where every channel is asynchronous but reliable. This section considers the case where the channels are not only asynchronous but also unreliable; more precisely, they are only fair. Such a system has been introduced in Chapter 4, where it is denoted $\mathcal{AS\_F}_{n,t}[\emptyset]$.

Reminder #1: fair channel   A fair channel, connecting p_i to p_j, is defined by the operations "send m to p_j" and "receive () from p_i" that satisfy the following properties.

- Validity. If p_j receives a message msg from p_i, then msg has been previously sent by p_i to p_j.

- Integrity. For any message msg, if p_j receives msg from p_i an infinite number of times, then p_i has sent msg to p_j an infinite number of times.

- Termination. For any message msg, if p_i sends an infinite number of times msg to p_j, if p_j is non-faulty and executes "receive () from p_i" infinitely often, it receives msg from p_i an infinite number of times.

Reminder #2: Uniform reliable broadcast and failure detectors   As we have seen, URB assumes that all the messages that are URB-broadcast are different. It is TO-URB without the "total order message delivery" property. The following important results, that are on URB and failure detectors, have been presented in Chapter 4.

- URB can be implemented in $\mathcal{AS\_F}_{n,t}[t < n/2]$ and cannot in $\mathcal{AS\_F}_{n,t}[t \geq n/2]$.

- When we consider the failure detector-based approach, URB can be implemented in $\mathcal{AS\_F}_{n,t}[\Theta]$. Θ is the weakest class of failure detectors that allows URB to be solved despite fair channels, whatever the value of t.

It follows from these results that Theorem 5.3 can be extended as follows.

Theorem 5.4   *Consensus and TO-URB are equivalent in both $\mathcal{AS\_F}_{n,t}[t < n/2]$ and $\mathcal{AS\_F}_{n,t}[\Theta]$.*

The rest of section shows that TO-URB can be built in $\mathcal{AS\_F}_{n,t}[\emptyset]$ as soon as this system is enriched with consensus objects. This means that, in these systems, it is not necessary to build an intermediate URB abstraction to obtains TO-URB. TO-URB can be obtained directly from consensus objects. In the following, both the case of binary consensus and the case of multivalued consensus are considered.

5.3.2   URB AND TO-URB IN $\mathcal{AS}\_\mathcal{F}_{n,t}[BIN\_CONS]$

We show here that the URB problem can be solved in the system model $\mathcal{AS}\_\mathcal{F}_{n,t}[\emptyset]$ enriched with binary consensus objects. This system model is denoted $\mathcal{AS}\_\mathcal{F}_{n,t}[BIN\_CONS]$. Said another way, this construction shows that binary consensus is powerful enough to cope with asynchrony, fair channels, and half or more process crashes when one has to construct the URB abstraction. (The interest of this construction is more theoretical than practical.)

The construction is described in Figure 5.5. It assumes that each message m that is URB-broadcast can be encoded in an integer such that no two messages have the same encoding (which is always possible with a perfect hash function).

Local variables   Each process p_i manages the following variables.

- $received_i$ is a set (initialized to $\emptyset$) containing the messages (integers) that p_i has received.
- $URB\_delivered_i$ is a set (initialized to $\emptyset$) containing the messages (integers) that p_i has URB-delivered.
- $level_i$ is an integer (initialized to 0) that is at the core of the construction. It is used to repeatedly scan the integers in such a way that every integer (message) that has been received (i.e., belongs to $received_i$) is eventually URB-delivered.

Global variables   The processes communicate by exchanging messages through fair channels and cooperate through binary consensus objects. These objects are denoted $BC[a, b]$ where $0 \le a < +\infty$ and $0 \le b \le a$. A process accesses an object $BC[a, b]$ by invoking (at most once) $BC[a, b].\mathsf{bin\_propose}\,(prop)$ where $prop$ is the value it proposes to that binary consensus instance.

Process behavior   When a process p_i wants to URB-broadcast a message or receives a message, it deposits it in $received_i$. The rest of its behavior is made up of two tasks.

The first task is to overcome the fact that channels are not reliable. To that end, p_i regularly sends to each other process (through the fair channels connecting it to these processes) each message (integer) it has received but not yet URB-delivered. This repetitive sending, plus the termination property of a fair channel (namely, a message sent infinitely often is received infinitely often), guarantees that any message in $received_i \setminus URB\_delivered_i$ is eventually received by every non-faulty process.

The second task is the heart of the construction. Process p_i proceeds by levels. At level $level_i = a$, it scan all the integers x (possible messages) between 0 and a. If such a message x has already been delivered, it has nothing to do. Otherwise, p_i strives to URB-deliver message x if it does correspond to a message that it has received. To that end, p_i uses the underlying binary consensus object $BC[level_i, x]$ to eliminate the integer x if it does not correspond to a message that has been received. More precisely, if x is a message that has been received, p_i proposes 1 to the binary consensus instance; otherwise, it proposes 0. If the value returned by $BC[level_i, x]$ is 1, p_i URB-delivers x; otherwise, it does not. Finally, when all the integers x such that $0 \le x \le level_i = a$, have

```
init: received_i ← ∅; URB_delivered_i ← ∅; level_i ← 0.

operation URB_broadcast (v): received_i ← received_i ∪ {v}.

when MSG (v) is received: received_i ← received_i ∪ {v}.

repeat forever
    for each v ∈ received_i \ URB_delivered_i do
        for each j ≠ i do send MSG (v) to p_j end for
    end for
end repeat.

repeat forever
    for x from 0 to level_i do
        if (x ∉ URB_delivered_i) then
            if (x ∈ received_i) then prop ← 1 else prop ← 0 end if;
            r ← BC[level_i, x].bin_propose (prop);
            if (r = 1) then URB_delivered_i ← URB_delivered_i ∪ {x};
                            URB_deliver (x);
            end if
        end if
    end for;
    level_i ← level_i + 1
end repeat.
```

Figure 5.5: An algorithm that constructs the URB abstraction in $\mathcal{AS\_F}_{n,t}[BIN\_CONS]$ (code for p_i)

been scanned, p_i progresses to level $level_i + 1$. In that way, whatever the time a message (integer) is URB-broadcast and its value, the termination property of URB can be ensured.

Theorem 5.5   *The algorithm described in Figure 5.5 constructs an URB abstraction in* $\mathcal{AS\_F}_{n,t}[BIN\_CONS]$.

Proof Claim C. The non-faulty processes execute the same infinite sequence of binary consensus instances. A faulty process executes a prefix of it.

Proof of claim C. It follows from the text of the algorithm that the first consensus instance executed by the processes is $BC[0, 0]$. Moreover, we have the following: (a) at least non-faulty processes execute it and each of them decides a value (consensus termination property), (agreement property of $BC[0, 0]$) (b) a single value is decided(agreement property of $BC[0, 0]$), and (c) that value is 0 or 1 (consensus validity property). There are two cases according to which value is decided.

- 1 is decided by $BC[0, 0]$. When a process p_i returns from $BC[0, 0].\text{bin\_propose}(prop)$, it URB-delivers 0, adds it to $URB\_delivered_i$, and proceeds to level 1. Moreover, after a process p_i has returned from $BC[0, 0].\text{bin\_propose}(prop)$, the local predicate $0 \in URB\_delivered_i$ remains forever true. It follows that no process will ever invoke $BC[a, 0].\text{bin\_propose}()$ with $a \geq 1$ (this is because the predicate $0 \in URB\_delivered_i$ is then used to "discard" these consensus objects that have become useless because 0 can no longer be URB-delivered again).

- 0 is decided by $BC[0, 0]$. In that case, 0 is not URB-delivered and the consensus objects $BC[a, 0]$ with $a \geq 1$ are not discarded.

It follows that the next consensus object accessed by processes will be $BC[1, 1]$ if 0 has been URB-delivered, and $BC[1, 0]$ if 0 has not been URB-delivered. The important point here is that the second binary consensus object will be the same for all processes.

Then, considering the second consensus object used by processes, the same reasoning shows that the processes that will invoke a third consensus object will invoke the very same consensus object. It follows by induction that the non-faulty processes execute the same infinite sequence of binary consensus instances, and a faulty process executes a prefix of it. End of proof of Claim C.

Proof of validity property. We have to show that if a message x is URB-delivered by a process, it has been previously URB-broadcast. If x is URB-delivered, there is a binary consensus instance $BC[level, x]$ that decided 1. It then follows from the consensus validity property that some process p_i has invoked $BC[level, x]$.bin_propose (1). Hence, we have $x \in received_i$. It is easy to see from the text of the algorithm that only values v that are URB-broadcast can be added to a set $received_i$, which completes the proof of URB validity property.

Proof of integrity property. We have to show that a process URB-delivers a message x at most once. This property follows directly from the following observations. First, for a message x to be URB-delivered at p_i, the predicate $(x \notin URB\_delivered_i)$ has to be satisfied. Second, when it URB-delivers a message, p_i adds it to the set $URB\_delivered_i$. Hence, after x has been URB-delivered, the predicate $(x \notin URB\_delivered_i)$ remains false forever. Hence, x cannot be URB-delivered several times.

Proof of termination property. Let us first show that if a process p_i URB-delivers a message x, any non-faulty process URB-delivers x. If p_i URB-delivers x, there is a consensus instance $BC[y, x]$ that decides 1. Moreover, every non-faulty process executes that instance (claim C). It then follows that every non-faulty process URB-delivers x.

Let us now show that, if a non-faulty process p_i URB-broadcasts x, every non-faulty process URB-delivers x. The proof is by contradiction. Let us suppose that x is never URB-delivered by any process (otherwise, the previous case applies). As the channels from p_i to each other process are fair, there is a finite time τ' after which every non-faulty process p_j is such that $x \in received_j$. Moreover, there is a time τ'' after which all faulty processes have crashed. As x is never URB-delivered by a process, it follows from claim C that there is a time $\tau \geq \max(\tau', \tau'')$ after which there is a level y such that all the processes propose 1 to the consensus instance $BC[y, x]$. Due to the consensus agreement property, every non-faulty process decides 1 when it invokes that instance. It follows that each non-faulty process URB-delivers x, contradicting the initial assumption. $\square_{Theorem\ 5.5}$

The next theorem is an immediate consequence of claim C that appears in proof of Theorem 5.5. (This claim states that the processes invoke the underlying binary consensus in the same order.)

Theorem 5.6   *The algorithm described in Figure 5.5 constructs a TO-URB abstraction in* $\mathcal{AS}\_\mathcal{F}_{n,t}[BIN\_CONS]$.

This theorem demonstrates that the computational power of binary consensus is strong enough to cope with the net effect of asynchrony, any number of process crashes, and unreliable (but fair) channels.

5.3.3   TO-URB IN $AS\_\mathcal{F}_{n,t}[CONS]$

As proved by the previous construction, binary consensus is sufficient to build TO-URB on top of fair channels. An interesting question is then the following: is there an advantage to use multivalued consensus instead of binary consensus? The answer is "yes", in the sense that we obtain a more efficient construction.

---

init: $sn_i \leftarrow 0$; $TO\_deliverable_i \leftarrow \epsilon$; $received_i \leftarrow \emptyset$.

operation TO_broadcast (v): $received_i \leftarrow received_i \cup \{v\}$.

when ($TO\_deliverable_i$ contains messages not yet TO-delivered):
    Let m be the first message of $TO\_deliverable_i$ not yet TO-delivered;
    TO_deliver (m).

when MSG (v) **is received**: $received_i \leftarrow received_i \cup \{v\}$.

repeat forever
    for each $v \in (received_i \setminus TO\_delivered_i)$ **do**
        for each $j \neq i$ **do** send MSG (v) to p_j **end for**
    end for
end repeat.

repeat forever
    let $seq_i = (received_i \setminus TO\_deliverable_i)$;
    order (arbitrarily) the messages in seq_i;
    $sn_i \leftarrow sn_i + 1$;
    $res_i \leftarrow CS[sn_i].$propose (seq_i);
    $TO\_deliverable_i \leftarrow TO\_deliverable_i \oplus res_i$
end repeat.

Figure 5.6: Building a TO-URB abstraction in $AS\_\mathcal{F}_{n,t}[CONS]$ (code for p_i)

The construction   Such a construction is described in Figure 5.6. It is a "merge" of the construction of Figure 5.3 (that builds TO-broadcast in $AS_{n,t}[CONS]$) and the construction of Figure 5.5 (that builds URB in $AS\_\mathcal{F}_{n,t}[BIN\_CONS]$).

Processes directly use fair channels (as in Figure 5.5), and they invoke periodically consensus instances (as in both constructions). The local variables have the same meaning as their counterparts in Figures 5.5 and 5.6. The main difference with respect to the TO-URB construction designed for $AS_{n,t}[CONS]$ lies in the fact that now a process invokes a new instance even if the set *received$_i$* \ *TO_deliverable$_i$* is empty. It follows that, differently from the construction in Figure 5.5, this construction is not "quiescent with respect to the number of consensus instances".

The proof of this construction is easily obtained by merging the proofs of Theorem 5.1 and Theorem 5.6.

Why a process has to forever invoke consensus   Let us consider a system with 4 processes p_1, p_2, p_3 and p_4. Process p_1 TO-broadcasts m. It sends m to each other process, but only p_2 receives it (the messages to p_3 and p_4 are lost). Processes p_1 and p_2, that have then $seq_1 = seq_2 = \langle m \rangle$, invoke $CS[1].$propose $(\langle m \rangle)$. Then, both URB-deliver m and crash. Moreover, suppose that no more messages are ever TO-broadcast. It is easy to see that, if a process p_i participates in its next consensus instance only if $seq_i \neq \emptyset$, the construction does not work.

5.4   THE UNIVERSALITY OF CONSENSUS

5.4.1   THE STATE MACHINE APPROACH

Provide a service to clients   Practical systems provide clients with services. A *service* is usually defined by a set of commands (or requests) that each client can invoke. It is assumed that a client invokes one command at a time (hence, a client is a sequential entity). The state of the service is encoded in internal variables that are hidden to the clients. From the clients point of view, the service is defined by its commands.

A command (request) may cause a modification of the state of the service. It may also produce outputs that are sent to the client that invoked the command. It is assumed that the outputs are completely determined by the initial state of the service and the sequence of commands that have already been processed.

Replicate to tolerate failures   If the service is implemented on a single machine, the failure of that machine is fatal for the service. So, a natural idea consists in replicating the service on physically distinct machines. More generally, the *state machine replication* technique is a methodology for making fault-tolerant a service offered to clients. The state of the service is replicated on several machines that can communicate with one another through a network.

Ideally, the replication has to be transparent to the clients. Everything has to appear as if the service was implemented on a single machine. This is called the *one copy equivalence* consistency condition. To attain this goal, the machines have to coordinate themselves. The main issue consists in ensuring that all the machines execute the commands in the same order. In that way, as the commands are deterministic, the copies of the state of the service will not diverge despite the crash of some of the machines. It is easy to see that, once each command issued by a client is encapsulated in a message, ensuring the *one copy equivalence* consistency condition amounts to construct a TO-URB abstraction among the machines.

Of course, according to the type of service, it is possible to partially weaken the total order requirement (for example, for the commands that are commutative). Similarly, for some services, the commands that do not modify the state of the service are not required to be always processed by all replica.

5.4.2   CONSENSUS IS UNIVERSAL FOR BUILDING OBJECTS WITH A SEQUENTIAL SPECIFICATION

Let us consider all concurrent objects that have a sequential specification. Let us remember that this means that the correct behaviors of such objects can be described by a (possibility infinite) set of traces on their operations. The types of services described in the previous section are examples of objects with a sequential specification (each command is actually an object operation). As we have already seen, classical examples of concurrent objects defined by a sequential specification are atomic registers, and concurrent stacks, trees, or queues objects.

Considering an asynchronous distributed system prone to process crashes, a simple way to make such an object tolerant to process (machine) crash consists in replicating the object on each machine and using the TO-URB abstraction to ensure that the alive machines apply the same sequence of operations to their copy of the object. This section develops this approach.

The nature of the object   The object, the implementation of which we want to make fault-tolerant, is defined by an initial state s_0, a finite set of m operations and a sequential specification. We consider that the operations are *total*, which means that any operation can be invoked in any state of the object. As an example, let us consider an unbounded stack. It has two operations, push() and pop(). As the stack is unbounded, the push() operation can always be invoked, and is, consequently, total. It is easy to define a pop() operation that is total by defining a meaning for pop() when the stack is empty (for example, pop() returns a default value (e.g., $\top$) when the stack is empty). (For a reason that will become clear below, the only constraint on that default value is that it has to be different from the control value $\bot$ used in Figure 5.7.)

An operation has the form $\mathsf{op}_x(param_x, result_x)$, with $1 \leq x \leq m$; $param_x$ is the list (possibly empty) of the input parameters of $\mathsf{op}_x()$, while $result_x$ denotes the result it returns to the invoking process. Instead of defining the set of all traces that describe the correct behavior of the object, its sequential specification can be defined by associating a pre-assertion and a post-assertion with each operation $\mathsf{op}_x()$. Assuming that $\mathsf{op}_x()$ is executed in a concurrency-free context, the pre-assertion describes the state of the object before the execution of $\mathsf{op}_x()$, while the post-assertion describes both its state after $\mathsf{op}_x()$ has been executed and the corresponding value of $result_x$ returned to the invoking process.

A sequence of operations applied to the object can be encoded by the values of variables that define its current state. The semantics of an operation can consequently be described by a transition function $\delta()$. This means that, s being the current state of the object, $\delta(s, \mathsf{op}_x(param_x))$ returns a pair (s', res) from a non-empty set of pairs $\{(s1, res1), \ldots, (sx, resx)\}$. Each pair of this set defines a possible output where s' is the new state of the object and res is the output parameter value returned to the invoking process (i.e., the value assigned to $result_x$).

If, for each operation op_x and for any state s of the object, the set $\{(s1, res1), \ldots, (sx, resx)\}$ contains exactly one pair, the object is deterministic. Otherwise, it is non-deterministic.

The universal construction for a deterministic object   A *universal construction* is an algorithm that, given the sequential specification of an object, builds a fault-tolerant implementation of it. Such a construction, described in Figure 5.7, relies heavily on the TO-URB communication abstraction.

Each process p_i plays two roles: a client role for the upper layer application process it is associated with and a server role associated with the local implementation of the object. To that end, p_i manages a copy of the object in its local variable $state_i$.

When the upper layer application process invokes $\mathsf{op}(param)$, p_i builds a message (denoted msg_sent) containing that operation and the identity i, and TO-broadcasts it. Given such a message m, $m.op$ denotes the operation it contains, while $m.proc$ is the identity of the process that issued that operation. Then, p_i waits until the result associated with the invocation has been computed. Finally, it returns this result to the upper layer application process.

The server role of p_i consists in implementing a local copy of the object (kept in $state_i$). This is realized by a background task T that is an infinite loop. During each iteration, p_i first TO-delivers a message msg_rec (let us observe that this can entail T to wait if presently there is no message to be TO-delivered). Then, p_i invokes the transition function $\delta(state_i, msg\_rec.op)$ that computes the new local state of the object and the value returned to the invocation of the operation $msg\_rec.op$ that has been issued by the process whose identity is $msg\_rec.proc$. If this process is p_i, T deposits the result in $result_i$. In all cases, the task starts another iteration.

The **wait until** statement and the invocation of TO_deliver() can entail p_i to wait. It is assumed that the application process associated with p_i is sequential, i.e., after it has invoked an operation, it waits for the result of that operation before invoking another one.

```
when the operation op (param) is locally invoked by the application process:
    result_i ← ⊥;
    let msg_sent = ⟨op (param), i⟩;
    TO_broadcast (msg_sent);
    wait until (result ≠ ⊥);
    return (result_i).

background task T:
    repeat forever
        msg_rec ← TO_deliver();
        (state_i, res) ← δ(state_i, msg_rec.op);
        if (msg_rec.proc = i) then result_i ← res end if
    end repeat.
```

Figure 5.7: A TO-URB-based universal construction (code for p_i)

Due to the properties of the underlying TO-broadcast abstraction, it is easy to see that (1) the non-faulty processes apply the same sequence of operations to their local copy of the object, (2) any faulty process applies a prefix of this sequence to its local copy, and (3) this sequence includes all the operations issued by the non-faulty processes and the operations issued by each faulty process until it crashes (the last operation issued by a faulty process can belong or not to this sequence; it depends on the run).

The case of a non-deterministic object   There are two ways to deal with non-deterministic objects. The first is to ignore non-determinism. This can easily be done by using a non-genuine construction, i.e., a construction that implements any deterministic reduction of the object. This can be very easily done as follows. For each transition such that $\delta(s, \mathsf{op}_x(param_x))$ returns any pair from a non-empty set $\{(s1, res1), \ldots, (sx, resx)\}$, the set $\{(s1, res1), \ldots, (sx, resx)\}$ is arbitrarily reduced to a single of its pairs.

Differently, a genuine construction keeps the non-determinism of the object specification. Such a construction can easily be obtained by replacing the deterministic line

$$(state_i, res) \leftarrow \delta(state_i, msg\_rec.op)$$

by the following line:

$$pair_i \leftarrow \delta(state_i, msg\_rec.op); sn_i \leftarrow sn_i + 1; (state_i, res) \leftarrow CS.[sn_i].\mathsf{propose}\,(pair_i),$$

where the unique value of the pair $(state_i, res)$ is determined with the help of a consensus object $CS.[sn_i]$. The local variable sn_i (initialized to 0) is used to identify the consecutive consensus objects $CS.[1], CS.[2], \ldots$ For the sn_i-th pair it has TO-delivered and deposited in msg_rec, each process p_i first computes, with the help of the transition function, a proposal (denoted $pair_i$) for the pair $(state_i, res)$. Each process p_i then proposes $pair_i$ to the consensus object $C[sn_i]$. The single value decided from that consensus object is then deposited by p_i in $(state_i, res)$. It follows from the properties of the consensus object that all the processes associate the same pair $(state, res)$ with the sn_i-th TO-delivered operation.

Universality of consensus   Figure 5.7 has described a universal construction that makes an object fault-tolerant. The name "universal" comes from the fact that the construction works for any object that has total operations and is defined by a sequential specification.

It is because there is a construction based on the TO-broadcast abstraction, and such an abstraction can be built in $\mathcal{AS}_{n,t}[CONS]$, that the consensus object is called *universal*.

Said differently, let μ be any object type, with total operations, that is defined by a sequential specification. Consensus objects allow the construction of a concurrent object of type μ (i.e., an object that can be accessed concurrently by processes) in an asynchronous system prone to any number of process crashes.

5.5   CONSENSUS VS NON-BLOCKING ATOMIC COMMIT

This section shows how consensus can help solve the non-blocking atomic commit problem in asynchronous systems enriched with an appropriate failure detector. (It is important to notice that this does not mean that consensus and non-blocking atomic commit are equivalent in a pure asynchronous system $\mathcal{AS}_{n,t}[\emptyset]$. See Section 5.5.3.)

5.5.1   THE NON-BLOCKING ATOMIC COMMIT PROBLEM

This problem (in short, NBAC) is a particular agreement problem in which each process votes (*yes* or *no*) and the processes have to validate their previous local computations (COMMIT) or back track to a predetermined previous state (ABORT). The validation/backtracking alternative is governed by the votes issued by the processes and the failure pattern. A vote *yes* means that the issuing process proposes to validate the local computations because everything went well on its side, while a vote *no* means that the issuing process cannot validate its local computation (because something went wrong on its side).

Definition   More precisely, the NBAC problem is a one-shot problem (each process invokes at most once the operation) defined by the following properties. It is assumed that each alive process invokes *NBAC*.propose(v) where *NBAC* is the object associated with the considered NBAC problem instance, and v is the value (*yes* or *no*) of its vote. If p_i does not crash, its invocation *NBAC*.propose(v) returns it a value.

- Validity. A decided value is COMMIT or ABORT. Moreover,

    - Justification. If a process decides COMMIT, all the processes have voted *yes*.

    - Obligation. If all the processes vote *yes* and there is no crash, no process decides ABORT.

- Integrity. A process decides at most once.

- Agreement. No two processes decide different values.

- Termination. Each non-faulty process decides.

This problem has the same agreement, integrity and termination properties as the consensus problem. It differs from it in the validity property, namely, a decided value is not a proposed value (vote) but a value that depends on both the proposed values *and* the failure pattern. Differently, the properties defining the consensus problem do not refer directly to the failure pattern.

A remark on non-determinism   Let us remark that if the obligation property was missing, nothing would prevent the processes to always decide ABORT. Hence, the idea of the definition is that, if everything went well (i.e., all the processes voted *yes*, and there is no crash) then the processes have no choice: they have to commit their local computations.

Differently, if a process voted *no* (whether it crashes or not) the decision can be only ABORT. The reader can check that if a process crashes before voting, the only possible decision is also ABORT. In the cases where all the processes have voted *yes* and at least one of them crashes, the decision can be COMMIT or ABORT. Hence, in some cases, the decision is fixed, while in other cases the decision depends on the actual run. In that precise sense, and similarly to consensus, NBAC allows non-determinism to be solved: the decided value cannot always be computed from a deterministic function on the proposed values, it depends on the asynchrony and failure pattern that occur during the considered run.

Sequential vs non-sequential specification   The specification of a concurrent object such as a register, a stack or a queue is sequential in the sense that all the correct behaviors of the object can be described by the sequences on their operations that are allowed. As an example, a stack, a tree, a set, a register, or a queue can be defined by a sequential specification.

It is important to notice that the NBAC problem has no sequential specification. There is no sequence of $NBAC.\mathsf{propose}()$ invocations that defines the correct behavior of the NBAC object. The specification is concurrent in the sense that the value output by an NBAC object involves "some input" from each process (either its vote, or an information on the fact that it has crashed).

5.5.2   CONSENSUS-BASED NBAC

Anonymously perfect failure detector   Let $?P$ be the class of failure detectors that provide each process p_i with a variable $failure_i$, whose range is $\{red, green\}$ and that p_i can only read (red means "a failure has occurred", while "green" means "no failure has yet occurred"). The set of variables $\{failure_i\}_{1 \leq i \leq n}$ satisfies the following properties. Let us remember that, given a failure pattern F, $Faulty(F)$ and $Correct(F)$ denote the set of processes that are faulty and non-faulty in F, respectively. Moreover, $failure_i^\tau$ is the value of $failure_i$ at time τ.

- Anonymous completeness. $(Faulty(F) \neq \emptyset) \Rightarrow (\forall i \in Correct(F): \exists \tau: \forall \tau' \geq \tau: failure_i^{\tau'} = red)$.

- Anonymous accuracy. $\forall \tau: (F(\tau) = \emptyset) \Rightarrow (\forall i: failure_i^\tau = green)$.

The completeness property states that if a process crashes, the non-faulty processes will be informed of a crash, while the accuracy property states that no process is informed of a crash before a crash does occur. The anonymity attribute is due to fact that, if crashes occur, no process ever knows the identity of the crashed processes.

Notation   Let $\mathcal{AS}_{n,t}[?P, CONS]$ be an asynchronous system where any number t of processes can crash, and where the processes can use underlying consensus objects and a failure detector of the class $?P$. This means that, in this type of system, the consensus objects and $?P$ are given for free.

Solving NBAC in $\mathcal{AS}_{n,t}[?P, CONS]$ The algorithm described in Figure 5.8 constructs an NBAC object in asynchronous systems prone to any number of process crashes, enriched with a failure detector of the class $?P$ and consensus objects (one consensus object is actually sufficient).

The NBAC object that is built is denoted $NBAC$. The underlying consensus object is denoted CS. It is assumed that each non-faulty process invokes $NBAC.\mathsf{propose}(v)$ where v is its vote. When it invokes it, a process p_i first sends its vote to each process, including itself (the broadcast MY_VOTE (v_i) operation is a best effort broadcast: if p_i crashes during the broadcast, an arbitrary subset of the processes receive the message).

---

operation *NBAC*.propose (v_i): % the vote v_i is *yes* or *no* %
    broadcast MY_VOTE (v_i);
    wait until $\big(\,$(MY_VOTE ($-$) received from each process) $\vee$ (*failure$_i$* = *red*)$\big)$;
    if $\big(\,$a vote *yes* has been received from every process$\big)$
        then *output$_i$* $\leftarrow$ *CS*.propose (COMMIT)
        else *output$_i$* $\leftarrow$ *CS*.propose (ABORT)
    end if;
    return (*output$_i$*).

Figure 5.8: An algorithm that constructs an NBAC object in $\mathcal{AS}_{n,t}[?P, CONS]$ (code for p_i)

Then, p_i waits until either it has received a vote from each process, or it is informed of a crash. Then, if it has received a *yes* vote from all, it proposes COMMIT to the underlying consensus object; otherwise, it proposes ABORT to that object. Finally, p_i returns the value output by the consensus object.

Theorem 5.7   *The algorithm described in Figure 5.8 constructs an NBAC object in $\mathcal{AS}_{n,t}[?P, CONS]$.*

Proof As a process returns at most once, the NBAC integrity property is guaranteed. Moreover, as a process returns the value obtained from the underlying consensus object, the NBAC agreement property is inherited from consensus agreement.

Let us now consider the NBAC termination property. If no process is faulty, they all broadcast their vote, and whatever the value of the votes, their **wait until** statements terminate. If a process is faulty, the local variables *failure$_i$* of the non-faulty processes are eventually assigned the value *red*, and their **wait until** statements terminate. Hence, whatever the case, all non-faulty processes eventually invoke the consensus object and, due to its termination property, do terminate their invocation, which proves the NBAC termination property.

As far as the validity property is concerned, it follows from the consensus validity property that only the value COMMIT or the value ABORT can be decided. As far as the justification property is concerned, we have the following. If a process decides COMMIT, it follows from the consensus validity property that a process p_i has proposed COMMIT to the consensus object. We conclude then, from the text of the algorithm, that p_i has received a vote *yes* from each process, which concludes the proof of the justification property.

Let us finally consider the obligation property. If there is no crash and all processes vote *yes*, they all propose COMMIT to the consensus object. As a single value is proposed to the consensus object C, only that value can be decided from CS, and consequently all processes eventually return COMMIT, which concludes the proof of the NBAC obligation property. $\square_{Theorem\ 5.7}$

5.5.3 CONSENSUS VS NBAC

The previous section has shown how the NBAC problem can be solved in $\mathcal{AS}_{n,t}[\emptyset]$ enriched with both a failure detector of the class $?P$ and a consensus object. The algorithm described in Figure 5.8 is a reduction of NBAC to consensus in the model $\mathcal{AS}_{n,t}[?P]$.

This does not mean that the consensus problem and the NBAC problem can be compared in $\mathcal{AS}_{n,t}[\emptyset]$. Actually, they are incomparable in $\mathcal{AS}_{n,t}[\emptyset]$. More precisely, there is a failure detector class *FD1* such that the NBAC problem can be solved in $\mathcal{AS}_{n,t}[FD1]$ while consensus cannot, and there is failure detector class *FD2* such that the consensus can be solved in $\mathcal{AS}_{n,t}[FD2]$ while NBAC cannot. These classes of failure detectors are not addressed in this book.

Let us finally remember that the consensus problem has a sequential specification while the NBAC problem has not.

5.6 CONSENSUS IMPOSSIBILITY IN $\mathcal{AS}_{n,t}[\emptyset]$

This section shows that the consensus problem cannot be solved in $\mathcal{AS}_{n,t}[\emptyset]$. Solving it requires a distributed system model "stronger" than $\mathcal{AS}_{n,t}[\emptyset]$. (This is the famous FLP impossibility result.)

5.6.1 THE INTUITION THAT UNDERLIES THE IMPOSSIBILITY

To stop waiting or not to stop waiting, that is the question   The impossibility of solving some distributed computing problems comes from the uncertainty created by the net effect of asynchrony and failures. This uncertainty makes it impossible to distinguish a crashed process from a process that is slow or a process with which communication is slow.

Let us consider a process p that is waiting for a message from another process q. In the system model $\mathcal{AS}_{n,t}[\emptyset]$, the main issue the process p has to solve is to stop waiting for the message from q or to continue waiting. Basically, allowing p to stop waiting can entail a violation of the safety property of the problem if q is currently alive, while forcing p to wait the message from q can prevent the liveness property of the problem to be satisfied (if q has crashed before sending the required message).

Synchrony rules out uncertainty   Let us consider a synchronous system involving two processes p_i and p_j. Synchronous means that the transfer delays are upper bounded (let Δ be the corresponding bound) and there is a lower bound and an upper bound on the speed of the processes. In order to simplify (and without loss of generality), we consider here that processing time are negligible with respect to message transit times and are consequently equal to 0.

In such a synchronous context, let us consider a problem P where each process has an initial value (v_i and v_j, respectively), and they have to compute a result that depends on these values as follows. If no process crashes, the result is $f(v_i, v_j)$. If p_j (resp., p_i) crashes, the result is $f(v_i, v_j)$ or $f(v_i, \perp)$ (resp., $f(\perp, v_j)$).

Each process sends its value and waits for the value of the other process. When it receives the other value, a process sends its value if not yet done. In order not to wait forever, the value of the other process (say p_j), the process p_i uses a timer as follows. It sets the timer to 2Δ when it sends its value. If it has not received the value of p_j when the timer expires, it concludes that p_j has crashed before sending its value and returns $f(v_i, \bot)$. In the other cases, it has received v_j and returns $f(v_i, v_j)$. These two cases are described in Figure 5.9 (in the figure at the right, the cross on p_j's axis indicates its crash).

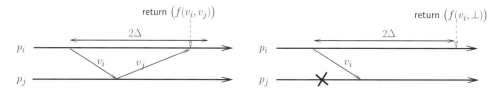

Figure 5.9: Synchrony rules out uncertainty

The execution on the left is failure-free, and p_j sends its value at the latest, i.e., when it receives the value v_i from p_i. In that case, p_i returns $f(v_i, v_j)$ (and the timer is useless). Differently, in the execution on the right, p_j has crashed before sending its value, and, consequently, p_i returns $f(v_i, \bot)$ when the timer expires. (If p_j had sent its value before crashing, p_i would have received it and would have returned $f(v_i, v_j)$ when receiving v_j). The uncertainty on the state of p_j is controlled by the timeout value. The timer is conservatively set in both cases, as p_i does not know in advance if p_j has crashed or not.

... While asynchrony cannot   Let us now consider that, while processing times remain equal to 0, message transfer delays are finite but arbitrary. So, the system is asynchronous as far as messages are concerned.

A process can use a local clock and an "estimate" of the round-trip delay, but, unfortunately, there is no guarantee that (whatever its value) this estimate be an upper bound on the round trip delay in the current execution (otherwise, the system would be synchronous).

Using such an "estimate", several cases can occur. It is possible that, in the current execution, the estimate is actually a correct estimate. In that case, the synchrony assumption used by the processes is correct, and we are luckily in the case of the previous synchronous system described in Figure 5.9.

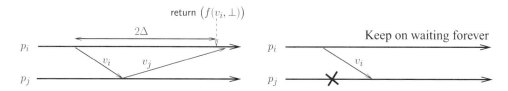

Figure 5.10: To wait or not to wait in presence of asynchrony and failures?

Unfortunately, as already said, there is no guarantee that (whatever its value) the estimate value used is a correct estimate. This is described on the left side of Figure 5.10, where p_i returns

$f(v_i, \perp)$ when the timer expires, while it should return $f(v_i, v_j)$. In that case, the incorrectness of the estimate value entails the violation of the safety property of the problem. So, timers cannot be used safely. But if p_i does not use a timer while p_j has crashed before sending its value (right side of Figure 5.10), it will wait forever, violating the liveness property of the problem.

This simple example shows that it can be impossible to guarantee both the safety property and the liveness property of a problem P, when one has to solve P in an asynchronous system.

5.6.2   REFINING THE DEFINITION OF $\mathcal{AS}_{n,1}[\emptyset]$

Before proving the impossibility result in the next sections, this section refines the definition of the underlying asynchronous model $\mathcal{AS}_{n,1}[\emptyset]$. Let us remark that we now assume $t = 1$.

Modeling the communication system   The system consists of a set of n processes that communicate by sending and receiving messages with the operations "send m to $proc$" and "receive ()". Each message m is assumed to contain the identity of its sender ($m.sender$) and the identity of its destination process ($m.dest$). Moreover, without loss of generality, all messages are assumed to be different (this can easily be done by adding sequence numbers).

When a process sends a message to a process p_i, that message is deposited in a set denoted *buffer*. When a process p_i invokes the receive operation, it obtains either a message m such that $m.dest = i$ that has been deposited into *buffer*, or the default value $\perp$ that indicates "no message". If the message value that is returned is not $\perp$, the corresponding message is withdrawn from *buffer*. It is possible that *buffer* contains messages m such that $m.dest = i$, while p_i obtains $\perp$. The fact that a message can remain an arbitrary time in *buffer* is used to model communication asynchrony (but, while arbitrary, this time duration is finite, see below).

The network is reliable in the sense that there is neither message creation, nor message duplication. Moreover, the "no loss" property of the communication system is modeled by the following *fairness* assumption: given any process p_i and any message m that has been deposited into *buffer* and is such that $m.dest = i$, if p_i executes receive() infinitely often, it eventually obtains m.

Modeling the processes   The behavior of a process is defined by an automaton that proceeds by executing steps. A step is a represented by a pair (i, m) where i is a process name and m a message or the default value $\perp$. When it executes the step (i, m), process p_i performs atomically the following:

- Either it receives a message m previously sent to it (in that case $m \in buffer$, $m.dest = i$ and m is then withdrawn from *buffer*), or it "receives" the value $m = \perp$ (meaning that there is no message to be received yet).

- Then according to the value received (a message value or $\perp$), it sends a finite number of messages to the processes (those are deposited in *buffer*), and it changes its local state.

Hence, (until it possibly crashes) each process executes a sequence of steps (as defined by its automaton), and each step takes one global state to another. Let σ_i be the current local state of p_i. The execution of its next step by p_i entails its progress from σ_i to a new local state σ_i'. Let us observe that the behavior of a process is deterministic. The next state of p_i and the message it sends (if any) are entirely determined by its initial state and the sequence of messages and $\bot$ values that it has received so far.

Input vector   Given a consensus instance, let v_i be the value proposed to that consensus instance by process p_i. That value is part of its initial local state. The corresponding input vector, denoted $Input[1..n]$, is the vector such that $Input[i] = v_i, 1 \leq i \leq n$. When considering binary consensus, the set of all possible input vectors is the set $\{0, 1\}^n$.

System global state   A *global state* Σ (also called *configuration*) is a vector of n local states $[\sigma_1, \ldots, \sigma_n]$ (one per process p_i), plus a set of messages that represents the current value of *buffer* (those messages are the messages that are in transit with respect to the corresponding global state). A *non-faulty* global sate is a global state in which no process has crashed.

An initial global state Σ_0 is such that each $\sigma_i, 1 \leq i \leq n$, is an initial local state of p_i, and *buffer* is the empty set.

A step $s = (i, \bot)$ can be applied to any global state Σ. A step $s = (i, m)$ where $m \neq \bot$ can be applied to a global state Σ only if *buffer* contains m. If an applicable step s is applied to global state Σ, the resulting global state is denoted $\Sigma' = s(\Sigma)$.

Schedule, reachability and accessibility   A *schedule* is a (finite or infinite) sequence of steps $s_1, s_2, \ldots$ issued by the processes. A schedule σ is *applicable* to a global state Σ, if for all $i \geq 1$ (and $i \leq |\sigma|$ if σ is finite), s_i is applicable to Σ_{i-1} where $\Sigma_0 = \Sigma$ and $\Sigma_i = \sigma_i(\Sigma_{i-1})$.

A global state Σ' is *reachable* from Σ if there is a finite schedule σ such that $\Sigma' = \sigma(\Sigma)$. A global state is *accessible* if it is reachable from an initial global state.

Runs of an algorithm   The algorithm A that solves consensus despite asynchrony and one process crash is encoded in a set of n automata, one per process (as defined previously). The local state of each process p_i contains a local variable $decided_i$. That variable, initialized to $\bot$, is a one-write variable that is assigned by p_i to the value it decides upon.

It is assumed that the algorithm executed by a process is such that, after it has decided (if it ever decides) a non-faulty process keeps on executing steps forever. Hence, a correct process executes an infinite number of steps. Given an initial global state, a *run* is an infinite schedule that starts from this global state.

In the context of the impossibility proof, a run is *admissible* if at most one process crashes and all messages that have been sent to the non-faulty processes are eventually received.

A tree of admissible runs   Given an initial state Σ_0 and a consensus algorithm A, all its possible runs define a tree, denoted $\mathcal{T}(A, \Sigma_0)$, where each node represents a global state of A, and each edge represents a step by a process.

5.6.3   NOTION OF VALENCE OF A GLOBAL STATE

The impossibility proof considers the binary consensus problem, i.e., the case where only two values (0 and 1) can be proposed. It is a proof by contradiction: it assumes that there is an algorithm A that solves binary consensus in $\mathcal{AS}_{n,1}[\emptyset]$, and exhibits a contradiction. Trivially, as binary consensus cannot be solved when one process can crash, it cannot be solved either when $t \geq 1$ processes can crash, and multivalued consensus cannot be solved either for $t \geq 1$.

Given an initial global state Σ_0, let us consider the tree $\mathcal{T}(A, \Sigma_0)$. It is possible to associate a *valence* notion with each state Σ of this tree, defined as follows. The valence of a node (global state) $\Sigma \in \mathcal{T}(A, \Sigma_0)$ is the set of values that can be decided upon in a global state reachable from Σ. Let us observe that, due to the termination property of the consensus algorithm A, the set $valence(\Sigma)$ is not empty. As the consensus is binary, it is equal to one of the following sets: $\{0\}$, $\{1\}$ or $\{0, 1\}$. More explicitly:

- Σ is *bivalent* if the eventual decision value of the consensus is not yet fixed in Σ. This means that, when considering $\mathcal{T}(A, \Sigma_0)$, the bivalent global state Σ is the root of a subtree including both global states where processes decide value 1, and global states where processes decide value 0. Said differently, an external observer (who would have an instantaneous view of the process states and the channel states) cannot determine the value that will be decided from Σ.

- Σ is *univalent* if the eventual decision value is fixed in Σ: all runs starting from Σ decide the same value. If that value is 0, Σ is *0-valent*; otherwise, it is *1-valent*. Hence, if Σ is x-valent ($x \in \{0, 1\}$), all nodes of the subtree of $\mathcal{T}(A, \Sigma_0)$ that is rooted at Σ are x-valent. This means that, given Σ, an external observer could determine the single value that can be decided from that global state. Let us observe that it is possible that no local state σ_i of Σ allows the corresponding process p_i to know that Σ is univalent.

A part of a tree $\mathcal{T}(A, \Sigma_0)$ for a system of two processes is described in Figure 5.11. (As there are only two processes, each global state has at most two successors.) Each node (global sate) is labeled with the set of values that can be decided from it. If this set contains a single value, the corresponding global state is univalent (and then all its successors have the same valence). Otherwise, it is bivalent.

The notion of valence captures a notion of non-determinism. Said differently, if state Σ is univalent, "the dice are cast": the decision value (that is perhaps not yet explicitly known by processes) is determined. If Σ is bivalent, "the dice are not yet cast": the decision value is not yet determined (it still depends on the run that will occur from Σ, which in turn depends on asynchrony and the failure pattern).

5.6.4   CONSENSUS IS IMPOSSIBLE IN $\mathcal{AS}_{n,1}[\emptyset]$

As already indicated, the proof is by contradiction: assuming that there is an algorithm A that solves binary consensus in $\mathcal{AS}_{n,1}[\emptyset]$, it exhibits a contradiction. More precisely, the proof shows that there

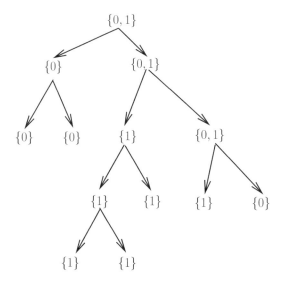

Figure 5.11: Bivalent vs univalent global states

is an initial global state Σ_0 such that $\mathcal{T}(A, \Sigma_0)$ has an infinite run of A whose all global states are bivalent. Said another way, assuming that A always preserves the safety property (at most one value is decided) implies that it has executions that never decide.

Bivalent initial state   The next lemma shows that, whatever the consensus algorithm A, there is at least one input vector *Input*[$1.n$] such that the corresponding initial global state is bivalent. This means that, while the value decided by A is determined by the input vector only, when the corresponding initial global state Σ_0 is univalent, this cannot be true for all the input vectors.

Lemma 5.8   *Every consensus algorithm A has a bivalent initial global state.*

Proof Let C_0 be the initial global state in which all processes propose 0 (so its input vector is $[0, \ldots, 0]$), and C_i, $1 \le i \le n$, the initial global state in which the processes from p_1 to p_i propose the value 1, while all the other processes propose 0. So, the input vector of C_n is $[1, \ldots, 1]$ (all processes propose 1).

These initial global states constitute a sequence in which any two adjacent global states C_{i-1} and C_i, $1 \le i \le n$, differ only in the value proposed by the process p_i: it proposes the value 0 in C_{i-1} and the value 1 in C_i. Moreover, it follows from the validity property of the consensus algorithm A, that C_0 is 0-valent, while C_n is 1-valent.

Let us assume that all the previous configurations are univalent. It follows that, in the previous sequence, there is (at least) one pair of consecutive configurations, say C_{i-1} and C_i, such that C_{i-1} is

0-valent and C_i is 1-valent. Assuming that there is a consensus algorithm A in $\mathcal{AS}_{n,1}[\emptyset]$, we exhibit a contradiction.

Assuming that no process crashes, let us consider a run of A that starts from global state C_{i-1}, in which process p_i executes no step for an arbitrarily long period (the end of that period is defined below). Let us observe that, as the algorithm A can cope with one process crash, no process executing A (but p_i) is able to distinguish the case where p_i is slow and the case where it has crashed.

As (by assumption) the algorithm satisfies the consensus termination property despite up to one crash, all the processes (but p_i) decide after a finite number of steps. The sequence of steps that starts at the very beginning of the run and ends when all the processes have decided (but p_i, which has not yet executed a step), defines a schedule σ. (See the upper part of Figure 5.12 where, within the input vector C_{i-1}, the value proposed by p_i is inside a box.) As C_{i-1} is 0-valent, the global state $\sigma(C_{i-1})$ is also 0-valent (let us recall that $\sigma(C_{i-1})$ is the global state attained by executing the sequence σ from C_{i-1}). Finally, after all the steps of σ have been executed, p_i starts executing and decides. As $R(C_{i-1})$ is 0-valent, p_i decides 0.

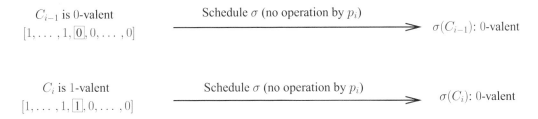

Figure 5.12: There is a bivalent initial configuration

Let us observe (lower part of Figure 5.12) that the same schedule σ can be produced by the algorithm A from the global state C_i. This is because (1) as the global states C_{i-1} and C_i differ only in the value proposed by p_i, and (2) p_i executes no step in σ, the decided value cannot depend on the value proposed by p_i. It follows that, as $\sigma(C_{i-1})$ is 0-valent, the global state $\sigma(C_i)$ is also 0-valent. But as the global state C_i is 1-valent, we conclude that $\sigma(C_i)$ is necessarily 1-valent, which contradicts the initial assumption and concludes the proof of the lemma. $\square_{Lemma\ 5.8}$

A remark on the validity property: strengthening the lemma In addition to the fact that at most one process can crash, the previous lemma is based on the validity property satisfied by the algorithm A that states that the decided value is one of the proposed values (from which we have concluded that C_0 and C_n are 0-valent and 1-valent, respectively).

The reader can check that the lemma remains valid if the validity property is weakened as follows: "there are runs in which the value 0 is decided, and there are runs in which the value 1 is decided". This validity property is weaker because it does not prevent a consensus algorithm from deciding 0 when all the processes propose 1. Despite its weakness, this property is sufficient to conclude that, if we assume that all the initial global states are univalent, then there is at least one initial global state that is 0-valent and at least one initial global state that is 1-valent. The proof of the lemma follows easily from this simple observation.

The lemma is then stronger (i.e., it applies to more runs) because it requires weaker assumptions (validity property satisfied by the consensus algorithm A).

Remark: crash vs asynchrony   The previous proof is based on the assumption that, despite asynchrony and the possibility for one process to crash, the algorithm A allows all the correct processes to decide and terminate. This allows the proof to play with process speed and consider a schedule σ during which a process p_i executes no step. We could have instead considered that p_i has initially crashed (i.e., p_i crashes before executing any step). During the schedule σ, the consensus algorithm A has no way to know in which case the system really is (has p_i initially crashed or is it only very slow?). This shows that, for some problems, asynchrony and process crashes are two facets of the same "uncertainty" algorithms have to cope with.

Lemma 5.9   *Let Σ be a non-faulty bivalent global state, and let $s = (i, m)$ be a step that is applicable to Σ. Then, there is a finite schedule σ (not including s) such that $s(\sigma(\Sigma))$ is bivalent.*

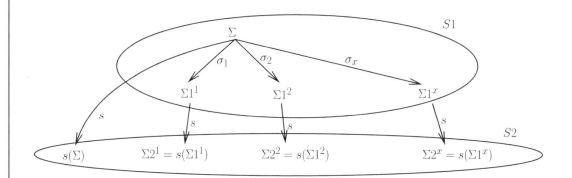

Figure 5.13: Illustrating the definitions used in Lemma 5.9

Proof Let $S1$ be the set of global states reachable from Σ with a finite schedule not including s, and $S2 = s(S1) = \{s(\Sigma 1) \mid \Sigma 1 \in S1\}$ (see Figure 5.13.) We have to show that $S2$ contains a non-faulty bivalent global state.

Let us first notice that, as s is applicable to Σ, it follows from the definition of $S1$ and the fact that messages can be delayed for arbitrarily long periods, that s is applicable to every global state $\Sigma' \in S1$. The proof is by contradiction. Let us assume that every global state $\Sigma 2 \in S2$ is univalent.

Claim C1. $S2$ contains both 0-valent and 1-valent global states.
Proof of the claim. Since Σ is bivalent, for each $v \in \{0, 1\}$, there is a finite schedule σ_v that is

applicable to Σ and such that the global state $C_v = \sigma_v(\Sigma)$ is v-valent. We consider two cases according to the fact that σ_v contains s or not.

$$\Sigma \xrightarrow{\quad \sigma_v \quad} C_v = \sigma_v(\Sigma) \xrightarrow{\quad s \quad} \Sigma 2 = s(C_v)$$

$$\Sigma \xrightarrow{\quad \sigma 1_v \quad} \xrightarrow{\quad s \quad} \Sigma 2 \xrightarrow{\quad \sigma 2_v \quad} C_v = \sigma 2_v(\Sigma 2)$$

Figure 5.14: $\Sigma 2$ contains 0-valent and 1-valent global states

- Case 1: σ_v does not contain s (top part of Figure 5.14). In that case, taking $\Sigma 2 = s(C_v)$, we trivially have $\Sigma 2 \in S2$. As C_v is v-valent, it follows that $\Sigma 2$ also is v-valent.
- Case 2: σ_v contains s (bottom part of Figure 5.14). Then, there are two schedules $\sigma 1_v$ and $\sigma 2_v$ such that $\sigma_v = \sigma 1_v \, s \, \sigma 2_v$. In that case, taking $\Sigma 2 = s(\sigma 1_v(\Sigma))$, we trivially have $\Sigma 2 \in S2$. As all global states in $S2$ are univalent, $\Sigma 2$ is univalent. Finally, as $C_v = \sigma 2_v(\Sigma 2)$ is v-valent, it follows that $\Sigma 2$ also is v-valent. End of the proof of the claim C1.

Claim C2. Let two global states be *neighbors* if one is reachable from the other in a single step. There exist two neighbors $\Sigma 1'$, $\Sigma 1'' \in S1$ such that $\Sigma 2' = s(\Sigma 1')$ is 0-valent and $\Sigma 2'' = s(\Sigma 1'')$ is 1-valent.

Proof of the claim. Considering the global states in $S1$ as the nodes of a graph G in which any two adjacent nodes are connected by an edge, let us label a node X in G with $v \in \{0, 1\}$ if and only if $s(X) \in S2$ is v-valent. As by assumption any global state in $S2$ is univalent, every node of G has a well-defined label. It follows from Claim C1 that there are nodes labeled 0 and nodes labeled 1. Moreover, as Σ belongs to $S1$ (this is because the empty schedule is a finite schedule), it also belongs to G and has, consequently, a label. Finally, as (a) there a path between any two nodes of G (through the node associated with Σ), and (b) all nodes of G are labeled 0 or 1, there are necessarily two adjacent nodes that have distinct labels. End of the proof of the claim.

Let two neighbors $\Sigma 1'$, $\Sigma 1'' \in S1$ such that $\Sigma 2' = s(\Sigma 1')$ is 0-valent and $\Sigma 2'' = s(\Sigma 1'')$ is 1-valent (due to Claim C2, they exist). Moreover, let $s' = (i', m')$ be the step such that $\Sigma 1'' = s'(\Sigma 1')$ (Figure 5.15). We consider two cases.

- Case $i \neq i'$. As the steps s and s' are independent (s is not the reception of a message sent by s' and s' is not the reception of a message sent by s), it follows that $\Sigma 2'' = s'(s(\Sigma 1')) = s(s'(\Sigma 1'))$, which means that $\Sigma 2''$ has to be bivalent. This contradicts the fact that $\Sigma 2''$ is 1-valent, and proves the lemma for that case.
- Case $i = i'$. Let us consider Figure 5.16 where, according to the previous notations, the global state $\Sigma 2'$ is 0-valent, while $\Sigma 2''$ is 1-valent. Let us consider a schedule that starts from $\Sigma 1'$ in which p_i takes no steps and all other processes decide. Such a schedule exists because the

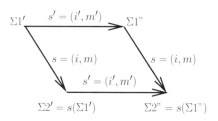

Figure 5.15: Valence contradiction when $i \neq i'$

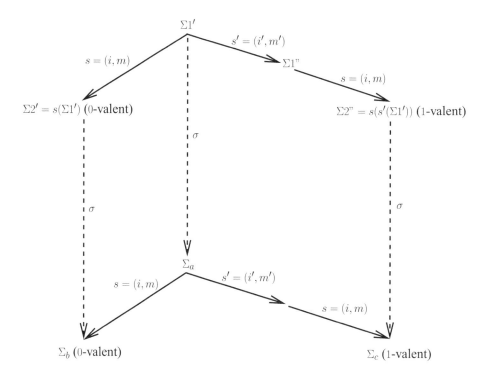

Figure 5.16: Valence contradiction when $i = i'$

algorithm A is correct, and it copes with one process crash. In that schedule, everything appears as if p_i has crashed in $\Sigma 1'$. It follows that $\Sigma_a = \sigma(\Sigma 1')$ is univalent.

As σ includes no step by p_i, the very same schedule σ can be applied to both $\Sigma 2'$ and $\Sigma 2''$ and we obtain the following.

– $\Sigma_b = \sigma(s(\Sigma 1')) = s(\sigma(\Sigma 1')) = s(\Sigma_a)$. This is because, as σ and s are independent, when the schedule $s\,\sigma$ and the schedule $\sigma\,s$ are applied to the same global state ($\Sigma 1'$), they necessarily produce the same global state (Σ_b).

– $\Sigma_c = \sigma(s(s'(\Sigma 1'))) = s(s'(\sigma(\Sigma 1'))) = s(s'(\Sigma_a))$. As before, this is because, as the schedules σ and $s'\,s$ are independent, when the schedule $s'\,s\,\sigma$ and the schedule $\sigma\,s'\,s$ are applied to the same global state ($\Sigma 1'$), they necessarily produce the same global state (Σ_c).

It follows that we have $\Sigma_b = s(\Sigma_a)$ and $\Sigma_c = s(s'(\Sigma_a))$.

As $\Sigma 2'$ is 0-valent, so is Σ_b. Similarly, as $\Sigma 2''$ is 1-valent, so is Σ_c. It then follows from $\Sigma_b = s(\Sigma_a)$ and $\Sigma_c = s(s'(\Sigma_a))$ that Σ_a is bivalent, contradicting the fact that is univalent and concludes the proof of the lemma.

$\square_{Lemma\ 5.9}$

Theorem 5.10   *There is no consensus algorithm A in $\mathcal{AS}_{n,1}[\emptyset]$.*

Proof The proof consists in building an infinite run in which no process decides. The idea is the following. The algorithm A is started in a bivalent global state (that exists due to Lemma 5.8), and then the steps executed by the processes are selected in such a way that the processes proceed from a bivalent global state to a new bivalent state (that exists due to Lemma 5.9). This run has to be admissible (there is at most one process crash, and any message send by a correct process is be eventually received).

The admissible run that is built is actually a failure-free run (each process takes infinitely many steps). The processes are initially placed in queue (in arbitrary order).

1. The initial global state Σ is any bivalent global state. The run R is initialized to the empty sequence. Then, repeatedly, the following sequence is executed.

2. Let p_i be the process at the head of the queue. If the input buffer of p_i contains a message m such that (i, m) is applicable to Σ, then let $s = (i, m)$ be the oldest such step, else let $s = (i, \bot)$.

3. Let us select σ be a schedule such that $s(\sigma(\Sigma))$ is bivalent (such a global state exists due to Lemma 5.9).

4. Assign $s(\sigma(\Sigma))$ to Σ, update R to the sequence $R\,\sigma\,s$, move p_i at the end of the queue, and go to item 2.

It is easy to see that the run R is admissible (no process crash, and any message is delivered and processed). Moreover, the run is infinite and no process ever decides, which concludes the proof of the impossibility result.

$\square_{Theorem\ 5.10}$

Strengthening the impossibility   In order to obtain a stronger impossibility result, it is possible to consider a weaker version of the problem. The reader can check that the consensus impossibility result is still valid when the consensus termination property is weakened into "some process eventually decides" (instead of "all non-faulty processes decide").

5.7   BIBLIOGRAPHIC NOTES

- The first explicit formulation of the consensus problem, has appeared in the context of synchronous systems under the name *Byzantine generals problem*. It is due to Lamport, Shostack and Pease [111].

- A strong connection relating distributed agreement problems and error-correcting codes is established in [70]. An informal introduction to agreement problems is presented in [150].

- The state machine approach has been first proposed and developed by Lamport [107, 108]. A survey appears in [154]. The total order broadcast abstraction (TO-URB) has been formalized in [93].

- The construction of the TO-URB abstraction in $\mathcal{AS}_{n,t}[CONS]$ is due to Chandra and Toueg [34], who have also shown that the TO-URB problem and the consensus problem are equivalent in $\mathcal{AS}_{n,t}[\emptyset]$.

  Consensus-based total order multicast has been studied in [69]. The use of total order broadcast for quorum-based data replication is investigated in [152]. Consensus-based total order broadcast algorithms can save consensus executions in some execution patterns. Such an approach is presented in [135].

- The universality of consensus objects to build any concurrent object, defined by a sequential specification, in asynchronous systems prone to process crashes is due to Herlihy [96].

- The non-blocking atomic commit problem originated in databases [23, 81, 156]. The first investigations of its relation with the consensus problem are due to Hadzilacos [92] and Guerraoui [82].

  The class $?P$ of anonymous failure detectors is due to Guerraoui [84]. The weakest class of failure detectors to solve the non-blocking atomic commit problem is described in [48] where it is shown that none of these problems can help solving the other in $\mathcal{AS}_{n,t}[\emptyset]$.

- The construction of uniform reliable broadcast from binary consensus objects and the construction of total order uniform reliable broadcast from multivalued consensus objects in asynchronous systems with fair channels are due to Zhang and Chen [162].

- The impossibility of solving consensus in asynchronous message-passing systems prone to even a single process crash failure is due to Fischer, Lynch and Paterson [68]. This fundamental result is known in the literature under the acronym FLP. It is one of the most celebrated results of fault-tolerant distributed computing.

- The first proof of the impossibility of consensus in asynchronous read/write shared memory systems prone to even a single process crash appeared in [116]. Another proof is given in [96]. See also [97].

CHAPTER 6

Consensus Algorithms for Asynchronous Systems Enriched with Various Failure Detectors

This chapter is devoted to consensus algorithms in asynchronous message-passing systems prone to process crashes, enriched with various types of failure detectors (oracles that provide processes with information on failures). All these algorithms assume that each non-faulty process p_i proposes a value to the consensus instance, i.e., invokes the operation "propose (v_i)" where v_i is the value it proposes to that instance.

Many algorithms are presented, each designed for an appropriately enriched version of the base system model $\mathcal{AS}_{n,t}[\emptyset]$. Before entering into the technical developments, this list of items describes the structure of the chapter.

- First, Section 6.1 considers $\mathcal{AS}_{n,t}[\emptyset]$ enriched with a perfect failure detector. It presents two consensus algorithms for that model, that works for any value of t. In the first algorithm the processes decide in $t + 1$ asynchronous rounds (communication steps), The second algorithm allows for early decision, namely, a process decides (and stops) in at most $\min(f + 2, t + 1)$ rounds (where f is the actual number of process crashes).

- Section 6.2 introduces the weakest failure detector class (Ω) that allows consensus to be solved in $\mathcal{AS}_{n,t}[t < n/2]$. Then, Section 6.3 presents a consensus algorithm suited to $\mathcal{AS}_{n,t}[t < n/2, \Omega]$ and studies its properties.

- Section 6.4 considers then the case where, instead of a failure detector, the underlying system $\mathcal{AS}_{n,t}[t < n/2]$ is enriched with a random number generator; hence the system becomes a randomized system. Several binary consensus algorithms for different types of randomized systems are presented.

  The notion of an hybrid system is also presented. Such a system is enriched with both a failure detector of the class Ω and a random number generator. A corresponding algorithm is described and analyzed.

- Assuming that the underlying system $\mathcal{AS}_{n,t}[\emptyset]$ is enriched with a binary consensus algorithm, Section 6.5 presents two algorithms that solve multivalued consensus on top of such an enriched system.

- Section 6.6 investigates the cases where consensus can be solved in one communication step.

- Finally, Section 6.7 addresses anonymous asynchronous systems. It presents failure detector classes suited to this type of systems and associated consensus algorithms.

As we have seen in previous chapters, the operation '"broadcast m" that is used is not a reliable broadcast abstraction. It is only a shortcut for "**for each** $j \in \{1, \ldots, n\}$ **do** send m to p_j **end for**". (The sending by a process of a message to itself can be trivially eliminated. We nevertheless keep this sending in order to have a simpler statement of the algorithms that are presented.)

6.1   ENRICHING THE ASYNCHRONOUS SYSTEM WITH A PERFECT FAILURE DETECTOR

This section presents a few simple algorithms that solve the consensus problem in $\mathcal{AS}_{n,t}[P]$ where P is the class of perfect failure detectors.

Let us remember that any failure detector of that class P provides each process p_i with a set $suspected_i$ that (1) eventually contains all crashed processes (completeness), and (2) never contains a process before it crashes (strong accuracy).

6.1.1   A SIMPLE ALGORITHM BASED ON A ROTATING COORDINATOR

Principle and description of the algorithm   An algorithm that constructs a consensus object in $\mathcal{AS}_{n,t}[P]$ is described in Figure 6.1, where v_i is the value proposed by process p_i. This algorithm is coordinator-based: the processes proceed in consecutive asynchronous rounds, and each round is coordinated by a process. More precisely, we have the following:

- Each process p_i executes a sequence of $(t + 1)$ asynchronous rounds at the end of which it decides (if it has not crashed before). As rounds are asynchronous (they are not given for free by an external device) each p_i has to manage a local variable r_i that contains its current round number. Let us observe that, due to asynchrony, nothing prevent two processes to be at different rounds at the same time.

- Each process p_i manages a local variable est_i that contains its current estimate of the decision value (so, est_i is initialized to the value it proposes, namely v_i). Each round is statically assigned a coordinator: round r is coordinated by process p_r. This means that, during that round, p_r tries to impose its current estimate as the decision value. To that end, p_r broadcasts the message $\text{EST}(est_r)$.

  If a process receives $\text{EST}(est)$ from p_r during round r, it updates its estimate of the decision value est_i to the value of the estimate est it has received, and then proceeds to the next round. If it suspects p_r, it proceeds directly to the next round.

  Let us notice that a message does not carry its sending round number.

Theorem 6.1   *The algorithm described in Figure 6.1 solves the consensus problem in $\mathcal{AS}_{n,t}[P]$.*

```
operation propose (v_i):
    est_i ← v_i; r_i ← 1;
    while r_i ≤ t + 1 do
        begin asynchronous round
        if (r_i = i) then broadcast EST (est_i) end if;
        wait until ((EST (est) received from p_{r_i}) ∨ (r_i ∈ suspected_i));
        if (EST (est) received from p_{r_i}) then est_i ← est end if;
        r_i ← r_i + 1
        end asynchronous round
    end while;
    return (est_i).
```

Figure 6.1: A coordinator-based consensus algorithm for $\mathcal{AS}_{n,t}[P]$ (code for p_i)

Proof The proof of the integrity property (a process decides at most once) is trivial: if it does not crash before the end of the last round, a process decides when it executes the return () statement that terminates its participation to the algorithm. The proof of the validity property (a decided value is a proposed value) follows from the observation that any EST() message carries the current value of an est_i local variable, and initially these variables contain only proposed values.

Proof of the termination property. The proof consists in showing that no non-faulty process blocks forever in the **wait until** statement executed during a round. Let us consider the first round. If p_1 is non-faulty it invokes propose (v) and, consequently, sends the message EST (v_1) to each process that (as the channels are reliable) eventually receives it. If p_1 crashes, we eventually have $1 \in suspected_i$ (let us remember 1 is p_1's identity). It follows that no process p_i can block forever during the first round and consequently each non-faulty process enters the second round. Applying inductively the same reasoning to rounds 2, 3, etc., until $t + 1$, allows us to conclude that each non-faulty process returns (decides) a value.

Proof of the agreement property. As t is an upper bound on the number of faulty processes, it follows that at least one among the $(t + 1)$ processes $p_1, \ldots, p_{t+1}$, is non-faulty. Let p_x be the first of these non-faulty processes. Due to the termination property, p_x executes the round $r = x$. As it is the coordinator of this round, it sends its current estimate $est_x = v$ to every process. As it is non-faulty, no process p_i suspects it, which implies that the predicate $x \in suspected_i$ remains forever false. Consequently, each process p_i receives EST (v) and executes $est_i ← v$. It follows that all processes that terminate round x have the same estimate value v. The agreement property follows from the observation that no value different from v can thereafter be sent in a later round. $\square_{Theorem\ 6.1}$

Cost   It is easy to see that the algorithm requires $(t + 1)$ (asynchronous) rounds. Moreover, in each round, at most one process broadcasts a message whose size is independent of the algorithm. So, in the worst case (no crash), $n(t + 1)$ messages are sent (considering that a process does send message to itself). Let $|v|$ be the bit size of a proposed value. The bit communication complexity of the P-based consensus algorithm is consequently $n(t + 1)|v|$.

P is not the weakest failure detector class to solve consensus   Let us consider the failure detector class denoted S defined by the following properties:

- Completeness. Each set $suspected_i$ eventually contains all faulty processes. (Same as for P.)

- Weak accuracy. Some correct processes is never suspected.

On the one hand, both P and S have the same completeness property (this property is used to prevent the processes that use them to block forever waiting for messages from crashed processes). On the other hand, the accuracy property of S is strictly weaker than the one of P. A failure detector of the class P never suspects a process before it crashes, while a failure detector of the class S can erroneously suspect not only faulty processes before they crash, but also (intermittently or forever) all but one non-faulty processes. Hence, it is not possible to build a failure detector of the class P in $\mathcal{AS}_{n,t}[S]$. The class P is strictly stronger than the class S.

The reader can check that the algorithm described in Figure 6.1 solves the consensus problem in $\mathcal{AS}_{n,t}[S]$, when each process is required to execute n rounds (instead of $t + 1$).

The proof is the same as for this algorithm. The important point is that, due to the accuracy property of S and the fact that $t = n - 1$, one of the $t + 1 = n$ coordinators is necessarily a non-faulty process that is never suspected.

The class S is strictly weaker than the class P. This follows from the observation that S does not prevent a correct process from being always suspected. Hence, P cannot be the weakest class of failure detectors that allows solving consensus in an asynchronous system prone to process crashes.

Fairness with respect to the processes   When we consider the algorithm described in Figure 6.1, only the processes $p_1, \ldots, p_{t+1}$ are round coordinators and, consequently, the value decided can only be one of the values they propose. No value proposed by processes p_{t+2} until p_n can ever be decided (except the ones of them that, incidentally, are proposed by a coordinator). In that sense, the construction is *unfair* with respect to the set of processes. Hence, the definition of the following fairness property.

A consensus algorithm is *fair with respect to the processes* if the value that is decided is not predetermined by process identities. If the value v proposed by process p_i is decided, the same value v proposed by the same process could have been decided if, instead of having the identities $1, 2, \ldots, n$ the processes had the identities $\pi(1), \pi(2), \ldots, \pi(n)$ where $\pi()$ is any permutation of the set $\{1, 2, \ldots, n\}$. Fairness guarantees independence between the value that is decided and the identity of the process that proposes it. While this property does not belong to the consensus definition, some applications can benefit from it.

Shuffling the inputs in order to ensure fairness   A simple way to ensure the fairness property consists in adding a preliminary communication round before the **while** loop. During this shuffling round, each process sends its value to the $(t + 1)$ statically defined coordinators, and a coordinator adopts the first value it receives (from any process). The code of this preliminary round is the following for p_i.

```
broadcast SHUFFLE (est_i):
if i ∈{1, . . . , t + 1} then
        wait (SHUFFLE (est) from any process p_j );
        est_i ← est
end if.
```

It is easy to see that this shuffling of the proposed values can assign arbitrarily any proposed value with any coordinator. From an operational point of view, the result of this re-assignment depends on the failure pattern and asynchrony pattern. The P-based algorithm obtained that way is fair (and simple), but requires $(t + 2)$ rounds.

6.1.2   A FAIR ALGORITHM IN $(t + 1)$ ROUNDS

It is actually possible to design a fair P-based algorithm that requires only $t + 1$ rounds. Such an algorithm is described below in Figure 6.3. Let us remember that $t + 1$ rounds is a lower bound for consensus in synchronous systems prone to up to t process crashes (see bibliographic notes). Hence, the algorithm that is presented for $\mathcal{AS}_{n,t}[P]$ shows that, as far as consensus is concerned, the same efficiency can be attained in $\mathcal{AS}_{n,t}[P]$.

Synchronous system   In a round-based synchronous system the round notion is given for free. Processes progress in a lock-step manner: they all execute the same round at the same time. During a round r a process executes the following steps.

- First p_i sends a round r message to the other processes. If it crashes while executing this step, an arbitrary subset of processes receive its round r message.
- Then, p_i waits for round r messages from other processes.
- And finally p_i executes local computation.

The progress from a round r to round $r + 1$ is not managed by each process separately (as done in an asynchronous system), but governed by the system that directs the processes to proceed from r to $r + 1$. The most important feature of a synchronous system is that a message sent in a round is received in the very same round. It follows that if a process p_i does not receive a round r message from a process p_j, it can safely conclude that p_j has crashed; the absence of message indicates a process crash.

Strengthening the definition of P   In order to point out differences between a synchronous system and an asynchronous system enriched with P, let us consider Figure 6.2 where the round boundaries are indicated by bold lines. There are two processes p_i and p_j. During round $(r - 1)$, each receives

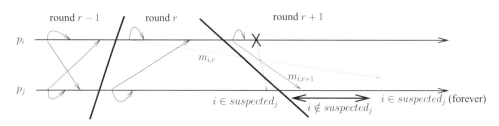

Figure 6.2: Rounds, asynchrony and perfect failure detector

two messages and proceeds to round r. During round r, p_i sends the message $m_{i,r}$, receives two messages, and proceeds to round $(r + 1)$. Moreover, in round $(r + 1)$, p_i sends the message $m_{i,r+1}$ and crashes. On its side, during round r, after having sent a message to p_i, the process p_j waits for a message from p_i. But, in the scenario described on the figure, the corresponding message $m_{i,r}$ is very slow (asynchrony), and p_j is informed of the crash of p_i before receiving $m_{i,r}$. As P provides it with safe suspicions, p_j stops waiting and proceeds to round $(r + 1)$.

Then during round $(r + 1)$ the following can happen. Let us remember that any failure detector of the class P ensures that no process is suspected before it crashes (accuracy property), and if a process p_i crashes, there is a time after which i remains forever in $suspected_j$ (completeness property). This does not prevent the scenario described in the figure that depicts a finite period during which i does not belong to $suspected_j$. This period starts when i is added to $suspected_i$ for the first time, and it ends when it is added to $suspected_j$ for the last time. If this occurs, p_j does not suspect p_i when it receives the message $m_{i,r+1}$ (and consequently considers that message): p_j has then received from p_i a round $(r + 1)$ message and no round r message.

This behavior can never occur in a synchronous system. (In a synchronous system, the round boundary lines are "orthogonal" with respect to the time axis.) The message $m_{i,r}$ would be received by p_j during round r, and the message $m_{i,r+1}$ during round $(r + 1)$. In a synchronous system with the crash pattern presented in Figure 6.2, p_j would discover the crash of p_i during round $(r + 2)$: as it will not receive a round $(r + 2)$ message from p_i, p_j will conclude that p_i has crashed during round $(r + 1)$ or $(r + 2)$.

A fair consensus algorithm for $\mathcal{AS}_{n,t}[P]$ The idea is to simulate the behavior of a synchronous consensus algorithm in $\mathcal{AS}_{n,t}[P]$. In order to guarantee the fairness property, the algorithm is based on the following principle that consists in directing each process to broadcast its current estimate during each round (this is called a *flooding technique*). Moreover, a deterministic function is used to select the decided value (e.g., a process decides the smallest value it has even seen).

In order to prevent the bad phenomenon described in Figure 6.2, each process p_i manages a set $crashed_i$ (that is initially empty). Differently from the set $suspected_i$, the set $crashed_i$ is monotone, i.e., $\forall \tau, \tau' : (\tau \leq \tau') \Rightarrow (crashed_i^\tau \subseteq crashed_i^{\tau'})$ (where $crashed_i^x$ is the value of $crashed_i$ at time x). To implement $crashed_i$, p_i manages a thread that forever executes $crashed_i \leftarrow$

$crashed_i \cup suspected_i$. It is easy to see, that the sets $\{crashed_i\}_{1 \leq i \leq n}$ of the processes satisfy the completeness and accuracy properties of P plus the monotonicity property that rules out the bad phenomenon described in Figure 6.2. This thread is not described in Figure 6.3.

Each process p_i manages the following local variables.

- est_i: p_i's current estimate of the decision value. Its initial value is v_i (value proposed by p_i).
- r_i: p_i's current round number. Its initial value is 1.
- Let us recall that p_i can read $crashed_i$ that is a monotone version of $suspected_i$.

The scope of the other auxiliary local variables is one round. Their meaning follows clearly from their identifier.

```
operation propose (v_i):
(1)   est_i ← v_i; r_i ← 1;
(2)   while r_i ≤ t + 1 do
(3)          begin asynchronous round
(4)          broadcast EST (r_i, est_i);
(5)          wait until (∀j ∉ crashed_i: (EST (r_i, −) received from p_j);
(6)          let rec_from_i = {1, ..., n} \ crashed_i;
(7)          let est_rec_i = {est received during r_i from the processes in rec_from_i};
(8)          est_i ← min(est_rec_i);
(9)          r_i ← r_i + 1
(10)         end asynchronous round
(11)  end while;
(12)  return (est_i).
```

Figure 6.3: A fair consensus algorithm for $\mathcal{AS}_{n,t}[P]$ (code for p_i)

As in a round-based synchronous system, the behavior of a process p_i during a round r is made up of two phases, a communication phase followed by a local computation phase.

- Communication phase. A process p_i first broadcasts EST (r_i, est_i) to inform the other processes on its current state. Then, it waits until it has received a message EST $(r_i, −)$ from each process p_j but the processes that, to its knowledge, have crashed. Let rec_from_i denote the set of processes from which p_i considers and processes the messages it has received.

- Computation phase. Then p_i computes its new estimate value, that is the smallest value carried by a message it has received from a process in rec_from_i.

Notation   Let $min(r)$ denote the smallest value of the current estimates of the processes that terminate round r (i.e., after the updates of est_i during round r). Moreover, $min(0)$ denotes the smallest proposed value.

Theorem 6.2   *The algorithm described in Figure 6.3 solves consensus in* $\mathcal{AS}_{n,t}[P]$. *Moreover, the decided value is* $min(t)$.

Proof

Proof of the validity property. This property follows trivially from the following observations: (a) a process decides the current value of its estimate, (b) the initial values of the estimates are the proposed values, and (c) when updated, a local estimate is set to the minimum of a set of current estimates it has received.

Proof of the termination property. Due to the completeness property of the failure detector, a process cannot be blocked forever in the **wait** statement of line 5. Consequently, all correct processes terminate round $t + 1$ and decide.

Proof of the agreement property. In order to establish this property, we first prove a claim that captures the synchronization provided by the net effect of the **wait** statement and the use of a class P failure detector.

Claim C1. For any r, $1 \leq r \leq t + 1$, when a process p_i terminates round r (this occurs when it sets r_i to $r + 1$), there is no alive process in a round $r' < r$. (At any time, any two alive processes are separated by at most one round.)

Proof of the claim C1. The claim follows from the accuracy property of P. If p_j is alive and executing round $r - 1$ or a smaller round (or is alive and has not yet started if $r = 0$), we have $j \notin suspected_i$, which implies $j \notin crashed_i$. It then follows from the predicate "$\forall j \notin crashed_i$: (EST $(r_i, -)$) received from p_j" (**wait** statement) that controls the progress of p_i from r to $r + 1$, that p_i cannot proceed to $r + 1$. End of proof of claim C1.

The proof of the agreement property is by contradiction. Let us suppose that some process decides a value different from $min(t)$. We show that there are then $(t + 1)$ crashes, which contradicts the model definition. To that end, let us consider the following definitions where r is any round number such that $1 \leq r \leq t + 1$.

- $Q(r) = \{ p_x \mid est_x \leq min(t)$ when p_x starts round r $\}$.
- $R(r) = Q(r) \setminus (R(0) \cup R(1) \dots R(r - 1))$ with $R(0) = \emptyset$. $R(r)$ is the set of processes p_x that start round r with $est_x \leq min(t)$ but did not start a round $r' < r$ with $est_x \leq min(t)$.

By a slight abuse of language, we say that, when a process decides, it is executing the communication-free round $t + 2$. Hence, a process that crashes after having decided crashes during round $t + 2$.

Claim C2. If agreement is violated at the end of round $(t + 1)$, $\forall r : 1 \leq r \leq t + 1$: (i) $|R(r)| \geq 1$, and (ii) all processes in $R(r)$ crash while executing round r or $(r + 1)$.

It follows from claim C2 that, for each round r, $1 \leq r \leq t + 1$, at least one process crashes during r or $r + 1$, from which we conclude that $(t + 1)$ processes crash. This contradicts the fact that at most t processes may crash and proves, consequently, the agreement property.

Proof of claim C2. The proof is by induction on r. Let us first consider the base case $r = 1$.

- Proof of (i): $|R(1)| \geq 1$. As $min(t)$ is the smallest estimate value at the end of round t, and the algorithm does not create estimate values, there is at least one process whose proposed value is equal to $min(t)$.

- Proof of (ii): all processes in $R(1)$ crash while executing round 1 or round 2. Let us assume by contradiction that there is a process $p_i \in R(1)$ that does not crash while executing round 1 or round 2 (hence, p_i terminates round 2). Due to the claim C1, there is no process alive in round 1 when p_i terminates $r = 2$. It follows that all processes that have terminated the first round have received and processed the message EST $(1, est_i)$, with $est_i \leq min(t)$. Consequently, every process p_j that enters the second round has updated its estimate est_j to a value $\leq min(t)$ before entering the second round. Since estimates can only decrease during the execution, this implies that any process p_j that starts the last round has an estimate $est_j \leq min(t)$. By the very definition of $min(t)$ it means that such an estimate $est_j = min(t)$. Hence all processes that start the last round have the same estimate, $min(t)$ and then no other value can be decided. It contradicts the fact that (by assumption) some process decides a value different from $min(t)$. This contradiction concludes the proof of item (ii) for the base case.

Let us now consider the induction step. So, assuming that items (i) and (ii) are satisfied from the first round until round $r - 1$, let us show that they are satisfied for round $r \leq t + 1$.

- Proof of (i): $|R(r)| \geq 1$. Let p_i be a process that terminates round r and such that $est_i \leq min(t)$ at the end of round r. Due to the definition of $min(t)$ and the fact that there is no creation of value, such a process necessarily exists. There are two cases.
  Case 1: $p_i \in Q(r)$. As p_i terminates round r, and no process in $R(r - 1), R(r - 2), \ldots, R(1)$ terminates round r (induction assumption), it follows that $p_i \notin R(0) \cup R(1) \ldots R(r - 1)$. By the definition of $R(r)$, it follows that $p_i \in R(r)$. Hence, $|R(r)| \geq 1$, which proves item (i) for the case.
  Case 2: $p_i \notin Q(r)$. As $p_i \notin Q(r)$, it follows that p_i has received a message EST (r, est_j) from a process p_j such that $est_j \leq min(t)$ at the beginning of r, i.e., $p_j \in Q(r)$.
  Claim C3 : $p_j \notin Q(r - 1)$.
  Assuming C3, as $p_j \notin Q(r - 1)$ and due to the fact that est_j can only decrease during an execution, $p_j \notin Q(r')$ for all $r' < r$. Since $p_j \in Q(r)$ we have $p_j \in R(r)$, and, consequently, $|R(r)| \geq 1$, which proves item (i) for Case 2.

  Proof of the claim C3. As p_i has received EST (r, est_j) with $est_j \leq min(t)$ from process p_j during round r, we conclude from the monotonicity property of the set $crashed_i$, that p_i has received a message EST $(r - 1, -)$ from process p_j during round $r - 1$. Let us assume by contradiction that $p_j \in Q(r - 1)$. It then follows that p_i has received EST $(r - 1, est_j)$ from

p_j during round $r - 1$ with $est_j \leq min(t)$, and, consequently, we have $est_i \leq min(t)$, at the end of round $r - 1$, i.e., $p_i \in Q(r)$ which contradicts the assumption associated with Case 2. Hence, $p_j \notin Q(r - 1)$. End of proof of claim C3.

- Proof of (ii) of claim C2: All processes in $R(r)$ crash while executing round r or round $r + 1$. The proof of this item is verbatim the proof as for the base case after changing round numbers 1 and 2 by round numbers r and $r + 1$, respectively. So, it is not repeated here. End of proof of claim C2.

$\square_{Theorem\ 6.2}$

6.1.3 EARLY DECISION

Motivation Failures do occur but are not frequent. Hence, it is interesting to have a consensus algorithm for the model $\mathcal{AS}_{n,t}[P]$, in which the processes decide and halt in very few rounds when there are few failures. This is the *early decision/halting* notion. Let f be the number of processes that crash in a run, $0 \leq f \leq t$. This section presents an algorithm that directs the processes to decide and stop in $min(f + 2, t + 1)$ rounds when executed in the model $\mathcal{AS}_{n,t}[P]$. This means that a process decides and stops in two rounds in failure-free runs.

The lower bound on the number of rounds for early deciding/stopping consensus in synchronous systems $min(f + 2, t + 1)$. The algorithm that follows shows that this bound can be attained in asynchronous systems such as $\mathcal{AS}_{n,t}[P]$.

An early deciding/stopping algorithm The principle that underlies the proposed early-deciding/stopping algorithm (described in Figure 6.4) is as follows. A process decides as soon as it knows that (1) its current estimate of the decision value is the smallest estimate value present in the system, and (2) at least one non-faulty process knows that value. This algorithm extends the previous algorithm as follows. A line tagged (x) or (x') corresponds to line (x) in the non early-deciding algorithm. The lines tagged (Ny) are new lines that ensure early decision/stopping. In addition to the previous local variables, the algorithm uses the following ones.

- i_know_i is a boolean, initialized to *false*. This boolean is set to *true* at the end of a round r, if p_i learned -during that round- that its current estimate est_i contains the smallest estimate value among the processes that start round r. This means that est_i contains the smallest value still present in the system. This boolean is stable (once true, it remains true forever).

- $they\_know_i$ is a set, initialized to $\emptyset$. This set contains the identities of the processes that, to p_i's knowledge, have the smallest estimate value present in the system.

Behavior of a process As in the previous algorithm, the behavior of a process p_i during a round r is made up of two phases, a communication phase followed by a local computation phase.

- Communication phase. A process p_i first broadcasts EST (r_i, est_i, i_know_i) to inform the other processes on its current state. Then, it waits until it has received a message EST $(r_i, -, -)$

```
operation propose (v_i):
(1')    est_i ← v_i; r_i ← 1; they_know_i ← ∅; i_know_i ← false;
(2)     while r_i ≤ t + 1 do
(3)         begin asynchronous round
(4')            broadcast EST (r_i, est_i, i_know_i);
(5')            wait until (∀j ∉ ((crashed_i ∪ they_know_i) \ {i}): (EST (r_i, −, −) received from p_j);
(N1)            let crashed_or_knowing_i be the set (crashed_i ∪ they_known_i) when the wait terminates;
(6')            let rec_from_i = {1, . . . , n} \ crashed_or_knowing_i;
(7)             let est_rec_i = {est received during r_i from the processes in rec_from_i};
(8)             est_i ← min(est_rec_i);
(N2)            they_know_i ← they_know_i ∪ {x | EST (r_i, −, true) rec. from p_x with x ∈ rec_from_i};
(N3)            if ((|crashed_i ∪ they_know_i| ≥ t + 1) ∧ i_know_i) then return (est_i) end if;
(N4)            let some_knows_i = (∃ EST (r_i, −, true) received from p_x with x ∈ rec_from_i);
(N5)            i_know_i ← (some_knows_i) ∨ (|rec_from_i| ≥ n − r_i + 1);
(9)             r_i ← r_i + 1
(10)        end asynchronous round
(11)    end while;
(12)    return (est_i).
```

Figure 6.4: Early deciding/stopping consensus in $\min(f + 2, t + 1)$ rounds in $\mathcal{AS}_{n,t}[P]$ (code for p_i)

from each process p_j but the processes that, to its knowledge, have crashed or know the smallest estimate value. Moreover, we assume that it always receives its own message (while not necessary, this assumption simplifies the proof). Now, rec_from_i denotes the set of processes from which p_i considers and processes the messages it has received (those are the messages from itself and the processes not in $crashed_i \cup they\_know_i$).

Let us observe that a process p_k that knows the smallest estimate value can have decided and stopped in a previous round, and consequently, p_i could block forever if it was directed to wait for a message from p_k.

- Computation phase. Then p_i computes its new estimate value, that is the smallest value carried by a message it has received from a process in rec_from_i. It also updates the set $they\_know_i$ according to the boolean values carried by the EST $(r_i, −, −)$ messages it has received from the processes in rec_from_i. Then p_i strives to early decide. To that end, it does the following.

    – If it knows the smallest among the estimate values of the processes that start round r (i.e., i_know_i is true), and knows also that value is know by at least one non-faulty process (i.e., $|crashed_i \cup they\_know_i| \ge t + 1$), then p_i decides and stops its participation to the algorithm.

    – Otherwise, p_i updates its local state before starting a new round. To that end, it first computes the value of i_know_i. If p_i has received a message EST $(r_i, v, true)$, it has learned from another process that v is the smallest estimate value, and consequently sets i_know_i to true.

As we will see in the proof, if $|rec\_from_i| \geq n - r + 1$, then p_i discovers that the current value of its estimate is the smallest estimate value in the system. In that case, it sets i_know_i to the value *true*.

Theorem 6.3 *Let f be the number of processes that crash in a run ($0 \leq f \leq t$). The algorithm described in Figure 6.4 solves consensus in at most* $\min(f + 2, t + 1)$ *rounds in* $\mathcal{AS}_{n,t}[P]$.

Notation Let xxx_i be a local variable of process p_i. It is easy to see, that such a variable is updated at most once in a round r. The notation $xxx_i(r)$ is used to denote its value at the end of round r.

Proof The proof of the validity property is the same as in Theorem 6.2. Before proving the other properties, a few claims are proved.

Claim C1. $i\_know_i(r) \Rightarrow (est_i(r) = min(r - 1))$ (i.e., at the end of round r, p_i knows the smallest estimate value that was present in the system at the end of $r - 1$).
Proof of claim C1. The proof is by induction on the round number.

- If a process p_i updates its boolean i_know_i to true during round 1 (we have then $|rec\_from_i| = n$), it has received n messages containing the n initial estimates. Hence p_i knows the minimum value in the system amongst all the estimate values.

- Let p_i be a process that updates its boolean i_know_i to true during round r. There are two cases.

  – p_i has received a message EST $(r, -, true)$ from p_j. It means that p_j has updated its boolean i_know_j to true in a previous round, and then by induction, p_i knows the minimum value.

  – p_i has received $n - r + 1$ messages in round r and it has never received (in round r or in previous rounds) a message EST $(-, -, true)$. From p_i's point of view, the execution is similar to an execution of the algorithm described in Figure 6.3 in which we would have $t = r - 1$. This follows from the fact that (a) line N5 updates i_know_i only in round r, and (b) lines N1, N2, N3, and N4 do not modify local variables up to round r (they are consequently useless up to that round). Moreover, due to the current values of $i\_know_i = false$ and $they\_know_i = \emptyset$ before line N5 of round r, (1) the lines tagged (x') behave as the line tagged (x) in the algorithm of Figure 6.3, and (2) we have $|rec\_from_i(r)| \geq n - r + 1$. Consequently, at the end of round r, i_know_i is equal to *true*, and it follows from Theorem 6.2 that we have then $est_i(r) = min(r - 1)$ (smallest estimate value of processes that terminate round $r - 1$). End of proof of claim C1.

Claim C2. No process blocks forever in a round.

Proof of claim C2. Let us assume by contradiction that a process blocks forever in a round. Let r be the first round during which a process p_i blocks forever. This happens in the **wait** statement where p_i waits for messages EST $(r, -, -)$ from processes that currently are not in $crashed_i \cup they\_know_i$. If a process p_j crashes, it eventually appears in the set $crashed_i$ (let us remember that this set can only increase). Hence, a process that crashes cannot prevent p_i from progressing. If p_j is non-faulty, there are two cases.

- Case 1: p_j has not decided during a round $r' \leq r$. In that case, as by assumption r is the first round during which processes block forever, it follows that p_j sends a message EST $(r, -, -)$. Consequently, such a process p_j cannot block forever p_i in round r.

- Case 2: p_j has decided during a round $r' < r$. Before deciding during r', p_j sent EST $(r', -, true)$ to p_i, and (as p_j does not crash) p_i received and processed this message. Hence, $j \in they\_know_i(r')$. As the set $they\_know_i$ never decreases, and $r' < r$, it follows that $j \in they\_know_i(r - 1)$ (that is the value of $they\_know_i$ when p_i waits during round r). Hence, in that case also, p_i has not to wait for a message from p_j. End of proof of claim C2.

Proof of agreement property. Let r be the first round during which a process (say p_i) decides. Due to Claim C1, we have $est_i(r) = min(r - 1)$. If p_j decides at round r, we also have $est_j(r) = min(r - 1)$, from which we conclude that the processes that decide at round r, decide the same value.

Let p_k be a process that proceeds to round $r + 1$. Let us observe that, when p_i decides, we have $|crashed_i \cup they\_know_i| \geq t + 1$, from which we conclude that there is a non-faulty process p_x that sent EST $(r', est_x(r' - 1), i\_knows_x(r' - 1))$ (with $i\_knows_x(r' - 1) = true$) during round $r' < r$. As p_x is non-faulty, it follows that every non-crashed processes received this message during round r'. Due to Claim C1, we have $i\_knows_x(r' - 1) \Rightarrow (est_i(r' - 1) = min(r' - 2))$. (Notice that $r' > 1$ because any i_know_x is initially equal to *false*).

As p_i received $(r', est_x(r' - 1), true)$, it follows that $est_i(r) = est_x(r' - 1)$. Consequently, any process p_k that proceeds to round $r + 1$ is such that $est_k(r) = est_x(r' - 1) = est_i(r)$, i.e., the estimate values of all the processes that proceed to round $r + 1$ are equal to $est_i(r)$. It follows that no value different from $est_i(r)$ can be decided in a round $r'' \geq r$, which completes the proof of that agreement property.

Proof of termination property. Due to Claim C2, no process blocks forever in a round. It follows that if a process neither crashes, nor decides at a round $r < t + 1$, it proceeds to round $t + 1$ during which it decides (in the worst case at the last line of the algorithm).

Proof of early decision property. Let us first observe that a process executes at most $t + 1$ rounds. Hence, considering that $f < t$ processes crash, we have to show that no process decides after round $(f + 2)$. There are two cases.

- Case 1: a correct process p_c sends EST $(r, -, true)$, during a round $r \leq f + 1$. As p_c is non-faulty, every process that executes round r receives this message during round r. It follows that we have $i\_know_i(r) = true$ at each process p_i that terminates round r. Consequently, every process p_j that executes round $r + 1 (\leq f + 2)$ sends EST $(r + 1, -, true)$, and hence we have $|crashed_j(r + 1) \cup they\_know_j(r + 1)| = n$. It follows that the early decision predicate is satisfied, and every process that executes round $r + 1$ decides (and stops).

- Case 2: no correct process sends EST $(r, -, true)$ during a round $r \leq f + 1$. In that case, no correct process appears in a set $they\_know_x(r)$ for $r \leq f + 1$. Moreover, as f processes crash, and no correct process has decided, at least $(n - f)$ processes send messages during each round. Hence, at any round, we have $|rec\_from_i| \geq n - f$.

  Any process p_i that, during round $f + 1$, evaluates the predicate $|rec\_from_i| \geq n - r + 1$ finds that it is satisfied (because we have then $|rec\_from_i| \geq n - f = n - r + 1$). Consequently, every process p_i that terminates round $f + 1$, sets i_know_i to true.

  Then, for any process p_i that does not crash during $r = f + 2$, and any process p_j, we have $j \in crashed_i$ or $j \in rec\_from_i$ when p_i terminates its **wait** statement. Moreover, if $j \in rec\_from_i$, p_i has received EST $(f + 2, -, true)$ from p_j. It follows that $|crashed_i(f + 2) \cup they\_know_i(f + 2)| = n$. Consequently, during round $f + 2$, p_i executes return(), i.e., it decides and stops.

  $\square_{Theorem\ 6.3}$

6.2　THE WEAKEST FAILURE DETECTOR CLASS TO SOLVE CONSENSUS

The weakest failure detector class to solve consensus　As we have seen, the class P of perfect failure detectors is not the weakest class of failure detectors that permit to solve consensus. Neither is the class S previously described. This means that these failure detector classes provide the processes with more information on failures than what is sufficient to solve consensus in an asynchronous message-passing system prone to process crashes.

The weakest failure detector class to solve consensus in such a system is the combination of two failure detector classes Σ and Ω and is consequently denoted $\Sigma \times \Omega$. It provides each process with two outputs, one associated with Σ, the other one with Ω.

- The class Σ is the class of quorum failure detectors introduced in the second chapter, where it has been shown to be the weakest failure detector class for constructing a shared register in a crash-prone asynchronous message-passing system.

  A failure detector of the class Σ provides each process with a quorum local variable (set of process identities) such that each quorum eventually contains only non-faulty processes, and the values of any two quorums, each considered at any time, do intersect.

- The class Ω, formally defined below, is the class of *eventual leader* failure detectors. It provides each process with a local variable such that eventually all these local variables contain forever the identity of the same non-faulty process.

The class Ω of eventual leader failure detectors   This class of failure detectors provides each process p_i with a local variable $leader_i$ such that the set of local variables $\{leader_i\}_{1 \leq i \leq n}$ collectively satisfy the following properties.

Let $leader_i^\tau$ be the value of $leader_i$ at time τ (considering the failure detector history H associated with Ω we have $H(i, \tau) \equiv leader_i^\tau$). Let us remember a few definitions stated in Chapter 2. F denotes a crash pattern ($F(\tau)$ is the set of processes crashed at time τ), $Faulty(F)$ the set of processes that crash in the failure pattern F, and $Correct(F)$ the set of processes that are non-faulty in the failure pattern F.

- Validity. $\forall i: \forall \tau: leader_i^\tau$ contains a process identity.

- Eventual leadership. $\exists \ell \in Correct(F), \exists \tau: \forall \tau' \geq \tau: \forall i \in Correct(F): leader_i^{\tau'} = \ell$.

These properties state that a unique leader is eventually elected; this leader is not a faulty process, but there is no knowledge of when this leader is elected. Several leaders can co-exist during an arbitrary long (but finite) period of time, and there is no way for a process to know when this anarchy period is over. During the anarchy period, it is possible that crashed processes are considered as leaders by non-faulty processes and different processes may have different leaders.

The proof that Ω is the weakest class of failure detectors that allows the consensus problem to be solved despite asynchrony, and at most, t process crashes (with $1 \leq t < n/2$) is pretty involved and very technical. It is not presented here.

The system model $\mathcal{AS}_{n,t}[t < n/2, \Omega]$ As we have seen in second chapter, the assumption of a majority of non-faulty processes allows implementing a failure detector of the class Σ. Hence, in the following, we consider only systems that satisfy the assumption $t < n/2$. The asynchronous model considered is consequently $\mathcal{AS}_{n,t}[t < n/2, \Omega]$, i.e., $\mathcal{AS}_{n,t}[t < n/2]$ enriched with any failure detector of the class Ω.

Let p_i and p_j be any pair of processes. An algorithm can easily benefit from the assumption $n > 2t$ to force p_i and p_j to receive at least one message broadcast by the same process. To that end, let us direct p_i and p_j to wait for messages broadcast by $n - t$ distinct processes, and let Q_i (resp., Q_j) be the set of processes from which p_i (resp., p_j) receives a message. We have $|Q_i| = |Q_j| = n - t > n/2 > t$ (each set Q_i and Q_j is a majority set). Hence, $Q_i \cap Q_j \neq \emptyset$, and there is at least one process that belongs to both Q_i and Q_j.

As a quorum failure detector provides the processes with the same intersection property (without assuming the requirement of a majority of correct processes), the algorithms described in this chapter remain correct when the non-empty intersection property provided by $t < n/2$ is obtained by a quorum failure detector. As it is very simple (and some examples have been given in Chapter 4 devoted to the construction of the URB-broadcast abstraction in presence of fair channels), the replacement of the assumption $t < n/2$ by a failure detector of the class Σ in these algorithms is left to the reader.

6.3 A ZERO-DEGRADING CONSENSUS ALGORITHM FOR $\mathcal{AS}_{n,t}[t < n/2, \Omega]$

The Ω-based consensus algorithm presented in this section satisfies several noteworthy properties, including the zero-degradation property. That property will be defined in Section 6.3.4 (intuitively, this property says that failures that occurred before a consensus instance is started must not impact on the efficiency of that instance).

6.3.1 PRESENTATION OF THE ALGORITHM

Structure of the algorithm Each process p_i proceeds through consecutive asynchronous rounds. Each round is made up of two phases. During the first phase of a round, the processes strive to select the same value called estimate value. This is done with the help of the failure detector Ω. Then, they try to decide during the second phase. This occurs when they obtain the same value at the end of the first phase. Let us observe that, as the rounds are asynchronous, it is possible that not all the processes are at the same round at the same time.

Moreover, when a process is about to decide a value v, it first broadcasts a message DECIDE(v), and then decides by executing the statement return(v). When a process receives a message DECIDE(v), if forwards (i.e., broadcasts) it before deciding. Let us remember that when a processes executes return(v), it terminates participating in the algorithm. The reception of a message DECIDE () can occur at any time. As we will see later, this is to prevent permanent blocking that could otherwise occur. (When a process broadcasts a message DECIDE(v), it can save the sending to itself and to the process from which it receives that message, if it is the case.)

Local variables Each process p_i manages the following local variables.

- r_i: current round number.
- $est1_i$: local estimate of the decision value at the beginning of the first phase of a round.
- $est2_i$: local estimate of the decision value at the beginning of the second phase of a round.
- $my\_leaders_i$ and rec_i are auxiliary variables used by p_i in the first phase and the second phase of a round, perspectively.

The special value $\bot$ denotes a default value which cannot be proposed by a process.

The behavior of a process during the first phase of a round The algorithm executed by every process p_i is described in Figure 6.5. The aim of the first phase of a round r is to provide the processes with the same value v in their local estimate $est2_i$. When this occurs, a decision will be obtained during the second phase of the round r. As we are about to see, this aim is always attained when the eventual leader is elected.

```
operation propose (v_i):
    est1_i ← v_i; r_i ← 0;
    while true do
        begin asynchronous round
        r_i ← r_i + 1;
        % │ Phase 1 │: select a value with the help of the oracle Ω %
            my_leader_i ← leader_i; % read local Ω output %
            broadcast PHASEI (r_i, est1_i, my_leader_i);
            wait until (    [PHASEI (r_i, −, −) received from n − t processes]
                            ∧ [PHASEI (r_i, −, −) received from p_{my_leader_i} ∨ my_leader_i ≠ leader_i]);
            if ([∃ℓ: PHASEI (r_i, −, ℓ) received from > n/2 processes] ∧ [(r_i, v, −) received from p_ℓ])
                            then est2_i ← v else est2_i ← ⊥ end if;
        % Here, we have ((est2_i ≠ ⊥) ∧ (est2_j ≠ ⊥)) ⇒ (est2_i = est2_j = v) %
        % │ Phase 2 │: try to decide a value from the est2 values %
            broadcast PHASE2 (r_i, est2_i);
            wait until (PHASE2 (r_i, −) received from n − t processes);
            let rec_i = {est2 | PHASE2 (r_i, est2) has been received};
            case (rec_i = {v})      then broadcast DECIDE(v); return (v)
                 (rec_i = {v, ⊥}) then est1_i ← v
                 (rec_i = {⊥})     then skip
            end case
        end asynchronous round
    end while.

    when DECIDE(v) is received: broadcast DECIDE(v); return (v).
```

Figure 6.5: A zero-degrading consensus algorithm for $\mathcal{AS}_{n,t}[t < n/2, \Omega]$ (code for p_i)

So, the main issue of this first phase is to prevent the violation of the safety property (no two different values are decided) while Ω is still in its anarchy period during which the unique eventual non-faulty leader is not yet elected. To preserve the safety property, the first phase guarantees that a property, called *quasi-agreement*, is always satisfied just before the processes enter the second phase of the round r. Let $est2_x[r]$ be the value of $est2_x$ when p_x starts the second phase of round r. This property is defined as follows:

$$((est2_i[r] \neq \bot) \wedge (est2_j[r] \neq \bot)) \Rightarrow (est2_i[r] = est2_j[r] = v).$$

The predicate $est2_i[r] = v$ means that, from p_x's point of view, v can be decided, $est2_i[r] = \bot$ means that, from p_x's point of view, no value can be decided. The quasi-agreement states that the processes that enter the second phase of a round propose to decide on the same value (case $est2_i[r] = est2_j[r] = v$), or propose to proceed to the next round (case $est2_i[r] = \bot$).

In order the quasi-agreement property be satisfied at the end of the first phase of each round $r_i = r$, a process p_i does the following.

- First, it reads the local variable $leader_i$ provided by the failure detector Ω, and it keeps its value in my_leader_i. Then, it sends to the other processes the relevant part of its state (namely, here the values of $est1_i$ and my_leader_i) by broadcasting the message PHASE1 $(r, est1_i, my\_leader_i)$ (let us remember that the broadcast() operation is not reliable).

- Then p_i waits for $n - t$ messages PHASE1 $(r, -, -)$. Let us notice that, as up to t processes may crash, this is the maximum number of messages that a process can wait for without risking to be blocked forever. Let us also notice that, as $t < n/2$, any set of $n - t$ processes defines a majority and any majority includes at least one non-faulty process.

Process p_i waits also until either it has received a message PHASE1 $(r, -, -)$ from the process it considers as its current leader ($p_{my\_leader_i}$), or its current leader has changed ($my\_leader_i \neq leader_i$).

- When the previous broadcast/receive steps have been executed, p_i assigns a value to $est2_i$. In order the predicate be satisfied, this value is computed as follows. If there is a process p_ℓ such that

    1. a majority of processes -i.e., more than $n/2$- consider p_ℓ as their leader (this is witnessed by the messages PHASE1 $(r, -, \ell)$ they sent), and

    2. a message PHASE1 $(r, v, -)$ has been received from that process p_ℓ,

then p_i sets $est2_i$ to v (that is the value of $est1_\ell$ when p_ℓ started round r). Otherwise, p_i sets $est2_i$ to $\perp$. As any two majorities of processes intersect, it is not possible for two majorities to consider different processes as their unique leader, from which we conclude that it is not possible to have $est2_i[r] = v \neq \perp$ and $est2_j[r] = v' \neq \perp$ with $v \neq v'$.

Let us remark that it is possible that, at a round r, a process p_ℓ is considered as leader by a majority of processes, while it does not consider itself as leader (we have then $my\_leader_\ell \neq \ell$).

The behavior of a process during the second phase of a round   The second phase of round r obeys the same communication pattern as the first phase. A process p_i first broadcasts the relevant part of its state (message PHASE2 $(r, est2_i)$), and then it waits for a message PHASE2 $(r, -)$ from $n - t$ processes.

It follows from the first phase of round r that any message PHASE2 $(r_i, est2)$ broadcast by a process is such that $est2 = \perp$, or $est2 = v \neq \perp$ (no two messages can carry different non-$\perp$ values). It follows that the set rec_i of values received by p_i can be equal to only $\{v\}$, $\{v, \perp\}$, or $\{\perp\}$.

- If $rec_i = \{v\}$, p_i informs the other processes that it decides v (by broadcasting DECIDE (v)), and then decides v by executing return (v).

- If $rec_i = \{v, \perp\}$, p_i considers v as its new estimate value $est1_i$ (this is because some other process might have decided v), and proceeds to the round $r + 1$.

- If $rec_i = \{\perp\}$, p_i proceeds to the next round (without modifying $est1_i$).

It is important to notice that, at any round r, the local predicates $rec_i = \{v\}$ and $rec_j = \{\perp\}$ are mutually exclusive (if one is true, the other is necessarily false). This is an immediate consequence of the fact that any two majorities intersect: if p_i broadcasts DECIDE (v), it has received the message

PHASE2 (r_i, v) from a majority of processes. Hence, each other process p_j receives at least one message PHASE2 (r_i, v) and cannot have $rec_j = \{\bot\}$.

Why inform the other processes before deciding?   A process that decides stops participating in the consensus algorithm. According to the failure pattern, the behavior of the failure detector, and asynchrony, it is possible that not all the processes that decide do it during the same round. Hence, given processes that decide during r, it is possible that processes proceed to $r + 1$ and, during that round, wait forever for messages from non-faulty processes that have terminated during round r. The broadcast of the decided value, before deciding it, permits to break the round notion and prevents the previous bad scenarios from occurring. It guarantees that, as soon as a process p_i decides, all the non-faulty processes eventually decide.

6.3.2   PROOF OF THE ALGORITHM

Theorem 6.4   *The algorithm described in Figure 6.5 solves the consensus problem in $\mathcal{AS}_{n,t}[t < n/2, \Omega]$.*

Proof Proof of the validity and integrity properties. The integrity is trivial since a process decides when it executes the statement return() and this statement terminates its participation to the algorithm.

As far as the validity property is concerned, let us observe that any message DECIDE (v) carries a value $v \neq \bot$. Hence, $\bot$ cannot be decided. A value that is decided is a non-$\bot$ value that comes from a local variable $est2_i$, which in turn comes from a local variable $est1_j$. As initially the local variables $est1_j$ contain only proposed values, and then the algorithm copies values from $est1_x$ to $est2_y$ and vice-versa, the validity property follows.

Proof of the termination property. Claim C1. No non-faulty process blocks forever in a round.

Given C1, the proof is by contradiction. Let us assume that no process decides. It follows from the eventual leadership property of Ω, the claim C1, and the fact that faulty processes eventually crash (otherwise, they would not be faulty), that there is a finite round r from which (1) only the non-faulty processes are alive, and (2) these processes have forever the same non-faulty leader (say p_ℓ) in their local variables my_leader_i. So, let us consider, the non-faulty processes (that are more than $n/2$) when they execute the round r. Each of them (including p_ℓ) broadcasts PHASEI $(r, -, \ell)$ and receives only messages PHASEI $(r, -, \ell)$. Moreover, it receives at least $(n - t)$ such messages. It follows that the predicate "$(\exists \ell$: PHASEI $(r_i, -, \ell)$ received from more than $n/2$ processes$) \wedge ((r_i, v, -)$ received from $p_\ell)$" is satisfied at each process p_i. Consequently, each process sets $est2_i[r]$ to v, and during the second phase of round r only value v is sent. It follows that the set rec_i of each process is equal to $\{v\}$. Hence, each non-faulty process decides, which concludes the proof of the termination.

Proof of the claim C1. If a process decides, it has previously broadcast a message DECIDE (). As the channels are reliable, each correct process receives this message and decides. It follows that, if a process decides, no non-faulty process remains blocked forever in a round.

Let us now consider the case where no process decides. The proof is by contradiction. Assuming that no process decides, let r be the smallest round in which a non-faulty process p_i blocks forever. So, p_i blocks in the **wait** statement in the first phase or the second phase of round r. As no non-faulty process blocks forever in a round $r' < r$ (definition of r), it follows that p_i receives $(n - t)$ PHASE1 $(r, -, -)$ messages. Moreover, if its current leader $p_{my\_leader_i}$ is non-faulty it receives a message PHASE1 $(r, -, -)$ from this process. If $p_{my\_leader_i}$ is faulty, we eventually have $my\_leader_i \neq leader_i$ (due to the eventual leadership of Ω). It follows that no non-faulty process p_i can block forever in the first phase of round r. A similar reasoning applies to the second phase of round r: p_i receives at least $(n - t)$ PHASE2 $(r, -)$ messages from the non-faulty processes, and it cannot be blocked forever in this phase either. It follows that r is not the smallest round in which a non-faulty process blocks forever, which contradicts the definition of r and proves the claim. End of the proof of the claim C1.

Proof of the agreement property. Let r be the smallest round during which a process broadcasts a message DECIDE (v). We claim that, if any process broadcasts DECIDE (v') at round r, we have $v' = v$ (Claim C2), and the local estimates $est1_i$ of all the processes that proceed to $r + 1$ are such that $est1_i = v$ (Claim C3). It follows from these claims that no value different from v can be ever be decided, which proves the agreement property.

Proof of the claim C2. Let p_i (resp., p_j) a process that sends a message DECIDE (v) (resp. DECIDE (v')) at round r. It follows from the text of the algorithm that p_i has received $n - t$ messages PHASE2 (r, v) and p_j has received $n - t$ messages PHASE2 (r, v'). As $n - t > n/2$, and a process broadcasts at most one message PHASE2 $(r, -)$, p_i and p_j have received the same message PHASE2 (r, v'') from some process p_x (that belongs to the intersection of the two majorities of $n - t$ processes). It follows that $v'' = v = v'$, which proves the claim. End of the proof of the claim C2.

Proof of the claim C3. We have to prove that, if a process p_i broadcasts a message DECIDE (v) during a round r and p_j proceeds to round $r + 1$, we have $est1_j = v$ when p_j starts round $r + 1$.

As p_i broadcasts a message DECIDE (v) during a round r, there are at least $(n - t)$ processes that have sent a message PHASE2 (r, v). As any two majorities intersect and $n - t > n/2$, it follows that p_j has received at least one message PHASE2 (r, v) among the $(n - t)$ PHASE2 $(r, -)$ it has received during the second phase of round r. Moreover, it follows from the quasi-agreement property (which has been implicitly proved in the description of the algorithm), that p_j receives both v and $\perp$ (and no other value) in the second phase of round r, i.e., we have $rec_j = \{v, \perp\}$ (rec_j cannot be equal to $\{v\}$; otherwise, it would have broadcast DECIDE (v) during r). It follows that p_j updates $est1_j$ to v before proceeding to round $r + 1$. End of the proof of the claim C3. $\square_{Theorem\ 6.4}$

Remark   The reader can check that the proof of the consensus agreement property (safety) relies only on the majority of correct processes assumption (or on the intersection property of the quorum failure detector of the class Σ if such a failure detector is used instead of the "majority of correct processes" assumption). Differently, the proof of the termination property relies only on the use of the eventual leader oracle of the class Ω. This is in agreement with the FLP impossibility result: without the additional power provided by Ω, it is not possible to design a consensus algorithm that always terminates in $\mathcal{AS}_{n,t}[t < n/2]$.

6.3.3   THE CONSENSUS PROBLEM VS Ω

When a failure detector of the class Ω is used, no process ever knows from which time instant the failure detector provides forever the processes with the identity of the same correct process. A failure detector is a service that never terminates. Its behavior depends on the failure pattern, and Ω has no sequential specification.

Differently, when processes execute a consensus algorithm, there is time instant from which they do know that a value has been decided (for a process, this occurs when it invokes the return () statement). There is a single decided value, but that value can be the value proposed by a faulty process. To, summarize, consensus is a function while a failure detector is not.

6.3.4   FIRST CLASS PROPERTIES: INDULGENCE AND ZERO-DEGRADATION

Indulgence   Let A be an algorithm that is based on a failure detector of a class C. A is *indulgent with respect to the failure detector class C* if its safety property is never violated, whatever the behavior of the failure detector (of the class C) it uses. This means that, if the failure detector never meets its specification, it is possible that A does not terminate, but if it terminates it returns correct results. Said differently, if the underlying failure detector behaves arbitrarily, the termination property of A can be compromised, but its safety property is never violated.

As shown by the remark as the end of the previous section, the algorithm described in Figure 6.5 is indulgent with respect to Ω. On the one hand, in the executions in which the eventual leadership property is not satisfied, it is possible that the algorithm does not terminate. On the other hand, all the executions that terminate do satisfy the consensus safety property. These executions include all the executions where the failure detector satisfies the eventual leadership property plus some executions where it does not (as an exercise, the reader is invited to check that such executions do exist.)

Zero-degradation   Let a failure detector of the class Ω be *perfect* if the eventual leadership property is satisfied from the very beginning of the execution. With such a failure detector, it is possible to evaluate the efficiency of an Ω-based algorithm without being bothered by the erratic behavior of Ω during a finite but a arbitrary long period.

Let us consider a failure-free execution with a failure detector of the class Ω that has a perfect behavior. It is easy to check that processes decide at the end of the first round, i.e., after two consecutive communication steps, which is optimal. In that sense, the algorithm is *failure detector-efficient*. (We do not consider the cost due to DECIDE () messages as, in the previous scenario, they are not needed for a process to decide).

Consensus is typically used in a repeated form, and a process failure during one consensus instance appears as an *initial* failure in a subsequent consensus instance. Assuming its underlying failure detector behaves perfectly, a consensus algorithm is *zero-degrading* if a crash in one consensus instance does not impact the performance of any future consensus instance. It is easy to check that the algorithm described in Figure 6.5 satisfies the zero-degradation property: if the failure detector behaves perfectly, processes decide in two communication steps whatever the number of processes that have crashed before (or during) this consensus instance.

A non-zero degrading algorithm Let us consider the failure detector class $\diamond S$. A failure detector of $\diamond S$ provides each process p_i with a set $suspected_i$, such that there is a finite time after which (1) the set $suspected_i$ of any non-faulty process contains the identity of every faulty process, and (2) there is a non-faulty process that does not belong to the sets $suspected_i$.

$\diamond S$ and Ω have the same computational power. This means that it is possible to build (1) a failure detector of the class Ω in $\mathcal{AS}_{n,t}[\diamond S]$, and (2) a failure detector of the class $\diamond S$ in $\mathcal{AS}_{n,t}[\Omega]$.

If, instead of a failure detector of the class Ω, we have a failure detector of the class $\diamond S$, the replacement of the first phase of the algorithm presented in Figure 6.5 by the following statements produces a consensus algorithm that works in $\mathcal{AS}_{n,t}[t < n/2, \diamond S]$.

> % Phase 1: select a value with the help of the oracle $\diamond S$ %
> **let** $coord = (r_i \mod n)$; % round coordinator %
> **if** $(coord = i)$ **then** broadcast PHASE1 $(r_i, est1_i)$ **end if**;
> **wait until** $((\text{PHASE1 } (r_i, est) \text{ received from } p_{coord}) \wedge (coord \in suspected_i))$;
> **if** $(\text{PHASE1 } (r_i, est) \text{ received from } p_{coord})$ **then** $est2_i \leftarrow v$ **else** $est2_i \leftarrow \perp$ **end if**;
> % Here, we have $((est2_i \neq \perp) \wedge (est2_j \neq \perp)) \Rightarrow (est2_i = est2_j = v)$ %.

This $\diamond S$-based algorithm is coordinator-based: each round has a coordinator p_{coord} that tries to impose its value as the value to be decided. It is easy to see that the quasi-agreement property is satisfied.

A failure detector of the class $\diamond S$ is perfect if, from the very beginning, some non-faulty process p_x is never suspected by any process. It is easy to see that the previous $\diamond S$-based algorithm is not zero-degrading. This is because, useless rounds can be executed before p_x becomes the coordinator of the round r such that $r \mod n = x$.

6.3.5 SAVE BROADCAST INSTANCES

Although crash failure do occur, they are rare. So, the following question naturally arises: "Is it possible to make more efficient the previous consensus algorithm when few processes may crash?" This section answers positively this question by showing that the broadcast of DECIDE () messages can be saved when $t < n/3$. Hence the improvement presented in this section is for the system model $\mathcal{AS}_{n,t}[t < n/3, \Omega]$.

Modified algorithm The improvement appears in the local processing done by a process during the second phase of a round. Let $\#(v)$ denote the number of PHASE2 $(r, -)$ messages received by p_i that carry the same value v. Let us remember that, due to the quasi-agreement property, at the end of round r, (1) a set rec_i contains at most two values, namely the default value $\perp$ and a non-$\perp$ value v, and (2) if two sets rec_i and rec_j contain non-$\perp$ values a and b, we have $a = b$.

The improvement is as follows (Figure 6.6). If a process p_i receives more than $2t$ messages PHASE2 (r, v), it unilaterally decides v without informing the other processes by broadcasting a message DECIDE (). The other cases are the same as in Figure 6.5. Hence, when during a round no $est2_i$ variable is equal to $\perp$, each process decides without broadcasting the decide value.

```
broadcast PHASE2 (r_i, est2_i);
wait until (PHASE2 (r_i, −) received from n − t processes);
let rec_i = {est2 | PHASE2 (r_i, est2) has been received};
case (∃v ≠ ⊥ : v ∈ rec_i ∧ 2t + 1 ≤ #(v))      then return (v)
     (∃v ≠ ⊥ : v ∈ rec_i ∧ t < #(v) < 2t + 1)  then broadcast DECIDE(v); return (v)
     (∃v ≠ ⊥ : v ∈ rec_i ∧ #(v) ≤ t)           then est1_i ← v
     (rec_i = {⊥})                              then skip
end case.
```

Figure 6.6: The second phase for $\mathcal{AS}_{n,t}[t < n/3, \Omega]$ (code for p_i)

Theorem 6.5 *The algorithm obtained by replacing the second phase of Figure 6.5 by the code of Figure 6.6 solves the consensus problem in $\mathcal{AS}_{n,t}[t < n/3, \Omega]$.*

Proof If no process executes the first line of the **case** statement of Figure 6.6, the proof is similar to the one of the algorithm of Figure 6.5.

So, let p_i be a process that executes the first line of the **case** statement of Figure 6.6; it decides v without informing the other processes. This means that p_i has received at least $2t + 1$ messages PHASE2 (r, v), from which we conclude that any process p_j that executes this round receives at least $t + 1$ of these messages PHASE2 (r, v). Hence, p_j is such that $(\exists v \neq \perp : v \in rec_i \land t < \#(v))$. Consequently, p_j executes either the first or the second line of the **case** statement, and necessarily decides v, which proves that the new second phase neither violates the consensus agreement property nor prevents its termination property. □$_{Theorem\ 6.5}$

6.4 CONSENSUS IN RANDOM MODELS

6.4.1 ASYNCHRONOUS RANDOM MODELS

In a randomized computation model, in addition to deterministic statements, the processes can make random choices, based on some probability distribution. In our context, this means that the system model $\mathcal{AS}_{n,t}[\emptyset]$ (asynchronous system with up to t process crashes) is enriched with an appropriate random oracle. We consider two types of such oracles.

The random asynchronous model $\mathcal{AS}_{n,t}[R]$ This model is characterized by the fact that each process has access to a random number generator. Such an oracle (denoted R) is defined by an operation denoted random() that returns to the invoking process the value 0 or 1, each with probability 0.5.

It is important to remark that the random number generators associated with the processes are purely local, i.e., each one is independent from the others.

The random asynchronous model $\mathcal{AS}_{n,t}[CC]$ In this model, the processes have access to an oracle called *common coin*. Such an oracle can be seen as a global entity that delivers the same sequence of random bits $b_1, b_2, \ldots, b_r, \ldots$ to the processes, each bit b_r having the value 0 or 1 with probability 0.5.

More explicitly, this oracle provides processes with a primitive denoted random() that returns a random bit each time it is called by a process. The sequence of random bits output by the common coin satisfies the following global property: The r-th invocation of random() by any process p_i returns it the bit b_r. This means the same random bit is returned to any process as the result of its r-th invocation of random() whatever the time of that invocation (hence the name *common* coin).

Such a common coin can be realized by providing the processes with the same pseudo-random number generator algorithm and the same initial seed.

6.4.2 RANDOMIZED CONSENSUS

The termination property of the consensus problem states that there is a finite time after which every non-faulty process has decided. In a randomized system, this property can be ensured only with some probability. More precisely, randomized consensus is defined by the same validity, integrity and agreement properties as consensus plus the following termination property, denoted R-termination.

- R-termination. With probability 1, every non-faulty process decides.

When using a round-based algorithm, the R-termination property can be restated as follows:

$$\forall i : p_i \in Correct(F) : \lim_{r \to +\infty} \left(Proba\,[p_i \text{ decides by round } r] \right) = 1.$$

As we have seen in the previous chapter, solving consensus amounts to solve the non-determinism created by asynchrony and failures. Failure detectors are a type of oracles that allows such a non-determinism to be eventually solved. Random numbers may be seen as a type of "oracles" that makes it possible to address problems caused by non-determinism.

The uncertainty is caused by asynchrony, failures and the possibility of different input vectors. In the following, assuming a worst-case adversary (controlling asynchrony and failures) and a worst-case input, we analyze the probabilities coming only from random numbers.

6.4.3 BINARY CONSENSUS IN $\mathcal{AS}_{n,t}[t < n/2, R]$

The section presents a randomized binary consensus algorithm for an asynchronous system where each process has a local random bit generator and where a majority of processes are correct.

A binary randomized consensus algorithm The structure of the algorithm (that is described in Figure 6.7) is exactly the same as the one of the Ω-based algorithm described in Figure 6.5. The processes proceed by executing asynchronous rounds, and each round is made up of two phases. The local variables have the same meaning in both algorithms.

During the first phase, each process p_i broadcasts its current estimate (that is kept in its local variable $est1_i$). If process p_i receives the same estimate value from more than $n/2$ processes, it adopts it as the value of $est2_i$. Otherwise, it sets $est2_i$ to $\bot$. It is easy to see that the quasi-agreement property $\big((est2_i[r] \neq \bot) \wedge (est2_j[r] \neq \bot)\big) \Rightarrow (est2_i[r] = est2_j[r] = v)$ is satisfied at the end of the first phase of round r, and, consequently, a set rec_i used in the second phase can only be equal to $\{v\}$, $\{v, \bot\}$, or $\{\bot\}$.

The second phase is nearly the same as in Figure 6.5. The only difference is the last case of the **case** statement. Now, when, $rec_i = \{\bot\}$, process p_i assigns a random bit to $est1_i$. This is the place where randomness is used to solve non-determinism.

```
operation propose (v_i): % v_i ∈ {0, 1} %
    est1_i ← v_i; r_i ← 0;
    while true do
        begin asynchronous round
        r_i ← r_i + 1;
        % Phase 1 : from all to all %
            broadcast PHASE1 (r_i, est1_i);
            wait until ( PHASE1 (r_i, −) received from n − t processes );
            if (the same estimate v has been received from > n/2 processes)
                        then est2_i ← v else est2_i ← ⊥ end if;
        % Here, we have ((est2_i ≠ ⊥) ∧ (est2_j ≠ ⊥)) ⇒ (est2_i = est2_j = v) %
        % Phase 2 : try to decide a value from the est2 values %
            broadcast PHASE2 (r_i, est2_i);
            wait until (PHASE2 (r_i, −) received from n − t processes);
            let rec_i = {est2 | PHASE2 (r_i, est2) has been received};
            case (rec_i = {v})       then broadcast DECIDE(v); return(v)
                 (rec_i = {v, ⊥}) then est1_i ← v
                 (rec_i = {⊥})     then est1_i ← random()
            end case
        end asynchronous round
    end while.

    when DECIDE(v) is received: broadcast DECIDE(v); return(v).
```

Figure 6.7: A binary consensus algorithm for $\mathcal{AS}_{n,t}[t < n/2, R]$ (code for p_i)

When all the proposed values are equal   Let us consider the particular case where a single value v is proposed. It is easy to see that at the end of the first phase of the first round the variables $est2_i$ of the alive processes are equal to v. It follows that a process that does not crash decides when it terminates the second phase of its first round, and the decision is obtained in two communication steps. Let us observe that, in a very interesting way, the random oracle R is not used in that case.

It follows from the previous observation that, when a single value is proposed, there is no non-determinism at all. Hence, the random oracle is used only when both the values 0 and 1 are proposed. Actually, when both values are proposed, the random oracle is used during round r to help the processes by giving them a chance to start the round $r + 1$ with the same value in their local variables $est1_i$. When this occurs, the processes decide in the round $r + 1$.

What does a random oracle break?   As consensus is impossible in $\mathcal{AS}_{n,t}[t < n/2]$, an additional power is necessary. Here this power is given by the random oracle R.

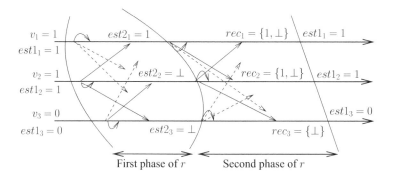

Figure 6.8: What is broken by the random oracle R

The example given in Figure 6.8 explains how the random oracle is used to breaks symmetry. There are three processes p_1, p_2 and p_3 and $t = 1$. The estimates at the beginning of round r are $est1_1 = est1_2 = 1$ and $est1_3 = 0$. During the first phase of round r, the processes broadcasts their estimates. As $t = 1$, each process waits for two messages PHASE I $(r, -)$. The messages that are received by a process are denoted by bold arrows, while the ones that arrive too late are denoted with dotted arrows. It follows that we have at the end of the first phase $est2_1 = 1$, $est1_2 = est1_3 = \perp$. Then, according to the message exchange pattern that occurs during the second phase of round r, we obtain $rec_1 = rec_2 = \{1, \perp\}$ and $rec_3 = \{\perp\}$. If, instead of executing the statement "$est1_3 \leftarrow$ random()", the process p_3 does not modify its $est1_3$ local estimate $est1_3$ (as shown on Figure 6.8), these estimates have the same values as at the beginning of round r, and this can repeat forever, preventing termination. If, as done if the algorithm of Figure 6.7, p_3 executes "$est1_3 \leftarrow$ random()", it selects the value 1 with probability $1/2$, and, consequently, the processes decide during the next round with probability $1/2$.

Theorem 6.6   *The algorithm described in Figure 6.7 solves the randomized consensus problem in the system model $\mathcal{AS}_{n,t}[t < n/2, R]$.*

Proof The proof of the validity, integrity and agreement properties are the same as the ones done in the proof of Theorem 6.4. (This is not at all counter-intuitive as the Ω-based algorithm of Figure 6.5 and the R-based algorithm of Figure 6.7 have the same structure, and their underlying oracles are used only to ensure their termination property).

Proof of the R-termination property. As we have seen if, when they start a round r, the local estimates $est1_i$ of the processes are equal (say to the value v), then they decide the value v during r. The proof shows that, with probability 1, there is a round such that the processes start it with the same estimate value $est1_i$.

The proof uses the following claim: No process blocks forever in a round (Claim C). The proof of this claim is nearly the same as the proof of Claim C1 given in Theorem 6.4 (after suppressing the part that refers to the local variable my_leader_i). Hence, the proof of the claim is not repeated here, and it is left to the reader. (Let us only notice that this claim does not depend on the underlying oracle Ω or R.)

Let us observe that, while the probability that the estimates $est1_i$ of the non-faulty processes are equal at the end of a round depends on the execution, it is always greater or equal to $p = (1/2^n) > 0$. Let $P(r)$ be the probability that the processes have the same $est1_i$ values at the end of a round r' for $1 \leq r' \leq r$. We have

$$P(r) \geq p + (1-p)p + (1-p)^2 p + \cdots + (1-p)^{r-1} p = 1 - (1-p)^r.$$

Let us observe that, if no process has decided by some round, due to Claim C, the non-faulty process enter the next round. From this observation, combined to the fact that $\lim_{r \to +\infty} (1 - (1 - p)^r) = 1$, it follows that, with probability 1, there is a round at the end of which the $est1_i$ of the non-faulty processes are equal. When this occurs the processes that are alive decide during the next round (and this includes at least all the non-faulty processes). The R-termination property follows (namely, every non-faulty process decides with probability 1). $\square_{Theorem\ 6.6}$

Favor early termination   Given a round r, three scenarios are possible according to (1) the estimate values $est1_i$ (at the beginning of r) of the processes that execute round r, and (2) the asynchrony pattern. Such a pattern defines, for each process, which are the $n - t$ messages it receives and processes.

- Scenario 1. All the processes that terminate round r, decide at the end of round r. This occurs always when the processes start round r with the same estimate value. In that case, the scenario is independent of the asynchrony pattern. But this scenario can also happen in "favorable" asynchrony patterns which occur when "enough" (but not all) processes start round r with the same estimate value.

- Scenario 2. Some processes decide during round r, while the other processes proceed to round $r + 1$.

- Scenario 3. No process decides during round r, and the processes proceed to round $r + 1$.

It is actually possible to force the processes to always decide by the end a round r in scenarios that do not require them to start this round with the very same estimate value. These scenarios that are independent of the failure pattern are characterized by the following predicate (where v and $\bar{v}$ denote the values of the binary consensus):

$$Pred(r, \bar{v}) \equiv \big(\text{ less than } (n - t)/2 \text{ processes start round } r \text{ with } est1_i = \bar{v}\big).$$

As we are about to see, when $Pred(r, \bar{v})$ is true, the value v can be safely decided during round r.

From an operational point of view, exploiting this predicate requires an additional phase (numbered 0) that is inserted between the statement $r_i \leftarrow r_i + 1$ and the first phase. This phase is as follows.

> broadcast PHASE0 $(r_i, est1_i)$;
> **wait until** (PHASE0 $(r_i, -)$ received from $n - t$ processes);
> $est1_i \leftarrow$ most frequent estimate received in the $n - t$ PHASE0 $(r_i, -)$ messages.

(If v and $\bar{v}$ are equally received, any of them is selected.)

If both $Pred(r, \bar{v})$ and $Pred(r, v)$ are false, phase 0 consists in a simple exchange of estimate values. So, let us assume that one of them is true (say $Pred(r, \bar{v})$) and let p_i be any process that terminates round r. As p_i receives $(n - t)$ PHASE0 $(r_i, -)$ messages, and less than $(n - t)/2$ of them carry $\bar{v}$, it follows that p_i has received the value v more than $(n - t)/2$ times, and, consequently, it sets $est1_i$ to v. As p_i is any process that executes round r, it follows that the local estimate $est1_i$ of the processes that terminate phase 0 of this round are equal to v. As we have seen, when this occurs, they decide the value v during round r.

Let us observe that the additional phase 0 is not required to be executed at each round. It can be executed only during predetermined rounds, e.g., only during the first round.

6.4.4   BINARY CONSENSUS IN $\mathcal{AS}_{n,t}[t < n/2, CC]$

The advantage of a common coin   In the system model $\mathcal{AS}_{n,t}[t < n/2, CC]$, the processes can use a common coin which is an object that provides them with a strong agreement, namely, the r-th invocation of the operation random() by any two processes returns them the same random bit b_r. As we are about to see, this property can be used to help the processes ensure the R-termination property of the randomized consensus problem.

A consensus algorithm based on a common coin   A binary consensus algorithm based on a common coin is described in Figure 6.9. Each process manages three local variables: r_i that contains its current round number; est_i that contains its current estimate of the decision value; and s_i that contains the random bit associated with the current round.

At every round r, the behavior of a process p_i is as follows.

- First, p_i obtains the value of the r-th random bit that it stores in s_i and broadcasts its current state (message EST (r, est_i)).
- Then, p_i waits for messages from $(n - t)$ processes. These messages carry estimate or decision values. They are EST $(r, -)$ messages and DECIDE $(-)$ messages (these messages are sent when a process decides, see below).
- Let $\#(v)$ denote the occurrence number of the value v carried in the messages EST $(r, -)$ and DECIDE $(-)$ message that have been received. Then, there are two cases.
    - If there is a value v received that is a majority value ($\#(v) > n/2$), p_i sets its estimate est_i to that value v. Then, if the value v is the value of the r-th random bit ($v = s_i$), p_i decides it.
    - If there is no majority value, p_i sets its estimate est_i to the value of r-th random bit kept in s_i.

When it is about to decide a value v, a process p_i first broadcasts a message DECIDE (v). The messages DECIDE () have the same goal as in the previous (deterministic and random) algorithms, namely prevent possible permanent blocking of processes. But, they attain their goal in a different way. Once a process p_i has received, in round r, a message DECIDE (v) sent by a process p_j, it considers this very same message in all rounds $r' \geq r$ until it decides. The message DECIDE (v) sent by p_j and received by p_i during round r, is a digest that replaces the messages EST (r, v), EST $(r + 1, v)$, etc., until p_i decides.

(Using a task to process the reception of a message DECIDE () -as in the previous algorithms- remains of course possible. This new way to process DECIDE () messages has been presented to show a different technique that saves the use of a second task.)

Theorem 6.7   *The algorithm described in Figure 6.9 solves the randomized consensus problem in the system model $\mathcal{AS}_{n,t}[t < n/2, CC]$.*

Proof The proof of the validity property (a decided value is a proposed value) and the integrity property (a process decides at most once) are the same as in the previous consensus algorithms and left to the reader. The proof of agreement and R-termination properties have exactly the same structure as in the proof of Theorem 6.6.

Proof of the agreement property. The proof is based on the following claims.
Claim C1. If all the processes that start a round r have the same estimate value v, they keep forever

```
operation propose (v_i): % v_i ∈ {0, 1} %
    est_i ← v_i; r_i ← 0;
    while true do
        begin asynchronous round
            r_i ← r_i + 1; s_i ← random();
            broadcast EST (r_i, est_i);
            wait until ( EST (r_i, −) or DECIDE (−) received from n − t processes );
            if (∃v : #(v) > n/2)
                then est_i ← v;
                    if (s_i = v) then broadcast DECIDE (v); return (v) end if
                else  est_i ← s_i
            end if
        end asynchronous round
    end while.
```

Figure 6.9: A binary consensus algorithm for $\mathcal{AS}_{n,t}[t < n/2, CC]$ (code for p_i)

that value in their estimates.

Claim C2. Let r be the first round during which a process decides (if any), and v the value it decides. (i) Any process that decides during r, decides the same value v, and (ii) the estimate value of any process that proceeds to round $r + 1$ is equal to v.

Let r be the first round during which a process decides the value v. Due to item (i) of claim C2, no other value is decided during round r. Due to item (ii) of claim C2, all the processes that proceeds to $r + 1$ have their estimate value equal to v. Due to the claim $C1$, from round $r + 1$, the estimate values remain forever equal to v from which it follows that no value different from v can be decided in a round $r' > r$, which concludes the proof of the agreement property.

Proof of claim C1. As all the processes that start round r have the same estimate value v (assumption), it follows that a process receives (in the **wait** statement) only messages carrying that value v. Moreover, as $t < n/2$, a process receives that value from more that $n/2$ processes. Hence, the predicate $(∃v : #(v) > n/2)$ is satisfied and, consequently, each process p_i that executes round r sets est_i to v, which proves the claim. End of proof of claim C1.

Proof of claim C2. Let p_i be a process that decides v during round r. It follows that (O1) p_i has received v from a majority of processes, and (O2) the random bit b_r provided by the common coin is such that $b_r = v$. If another process decides a value v', it has received v from a majority of processes, and as two majorities intersect we have $v = v'$ which proves item (i) of the claim.

Moreover, any process such that the predicate $(∃v : #(v) > n/2)$ is satisfied during r, decides v during that round. Consequently, if a process p_j proceeds to $r + 1$, its local predicate $(∃v : #(v) > n/2)$ is false. Hence it sets its estimate to the value b_r, which (due to O2) is equal to

v. This concludes the proof of the claim C2. End of proof of claim C2.

Proof of the R-termination property. Let us first observe that no process can block forever in a round. This follows from the following observations: (1) at most t processes may crash, (2) during a round a process waits for $(n - t)$ messages, and (3) a non-faulty process that has decided during a round r has sent a message DECIDE (v) that is a digest that replaces the messages EST (r', v) for any $r' \geq r$.

Claim C3. With probability 1, there is a round r at the end of which all the processes that start round $r + 1$, have the same estimate value.

Assuming claim C3, it follows from claim C1, that (with probability 1) the predicate $(\exists v : \#(v) > n/2)$ is satisfied at each process during each round $r' > r$. By the assumption that the common coin is random, it follows that (with probability 1) there is a round r' during which the value $b_{r'}$ output by the random oracle is such that $b_{r'} = v$. It then follows from the algorithm that, when this occurs, the processes that executes round r' decide v during r', which proves the R-termination property.

Proof of claim C3. Let us consider a run of the algorithm. There are three cases.

- Case 1. There is a round r such that all the processes that execute round r, execute the **else** part of the **if** statement. Hence, they all set their estimates est_i to the same random bit value b_r. Consequently, their estimates are equal at the end of r, which proves the claim.

- Case 2. There is a round r such that all the processes that execute round r, execute the **then** part of the **if** statement. Hence, they all sets their estimates est_i to the same value v (that is a majority value), which proves the claim.

- Case 3. The third case is when, in each round, some processes execute the **then** part of the **if** statement, while other execute the **else** part.

  Let us remember that the value of each random bit is 0 or 1, each with probability $p = 1/2$. Let $v[x]$ be the value of v that the processes that execute the **then** part of the **if** statement assign to their estimates during round x and b_x the value of the common coin output at round x. This means that $Proba[v[x] = b_x] = p = 0.5$. Let us compute the probability $P(r)$ that there is a round x, $1 \leq x \leq r$, during which we have $v[x] = b_x$. We have

$$P(r) = p + (1 - p)p + (1 - p)^2 p + \cdots + (1 - p)^{r-1} p = 1 - (1 - p)^r.$$

  It follows that $\lim_{r \to +\infty} P(r) = 1$, which proves the claim. End of proof of claim C3.

□ *Theorem* 6.7

Expected number of rounds   As we have seen, the termination is obtained in two stages. In the first stage, the processes that are alive adopt the same estimate value v, and in the second stage, the random bit has to be the same as the value v.

- As seen in the proof of the R-termination property, the situation in which the processes do not adopt the same value at the end of a round r is when some processes execute the **then** part of the **if** statement (and obtain the same value v), while others execute the **else** part (and obtain the same random bit b_r) and $v \neq b_r$. However, with probability $1/2$, we have $v = b_r$. Thus, the expected number of rounds for this to occur is bounded by 2.

- For the second stage, here again, the probability that the random bit be equal to the single estimate value of the processes is equal to $1/2$. Thus, the expected number of rounds for this to happen is also bounded by 2.

It follows that the expected number of rounds for the processes to decide is upper bounded by $2 + 2 = 4$ rounds.

6.4.5   BINARY CONSENSUS IN THE HYBRID MODEL $\mathcal{AS}_{n,t}[t < n/2, \Omega, R]$

Combining algorithms   Interestingly, it is possible to combine deterministic binary consensus algorithms with randomized binary consensus algorithms in order to obtain hybrid algorithms.

The combination of a deterministic binary consensus algorithm designed for the $\mathcal{AS}_{n,t}[t < n/2, \Omega]$ model, with a randomized binary consensus algorithm designed for the $\mathcal{AS}_{n,t}[t < n/2, R]$ model provides an algorithm that works in the hybrid model $\mathcal{AS}_{n,t}[t < n/2, \Omega, R]$. Such an algorithm satisfies the validity, integrity and agreement consensus properties, plus the following termination property.

- If the modules that are assumed to implement a failure detector of the class Ω do satisfy the specification of Ω (namely, after a finite time, they provide forever the processes with the same non-faulty leader), then each non-faulty process eventually decides.

  It is important to notice that the termination is then independent of the random oracle. This means that the misbehavior of the random oracle cannot prevent the correct processes from deciding.

- If the value of each variable *leader*$_i$ (local output of the failure detector of the class Ω) eventually contains the identity of a non-faulty process (different variables possibly containing different process identities), and the behavior of the random oracle agrees with its specification, then each correct process decide with probability 1.

  Let us observe that, in that case, the oracle Ω misbehaves as it does not ensure that eventually there is a single leader (the same for all processes). Several non-faulty leaders can co-exist (this property is required to prevent permanent blocking of a process).

Such an hybrid approach is particularly interesting because it allows the non-faulty processes (a) to always decide as soon as Ω behaves correctly and (b) to possibly decide earlier if additionally the random oracle R behaves correctly.

```
operation propose (v_i):
   est1_i ← v_i; r_i ← 0;
   while true do
      begin asynchronous round
      r_i ← r_i + 1;
      %  Phase 0 : select a value with the help of the oracle Ω %
         broadcast PHASE0 (r_i, est1_i);
         wait until ((∃ ℓ : leader_i = ℓ) ∧ (PHASE0 (r_i, v) received from p_ℓ));
         est1_i ← v;
      %  Phase 1 : from all to all %
         broadcast PHASE1 (r_i, est1_i);
         wait until (PHASE1 (r_i, −) received from n − t processes);
         if (the same estimate v has been received from > n/2 processes)
                        then est2_i ← v else est2_i ← ⊥ end if;
      % Here, we have ((est2_i ≠ ⊥) ∧ (est2_j ≠ ⊥)) ⇒ (est2_i = est2_j = v) %
      %  Phase 2 : try to decide a value from the est2 values %
         broadcast PHASE2 (r_i, est2_i);
         wait until (PHASE2 (r_i, −) received from n − t processes);
         let rec_i = {est2 | PHASE2 (r_i, est2) has been received};
         case (rec_i = {v})      then broadcast DECIDE(v); return(v)
              (rec_i = {v, ⊥})   then est1_i ← v
              (rec_i = {⊥})      then est1_i ←random()
         end case
      end asynchronous round
   end while.

   when DECIDE(v) is received: broadcast DECIDE(v); return (v).
```

Figure 6.10: A (hybrid) binary consensus algorithm for $\mathcal{AS}_{n,t}[t < n/2, \Omega, R]$ (code for p_i)

A hybrid algorithm   A consensus algorithm for the hybrid model $\mathcal{AS}_{n,t}[t < n/2, \Omega, R]$ is presented in Figure 6.10. Each round r is made up of three phases. It is easy to see that, if phase 0 is suppressed, the algorithm boils down to the randomized algorithm described in Figure 6.7.

The reader may check that, if we replace the invocation random() in the **case** statement in the third phase by the statement "skip", we obtain a deterministic consensus algorithm for the system model $\mathcal{AS}_{n,t}[t < n/2, \Omega]$. (The proof of this algorithm is close to the proof given for Theorem 6.4.)

It follows that the hybrid algorithm described in Figure 6.10 results actually from a simple combination of that algorithm with the randomized algorithm of Figure 6.7.

Theorem 6.8   *The algorithm described in Figure 6.10 solves the binary consensus problem in the hybrid system model $\mathcal{AS}_{n,t}[t < n/2, \Omega, R]$.*

Proof The proof of the validity and integrity properties are as for previous consensus algorithms. They are not repeated here. The proof of the agreement property follows from the quasi-agreement property, and the "majority of non-faulty processes" assumption used in the second and third phases of each round.

Proof of the termination property. The proof of this property is similar to the one done for previous algorithms. If a process decides, due to the DECIDE() messages, every non-faulty process decides. So, let us assume that no process ever decides.

Claim C. No non-faulty process blocks forever in a round. no process can block forever in a round. As no process decides, the claim follows from the fact that, at each round, (1) due to the fact that the oracle Ω eventually provides each process with a non-faulty leader, no process can block forever during phase 0, and (2) due to the "majority of correct processes" assumption, a process can block forever neither during phase 1 nor phase 2.

Assuming by contradiction that no process decides, let us consider the two following cases.

- Case 1: Ω eventually provides the processes with the same non-faulty leader. In that case, due to the claim, there is a round r after which a single non-faulty leader p_ℓ that has been elected. Hence, all the processes that execute phase 0 of round r (and this includes all the non-faulty processes -that are a majority-), wait for and receive the message PHASE0 $(r, est1_\ell)$. They all consequently update their estimate $est1_i$ to $est1_\ell$. From then on, there is a single estimate value in the system, and as we have seen in previous proofs, the processes decide by the end of round r.

- Case 2: Each variable $leader_i$ eventually contains the identity of a non-faulty process, different $leader_i$ variables containing different process identities. In that case, there is no guarantee that the processes execute a round with the same non-faulty leader process. The proof that each non-faulty process decides with probability 1 is then exactly the same as the one done for Theorem 6.6 and is not repeated here. (Let us remember that this proof is based on the fact that, due to the random choice of the next estimate value at the end of the third phase, there is a probability $p > 0$ that the processes start a round with the same estimate value).

$\square_{Theorem\ 6.8}$

6.5   FROM BINARY TO MULTIVALUED CONSENSUS

Presentation   Let $\mathcal{AS}_{n,t}[BIN\_CONS]$ denote the message-passing system model where binary consensus objects are given for free. This section addresses the following problem: how to solve the multivalued consensus problem in $\mathcal{AS}_{n,t}[BIN\_CONS]$.

Two algorithms are presented that construct a multivalued consensus object from base binary consensus objects. To prevent confusion, the "propose" operation of these base objects is denoted bin_propose (v). Both algorithms use the URB-broadcast communication abstraction to disseminate the values proposed by the processes. They differ in the strategy they use to benefit from the underlying binary consensus objects.

When comparing to classical synchronization techniques, we can say that the first algorithm that is presented is based on a "blocking" technique. This is because a process might be forced to wait in order to compute the binary value it will propose to an underlying binary consensus object. The bit that is proposed is related to the values of the proposals.

Differently, the second algorithm is based on a "non-blocking" technique. A process is never forced to wait before proposing a value to an underlying binary consensus object. The bit that is proposed is not related to the values that are proposed, but depends only on the fact that values have or not been URB-delivered.

As a consequence, the number of iterations (and, consequently, the number of base binary consensus objects) is bounded in the first algorithm (the bound is b, the bit size of the largest proposed value), while it is infinite (but unbounded) in the second algorithm.

Remark   Let us observe that none of the algorithms is restricted to some values of t. They work whatever the value of t, as soon as we can use binary consensus objects, and URB-broadcast can be implemented. Hence, these constructions are very general.

6.5.1   A BLOCKING STRATEGY BASED ON THE BIT REPRESENTATION OF THE PROPOSED VALUES

Preliminary notations   The arrays that are used are arrays of b bits, where b is the number of bits required to encode any value that can be proposed. It is assumed that b is known by the processes. Let $aa[1..b]$ be such an array. Let $0 \leq k < b$; $aa[1..0]$ denotes an empty array (it has no entry), and $aa[1..k]$ denotes the sub-array containing the entries from 1 to k. Finally, the predicate $aa[1..k] = bb[1..k]$ is true if and only if these two bit sub-arrays are component-wise equal. By definition, the predicate $aa[1..0] = bb[1..0]$ is always satisfied.

Principle of the algorithm   The algorithm is described in Figure 6.11. It is based on blocking strategy, in the sense that a process can be forced to wait for proposed values before proceeding.

Each process p_i URB-broadcasts the value v_i it proposes. When a process URB-delivers the value proposed by p_j, it stores its bit representation in a local variable $bin\_coding_i[j]$. Hence, once it has been updated, $bin\_coding_i[j][1..b]$ is an array of b bits containing the binary representation of the value proposed by p_j. Before the value proposed by p_j is URB-delivered, $bin\_coding_i[j]$ is equal to the default value $\bot$.

The principle of the algorithm is simple: the processes agree sequentially, one bit after the other, on each of the b bits of the proposed values, hence there are b binary consensus, one per bit of the proposed values. Moreover, in order for the decided array of bits to correspond to one of the proposed values, when the processes progress from bit k to bit $k + 1$, they consider only the values proposed -by processes p_j- whose k bit prefixes ($bin\_coding_i[j][1..k]$) are equal to the sub-array $res_i[1..k]$ on which they previously agreed.

Local variables and binary consensus objects   Each process manages three main local variables:

- $bin\_coding_i[1..n]$ managed as indicated above.

- k_i is an integer, initialized to 0, that is the index of current binary consensus.
- $res_i[1..b]$ is array of b bits that will contain the binary representation of the decided value.

Moreover, in order to agree on each of the b bits, the processes access an array of b base binary consensus objects, denoted $BC[1..n]$.

```
operation propose (v_i):
    bin_coding_i ← [⊥,...,⊥]; k_i ← 0;
    URB_broadcast PROPOSAL (v_i);
    repeat
        wait until (∃ x | (bin_coding_i[x] ≠ ⊥) ∧ (bin_coding_i[x][1..k_i] = res_i[1..k_i]));
        let X = {x | (bin_coding_i[x] ≠ ⊥) ∧ (bin_coding_i[x][1..k_i] = res_i[1..k_i])};
        k_i ← k_i + 1;   % next bit to agree on %
        let Y = {bin_coding_i[x][k_i] | x ∈ X};   % Y = {0}, or Y = {1}, or Y = {0, 1} %
        let bin_prop_i = any bit ∈ Y;
        res_i[k_i] ← BC[k_i].bin_propose(bin_prop_i);
    until (k_i = b) end repeat;
    return (decimal coding of res_i[1..b]).

when PROPOSAL(v) is URB_delivered from p_j:
    bin_coding_i[j] ← b-bit array-based binary representation of v.
```

Figure 6.11: Multivalued consensus in $\mathcal{AS}_{n,t}[BIN\_CONS]$ (code for p_i): construction #1

Behavior of a process As already indicated, a process p_i first URB-broadcasts the value v_i it proposes, and it waits until it has URB-delivered (at least) one proposed value. Then, p_i enters a loop that it executes b times (one loop iteration per bit). The integer k_i, $0 \le k_i < b$, is the number of bits on which the processes have already agreed upon. The value of these k_i bits is locally saved in the array prefix $res_i[1..k_i]$. The loop is follows.

- Process p_i waits until it knows proposed values (i.e., bit arrays such that $bin\_coding_i[x] \ne \perp$), whose binary coding of the k_i first bits (i.e., $bin\_coding_i[x][1..k_i]$) corresponds to the array of bits already decided (i.e., $res_i[1..k_i]$). Let X be the set of process identities of the corresponding proposed values. Due to the **wait** statement, the set X cannot be empty.
- Then, p_i proceeds to the next bit ($k_i \leftarrow k_i + 1$), and computes the set of bits that it can propose to the next binary consensus (i.e., $BC[k_i]$). This set Y is the non-empty set $\{bin\_coding_i[x][k_i] \mid x \in X\}$. Then p_i selects a bit from Y, proposes it to the consensus instance $BC[k_i]$, and stores the bit decided by that instance in $res_i[k_i]$. After this statement, there is an agreement on the k_i first bits of the decided value. If $k_i = b$, the decided value has been computed and p_i returns it. Otherwise, p_i proceeds to the next iteration.

Theorem 6.9 *The algorithm described in Figure 6.11 solves the multivalued consensus problem in the system model $\mathcal{AS}_{n,t}[BIN\_CONS]$.*

Proof (Sketch) The proof is tedious, so we give only a sketch of it. The integrity property follows directly from the fact that a process executes at most once the return() statement. The termination property follows from the termination property of the underlying URB-broadcast operation (that ensures that the non-faulty processes have URB-delivered at least the values they propose) and the termination property of the base binary consensus objects. The agreement property follows from the agreement on each bit provided by the b base binary consensus objects.

Finally, the validity property (a decided value is a proposed value) follows from the fact that, at each loop iteration k (where $k, 0 \leq k < b$, is the value of k_i at the beginning of the current iteration), the proposed values that are known by p_i (the values encoded in $bin\_coding_i[x]$ such that $bin\_coding_i[x] \neq \bot$) and whose prefix $bin\_coding_i[x][1..k]$ does not match the prefix $res_i[1..k]$ that has already been computed, are discarded by p_i before it selects the next bit it will proposes to then binary consensus $BC[k+1]$. $\square_{Theorem\ 6.9}$

6.5.2   A NON-BLOCKING STRATEGY BASED ON THE MESSAGES THAT HAVE BEEN DELIVERED

Principle of the algorithm   Differently from the previous algorithm where a process waits for messages before invoking a base binary consensus object, the algorithm proposed here never requires a process to wait for messages (but possibly, in the last iteration, just before deciding). As indicated previously, this second algorithm is non-blocking in the sense that a process is never forced to wait in order to determine the binary value it is about to propose to an underlying binary consensus object.

To make easier the presentation of the algorithm (described in Figure 6.12), we suppose that the process identities are $0, \ldots, n-1$, instead of $1, \ldots, n$ (this facilitates the use of the function modulo).

```
operation propose (v_i):
    proposals_i ← [⊥, . . . , ⊥]; k_i ← −1;
    URB_broadcast PROPOSAL (v_i);
    while (true) do
        k_i ← k_i + 1;
        let bin_prop_i = (proposals_i[k_i  mod n] ≠ ⊥);
        res_i ← BC[k_i].bin_propose(bin_prop_i);
        if (res_i) then wait (proposals_i[k_i  mod n] ≠ ⊥);
                       return (proposals_i[k_i  mod n])
        end if
    end while.

    when PROPOSAL(v) is URB_delivered from p_j: proposals_i[j] ← v.
```

Figure 6.12: Multivalued consensus in $\mathcal{AS}_{n,t}[BIN\_CONS]$ (code for p_i): construction #2

A process first URB-broadcasts the value v_i it proposes. When it URB-delivers the value proposed by p_j, process p_i stores that value in its local variable $proposal_i[j]$ (whose initial value is $\perp$).

Then p_i enters a loop made up of asynchronous rounds identified by the successive values of the index k_i, starting with $k_i = 0$. The principle of the algorithm is as follows. Let $x = (k_i \mod n)$. Hence, $x \in \{0, \ldots, n-1\}$ is the identity of a process. If p_i has received the value proposed by p_x (we have then $proposals_i[x] \neq \perp$) it proposes, the value *true* to the underlying binary consensus $BC[k_i]$, where $BC[1..]$ is an (unbounded) array of binary consensus objects. Otherwise, p_i proposes the value *false* to $BC[k_i]$.

- If $BC[k_i]$ returns *true*, the value proposed by p_x is decided. In that case, p_i waits for that value and returns it. Let us notice that, due to asynchrony, it is possible that the value proposed by p_x is decided while p_i has not yet URB-delivered it. If that value is decided, it has necessarily been URB-delivered by the processes that have proposed *true* to $BC[k_i]$.

- If $BC[k_i]$ returns *false*, the processes proceed to the next iteration.

Theorem 6.10   *The algorithm described in Figure 6.12 solves the multivalued consensus problem in the system model* $\mathcal{AS}_{n,t}[BIN\_CONS]$.

Proof   As in previous algorithms, the proof of the integrity property follows directly from the fact that a process invokes at most once the return() statement. The proof of the validity property follows directly from the validity property of the underlying URB-broadcast.

In order to prevent confusion, we use the word "bin-decide" when we consider a base binary consensus object, and the word "decide" when we consider multivalued consensus.

Proof of the agreement property. Let k be the first round during which a process p_i decides, and v_x the value it decides. Hence, we have $x = (k \mod n)$.

As p_i bin-decides during round k, it follows that all the invocations $BC[k].\mathsf{bin\_propose}()$ that terminate return the value *true*. It follows from the observation that each process executes the same sequence of rounds, and the fact that no process has bin-decided during a previous round ($< k$), that all the processes that execute round k bin-decide during that round. Due to the agreement property of the binary consensus object $BC[k]$, they bin-decide the value *true*. Hence, no process progresses to round $k + 1$. Finally, due to the '**wait** statement, no process p_j that executes round k can decide a value different from $v_{k \mod n}$ (i.e., v_x), which concludes the proof of the agreement property.

Proof of the termination property. Let us assume by contradiction that no process decides.
Claim C. No correct process remains forever blocked in a round. This claim follows directly from the termination property of each underlying binary consensus object.

Let p_x be a non-faulty process. Due to the termination property of the underlying URB-broadcast, there is a finite time after which the value proposed by p_x is URB-delivered to every non-faulty process. It follows from claim C that there is a round k after which (1) the faulty processes have crashed, and (2) the non-faulty processes have URB-delivered the value proposed by p_x. It also follows from claim C, and the use of the $\mod ()$ function, that the non-faulty processes enter a round k' such that $k' \geq k$ and $x = k' \mod n$. During round k', each non-faulty process proposes $true$ to the binary consensus object $BC[k']$. As all the processes that invokes $BC[k'].\text{bin\_propose}()$ propose $true$, it follows from the validity property of that object that the value bin-decided is $true$. Hence, every non-faulty process returns the value proposed by p_x, with contradicts the initial assumption, and concludes the proof of the termination property. $\square_{Theorem\ 6.10}$

6.6   CONSENSUS IN ONE COMMUNICATION STEP

6.6.1   AIM AND MODEL

Decision in one communication step   Both the algorithm presented in Figure 6.5 for the $\mathcal{AS}_{n,t}[t < n/2, \Omega]$ model and the algorithm presented in Figure 6.7 for the $\mathcal{AS}_{n,t}[t < n/2, R]$ model are based on the same design principle. They use asynchronous consecutive rounds made up of two phases where each phase is made up of a single communication step.

- During the first step, the processes try to agree on the same estimate value v, and a process that cannot agree on such a value considers instead the default value $\perp$. This has been captured by the *quasi-agreement* property.
- Then, during the second step, according to their new estimate values (that contain v or $\perp$) the processes strive to decide. If a process cannot decide, it proceeds to the next round.

It follows that, in the best case, the processes decide in one round, i.e., two communication steps. These algorithms allow up to $t = \lfloor (n-1)/2 \rfloor$ processes to crash in a run.

On another side, while failures do occur, they are rare in practice, which means that considering a model where the maximum number t of processes that may crash is much smaller than $\lfloor (n-1)/2 \rfloor$ is realistic. Hence, there is the following question: Is it possible to design a consensus algorithm that allows the processes to decide in one communication step in "favorable" circumstances in a system model where t is smaller than $\lfloor (n-1)/2 \rfloor$? Of course, this requires to precisely define which are the "favorable" circumstances in order to obtain a provably correct algorithm.

Model   This section presents such an algorithm, where "favorable" circumstances is when all the processes propose the same value. To ensure the "one communication step" in favorable circumstances, it requires that less than one third of the processes may be faulty. Moreover, it uses an underlying consensus algorithm as a subroutine to address the case where several values are proposed. Hence, the algorithm is for the message-passing model $\mathcal{AS}_{n,t}[t < n/3, CONS]$, in which the underlying consensus object is a "black box" given for free.

On non-determinism   As seen in Chapter 5 (section 1.4), the consensus problem is inherently non-deterministic, namely, the value that is decided cannot be computed from a deterministic function.

As we are about to see, decision in one communication step is possible when the same value is proposed by the processes. This is because these input vectors capture particular cases where consensus can be solved deterministically. More explicitly, there is no non-determinism when all the processes propose the same value.

6.6.2   A ONE COMMUNICATION STEP ALGORITHM

The algorithm   The algorithm is very simple. The corresponding operation is denoted one_step_propose () in order to differentiate it from the operation propose () of the underlying consensus object, denoted UC, that is used as a subroutine.

The algorithm is made up of two stages. The first stage consists of a single communication step, during which the processes exchange their proposals (messages PROPOSAL ()). If a process p_i receives "enough" copies of the same value (where "enough" means at least $n - t$), it decides that value. Let v be the value it decides when this occurs. As in previous algorithms, in order to prevent other processes to block forever, p_i has to broadcast a message EARLY_DEC(v)) before deciding (it decides when it invokes return (v)). These are the statements that appear in the **then** part of the **if** statement.

If a process p_i does not receive enough copies of the same value, it uses the underlying consensus subroutine to decide (invocation UC.propose ()). According to the asynchrony pattern and the values that are proposed, it is possible that some processes decide a value v during the first stage (i.e., in one communication step), while other processes do not see $(n - t)$ copies of the same value, and consequently invoke the underlying consensus. In order that the later processes do not decide a value different from the value v decided by the former ones, they have to propose v to the underlying consensus. This is done as follows: if, during the first stage, p_i has received $(n - 2t)$ times the same value v', it proposes v' to the underlying consensus. As we are about to see in the proof, if processes decide v during the first stage, we have then $v' = v$. These statements appear in the **else** part of the **if** statement.

```
operation one_step_propose (vᵢ):
    broadcast PROPOSAL (vᵢ);
    wait until (PROPOSAL (−) received from n − t processes);
    if (all these messages carry the same value, say v)
        then broadcast EARLY_DEC (v);
             return (v)
        else if ((n − 2t) messages carry the same value v) then propᵢ ← v else propᵢ ← vᵢ end if;
             decᵢ ← UC.propose (propᵢ);
             return (decᵢ)
    end if.

    when EARLY_DEC(v) is received: broadcast EARLY_DEC(v); return(v).
```

Figure 6.13: Consensus in one communication step in $\mathcal{AS}_{n,t}[t < n/3, CONS]$ (code for p_i)

Theorem 6.11 *The algorithm described in Figure 6.13 solves consensus in $\mathcal{AS}_{n,t}[t < n/3, CONS]$. Moreover, if no two processes propose different values, a correct process decides in one communication step.*

Proof The proof of the validity property follows from the observation that only proposed values are exchanged and from the validity of the underlying consensus (when it is used). The proof of the integrity property follows directly from the fact that a process executes at most one return() statement.

Proof of the termination property. If a process decides a value v in the **then** part of the **if** statement, it has previously broadcast a message EARLY_DEC (v). As the channels are reliable, every non-faulty process receives this message and decides (if it has not yet done).

So, let us consider that no process decides in the **then** part of the **if** statement. This means that (at least) every non-faulty process invokes the operation propose() on the underlying consensus object. Due to its termination property, no non-faulty process remains blocked inside this object. It follows that every non-faulty process decides a value.

Proof of the agreement property. If a process decides when it receives a message EARLY_DEC (v), it decides a value that another process is about to decide. Hence, we consider only the processes that decide when they execute return () in the **if** statement. There are three cases.

- Two processes p_i and p_j decide in the **then** part of the **if** statement. It follows that p_i has received $(n - t)$ copies of the same value v. Similarly for p_j that has $(n - t)$ copies of the same value v'. As $t < n/3$, we have $n - t > n/2$, which means that the message PROPOSAL (v) has been sent by a majority of processes, and similarly for the message PROPOSAL (v'). As two majority intersect, it follows that there is a process that has broadcast both PROPOSAL (v) and PROPOSAL (v'). As a process broadcasts only one PROPOSAL () message, we have $v = v'$. It follows that, if no process decides in the **else** part of the **if** statement, a single value can be decided.

- No process decides in the **then** part of the **if** statement. In that case, the processes that execute the **else** part of the **if** statement invoke the same underlying consensus object. If follows from its agreement property that this object returns them the same value. Hence, the dec_i values of the processes are equal, and no two processes decide different values.

- Some processes p_i decide in the **then** part of the **if** statement, while other processes decide in its **else** part. We then have the following.

  1. As process p_i decides in the **then** part, it has received $(n - t)$ messages PROPOSAL (v). This means that at most t messages PROPOSAL () carry a value different from v.

  2. As process p_j decides in the **else** part, it has received $(n - t)$ messages PROPOSAL (). Due to the previous item, at most t of these messages carry a value different from v (Observation O1). Moreover, in the worst case, these t values are equal (Observation O2). We conclude from O1 that p_j has received at least $(n - 2t)$ messages PROPOSAL (v). As $n - 2t > t$, it follows from $O2$ that v is the only value that p_j receives $(n - 2t)$ times. Consequently, p_j proposes v to the underlying consensus object.

3. It follows from the previous items that the processes that invoke the underlying consensus object propose it value v. Due to its validity property, only v can then be decided from this object.

Hence, in this third case, the proof of the agreement property follows from the fact that the processes that execute the **then** part decide the same value v, and the processes that execute the **else** part can decide only a value decided in the **then** part.

Proof of the one step communication property. This proof is trivial. At least $(n - t)$ processes start the algorithm. If the non-faulty processes propose the same value v, each receives at least $(n - t)$ copies of v and decide upon that value. In that case, the underlying consensus object is useless.
$\square_{Theorem\ 6.11}$

6.6.3   CONSIDERING ADDITIONAL ASSUMPTIONS

Additional assumptions   This section shows that, when additional assumptions are satisfied, the requirement $t < n/3$ can be weakened in $t < n/2$. These assumptions basically define "favorable circumstances" that allow the processes to decide in one communication step despite $t < n/2$. Two types of "favorable circumstances" are considered.

Existence of a privileged value   The first kind of "favorable circumstances" is value-oriented. It considers a statically predetermined value α. Hence α is known by the processes. The "favorable circumstances" are when processes see that α is majority among the proposed values. Then, they can decide it in one communication step. This additional assumption states implicitly that all the proposed values have not the same "power", namely α is more powerful than the others. The corresponding algorithm is described at the top of Figure 6.14.

Existence of a predefined set of processes   The second kind of "favorable circumstances" is control-oriented. It considers a statically predetermined set of processes S, such that $|S| > n/2$. S is initially known by the processes. For a process, the "favorable circumstances" are when it sees that all processes in S have proposed the same value. When this occurs, a process can decide in one communication step. The corresponding algorithm is described at the bottom of Figure 6.14. Let us notice that, as $|S| > n/2$, a process always receives the value of at least one process in S. The proofs of this algorithm and the previous one are similar to the proof given in Theorem 6.11.

Let us finally notice that, differently from the algorithm based on a predetermined set S, the algorithm based on a predetermined value α and the algorithm described in Figure 6.13 are *anonymous* in the sense that they do not use the identities of the processes.

operation one_step_propose (v_i):
  broadcast PROPOSAL (v_i);
  wait until $\bigl(\text{PROPOSAL } (-)$ received from a majority of processes$\bigr)$;
  if $\bigl($all the received values are equal to $\alpha\bigr)$
    then broadcast EARLY_DEC (α);
        return (α)
    else **if** (α has been received) **then** $prop_i \leftarrow \alpha$ **else** $prop_i \leftarrow v_i$ **end if**;
        $dec_i \leftarrow UC.$propose $(prop_i)$;
        return (dec_i)
  end if.

  when EARLY_DEC(v) **is received**: broadcast EARLY_DEC(v); return(v).

---

operation one_step_propose (v_i):
  broadcast PROPOSAL (v_i);
  wait until $\bigl(\text{PROPOSAL } (-)$ received from a majority of processes$\bigr)$;
  if $\bigl($ the same value v has been received from the processes in $S\bigr)$
    then broadcast EARLY_DEC (v);
        return (v)
    else $prop_i \leftarrow$ a value from a process $\in S$;
        $dec_i \leftarrow UC.$propose $(prop_i)$;
        return (dec_i)
  end if.

  when EARLY_DEC(v) **is received**: broadcast EARLY_DEC(v); return(v).

Figure 6.14: Enriching $\mathcal{AS}_{n,t}[t < n/2, CONS]$ with additional assumptions (code for p_i)

.

6.7   CONSENSUS IN ANONYMOUS ASYNCHRONOUS SYSTEMS

6.7.1   ANONYMOUS DISTRIBUTED SYSTEMS: THE MODEL $\mathcal{AAS}_{n,t}[\emptyset]$

Anonymous processes   In an anonymous system, processes have no identity, and they execute the very same algorithm. It follows that a process can use neither a "send m to p_j" operation, nor a "receive m from p_j" operation.

Anonymous communication   In order to communicate, the processes can use an unreliable broadcast operation, denoted "broadcast ()". This operation is given by the underlying system. Moreover, a process can receive messages by using the operation "receive ()".

    As in non-anonymous model, the "broadcast ()" operation is not reliable. If the sender crashes during that operation, it is possible that an arbitrary subset of the processes receive the message that has been broadcast. This operation is asynchronous in the sense that two processes that receive a message m can receive it at different times.

A process that receives a message cannot determine which process is its sender. Moreover, given any set of messages it has received, a process cannot determine whether these messages are from the same sender or from different senders.

Notation We continue using the notation $p_1, \ldots, p_n$ to denote the n processes. This is only for notational convenience in order to be able to distinguish processes. As an external observer, we are using process identities and time to explain and reason, but those notions are not known by the processes. The corresponding anonymous model is $\mathcal{AS}_{n,t}[\emptyset]$ without process identities. It is denoted $\mathcal{AAS}_{n,t}[\emptyset]$.

6.7.2 THE CLASS AP OF ANONYMOUS PERFECT FAILURE DETECTORS

The failure detector class AP The range $\mathcal{R}$ of the failure detector class AP is the set of integers $\{1, \ldots, n\}$. Let us remember that, given a failure pattern F, $F(\tau)$ is the set of processes that have crashed by time τ, $Fauty(F)$ is the set of processes that crash in a run whose failure pattern is F, and $H(i, \tau)$ is the failure detector history function that defines the failure detector output at p_i at time τ. The failure detectors of the class AP are defined by the following properties:

- Strong accuracy. $\forall \tau : \forall i \notin F(\tau) : H(i, \tau) \geq n - |F(\tau)|$.
- Completeness. $\exists \tau : \forall \tau' \geq \tau : \forall i \notin F(\tau') : H(i, \tau) = n - |Faulty(F)|$.

From an algorithm point of view, let us denote $aa\ell_i$ the output of the failure detector module at p_i ($aa\ell_i$ stands for *a*pproximate number of *a*live processes); p_i can only read $aa\ell_i$, and no other process can access it.

The strong accuracy property states that, at any time, $aa\ell_i$ is greater than or equal to the number of processes that have not crashed, while the completeness property states that $aa\ell_i$ is eventually equal to the number of processes that are non-faulty.

The class AP and the class P are equivalent in a non-anonymous system The definition of the class AP is motivated by the fact that it does correspond to the class P (perfect failure detectors), when we consider a non-anonymous system. More precisely, these classes are equivalent in a non-anonymous system. To show it, considering a non-anonymous system, two transformations are presented: a first one from P to AP, and a second one from AP to P.

Let us remember that a failure detector of the class P provides each process p_i with a set $suspected_i$ that never contains the identity of a process p_j before it crashes (strong accuracy), and contains eventually the identities of all the faulty processes (completeness).

From P to AP in a non-anonymous system. The transformation in that direction is trivial. The reader can easily check that taking the current value $n - |suspected_i|$ to define the current value of $aa\ell_i$, constructs a failure detector of the class AP.

From AP to P in a non-anonymous system. A transformation that builds a failure detector of the class P in $\mathcal{AS}_{n,t}[AP]$ is described in Figure 6.15. Interestingly, this transformation is bounded (be the execution finite or infinite, the local memory of each process requires only a bounded number of bits). Moreover, (1) the transformation is quiescent (i.e., there is a finite time after which no more messages are exchanged), and (2), additionally, the algorithm terminates in the runs where t processes crash.

In order to compute the value of $suspected_i$ (that is initialized to $\emptyset$), each process p_i manages two local variables:

- An integer k_i, initialized to 0, that represents its current knowledge on the number of processes that have crashed.

- An array $answered_i[1..n]$, initialized to $[0, \cdots, 0]$, such that $answered_i[j] = k$ means that k is the greatest inquiry number for which p_i has received the corresponding answer ALIVE (k).

The behavior of p_i is defined by two tasks. First, when p_i discovers there are more than k_i processes that have crashed, it updates accordingly k_i, and it broadcasts an inquiry message INQUIRY (k_i) to all the processes. Let us notice that this task can stop when $k_i = t$ as, due to the model definition, no more crash can occur. Let us also observe that the messages INQUIRY(k_i) are sent by p_i with increasing values, and due to the strong accuracy property of $aa\ell_i$, p_i knows that there are at most $n - k_i$ alive processes.

When p_i receives an INQUIRY (k) message from a process p_j it sends back to p_j an ALIVE (k) message to indicate that it is still alive. When it receives an answer ALIVE (k) from a process p_j, p_i learns that p_j has answered up to its k-th inquiry, and consequently updates $answered_i[j]$.

```
task T1: repeat wait until (n − aaℓᵢ > kᵢ);
              kᵢ ← n − aaℓᵢ; brodcast INQUIRY(kᵢ)
         until (kᵢ = t) end repeat.

         when INQUIRY(k) is received from pⱼ: send ALIVE(k) to pⱼ.
         when ALIVE(k) is received from pⱼ: answeredᵢ[j] ← max(answeredᵢ[j], k).
_____

task T2: repeat m ← kᵢ; % m is local to T2, while kᵢ is not %
              X ← {x such that answeredᵢ[x] ≥ m};
              if (|X| = n − m) then suspectedᵢ ← {1, . . . , n} \ X end if
         until (|suspectedᵢ| = t) end repeat.
```

Figure 6.15: Building P in $\mathcal{AS}_{n,t}[AP]$: a bounded transformation (code for p_i)

The core of the transformation is the task $T2$ that gives its current value to $suspected_i$. It is made up of a **repeat** statement that is executed until t processes are locally suspected. (When t processes have crashed, no more processes can crash and the task can terminate. If less than t processes crash, the task does not terminate.)

The body of the **repeat** statement is as follows. First, p_i sets a local variable m to k_i (the number of processes that, to the best of its knowledge, have crashed). Then, p_i computes the set X

made up of the processes that have answered its m-th inquiry or a more recent one . If the predicate $|X| = n - m$ is true, p_i can safely conclude that the $n - m$ processes that have answered its m-th inquiry were alive when they answered, which means that the m processes that have not answered have crashed and are exactly the ones in the set $\Pi \setminus X$ (let us recall that, while the tasks $T1$ and $T2$ proceed asynchronously, p_i broadcasts INQUIRY (m) only after it knows that m processes have crashed).

Theorem 6.12   *The algorithm described in Figure 6.15 constructs a failure detector of the class P in $\mathcal{AS}_{n,t}[AP]$.*

Proof Proof of the completeness property of P. Let us assume that p_i is a non-faulty process. We have to show that if a process p_j crashes, after some finite time, j permanently belongs to $suspected_i$. Let $f = |Faulty(F)|$.

There is a finite time τ, after which the f faulty processes have crashed and we have permanently $aa\ell_i = n - f$, which means that, after some finite time, p_i broadcasts a message INQUIRY(f). Due to the strong accuracy property of AP, this message is sent after the f processes have crashed. Consequently, no crashed process can answer this inquiry message. It follows that, when task $T2$ executes with $m = k_i = f$, the set X can only contain the $n - f$ non-faulty processes, and we have then $|X| = n - f = n - m$. Hence, $suspected_i$ is set to $\{1, \ldots, n\} \setminus X$, i.e., contains exactly the f faulty processes, which concludes the proof of the completeness property.

Proof of the strong accuracy property of P. Let p_i be any process. We have to show that no process is added to $suspected_i$ before crashing. Let $i_1, \ldots, i_m$ be the m process identities that are placed in $suspected_i$ during an iteration of task $T2$. It follows from the query/response mechanism (implemented by the INQUIRY/ALIVE messages) used when $k_i = m$, and the strong accuracy property of AP, that each of the $n - m$ other processes has answered after these m processes have crashed. Consequently, none of these $n - m$ processes can be part of the m crashed processes. Hence, the set of processes that defines the value of $suspected_i$ contains only crashed processes, which completes the proof of the strong accuracy property of P. $\square_{Theorem\ 6.12}$

6.7.3   CONSENSUS WITH AN ANONYMOUS PERFECT FAILURE DETECTOR

The algorithm   A consensus algorithm for the $\mathcal{AAS}_{n,t}[AP]$ model is described in Figure 6.16. This algorithm can be instantiated with any value of t, and it does not require the processes to know the value n. It is very close to the algorithm described in Figure 6.3 (that solves consensus in $\mathcal{AS}_{n,t}[P]$).

A process p_i invokes **propose**(v_i) where v_i is the value it proposes to the consensus. It terminates when it executes the **return**(est_i) statement, where est_i is the value it decides. The processes execute $(2t + 1)$ asynchronous rounds. In each round, each process p_i broadcasts its current estimate (denoted est_i and initialized to v_i) of the decision value and updates it with the minimum on the values it has received and taken into account in the current round.

```
operation propose(v_i):
    est_i ← v_i; r_i ← 1;
    while (r_i ≤ 2t + 1) do
        begin asynchronous round
            brodcast EST(r_i, est_i);
            wait until ( aaℓ_i messages EST(r_i, −) have been received );
            est_i ← min(est values received at the previous line);
            r_i ← r_i + 1;
        end asynchronous round
    end while;
    return(est_i).
```

Figure 6.16: Anonymous consensus in $\mathcal{AAS}_{n,t}[AP]$ (code for p_i)

Remark   When n is known by the processes and $t = n - 1$, the algorithm can be easily improved to allow the processes to decide in $2t$ rounds, thereby saving one round.

Misleading failure notification   Let us consider Figure 6.17 where the rounds $r - 1$, r and $r + 1$ are represented, the process p_a crashes during the round $r - 1$ (a crash is represented by a cross in the figure), and the process p_b crashes after it has broadcast its round r message (in the figure, the corresponding crash appears during the round $r + 1$). The asynchronous notification of each crash appears at p_i as a decrease of $aaℓ_i$; each is indicated with a dotted line. As p_a crashes during the round $r - 1$, it will not send round r messages, and so, during the round r, p_i has to wait for at least 3 messages ($aaℓ_i = 3$). Differently, p_i is notified of the crash of p_b (i.e., $aaℓ_i$ is decreased to 2) while it is waiting for round r messages. As a result, p_i waits for only two messages, and as it has received two round r messages (from p_b and itself), it terminates its participation to the round r. Such an early failure notification is called a *misleading* notification, and the message m sent by the corresponding crashed process is called a misleading message. More precisely, a message m sent at round r is *misleading* if it allows its receiver to terminate its round r, while the corresponding sender has crashed after or during the broadcast of m. These misleading notifications/messages come from the independence between the asynchronous rounds on one side, and the crash notifications supplied by failure detector AP on the other side. The following theorem captures the synchronization power the processes are provided with in the $\mathcal{AAS}_{n,t}[AP]$ model.

Theorem 6.13   *If x processes crash while executing round r, no process can proceed to round $r + 1$ while there are still $(x + 1)$ processes that are alive and execute round $r - 1$.*

Proof   let τ be the time at which the first process (say p_i) progresses from the round r to the round $r + 1$. Moreover, let $A(\tau)$ be the number of processes that are alive at time τ, and $R(\tau, r)$ be the number of processes that, at time τ, have entered a round $r' \geq r$. We have $R(\tau, r) = RA(\tau, r) +$

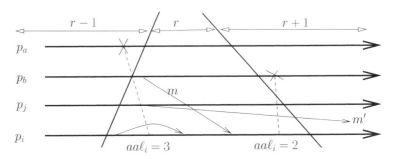

Figure 6.17: Misleading notification

$RC(\tau, r)$ where $RA(\tau, r)$ is the number of processes that, at τ, are alive and execute a round $r' \geq r$ (notice that only p_i starts executing $r' = r + 1$, the other processes of $RA(\tau, r)$ are executing r), and $RC(\tau, r)$ is the number of processes that have started executing the round r and have crashed by time τ).

- It follows from the safety property of ψ that, when the process p_i progresses from the round r to the round $r + 1$, we have $aa\ell_i(\tau) \geq A(\tau)$. Moreover, during the round r, p_i receives and processes only messages sent during the same round r, from which we conclude that $R(\tau, r) \geq aa\ell_i(\tau)$, and by transitivity we obtain $R(\tau, r) \geq A(\tau)$.

- At time τ, there are $A(\tau) - RA(\tau, r)$ alive processes that have not yet entered the round r. As $RA(\tau, r) = R(\tau, r) - RC(\tau, r)$ and $0 \leq RC(\tau, r) \leq x$, we conclude that there are at most $A(\tau) - R(\tau, r) + x$ alive processes that have not yet entered the round r.

Finally, as, at time τ, there are at most $A(\tau) - R(\tau, r) + x$ alive processes that have not yet entered the round r, and $R(\tau, r) \geq A(\tau)$, we conclude that $A(\tau) - R(\tau, r) + x \leq x$, which completes the proof of the theorem. $\qquad \Box_{Theorem\ 6.13}$

Corollary 6.14   *If no process crashes while executing round r, no process terminates round r (i.e., proceeds to $r + 1$ if $r < 2t + 1$, or decides if $r = 2t + 1$) while there are alive processes executing round $r - 1$.*

Theorem 6.15   *The algorithm described in Figure 6.16 solves the consensus problem in the anonymous asynchronous model $\mathcal{AAS}_{n,t}[AP]$.*

Proof Proof of the validity property. The proof of the validity property is a direct consequence of the following simple observations: (1) each local estimate est_i is initialized to a proposed value, (2) only estimate values are communicated, and (3) the new value of an estimate local variable is the minimum of the estimates values received and taken into account so far.

Proof of the termination property. Let us first observe that, due to the liveness properties of AP, during any round r no process can be blocked forever when it executes the **wait** statement. The termination property follows directly from this observation: every process that does not crash by the end of the $(2t + 1)$th round decides.

Proof of the agreement property. To prove this property we first prove the following claim.

Claim C. If no process crashes during two consecutive rounds r and $r + 1$, all the processes that terminate round r have the same estimate value.

Proof of claim C. Let r and $r + 1$ be two consecutive rounds without crash, and AR the set of processes that execute these two rounds. Let first observe that, due to Corollary 6.14 no process is alive in the round $r - 1$ when a process of AR proceeds to $r + 1$, and as no process crashes while executing the round $r + 1$, there is no misleading message. Finally, due to the safety property of ψ and the fact that no process that crashed before r can send round r messages, it follows that each process in AR receives a round r message from each process in AR and does not receive a round r message from any process not in AR. Consequently, during the round r, the processes of AR compute their new estimate as the smallest value from the same set, which proves the lemma. End of proof of claim.

To prove that no two processes decide different values, let us consider two cases.

- Case 1. In the sequence of $(2t + 1)$ rounds, there are two consecutive rounds without crash. Let r and $r + 1$ be these two rounds, with $\leq r \leq 2t$. It follows from Claim C that all the processes that proceed to the round $r + 1$ have the same estimate value. Hence, a single value can be decided at the end of the round $(2t + 1)$.

- Case 2. In the sequence of $(2t + 1)$ rounds, there are no two consecutive rounds without crash. This means that the odd rounds are crash-free, while each even round has exactly one crash. So, the t possible crashes occurred during the rounds $2, 4, \ldots, 2t$. As the last round is crash-free and there are no misleading messages during the round $2t + 1$, it follows (from the safety property of AP) that during that round every process receives a message from every process. They all consequently compute the same minimum value, which completes the proof of the agreement property.

$\square_{Theorem\ 6.15}$

On the cost of $(2t + 1)$ *rounds*   A simple run of the previous algorithm is depicted in Figure 6.18. This run, that considers $t = 2$, involves $n = 5$ processes and requires $2t + 1 = 5$ rounds for the non-faulty processes to decide. In that run, the process denoted p_1 crashes during the second round, and the process denoted p_2 crashes during the fourth round. Moreover, the message sent by p_1 during the first round is received only by itself, and its round 2 message is received only by p_2. Similarly for p_2 during the rounds 3 and 4. As we can see, if the algorithm stops at the 4th round, it does not solves the consensus problem. The behavior of the chain of processes p_1, p_2 during the first four

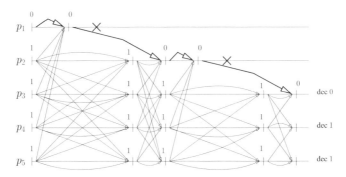

Figure 6.18: The algorithm requires $(2t + 1)$ rounds

Figure 6.18: The algorithm requires $(2t + 1)$ rounds

rounds (where the bold arrows are associated with the messages that carry the value 0) is similar to the chain of faulty processes that delays the decision until the round $(t + 1)$ in synchronous systems.

The fact that the algorithm requires $(2t + 1)$ rounds is not a particular feature of it, but a feature of all the algorithms that solve consensus in $\mathcal{AAS}_{n,t}[AP]$. This is because $(2t + 1)$ is a lower bound on the number of rounds to solve consensus in $\mathcal{AAS}_{n,t}[AP]$ (see the bibliographic notes). Hence, the previous algorithm is optimal.

6.7.4   CONSENSUS WITH AN ANONYMOUS EVENTUAL LEADER FAILURE DETECTOR

This section presents another consensus algorithm for anonymous systems. This algorithm assumes an anonymous eventual leader oracle.

The class $A\Omega$ of anonymous eventual leader oracles   Let us remember that any failure detector of the class of (non-anonymous) eventual leader oracles Ω provide each process p_i with a local variable *leader*$_i$ that contains a process identity and is such that, after an arbitrary but finite time, the variables *leader*$_i$ of the non-faulty processes contain forever the same identity, and this identity is the one of a non-faulty process.

It is easy to define an anonymous counterpart of Ω. This class of failure detectors (oracles), denoted $A\Omega$, provides every process p_i with a boolean variable *leader*$_i$ such that, after an arbitrary but finite time, there is one non-faulty process (say p_ℓ) whose boolean variable remains forever true, and the boolean variables of the other non-faulty processes remain forever false. Let us notice that, during the arbitrary long anarchy period, the local variables *leader*$_i$ can take arbitrary values (e.g., it is possible that they all are equal to *false*).

It is easy to see that Ω and $A\Omega$ are equivalent in a non-anonymous system (for any value of t).

Anonymous consensus in $\mathcal{AAS}_{n,t}[t < n/2, A\Omega]$ A consensus algorithm for the anonymous asynchronous model where a majority of processes remain non-faulty is described in Figure 6.20. This algorithm is obtained from very simple modifications of the algorithm described in Figure 6.10 that has been designed for the model $\mathcal{AS}_{n,t}[t < n/2, \Omega, R]$. More precisely, there is the following:

- As there is no random oracle, the invocation random() in Figure 6.10 is replaced by "skip".

- As Ω is replaced by $A\Omega$, the phase 0 is modified accordingly. During a round r, process p_i first waits until it discovers it is leader, or receives a message PHASE0(r, v). If it is currently leader (*leader*$_i$ is then equal to *true*), p_i keeps its estimate value $est1_i$ and broadcasts the message PHASE0$(r, est1_i)$ in order they strive to decide the value $v = est1_i$. Otherwise, it adopts the estimate value v it has received as the new value of its estimate $est1_i$. In that case, p_i also broadcasts the message PHASE0$(r, est1_i)$. This is to circumvent the possible crash of the process that sends the message PHASE0(r, v) it has received.

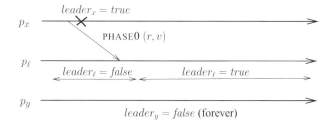

Figure 6.19: Why to forward PHASE0 () messages

As an example, let us consider Figure 6.19. Process p_x sends PHASE0 (r, v) to p_ℓ only, and then crashes. When, it receives this message, let us assume that p_ℓ proceeds to phase 1 of round r, without forwarding the message it has received. Moreover, let us assume that p_ℓ becomes the eventual leader after proceeding to phase 1 of round r and all other boolean *leader*$_y$ take the value *false*. It is easy to see that p_i remains blocked in round r waiting forever for a message PHASE0 $(r, -)$.

- All the other parts remain the same in Figure 6.10 and Figure 6.20.

Theorem 6.16   *The algorithm described in Figure 6.20 solves the consensus problem in* $\mathcal{AAS}_{n,t}[t < n/2, \Omega]$.

Proof The proof of the validity, integrity and agreement properties are the same as in the proof of the algorithm of Figure 6.10. They are not repeated here. (This is consistent with the fact that, when $t < n/2$, the failure detector is used only to ensure the termination property).

Proof of the termination property. The structure of the proof of this property is similar to the one done for previous algorithms. Let us first observe that, if a process decides, due to the DECIDE()

```
operation propose (v_i):
    est1_i ← v_i; r_i ← 0;
    while true do
        begin asynchronous round
        r_i ← r_i + 1;
        % Phase 0 : select a value with the help of the oracle AΩ %
            wait until ((leader_i) ∨ (PHASE0(r_i, v) received));
            if (PHASE0(r_i, v) received) then est1_i ← v end if;
            broadcast PHASE0 (r_i, est1_i);
        % Phase 1 : from all to all %
            broadcast PHASE1 (r_i, est1_i);
            wait until (PHASE1 (r_i, −) received from n − t processes);
            if (the same estimate v has been received from > n/2 processes)
                        then est2_i ← v else est2_i ← ⊥ end if;
        % Here, we have ((est2_i ≠ ⊥) ∧ (est2_j ≠ ⊥)) ⇒ (est2_i = est2_j = v) %
        % Phase 2 : try to decide a value from the est2 values %
            broadcast PHASE2 (r_i, est2_i);
            wait until (PHASE2 (r_i, −) received from n − t processes);
            let rec_i = {est2 | PHASE2 (r_i, est2) has been received};
            case (rec_i = {v})       then broadcast DECIDE(v); return (v)
                 (rec_i = {v, ⊥}) then est1_i ← v
                 (rec_i = {⊥})       then skip
            end case
        end asynchronous round
    end while.

    when DECIDE(v) is received: broadcast DECIDE(v); return (v).
```

Figure 6.20: A Consensus algorithm for $\mathcal{AAS}_{n,t}[t < n/2, A\Omega]$ (code for p_i)

messages, every non-faulty process receives such a message and consequently decides. So, let us assume that no process ever decides.

Claim C. No non-faulty process blocks forever in a round.

Proof of claim C. The proof is by contradiction. let r be the first round during which a non-faulty process (say p_i) blocks forever. Let us first consider phase 0 of round r. If p_i is the eventual leader it cannot be blocked forever in phase 0 of r. Hence, assuming that p_i is not the eventual leader, this means that p_i never receives a message PHASE0 (r_i, v). We consider several cases.

1. A non-faulty process p_x is (momentarily or permanently) designated as leader, and that process broadcasts PHASE0 $(r_i, est1_x)$ that is received by p_i. In that case, process p_i cannot block forever in the **wait** statement of phase 0.

2. A faulty process p_x (momentarily designated as leader) sends PHASE0 $(r_i, est1_x)$ to p_i (or to another process p_y that forwards the message PHASE0 $(r_i, est1_x)$ to p_i). In that case, process p_i cannot be blocked in the **wait** statement of phase 0.

3. No message PHASE0 $(r_i, est1_x)$ broadcast by a faulty process is received by p_i. In that case, the faulty processes either crash during round r or are never designated as leader during round

r. It then follows from the eventual leadership property of $A\Omega$, that there is a correct process that (momentarily or permanently) is designated as leader, and we are then in the scenario of Item 1.

It follows from the previous case analysis that no non-faulty process p_i can block forever during phase 0 of round r. Due to the "majority of correct processes" assumption, it follows that p_i can be blocked forever neither in the **wait** statement of phase 1 nor in the **wait** statement of phase 2. End of proof of claim C.

As (1) no process decides (assumption), (2) the non-faulty processes are never blocked in a round (Claim C), and (3), from their very definition, the faulty processes eventually crash, it follows that there is a round from which there are only non-faulty processes and one of them (say p_ℓ) is forever designated as the single leader. Let r be such a round.

During r, the leader p_ℓ is the only process such that $leader_\ell$ is equal to $true$, and it is consequently the first process that broadcasts PHASE0 (r, v). Moreover, as any other process p_j is such that $\neg leader_j$ from round r, such a process can only receive (and then forwards) PHASE0 (r, v). It follows that at the end of phase 0, the local estimates $est1_j$ are all equal to $v = est1_\ell$.

Hence, as we have seen in previous algorithms, the local estimates $est2_j$ are all equal to v at the end of phase 1. Then, during phase 2, every non-faulty process is such that $rec_j = \{v\}$, and consequently decides which contradicts the initial assumption and completes the proof of the termination property. $\quad\square_{Theorem\ 6.16}$

Number of communication steps   It is easy to see that, when the oracle $A\Omega$ is *perfect* (a single non-faulty leader is elected from the very beginning), a process decides at the end of the first round, i.e., after three communication steps. Moreover, this is independent of the value of t.

This is contrast with the algorithm described in Figure 6.16 designed for the $\mathcal{AAS}_{n,t}[AP]$ model, that requires $(2t + 1)$ rounds. This is not counter-intuitive, as the model $\mathcal{AAS}_{n,t}[AP]$ has no requirement such as $t < n/2$; the algorithm described in Figure 6.16 works for any value of t. Differently, there is no algorithm in $\mathcal{AAS}_{n,t}[t < n/2, \Omega]$ when $t \geq n/2$.

6.8   BIBLIOGRAPHIC NOTES
- The failure detector abstraction and a family of failure detector classes which includes the class of perfect failure detectors, have been introduced by Chandra and Toueg [34].
- The notion of early-deciding algorithms for agreement problems and the associated round complexity have first been addressed in the context of synchronous systems (e.g., [67, 52]). The early-deciding algorithm in the asynchronous model enriched with a perfect failure detector (class P) that has been presented is due to Bonnet and Raynal [31]. It extends results of the synchronous model to the system model $\mathcal{AS}_{n,t}[P]$.
- Proofs that $(t + 1)$ is a lower bound for the number of rounds in synchronous systems prone to process crash failures can be found in [11, 52, 57, 117, 126].

- A class of problems that can be solved efficiently in asynchronous systems enriched with P is described in [49]. A comparison of synchronous systems and asynchronous systems enriched with P, from the point of view of problem solvability and algorithm efficiency, is presented in [37].

- The proof that Ω is the weakest class of failure detectors to solve the consensus problem in asynchronous systems with a majority of non-faulty processes is due to Chandra, Hadzilacos and Toueg [33]. The proof that (Σ, Ω) is the weakest class of failure detectors to solve the consensus problem for any value of t has been given in [48].

- The notion of zero-degradation has been introduced by Dutta and Guerraoui [54]. The zero-degrading consensus algorithm for $\mathcal{AS}_{n,t}[t < n/2, \Omega]$ that has been presented is a variant of an algorithm due to Mostéfaoui and Raynal [134]. A versatile family of consensus algorithms based on different failure detectors proposed by Chandra and Toueg is presented in [101]. The saving of broadcast instances is due to [101]. The proof that 2 rounds are the lower bound for consensus in systems equipped with Ω is due to Keidar and Rajsbaum [105].

  The notion of zero-degradation is studied in [87]. Its combination with asynchrony to improve the efficiency of round-based consensus algorithms is investigated in [159]. Consensus algorithms suited to mobile ad hoc networks are presented in [160].

- The notion of indulgence is due to Guerraoui [83]. This notion has been investigated from a formal point of view in [86], and general frameworks to design indulgent Ω-based consensus algorithms are presented in [87, 89].

- Randomized binary consensus has been introduced simultaneously by Ben-Or [22] and Rabin [146]. The algorithm that has been presented is due to Ben-Or [22].

  The notion of common coin is due to Rabin [146]. The randomized algorithm based on such a shared object that had been presented is due to Friedman, Mostéfaoui and Raynal [72].

  A multivalued randomized consensus algorithm is presented in [60]. Hybrid consensus algorithms are presented in [10, 140]. Hybrid algorithms are interesting as they favor assumption coverage [144].

- The non-blocking algorithm that solves the multivalued consensus problem from binary consensus is from [139]. The notion of "one communication step" consensus has been introduced in [32].

- Consensus in asynchronous anonymous message-passing systems has been studied by Bonnet and Raynal who have proposed the algorithm that has been presented [29]. This paper shows that $(2t + 1)$ rounds are a lower bound on the number of rounds for that distributed computation model.

  The class of anonymous perfect failure detectors is a simple adaptation to anonymous systems of a failure detector class introduced in [133]. Anonymous consensus in a distributed message-passing model where the rounds are given for free is presented in [50].

The anonymous consensus algorithm based on $A\Omega$ is a simple variant of a non-anonymous Ω-based algorithm due to Mostéfaoui and Raynal [136].

- Other distributed computing models have been defined in the literature (e.g., [43, 51, 56, 75, 80, 106, 112, 158]). Among them, the Paxos family of agreement algorithms [39, 76, 112, 113] consider that messages can be lost and processes can crash and recover. The interested reader will find in [89] a framework for a restriction of these algorithms suited to asynchronous systems where channels are reliable and processes that crash never recover.

- An approach to solve consensus, despite asynchrony and process crashes, that is based on a restriction of the set of input vectors is defined [131]. Its combination with failure detectors to solve agreement problems is investigated [133].

CHAPTER 7

Constructing Failure Detectors

After having presented the two facets of a failure detector (modularity, and problem ranking), this chapter presents algorithms that build failure detectors in the system model $\mathcal{AS}_{n,t}[\emptyset]$ (or variants of it) enriched with additional appropriate behavioral assumptions. After having recalled a few notions stated in the second chapter, this chapter focuses on the failure detector classes P (perfect failure detectors), $\Diamond P$ (eventually perfect failure detectors), and Ω (eventual leader failure detectors). Its aim is to visit several behavioral assumptions and present algorithms based on different approaches and techniques that build failure detectors (with different power).

7.1 THE TWO FACETS OF FAILURE DETECTORS

This section complements the notions on failure detectors introduced in sections 4.1 and 4.2 of Chapter 2. Let us remember that a failure pattern is a function $F()$ such that $F(\tau)$ is the set of processes that have crashed up to time τ, and a failure detector is a device that provides each process p_i with a read-only local variable that gives p_i hints on failures. Formally, that variable is denoted $H(i, \tau)$, where $H()$ is the history function associated with the failure detector. When it reads $H(i, \tau)$, process p_i obtains its current content. A particular class of failure detectors provides each process p_i with a particular type of information on failures.

7.1.1 THE PROGRAMMING POINT OF VIEW: MODULAR BUILDING BLOCK

In asynchronous systems whose behavior is captured by the system model $\mathcal{AS}_{n,t}[\emptyset]$, physical time is not accessible to the processes. It is a resource needed to execute programs, but it is not a programming object that these programs can manipulate. This means that the timing assumptions, used by the underlying system layer to detect failures, are not known by the upper application layer.

As we have seen in Chapter 2 (section 4.1) the failure detector concept favors the separation of concerns. It consequently favors the following modular approach. Let FD be a given class of failure detectors and Pb a problem that can be solved as soon as we can benefit from information on failures provided by FD.

- On one side, enrich the system model $\mathcal{AS}_{n,t}[\emptyset]$ with an appropriate time-related assumption A that allows the construction of a failure detector of the class FD in the system model $\mathcal{AS}_{n,t}[A]$.

- On the other side, solve the problem Pb in the system model $\mathcal{AS}_{n,t}[FD]$.

As an example, let Pb be the problem of constructing an atomic register in an asynchronous message-passing system prone to any number of process crashes. We have seen in Chapter 2 that Pb can be solved in $\mathcal{AS}_{n,t}[\Sigma]$ (Σ is the class of quorum failure detectors). The construction of a failure detector of the class Σ and the construction of a register in $\mathcal{AS}_{n,t}[\Sigma]$ are two problems that can be solved independently, each in the appropriate model. More explicitly, the behavioral assumptions needed to construct Σ are not known in the model $\mathcal{AS}_{n,t}[\Sigma]$ (similarly, when one is using a high level programming language, she can no longer access machine instructions).

Such a separation of concerns favors algorithm design and proof, and program transportability. (Never forget that computer science is a science of abstraction.) This is made possible because (similarly to stacks, queues, and any computer science object) a failure detector class is defined by a set of properties that are independent of a particular implementation.

7.1.2   THE COMPUTABILITY POINT OF VIEW: PROBLEM RANKING

Ranking of failure detector classes   As we have seen, given a problem Pb and a model such that Pb cannot be solved in this model, the failure detector approach allows us to state the minimal information on failures the processes have to be provided with in order Pb can be solved in the considered model. An example of such a weakest class of failure detectors has been presented in Chapter 2, namely the class Σ that has been shown to be the weakest class of failure detectors that allow to build an atomic register in $\mathcal{AS}_{n,t}[t < n]$.

Given two classes of failure detectors $FD1$ and $FD2$, we say that $FD1$ is *weaker* than $FD2$ (or $FD2$ is *stronger* than $FD1$) if there is an algorithm E that builds a failure detector of the class $FD1$ in $\mathcal{AS}_{n,t}[FD2]$. This is denoted $FD1 \preceq FD2$ (or equivalently $FD2 \succeq FD1$). It means that the information on failures provided by a failure detector of the class $FD2$ "includes" the information on failures provided by the failure detectors of the class $FD1$. Actually, the algorithm E extracts this information from $FD2$. As an example, it is easy to design an algorithm E that builds a failure detector of the class Ω in $\mathcal{AS}_{n,t}[P]$, hence we have $\Omega \preceq P$.

The relation $\preceq$ is transitive and reflexive. If $FD1 \preceq FD2$ and $FD2 \preceq FD1$, both classes are equivalent. If $FD1 \preceq FD2$ and $\neg(FD2 \preceq FD1)$, then $FD1$ is *strictly weaker* than $FD2$ (denoted $FD1 \prec FD2$). As an example, it is possible to build a failure of the class Ω in $\mathcal{AS}_{n,t}[P]$ while it is not possible to build a failure of the class P in $\mathcal{AS}_{n,t}[\Omega]$. We have consequently w $\Omega \prec P$.

It is important to notice that not all the failure detector classes can be compared. As an example, while the class P is strictly stronger than both of them, Ω and Σ cannot be compared.

Ranking of problems   An interesting side of the ranking of failure detector classes lies in the ranking of problems it allows to be solved. This ranking is based on the notion of *weakest failure detector class* that permits to solve a given problem.

Let $Pb1$ be a distributed computing problem such that $FD1$ is the weakest class of failure detectors that allow to solve it. This means that there is an algorithm that solves $Pb1$ in $\mathcal{AS}_{n,t}[FD1]$. Similarly, let $Pb2$ be a distributed computing problem such that the class $FD2$ of failure detectors is the weakest that allow to solve it. Hence, there is an algorithm that solves $Pb2$ in $\mathcal{AS}_{n,t}[FD2]$.

We say that $Pb1$ *is less difficult than* $Pb2$ (or *easier* than $Pb2$) if the weakest class of failure detectors to solve $Pb1$ is weaker than the weakest class of failure detectors to solve $Pb2$, i.e., $FD1 \preceq FD2$. This is denoted $Pb1 \preceq Pb2$. If $Pb1$ is less difficult than $Pb2$ and $Pb2$ is less difficult than $Pb1$, the problems $Pb1$ and $Pb2$ are equivalent in the sense that they need the same information on failures to be solved, which means that -from a failure detector point of view- one can be solved as soon as the other can solved. If $Pb1$ is less difficult than $Pb2$ while $Pb2$ is not less difficult than $Pb1$, we say that $Pb1$ *is strictly less difficult than* $Pb2$ (denoted $Pb1 \prec Pb2$). We also say that $Pb2$ *is strictly stronger than* $Pb1$. This means that solving $Pb1$ requires less information on failures than solving $Pb2$.

As a simple example, the URB-broadcast problem can be solved in $\mathcal{AS}_{n,t}[\emptyset]$ (i.e., without any failure detector, which means with the trivial failure detector that produces arbitrary outputs). Differently, the construction of a register requires Σ as soon as a majority of processes may crash. It follows that, in message-passing systems with reliable channels and any number of process crashes ($t \leq n$), the URB-broadcast problem is strictly weaker than the construction of a register. (Let us notice that they are equivalent in reliable message-passing systems or in message-passing systems with a majority of non-faulty processes.)

This provides us with a failure detector-based method to establish a hierarchy among distributed computing problems.

7.2   IMPOSSIBILITY TO BUILD Ω IN $\mathcal{AS}_{n,t}[\emptyset]$

Reminder: definition of Ω   A failure detector of the class Ω (eventual leader) provides each process p_i with a local variable $leader_i$. These variables, that always contain a process identity, satisfy the following eventual leadership property: there is a finite time after which the variables $leader_i$ of the non-faulty processes contain forever the same identity and that identity is the one of a non-faulty process.

A direct impossibility proof   This section shows that it is impossible to build a failure detector of the class Ω in the system model $\mathcal{AS}_{n,t}[\emptyset]$. As $\Omega \prec \Diamond P \prec P$, it follows that neither $\Diamond P$ nor P can be built in $\mathcal{AS}_{n,t}[\emptyset]$.

As consensus can be solved in $\mathcal{AS}_{n,t}[t < n/2, \Omega]$, an "indirect" proof of this impossibility follows from the impossibility to solve consensus in $\mathcal{AS}_{n,1}[\emptyset]$. The proof given below is "direct" in the sense that it does not rely on the impossibility of another distributed computing problem.

Theorem 7.1   *No failure detector of the class Ω can be built in $AS_{n,t}[\emptyset]$ for $1 \leq t < n$.*

Proof   The proof is by contradiction. Let us assume that there is an algorithm that constructs a failure detector of the class Ω in $AS_{n,t}[\emptyset]$. The proof consists in constructing a crash-free execution in which there is an infinite sequence of leaders such that any two consecutive leaders are different, from which it follows that the eventual leadership property cannot be satisfied.

- Let R_1 be a crash-free execution, and τ_1 be the time after which some process p_{ℓ_1} is elected as the leader.

  Moreover, let R_1' be an execution identical to R_1 until $\tau_1 + 1$, and where p_{ℓ_1} crashes at $\tau_1 + 2$.

- Let R_2 be a crash-free execution identical to R_1' until $\tau_1 + 1$, and where the messages sent by p_{ℓ_1} after $\tau_1 + 1$ are arbitrarily delayed (until some time that we will specify later).

  As, for any process $p_x \neq p_{\ell_1}$, R_2 cannot be distinguished from R_1', it follows that some process $p_{\ell_2} \neq p_{\ell_1}$ is elected as the definitive leader at some time $\tau_2 > \tau_1$. After p_{ℓ_2} is elected, the messages from p_{ℓ_1} can be received.

  Moreover, let R_2' be an execution identical to R_2 until $\tau_2 + 1$, and where p_{ℓ_2} crashes at $\tau_2 + 2$.

- Let R_3 be a crash-free execution identical to R_2' until $\tau_2 + 1$, and where the messages from p_{ℓ_2} are delayed (until some time that we will specify later).

  Some process $p_{\ell_3} \neq p_{\ell_2}$ is elected as the definitive leader at some time $\tau_3 > \tau_2 > \tau_1$. After p_{ℓ_3} is elected, the messages from p_{ℓ_2} are received. Etc.

This inductive process, repeated indefinitely, constructs a crash-free execution in which an infinity of leaders are elected at times $\tau_1 < \tau_2 < \tau_3 < \ldots$ and such that no two consecutive leaders are the same process. It follows that there is no finite time after which the same correct process is forever elected as the single common leader. $\qquad \square_{Theorem\ 7.1}$

7.3   CONSTRUCTING A PERFECT FAILURE DETECTOR (CLASS P)

Ensuring only one of the properties of a perfect failure detector is trivial. To ensure the completeness property only (every process that crashes has to be suspected), it is sufficient to permanently suspect all the processes, while to ensure the strong accuracy property only (no process is suspected before it crashes), it is sufficient to never suspect any process. To ensure both properties, the main difficulty lies in ensuring strong accuracy because it is a *perpetual* property, it has never to be violated. (Differently, the completeness property is an *eventual* property, it specifies something that has to be eventually satisfied.)

This means that to be able to construct a perfect failure detector, the underlying system has to satisfy base properties. We examine three such base properties in the following.

7.3.1   USE AN UNDERLYING SYNCHRONOUS SYSTEM

A simple monitoring algorithm   A simple way to construct a perfect failure detector consists in using an auxiliary synchronous system. Let us remember that a synchronous system is characterized by upper bounds on communication delays and processing durations. (To simplify the presentation, we consider that processing durations are negligible with respect to communication delays, and we consequently consider that they are equal to 0. Alternatively, we could consider the processing time of a message is integrated in its transit time).

Each process p_i executes the very simple monitoring algorithm described in Figure 7.1. Regularly (every β time units, with $\beta > \Delta$), process p_i sends an INQUIRY() message to the processes it does not suspect, and it sets a timer to a value Δ that is an upper bound for the maximal round-trip delay (maximal duration that can elapse between the sending of a request and the reception of the corresponding reply). If it does not receive an answer from p_j before the timer expires, p_i adds j to $suspected_i$.

```
init: suspected_i ← ∅.

repeat  forever every β time units
        for each j ∉ suspected_i do send  INQUIRY(i) to p_j end for;
        crashed_i[1..n] ← [true, ..., true];
        set timer_i to Δ
end repeat.

when  INQUIRY(j) is received: send  ALIVE(i) to p_j.

when  ALIVE(j) is received: crashed_i[j] ← false.

when timer_i expires: suspected_i ← {x | crashed_i[x]}.
```

Figure 7.1: A simple process monitoring algorithm in a synchronous system (code for p_i)

Theorem 7.2   *The algorithm described in Figure 7.1 builds a perfect failure detector on top of a synchronous system for $0 \leq t < n$.*

Proof The completeness property of the class P follows from the observation that, if a process p_j crashes, and process p_i does not crash, due to the repeated sending of INQUIRY(i) messages, there is a finite time after which p_j no longer answers, and, consequently, the boolean $crashed_i[j]$ is set to *true* and keeps that value forever.

The strong accuracy property of P results from the fact that a process answers by return each INQUIRY() message it receives, processing times equal to 0, and the round-trip delay of an INQUIRY() message and its corresponding ALIVE() message is upper bounded by Δ. It follows from the conjunction of these properties that the message ALIVE() sent by a process p_j to a process p_i necessarily arrives before the timer has expired. $\square_{Theorem\ 7.2}$

Remark   The previous algorithm is not *indulgent* in the sense that, if there are "bad" periods during which the duration Δ is not a round-trip delay upper bound, the strong accuracy property can be violated. This is due to the fact that the strong accuracy property is a perpetual property (at any time, no alive process is suspected), and indulgence is not appropriate for perpetual properties.

The model   It is important to notice that the underlying synchronous system is hidden to the upper layer. The model in which the application processes evolve is $\mathcal{AS}_{n,t}[P]$. (This is similar to the speed of the hardware clock that remains unknown from the processes.)

Remark   The algorithm described in Figure 7.1 can be used in an asynchronous system as follows. The INQUIRY() and ALIVE() messages are defined as "very high priority" messages (sometimes called "datagrams" in network terminology) that overtake all the other messages on their way to destination (those are application messages sent by the processes). It becomes then possible to compute an upper bound for the round-trip delay of the INQUIRY() and ALIVE() control messages, while the transit delay of application messages remains finite but unbounded (i.e., asynchronous).

7.3.2   APPLICATIONS WITH A FAIR COMMUNICATION PATTERN

In some cases, the synchrony does not come from the underlying system but from the application itself. As we are about to see, such a synchrony can be used to implement a perfect failure detector.

Fair communication   Let communication be α-*fair* if any process p_i can receive at most α messages from any other process p_j without having received at least one message from each other non-crashed process.

    It is easy to see that fair communication with $\alpha = 1$ is close to the classical (synchronous) round-based lock-step system model, where in each round a process sends a message to each other process p_j and receives a message from each other non-crashed process p_j.

A fair communication-based construction of P   The algorithm described in Figure 7.2 builds a perfect failure detector. It assumes that α is known by all the processes. The data structure that is central to the algorithm is the local array $count_i[1..n, 1..n]$, managed by each process p_i, and the meaning of which is the following.

  • $(count_i[j, k] = x) \Leftrightarrow (p_i$ has received x messages from p_j since the last message it has received from $p_k)$.

    The set *suspected$_i$* built by the algorithm at every process p_i is initialized to $\emptyset$. When p_i receives a message from p_j, it does the following with respect to each process p_k that it does not suspect. It first increases $count_i[j, k]$. Then, it checks the predicate $count_i[j, k] > \alpha$. If this predicate is true, p_i has received more than α messages from p_j without having received a message from p_k. As this would contradict the fair communication assumption if p_k was alive, p_i concludes that p_k has crashed. Consequently, it adds the identity k to its set *suspected$_i$*. If the predicate is false, p_i resets $count_i[k, j]$ to 0 as, from now on, it has received no message from p_k since the last message from p_j.

Theorem 7.3   *Let us consider an application in which each correct process sends an infinite number of messages to each other process, and communication is α-fair. Assuming that α is known by the processes and $0 \leq t < n - 1$ (hence, there are at least two correct processes) The algorithm described in Figure 7.2*

```
init: suspected_i ← ∅;
        for each pair (j, k) do count_i[j, k] ← 0 end for.

when a message m is received from p_j:
        for each k ≠ j do
            if (k ∉ suspected_i) then
                count_i[j, k] ← count_i[j, k] + 1;
                if (count_i[j, k] = α + 1)
                    then suspected_i ← suspected_i ∪ {k}
                    else count_i[k, j] ← 0
                end if
            end if
        end for.
```

Figure 7.2: Building P from fair communication (code for p_i)

builds a perfect failure detector when communication is α-fair. Moreover, the algorithm has only bounded variables.

Proof The completeness property of the class P follows from the fact that a process p_k that crashes is discovered faulty by p_i because there is at least another non-faulty process p_j. More precisely, after p_k has crashed, it no longer sends messages, and, consequently, there is a finite time from which $count_i[j, k]$ is never reset to 0. On another side, as p_j is non-faulty, it sends forever messages. Consequently, after some finite time, the local predicate $count_i[j, k] > \alpha$ becomes true and p_i adds k to $suspected_i$. Finally, let us observe that, once added to $suspected_i$, no process identity is withdrawn from this set, which completes the proof of the completeness property.

The strong accuracy property of P follows from the fair communication assumption. This property states that, until p_k crashes (if it ever does), p_i receives at most α messages from any non-crashed process p_j between two consecutive messages from p_k. It follows that, until p_k crashes if ever it does, the predicate $count_i[j, k] > \alpha$ is always false when p_i receives a message from any process p_j.

It is easy to see that the value of a counter $count_i[j, k]$ varies between 0 and $\alpha + 1$, which establishes the property that all local variables have a bounded domain.   □$_{Theorem\ 7.3}$

7.3.3   THE THETA ASSUMPTION

The word "theta" is the name given by its authors to the assumption described below. It has not to be confused with the Θ failure detector class (and is not at all related to it).

The model   Considering an execution of a synchronous system, let δ^+ (resp., δ^-) be the maximal (resp. minimal) transit time for a message between any two distinct processes. Moreover, let $\theta = \lceil \frac{\delta^+}{\delta^-} \rceil$.

As we can see, θ actually characterizes an infinite set of runs, $R_1, R_2, \ldots$, each run R_x with its own pair of bounds (δ_x^+, δ_x^-) such that $\theta = \lceil \frac{\delta_1^+}{\delta_1^-} \rceil = \lceil \frac{\delta_2^+}{\delta_2^-} \rceil = \cdots$.

Let us now consider an infinite run where, while there are no bounds δ^+ and δ^- on message transfer delays, the run can be sliced in consecutive periods such that, during each period, θ is greater than or equal to the ratio of the maximal and the minimal transit times that occur during that period. As an example, this appears when both the maximal and the minimal transit times doubles from one period to the next one.

Notation   In the following, $\mathcal{AS}_{n,t}[\theta]$ denotes the system made of all the runs where the previous assumption on the ratio on the speed of messages, as captured by θ, is satisfied, and local processing takes no time. (This model is clearly asynchronous in the sense that its definition does not explicitly rely on physical time.)

Building a perfect failure detector in $\mathcal{AS}_{n,t}[\theta]$ As we are about to see, θ captures enough synchrony to implement a perfect failure detector, while hiding to the processes the uncertainty associated with message transfer delays.

The principle of the algorithm is similar to the previous one: a process p_i monitors each other process p_j and suspects it when, assuming p_j is alive, its behavior would falsify the assumption θ. The algorithm is described in Figure 7.3.

```
init: suspected_i ← ∅;
        for each j ≠ i do send PING (i) to p_j end for.

when a message PING (j) is received: send PONG (i) to p_j.

when a message PONG (j) is received:
        for each k ≠ j do
          if (k ∉ suspected_i) then
              count_i[j, k] ← count_i[j, k] + 1;
              if (count_i[j, k] > θ)
                  then suspected_i ← suspected_i ∪ {k}
                  else count_i[k, j] ← 0
              end if
          end if
        end for;
        send PING (i) to p_j.
```

Figure 7.3: Building P in $\mathcal{AS}_{n,t}[\theta]$ (code for p_i)

A process p_i executes a sequence of rounds (without using explicit round numbers) with respect to each other process. During each round with respect to p_j, process p_i sends it a message PING (i) and waits for the PONG (j) message that p_j echoes when it receives PING (i). Finally, when it receives this echo message, p_i starts a new round with respect to p_j by sending it a new PING (i) message.

The assumption θ and these PING/PONG messages actually generate an execution the communication of which is θ-fair (see Figure 7.4 where the messages between p_i and p_j take δ^- times units, while the ones between p_i and p_k take δ^+ times units). It follows that, when it receives PONG (j), p_i has simply to execute the same statements as the one described in Figure 7.2 before starting a new round with respect to p_j.

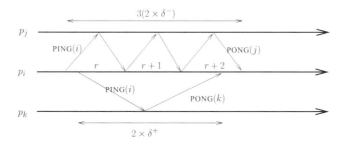

Figure 7.4: Example of message pattern in the theta model with $\theta = 3$

Theorem 7.4 *Let us assume that there are at least two non-faulty processes. The algorithm described in Figure 7.3 builds a perfect failure detector in the θ model.*

Proof Claim C. In any run, the assumption θ and the PING/PONG messages generate θ-fair communication.
The proof follows from this claim and Theorem 7.3.

Proof of claim C. Let us first observe that, until it crashes (if ever it does), a process p_k sends PING() messages and answers by return all the PING() messages it receives. It follows that any two processes permanently exchange messages until one of them crashes (there is no period without messages between any two alive processes).

As there are always messages exchanged between alive processes, it follows from the θ assumption on the maximal ratio on the speed of messages that, when p_i, p_j and p_k are alive, p_i receives at most θ messages from p_j without receiving a message from p_k, which means that communication is θ-fair. End of proof of claim C.

$\square_{Theorem\ 7.4}$

7.4   CONSTRUCTING AN EVENTUALLY PERFECT FAILURE DETECTOR (CLASS $\diamond P$)

7.4.1   FROM PERPETUAL TO EVENTUAL PROPERTIES

A failure detector of the class $\diamond P$ can be built in a system that satisfies an eventual version of the θ assumption or the α-fair communication assumption. These weakened versions are denoted $\diamond\theta$ and $\diamond\alpha$, respectively.

- The $\diamond\theta$ property states that there is a finite (but unknown) time after which the ratio of the upper and lower bounds on message transfer delays is bounded by θ.
- The $\diamond\alpha$ property states that there is a finite (but unknown) time after which communication is α-fair.

As an example, the algorithm presented in Figure 7.5 builds a failure detector of the class $\diamond P$ in a system that satisfies the $\diamond\alpha$ property. This algorithm is a straightforward extension of the algorithm described in Figure 7.2. The aim of the new statements is to correct the false suspicions that occur before communication becomes α-fair.

---

init: $suspected_i \leftarrow \emptyset$;
       for each pair (j, k) **do** $count_i[j, k] \leftarrow 0$ **end for**.

when a message m **is received from** p_j:
     if $(j \in suspected_i)$ **then** $suspected_i \leftarrow suspected_i \setminus \{j\}$ **end if**;
     for each $k \neq j$ **do**
       if $(k \notin suspected_i)$ **then**
         $count_i[j, k] \leftarrow count_i[j, k] + 1$;
         if $(count_i[j, k] > \alpha)$ **then** $suspected_i \leftarrow suspected_i \cup \{k\}$ **end if**
       end if;
       $count_i[k, j] \leftarrow 0$
     end for.

Figure 7.5: Building $\diamond P$ from eventual fair communication (code for p_i)

This algorithm can easily be extended to the case where the bound α exists but is not known by the processes (it is sufficient to increase α each time a false suspicion occurs).

7.4.2   EVENTUALLY SYNCHRONOUS SYSTEMS

Definition   Let an *eventually synchronous* system be a system whose runs satisfy the following properties.

- There is an upper bound δ on message transfer delays, but this bound (1) is not known, and (2) holds only after a finite (but unknown) time (called global stabilization time or GST).
- Local processing times are negligible with respect to message transfer delays, and they are consequently assumed to be of zero duration.

In the following, the notation $\mathcal{AS}_{n,t}[\Diamond Syn]$ is used to denote such a system model.

Let us observe that the previous property requires that, after a finite time, the system forever behaves synchronously. Actually, this is stronger than necessary from the point of view of the algorithms that use a failure detector of the class $\Diamond P$ (that this property allows to build). Let us consider a $\Diamond P$-based algorithm A that is executed consecutively several times. As $\Diamond P$ is useless between successive invocations of A, the property that allows the construction of a failure detector of the class $\Diamond P$ is not required to be satisfied during these periods. The "eventual synchrony" property states the existence of a global stabilization time (namely, "from which forever" ...) only because, to be as general as possible, its statement is formulated in a way that is independent of the way it is used.

A construction of a failure detector of $\Diamond P$ The algorithm is described in Figure 7.6. Each process p_i manages, with respect to each other process p_j, a timer $timer_i[j]$ and a timeout value $timeout_i[j]$. The initial value of $timeout_i[j]$ can be arbitrary; $timer_i[j]$ is initially set to $timeout_i[j]$.

Regularly (e.g., every β_i time units as measured by its local clock), process p_i sends a message ALIVE() to each other process p_j to indicate it is alive. When it receives a message ALIVE() from a process p_j, p_i stops suspecting p_j if it was the case. Moreover, in order to prevent future erroneous suspicions, p_i increases the timeout value currently associated with p_j. Finally, p_i resets $timer_i[j]$ to the current value of $timeout_i[j]$.

```
init: suspected_i ← ∅;
    foreach j ≠ i do
        timeout_i[j] ← arbitrary value; set timer_i[j] to timeout_i[j]
    end for.

repeat forever every β_i time units
    for each j ≠ i do send ALIVE (i) to p_j end for
end repeat.

when timer_i[j] expires: suspected_i ← suspected_i ∪ {j}.

when ALIVE (j) is received:
    if (j ∈ suspected_i) then
        suspected_i ← suspected_i \ {j};
        timeout_i[j] ← timeout_i[j] + 1
    end if;
    set timer_i[j] to timeout_i[j].
```

Figure 7.6: Building $\Diamond P$ in $\mathcal{AS}_{n,t}[\Diamond Syn]$ (code for p_i)

Theorem 7.5   *The algorithm described in Figure 7.6 builds an eventually perfect failure detector in an eventually synchronous system $\mathcal{AS}_{n,t}[\Diamond Syn]$ where $0 \le t < n$.*

Proof Let us first prove the completeness property. Let p_i be a non-faulty process and p_j a process that crashes. It follows that p_j sends a finite number of ALIVE(j) messages. When it receives the last of these messages, p_i resets $timer_i[j]$ for the last time. When $timer_i[j]$ expires for the last time, j is added to $suspected_i$, and as there are no more ALIVE(j) messages, j is never withdrawn from $suspected_i$.

To prove the eventual strong accuracy property, let us consider two non-faulty processes p_i and p_j. We have to show that, after some finite time, the predicate $j \notin suspected_i$ remains forever false.

As p_j is non-faulty, it sends an infinite number of ALIVE() messages to p_i. Each time it receives such a message, p_i suppresses j from $suspected_i$ if j was in this set. If this suppression occurs a finite number of times, the eventual strong accuracy property follows. Hence, let us suppose by contradiction that j is suppressed an infinite number of times from $suspected_i$. It follows that there is a time τ after which the value of $timeout_i[j]$ becomes strictly greater than $\beta_j + \delta$, which means that, from time τ, $timer_i[j]$ is always set to a value $> \beta_j + \delta$ (see Figure 7.7). Let us remember that from time GST, the value δ -that is unknown by the processes- is an upper bound on message transfer delays.

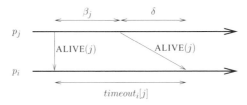

Figure 7.7: The maximal value of $timeout_i[j]$ after GST

Let $\tau' \geq \max(\text{GST}, \tau)$. It then follows from the definition of τ and GST that, after τ', any ALIVE(j) message arrives at p_i before $timer_i[j]$ expires, which concludes the proof. $\square_{Theorem\ 7.5}$

7.4.3   ON THE EFFICIENT MONITORING OF A PROCESS BY ANOTHER PROCESS

Motivation   The previous section has shown that the use of local timers can help implement an eventually perfect failure detector in an eventually synchronous system. While being correct, the algorithm that has been described suffers the following issues. Let us consider Figure 7.8 where process p_i monitors p_j, δ is an upper bound message transfer delay, and δ' is the current value of $timeout_i[j]$.

- Let us consider the left part of the figure. Process p_j has sent a message ALIVE(j) to p_i, and crashed just immediately after that sending. Moreover, this message takes δ time units to

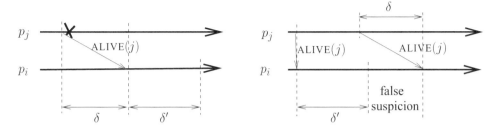

Figure 7.8: Possible issues with timers

travel to p_i. When p_i receives it, it sets its timer to δ'. Finally, as p_j has crashed, the timer will expire, and after the timer has expired, p_i starts suspecting p_j forever.

Let the *detection time* be the duration that elapses between the crash of a process (p_j) and the time when another process (p_i) starts suspecting it permanently. In the previous scenario, the detection time is equal to $\delta + \delta'$. As we can see, this scenario entails the worst detection time.

- Let us consider the right part of the figure. In that case, p_j is non-faulty, but the two consecutive messages ALIVE(j) it sends to p_i are such that the first arrives nearly immediately, while the second takes δ units of time.

  When it receives the first message, p_i sets its timer to δ'. As the second message has not yet arrived when the timer expires, p_i suspects p_j, and will stop suspecting it when it will receive the second message. This creates a *false suspicion* period.

Aim   The aim is to design an algorithm that solves the two previous issues, by reducing both the detection time of a crashed process, and the duration of false suspicion periods. The monitoring algorithm that is presented below attains these goals when the probabilistic distribution of message transfer delay is a priori know by the processes.

System model   Each pair of processes is connected by reliable channels, and message delays follow some probabilistic distribution. $E(delay)$ denotes the average transit time. The algorithm that appears below describes the monitoring of a process p_j by a process p_i. It can be trivially extended to the monitoring of all processes by process p_i.

A monitoring algorithm   It is easy to see that the issues described in Figure 7.8 are due to the fact that the timer is reset only when an ALIVE() message arrives; if a message is late, the timer is reset too lately. The belated arrival of the ALIVE() messages increases the uncertainty of the system.

This suggests to base a solution on an appropriate definition of the time instants at which a timer is reset. To that end, some monotonicity is created as follows.

- On the side of the monitored process p_j.

- Process p_j sends its ALIVE() messages at regular time intervals $\sigma_1, \sigma_2 \ldots$ where regularity is defined as follows: $\forall sn \geq 1 : \sigma_{sn+1} - \sigma_{sn} = \Delta$ (a positive value, known by both p_j and p_i).
- A sequence number sn is associated with each message. ALIVE(j, sn) is sent at local time σ_{sn}.

- On the side of the monitoring process p_i.
    - The sequence number associated with each message allows us to associate a lifetime with it. Operationally, this is captured by defining a time instant ρ_{sn} defining the deadline after which ALIVE(j, sn) is meaningless (because it arrives too late).
    - The sequence $\rho_0, \rho_1, \ldots$ is defined as follows. $\forall sn \geq 1 : \rho_{sn+1} = \rho_{sn} + \Delta$, and $\rho_1 = \sigma_1 + \Delta + d$. The value d is a predefined value that can be set to $E(delay) + d'$ (where d' is a "safety margin" added to the average transit delay).

      Only if it arrives before ρ_{sn}, the message ALIVE(j, sn) is taken into account. More precisely, let τ be a time instant at which p_i queries the status of p_j, with $\rho_{sn-1} < \tau \leq \rho_{sn}$. Process p_i trusts (i.e., does not suspect) p_j, if and only if it has received a message ALIVE(j, x) such that $x \geq sn$.

The corresponding algorithm is described in Figure 7.9. The variable $output_i$ takes the value *suspect* or *no suspect*. It is initialized to *suspect*. The local variable sn is initialized to 1, and (as already indicated) the initial value of ρ_1 is $\sigma_1 + \Delta + d$. Due to its very construction, this solution can not suffer from premature timeouts (such as the one depicted on the right part of Figure 7.8).

---

when *local time* $= \rho_{sn}$:
    if (no ALIVE(j, x) received with $x > sn$) **then** $output_i \leftarrow suspect$ **end if**;
    $sn \leftarrow sn + 1$; **let** $\rho_{sn} = \rho_{sn+1} + \Delta$.

when ALIVE(j, x) **is received**:
    if (*local time* $\leq \rho_{sn}$) $\wedge$ ($x \geq sn$) **then** $output_i \leftarrow no\ suspect$ **end if**.

Figure 7.9: A simple monitoring algorithm (p_i monitors p_j)

Illustration   Considering that p_j does not crash, Figure 7.10 depicts three possible scenarios.
- On the first scenario (top left part of the figure), the message ALIVE(j, sn) arrives before ρ_{sn-1}, hence before its deadline ρ_{sn}. Consequently, p_j is not suspected from the message arrival until ρ_{sn}.
- On the second scenario (top right part of the figure), the message ALIVE(j, sn) arrives after ρ_{sn-1} but before its deadline ρ_{sn}. As before, p_j is not suspected from the message arrival until ρ_{sn}, but differently from the previous scenario, it is suspected between ρ_{sn-1} and the message arrival.

- On the third scenario (bottom part of the figure), the message ALIVE(j, sn) arrives after ρ_{sn}, i.e., after its deadline. Consequently, p_j is suspected from ρ_{sn-1} until another message ALIVE(j, sn') arrives before its deadline $\rho_{sn'}$.

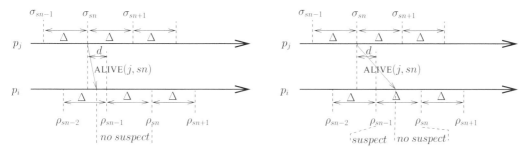

Message ALIVE(j, sn) arrives early   Message ALIVE(j, sn) arrives late but before the deadline

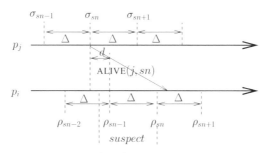

Message ALIVE(j, sn) arrives too late (after deadline)

Figure 7.10: The three cases for the arrival of ALIVE(j, sn)

Finally, if p_j crashes between the sending of ALIVE(j, sn) and the sending of ALIVE$(j, sn + 1)$, it is easy to see that p_i will suspect it permanently from time ρ_{sn}.

7.4.4   AN ADAPTIVE ALGORITHM

Adaptiveness   The algorithm of Section 7.4.2, which builds a failure detector of the class $\diamond P$ in an eventually synchronous system, is based on a broadcasting technique: regularly, each process sends an ALIVE() message to indicate that it is alive (or more precisely, it was alive when it sent the message). This section presents an algorithm based on a totally different approach based on a monitoring technique.

This algorithm directs each process p_i to observe each other process p_j and consequently detect its crash. This observation (monitoring) is *adaptive* (or lazy) in the sense that it uses the application messages sent by p_i to p_j and acknowledgments whenever it is possible. Additional control messages from p_i to p_j are used only in periods where all the application messages sent by p_i to p_j have been acknowledged.

Local clocks   Each process p_i uses a hardware clock (denoted h_clock_i) to measure round-trip delays. These clocks are purely local: they are not synchronized, and there is no assumption on their possible drift. The only assumption on the behavior of a clock is that, between two consecutive steps of p_i, it is increased at least by 1.

Monitoring   In addition to sending and receiving application messages, a process p_i can invoke query (j). That operation returns *suspect* or *no suspect*. In the first case, p_i adds j to $suspected_i$. In the second case, it withdraws j from $suspected_i$ if it was in this set.

Messages and local variables   The algorithm uses three types of protocol messages, namely APPL(msg), ACK(msg), and SUBST(msg). A protocol message msg is made up of two fields that contain a value and a local date.

- APPL(msg). In that case, the field $msg.content$ contains the application message m that p_i wants to send to p_j, and the field $msg.send\_time$ contains the local date at which this message is sent by p_i.
- ACK(msg). In that case, the field $msg.content$ is irrelevant, while $msg.send\_time$ contains the sending date of the message that is acknowledged (and not the sending date of the acknowledgment).
- SUBST(msg). This type of message acts as a substitute for an application message when all the application messages sent by p_i have been acknowledged by p_j.

Each process p_i manages two local data structures.

- $pending\_send\_time_i[1..n]$ is an array such that, for any $j \neq i$, $pending\_send\_time_i[j]$ is a set (initially empty) that contains the sending dates (as measured by h_clock_i) of the messages sent by p_i to p_j and not yet acknowledged.
- $max\_rtd_i[1..n]$ is an array such that $max\_rtd_i[j]$ is an integer variable (initially to 0) that contains the greatest round-trip delay of the messages that have been sent by p_i to p_j and have been acknowledged. (In practice, $max\_rtd_i[j]$ can be initialized to a round-trip delay known from previous executions.)

Process behavior   The algorithm is described in Figure 7.11. When p_i wants to send an application message m to p_j, a protocol message APPL(msg) is defined and sent to p_j. Moreover, the local sending date is added to $pending\_send\_time_i[j]$.

The processing of a protocol message that has been sent by a process p_j and is received by p_i depends on its type.

- The message is APPL(msg). In that case, its content $msg.content$ is delivered to the upper layer, and ACK(msg) is sent by return to p_j. It is important to notice that an ACK() message carries exactly the same value $msg.send\_time$ as the APPL() message that entails its sending.

- The message is SUBST(msg). In that case, the message is a pure control message. ACK(msg) is sent by return to p_j.

- The message is ACK(msg). In that case, the application message $msg.content$ sent by p_i to p_j is acknowledged by p_j. Process p_i computes the corresponding round-trip delay (that is equal to $h\_clock_i - msg.send\_time$) and updates accordingly $max\_rtd_i[j]$; p_i also suppresses the sending date $msg.send\_time$ from the set $pending\_send\_time_i[j]$.

Finally, the operation query(j) is realized as follows. There are two cases according to the current value of the set $pending\_send\_time_i[j]$.

- $pending\_send\_time_i[j] \neq \emptyset$. In that case, p_i computes a lower bound for the round-trip delay of the oldest message sent by p_i to p_j that has not yet been acknowledged. This lower bound lb is the current value of $h\_clock_i - \min(pending\_send\_time_i[j])$. Then, if $lb > max\_rtd_i[j]$, p_i suspects p_j. Otherwise, it returns $no\ suspect$.

- $pending\_send\_time_i[j] = \emptyset$. In that case, all the application messages sent by p_i to p_j have been acknowledged. Hence, p_i creates a substitute (control) message, sends it to p_j, and returns $no\ suspect$ to the current query concerning p_j.

Theorem 7.6   *The algorithm described in Figure 7.11 can be used to build an eventually perfect failure detector in an eventually synchronous system $\mathcal{AS}_{n,t}[\diamond Syn]$ where $1 \leq t < n$.*

Proof Proof of the completeness property. (This proof does not rely on the eventual synchrony of the system.) Let p_j be a process that crashes and p_i be a non-faulty process. As p_j crashes there is a time τ_a after which all the messages it has sent to p_i have been received. It follows that, after τ_a,
- (O1) $max\_rtd_i[j]$ remains always equal to some value R, and
- (O2) no value is suppressed from $pending\_send\_time_i[j]$.
We show that there is a time $\tau_b \geq \tau_a$ after which every invocation query (j) issued by p_i returns the value $suspect$ (which proves the completeness property). There are two cases.

- Case 1: at time τ_a, there is a message APPL (msg), or SUBST (msg), that has not been acknowledged by p_j. After τ_a, we have then:
  - (O3) The date $msg.send\_time$ remains forever in the set $pending\_send\_time_i[j]$, and
  - (O4) Due to O2 and O3, $\min(pending\_send\_time_i[j])$ remains forever $\leq msg.send\_time$.

  Let us consider the execution of an infinite sequence of query (j) issued by p_i after τ_a. We have the following:
  - (O5) Due to O3, during each query (j), p_i executes always the **else** part of the first **if** statement.

  Let $rt(1), rt(2), \ldots$ be the sequence of dates obtained by p_i when it reads h_clock_i (in the **else** part). Due to the monotonicity and the granularity of the local clock, we have $rt(1) < rt(2) < \ldots$ It follows that there is an integer x such that

```
when "send m to p_j" is invoked:
    create msg; msg.content ← m; msg.send_time ← h_clock_i;
    pending_send_time_i[j] ← pending_send_time_i[j] ∪ {msg.send_time};
    send APPL(msg) to p_j.

when TYPE(msg) is received from p_j:
    case TYPE=APPL   then deliver msg.content; msg.content ← ⊥;
                              send ACK(msg) to p_j
         TYPE=SUBST  then send ACK(msg) to p_j
         TYPE=ACK    then rt ← h_clock_i;
                              max_rtd_i[j] ← max(max_rtd_i[j], rt − msg.send_time);
                              pending_send_time_i[j] ← pending_send_time_i[j] \ {msg.send_time}
    end case.

operation query(j):
    if (pending_send_time_i[j] = ∅)
        then create msg; msg.content ← ⊥; msg.send_time ← h_clock_i;
             send SUBST(msg) to p_j;
             pending_send_time_i[j] ← {msg.send_time};
             return (no suspect)
        else rt ← h_clock_i;
             if (rt − min(pending_send_time_i[j]) > max_rtd_i[j])
                      then return (suspect)
                      else return (no suspect)
             end if
    end if.
```

Figure 7.11: A lazy algorithm that builds $\lozenge P$ in $\mathcal{AS}_{n,t}[\lozenge Syn]$ (code for p_i)

- (O6): $\forall y \geq x$: the predicate $(rt(y) > msg.send\_time + R)$ is true.

It follows from the observations (O1), (O4) and (O6) that there is a time $\tau_b \geq \tau_a$ after which the predicate $\big(rt - \min(pending\_send\_time_i[j]) > max\_rtd_i[j]\big)$ is always satisfied when p_i invokes query (j). Consequently, after τ_b, query (j) always returns *suspect*, which proves the case.

- Case 2: at time τ_a, each message APPL (msg) or SUBST (msg) sent by p_i to p_j, has been acknowledged by p_j. Hence, $pending\_send\_time_i[j] = \emptyset$ at τ_a. It follows that the first invocation of query (j) by p_i issued after τ_a, executes the **then** part of the first **if** statement. Process p_i creates a control message SUBST (msg), adds $msg.send\_time$ to $pending\_send\_time_i[j]$ and sends the message to p_j. We are then in Case 1 whose proof appears above.

Proof of the eventual strong accuracy property. This proof relies on the eventual synchrony property of the system. Let p_i and p_j be two non-faulty processes, and τ_{ub} a time after which there is an upper bound on message transfer delays. Moreover, let $\tau_a \geq \tau_{ub}$ be a time after which the

ACK () messages send by p_j to p_i, that are associated with the APPL () and SUBST () messages sent by p_i to p_j before τ_{ub}, have been received by p_i.

Claim C1. There is a time $\tau_b \geq \tau_a$ such that the predicate $\left(rt - \min(pending\_send\_time_i[j]) > max\_rtd_i[j]\right)$ is never satisfied after τ_b.

Let us consider an invocation query (j) issued by p_i after τ_b. If p_i executes the **then** part of the first **if** statement it returns the value *no suspect*. If it executes the **else** part, it follows from Claim C1 that the predicate $\left(rt - \min(pending\_send\_time_i[j]) > max\_rtd_i[j]\right)$ is false, and, consequently, p_i returns also the value *no suspect*, which establishes the eventual strong accuracy property.

Proof of claim C1. It follows from the definition of τ_{ub}, and the fact that $\tau_a \geq \tau_{ub}$, that, from time τ_a, message round-trip delays are upper bounded by some value Δ.

Let us consider the value of $rt - \min(pending\_send\_time_i[j])$ when, after τ_a, p_i evaluates the predicate in the **else** part of the first **if** statement (let us notice that, as p_i is in the **else** part, we necessarily have $pending\_send\_time_i[j] \neq 0$). Let msg be such that $msg.send\_time = \min(pending\_send\_time_i[j])$ (msg is a message typed APPL or SUBST that has been sent by p_i to p_j after τ_a and is not yet acknowledged).

Due to (a) the bound Δ, (b) the fact that ACK(msg) has not yet been received but will be received (because p_j is non-faulty and channels are reliable), and (c) the fact that rt is the current time value, it follows that $rt - msg.send\_time < RT_{msg} - msg.send\_time \leq \Delta$, where RT_{msg} is p_i's local time at which ACK(msg) will be received (which implies $rt < RT_{msg}$). There are two cases.

- Case 1: at τ_a, we have $max\_rtd_i[j] \geq \Delta$. In that case, we have $rt - msg.send\_time < RT_{msg} - msg.send\_time \leq \Delta \leq max\_rtd_i[j]$, and the claim follows.

- Case 2: at τ_a, we have $max\_rtd_i[j] < \Delta$. We claim (Claim C2) that after some finite time $\tau_c \geq \tau_a$, $max\_rtd_i[j]$ remains constant, equal to a value Δ'. This means that Δ' is an upper bound for the round-trip delays between p_i and p_j. We then have $RT_{msg} - msg.send\_time \leq \Delta'$, which terminates the proof of claim C1.

  Proof of claim C2. Let us suppose by contradiction that $max\_rtd_i[j]$ never stops increasing. (Due to the granularity assumption of the local clock h_clock_i, $max\_rtd_i[j]$ increases by steps ≥ 1.) It follows that the sequence of values taken by the quantity $\Delta - max\_rtd_i[j]$ is monotonically decreasing and eventually becomes negative. A contradiction as Δ is an upper bound for the round-trip delays between p_i and p_j. End of proof of claim C2. $\square$
  $\square_{Theorem\ 7.6}$

7.5 CONSTRUCTING AN EVENTUAL LEADER FAILURE DETECTOR (CLASS Ω)

This section presents algorithms that build failure detectors of the class Ω in different systems models. Each model is a variant of $\mathcal{AS}_{n,t}[\emptyset]$ enriched with an appropriate assumption. While some of these assumptions are weaker than others, let us remember that the existence of the "weakest synchrony assumptions" (if any) that allow Ω to be built is still an open problem (end of 2009).

7.5.1   ELECTING THE NON-FAULTY PROCESS WITH THE SMALLEST IDENTITY

A synchrony assumption   Similarly to previous chapters, the system is made up of n processes $p_1, \ldots, p_n$ such that i is the identity of p_i. We suppose (without loss of generality) that only message transfer takes time (the processing associated with a message reception can be seen as being part of its transfer time). Moreover, each pair of processes is connected by two directed channels, one in each direction. The channel from p_i to p_j is *eventually timely* if there is a finite time τ (that remains unknown to the processes), and a bound δ, such that, after time τ, each message sent by p_i to p_j is received by time $\tau + \delta$.

Let $\Diamond T$ denote the following assumption: the output channels of the non-faulty process with the smallest identity (let us denote it q) are eventually timely.

It is important to notice that q can be p_i in some runs and another process p_j in another run. The answer to "which process is q" depends on the failure pattern. Moreover, let us remark that the assumption $\Diamond T$ imposes a constraint only on the output channels of the non-faulty process with the smallest identity. The other channels can be asynchronous.

Notation   The previous system model made up of asynchronous crash-prone processes connected by unidirectional asynchronous channels, and where each run satisfies assumption $\Diamond T$ is denoted $\mathcal{AS}_{n,t}[\Diamond T]$. It follows from its definition that this system model is weaker than the eventually synchronous system model $\mathcal{AS}_{n,t}[\Diamond Syn]$ (which requires all the channels to be eventually timely).

Electing an eventual leader in $\mathcal{AS}_{n,t}[\Diamond T]$ In each run of such a system, the aim is to elect the non-faulty process with the smallest identity. The algorithm succeeds if its output channels are eventually timely (which is always the case when the system is eventually synchronous).

To that end, each process p_i maintains a local variable $leader_i$ that contains the identity of the process it currently considers as leader. Initially, each process p_i considers p_1 as leader (i.e., $leader_i = 1$). Then, if it suspects p_1, p_i considers p_2 as its current leader, etc. If it suspects all the processes with an identity smaller than its own identity, p_i considers it is leader and starts sending regularly (every β time units, where β is a predefined constant) a message LEADER(i) to the processes with a higher identity.

The suspicion mechanism is based on timeout values. Hence, each p_i manages an array of timeout values denoted $timeout_i[1..i-1]$. If $leader_i = j \neq i$ (we have then $1 \leq j < i$), and p_i has not received a message LEADER(j) during the last $timeout_i[j]$ time units, it suspects p_j to have crashed and accordingly updates $leader_i$ to $leader_i + 1$.

If p_i receives a message LEADER(j) while $leader_i = j$, it resets its timer $timer_i$ to the value kept in $timeout_i[j]$. Differently, if $j < leader_i$, it discovers that it has erroneously suspected

p_j. Consequently, p_i resets $leader_i$ to j, and increases $timeout_i[j]$ to prevent future erroneous suspicions. The corresponding algorithm is described in Figure 7.12.

---

init: for each $j \in \{1, \ldots, i-1\}$ **do** $timeout_i[j] \leftarrow$ default value **end for**;
    $leader_i \leftarrow 1$; set $timer_i$ to $timeout_i[1]$.

repeat every β **time units**
    if $(leader_i = i)$ **then**
        for each $j \in \{i+1, \ldots, n\}$ **do** send LEADER(i) to p_j **end for**
    end if
end repeat.

when LEADER(j) **is received**:
    case $(j = leader_i)$ **then** set $timer_i(i)$ to $timeout_i[j]$
            $(j < leader_i)$ **then** $leader_i \leftarrow j$;
                        $timeout_i[j] \leftarrow timeout_i[j] + 1$;
                        set $timer_i$ to $timeout_i[j]$
            $(j > leader_i)$ **then** skip
    end case.

when $timer_i$ **expires**:
    $leader_i \leftarrow leader_i + 1$;
    if $(leader_i \neq i)$ **then** set $timer_i$ to $timeout_i[leader_i]$ **end if**.

Figure 7.12: Building Ω in $\mathcal{AS}_{n,t}[\lozenge T]$ (code for p_i)

Theorem 7.7 *The algorithm described in Figure 7.12 builds a failure detector of the class Ω (eventual leader) in $\mathcal{AS}_{n,t}[\lozenge T]$ where $0 \leq t < n$.*

    The proof shows that, after a finite time, the non-faulty process $q = p_\ell$ with the smallest identity is elected as the permanent leader. This is a consequence of the assumption that this process has eventually timely output channels.

Proof In the claims that follow, time τ is the time defined in claim C1.

Claim C1. $\exists \tau$ after which $\forall i \in Correct(F): leader_i \geq \ell$.
Proof of claim C1. (This proof is independent of the timely behavior of some channels.) As ℓ is the smallest identity of a non-faulty process, there is a time τ' after which the output channels of p_ℓ are timely, the faulty processes have crashed (this includes $p_1, \ldots, p_{\ell-1}$), and the messages they sent have been received. Let p_i $(i \geq \ell)$ be any non-faulty process.

1. At time τ', $leader_i \geq \ell$. As, after τ', no process p_x with $x < \ell$ sends messages, p_i will never receive message LEADER(x). It follows that $leader_i$ will never be updated to a value smaller than ℓ. In that case let $\tau = \tau'$.

2. At time τ', $leader_i = x < \ell$. As p_x has crashed, p_i will never receive LEADER(x). Consequently, $timer_i$ (that has been set to $timeout_i[x]$ when $leader_i$ was set to x) expires and p_i

sets $leader_i$ to $x + 1$ at time τ''. If $x + 1 = \ell$, the first item applies, and the claim follows with $\tau = \tau''$. If $x + 1 < \ell$, this second item is repeated with $leader_i = x + 1 < \ell$. It follows that $leader_i$ is eventually set to $x + 2$. And this is repeated until $leader_i = \ell$, which defines the value of τ, and concludes the proof. End of proof of claim C1.

Claim C2. From time τ, $leader_\ell = \ell$ remains always true.
Proof of claim C2. It follows from the initialization ($leader_\ell \leftarrow 1$) and the statement executed when $timer_\ell$ expires, that $leader_\ell$ remains always smaller or equal to ℓ. The claim then follows from this observation combined with claim C1. End of proof of claim C2.

Claim C3. There is a time after which p_ℓ sends regularly and forever LEADER(ℓ).
Proof of claim C3. The proof follows from C2 and the code of the **repeat** statement. End of proof of C3.

Claim C4. Let p_i be a non-faulty process such that $i \neq \ell$. If there is a time $\tau' > \tau$ at which $leader_i > \ell$, then there is a time $\tau'' > \tau'$ at which $leader_i = \ell$.
Proof of claim C4. After time τ, p_ℓ sends forever LEADER(ℓ) every β time units to any process p_i such that $i > \ell$. The first message LEADER(ℓ) sent by p_ℓ after τ' is sent at the latest at time $\tau' + \beta$ and received by p_i at the latest at time $\tau'' = \tau' + \beta + \delta$ (where δ is the bound defined in the assumption $\Diamond T$). Due to claim C1, at τ'' we have $leader_i \geq \ell$. It then follows from the code of the algorithm that, if not yet done, p_i sets $leader_i$ to ℓ at time $\tau'' > \tau' > \tau$. End of proof of claim C4.

Claim C5. After time τ, any non-faulty process p_i updates $leader_i$ to a value different from ℓ, a finite number of times.
Proof of claim C5. Let us first observe that, due to claim C4, at $\tau'' > \tau$, if not yet done, p_i sets $leader_i$ to ℓ. Let us assume by contradiction that it then changes $leader_i$ from ℓ to values different from ℓ, an infinite number of times. It follows from C4 that $leader_i$ changes an infinite number of times from a value different from ℓ to ℓ.

It follows from the algorithm that $leader_i$ changes from ℓ to $\ell + 1$ if two messages LEADER(ℓ) are received by p_i more than $timeout_i[\ell]$ time units apart. Let us notice that after τ, two messages LEADER(ℓ) are received by p_i at most $\beta + \delta$ time units apart. Every time $leader_i$ is changed from ℓ to a value different from ℓ, $timeout_i[\ell]$ is increased by 1. It follows that after a finite time we have $timeout_i[\ell] > \beta + \delta$. After this has occurred, due to claim C4, we eventually have again $leader_i = \ell$. Then, $timeout_i[\ell]$ does not expire, which contradicts the assumption and proves the claim. End of proof of claim C5.

The theorem follows from claim C2 for process p_ℓ and claims C4 and C5 for the other non-faulty processes. These claims show that in $\mathcal{AS}_{n,t}[\Diamond T]$, there is a finite time after which all the non-faulty processes have the same leader and this leader is one of them. $\Box_{Theorem\ 7.7}$

Communication efficiency   The property "after the common leader has been elected, it is the only process to send messages" is called *communication efficiency*. This is an optimality property because, in order not to suspect the common leader once it has been elected, a process needs to receive forever (directly or indirectly) messages indicating that the leader is still alive. Let us observe that the previous algorithm is communication efficient.

Remark on fairness with respect to process identities   Due to the model $\mathcal{AS}_{n,t}[\Diamond T]$, the previous Ω algorithm is *unfair* in the sense that it favors processes based on their identities. To be more explicit, let us assume that f processes crash in a run. The processes $p_{f+2}, \ldots, p_n$ cannot be elected in that run. More generally, whatever the run, the processes $p_{t+2}, \ldots, p_n$ can never be elected because their identities are never the smallest identity of a non-faulty process. Moreover, if p_{t+2} is non-faulty and is also the only process that has eventually timely channels, the $\Diamond T$ assumption is not satisfied and the algorithm does not work. Differently, if the identities of p_{t+2} and p_1 were exchanged, then it would be elected. It is nevertheless important to notice that, when the algorithm is executed in an eventually synchronous model, a process is always elected (this is because, in such a system, all channels are eventually timely). The Ω algorithms that are presented in the next sections do not suffer from this unfairness problem.

Weakening the model   The reader can check that the algorithm presented in Figure 7.12 remains correct in a weakened version of $\mathcal{AS}_{n,t}[\Diamond T]$. The weakening is on the behavior on the channels, namely any channel can lose and duplicate (a finite number of times) messages, but the output channels of the non-faulty process with the smallest identity (after they become eventually timely).

7.5.2   EVENTUAL LEADER IN THE SYSTEM MODEL $\mathcal{AS}_{n,t}[\Diamond t\text{-source}]$

The $\Diamond t$-source assumption   This assumption is as follows: There is a non-faulty process q that has t output channels that are eventually timely. The corresponding system model is denoted $\mathcal{AS}_{n,t}[\Diamond t\text{-source}]$. As we can see, only t output channels of a non-faulty process are required to be eventually timely. All the other channels are reliable and asynchronous.

Let us observe that, after a process p_j has crashed, the channel from any process p_i to p_j is timely whatever the transit time of the messages sent by p_i. This is because, as p_j has crashed, everything appears as if each of these messages is received δ time units after been sent.

Electing an eventual leader in $\mathcal{AS}_{n,t}[\Diamond t\text{-source}]$ An algorithm that elects an eventual leader in the system model $\mathcal{AS}_{n,t}[\Diamond t\text{-source}]$ is described in Figure 7.13. The idea is to elect the less suspected (to have crashed) non-faulty process. As we are about to see, the $\Diamond t$-source assumption on the channels behavior provides enough synchrony to ensure that a non-faulty process will become common leader. The algorithm requires the processes to know the value of the system parameter t.

Each process p_i manages the following local variables.

- Two arrays $timer_i[1..n]$ and $timeout_i[1..n]$, such that $timeout_i[j]$ contains the current time-out value that p_i uses to monitor p_j, while $timer_i[j]$ is the associated local timer. Each $timeout_i[j]$ is initialized to a predefined value β and $timer_i[j]$ is initially set to that value.

  As a process p_i does not monitor itself, $timeout_i[i]$ and $timer_i[i]$ are useless.

- An array $count_i[1..n]$, such that $count_i[j]$ counts the number of suspicions of process p_j that have been committed (see below). The initial value of $count_i[j]$ is 0.

- An array $suspect_i[1..n]$, such that $suspect_i[j]$ contains the identities of the process that currently suspect p_j to have crashed. If enough processes suspect p_j, namely, $|suspect_i[j]| \geq n - t$, these suspicions are committed and p_i increases $count_i[j]$ by 1. The initial value of $suspect_i[j]$ is $\emptyset$.

```
init: for each k do
          count_i[k] ← 0; suspect_i[k] ← ∅; timeout_i[k] ← β;
          if (k ≠ i) then set timer_i[k] to timeout_i[k] end if
      end for.

repeat every β time units
      for each j ≠ i do send ALIVE(count_i) to p_j end for
end repeat.

when ALIVE(count) is received from p_j:
      for each k ∈ {1, ..., n} do count_i[k] ← max(count_i[k], count[k]) end for;
      set timer_i[j] to timeout_i[j].

when timer_i[k] expires:
      for each j ∈ {1, ..., n} do send SUSPECT(k) to p_j;
      timeout_i[k] ← timeout_i[k] + 1;
      set timer_i[k] to timeout_i[k].

when SUSPECT(k) is received from p_j:
      suspect_i[k] ← suspect_i[k] ∪ {j};
      if (|suspect_i[k]| ≥ (n - t)) then count_i[k] ← count_i[k] + 1; suspect_i[k] ← ∅ end if.

when leader_i is read by the upper layer:
      let (−, ℓ) = min ({(count_i[x], x)}_{1≤x≤n});
      return (ℓ).
```

Figure 7.13: Building Ω in $\mathcal{AS}_{n,t}[\Diamond t\text{-source}]$ (code for p_i)

A process p_i regularly sends a message ALIVE($count_i$) to each other process. This message has two aims: ALIVE() is to inform the other processes that p_i is still alive, while its content ($count_i$) provides them with its current suspicion view. Hence, when it receives a message ALIVE($count$) from a process p_j, p_i updates its suspicion array $count_i[1..n]$ and resets its timer $timer_i[j]$ to the current value of $timeout_i[j]$.

When $timer_i[k]$ expires, p_i suspects p_k to have crashed, but it does not commit this local suspicion. Instead, it sends to each process a message SUSPECT(k) to inform them on this local suspicion. Moreover, whether p_k has crashed or not, p_i increases $timeout_i[k]$ and resets $timer_i[k]$ to that new value.

When it receives SUSPECT(k) from any process p_j, p_i first adds j to $suspect_i[k]$ (the set of processes that locally suspect p_k). Then, if enough processes locally suspect p_k, i.e., $|suspect_i[k]| \geq (n - t)$, p_i commits these local suspicions and transforms them into a global suspicion by increasing $count_i[k]$. (The gossiping of the ALIVE($count_i$) messages is used to disseminate the committed suspicions.)

Finally, when $leader_i$ is read by the upper layer application process, the identity of the less suspected process is returned. As several processes can be equally suspected, process identities are used to tie-break, if needed. More precisely, the function $\min(X)$, where X is a set of pairs of integers (such that no two pairs have the same second element) returns the smallest pair according to lexicographical order, i.e., $(v1, x) < (v2, y) \equiv \big((v1 < v2) \vee (v1 = v2 \wedge x < y)\big)$.

Remark It is easy to see that process identities are used only to tie-break when several processes are equally less suspected. If there is a single process that is the less suspected, its identity does not participate in the fact it is elected. In that sense, the algorithm is fair with respect the process identities. On another side, as each non-faulty process sends forever messages, this algorithm is not communication-efficient.

The case $t = 1$ An interesting case, that is a common assumption in practice, is $t = 1$. In that case, Ω can be implemented if the system has only one eventually timely link. Consequently, this very weak synchrony assumption is sufficient to solve consensus in systems where at most one process may crash (i.e., consensus can be solved in $\mathcal{AS}_{n,1}[\Diamond 1\text{-source}]$).

Theorem 7.8 *The algorithm described in Figure 7.13 builds an eventual leader failure detector in the system model $\mathcal{AS}_{n,t}[\Diamond t\text{-source}]$.*

Proof Claim C1. $\forall i, j : count_i[j]$ never decreases. (The proof of this claim follows directly from the code of the algorithm.)

Claim C2. $\forall i, j$, if p_j is non-faulty and has t eventually timely output channels, then $count_i[j]$ is bounded.
Proof of claim C2. Let $p_{h(1)}, \ldots, p_{h(t)}$ be the t processes such that the channel from p_j to each $p_{h(x)}$ is eventually timely. It follows from the fact that these channels are timely and the management of the timers $timer_{h(x)}[j], 1 \leq x \leq t$, that there is a time after which no process $p_{h(x)}$ sends a message SUSPECT(j). Moreover, the process p_j never sends a message SUSPECT(j). It follows that, after some finite time, a set $suspect_i[j]$ can contain at most $(n - t - 1)$ identities, and, consequently, no process p_i can increase $count_i[j]$ because the predicate $|suspect_i[j]| \geq (n - t)$ remains false.

Finally, let us observe that, while the gossiping of the ALIVE($count_k$) messages can entail the increase of entries of some local arrays, it cannot by itself make these entries increase forever.

It follows from the previous arguments that, if p_j is non-faulty and has t eventually timely output channels, for any process p_i, $count_i[j]$ is bounded. End of proof of claim C2.

Claim C3. There is a time after which the bounded entries of the *count* arrays of the non-faulty processes remain forever equal.
Proof of claim C3. This is an immediate consequence of the gossiping of ALIVE(*count*) messages and the fact that, when such a message is received, each entry $count_i[k]$ is updated to $\max(count_i[k], count[k])$. End of proof of claim C3.

Claim C4. $\forall\ i, k$, if p_i is non-faulty and p_k is faulty, $count_i[k]$ is unbounded.
Proof of claim C4. Let p_j be any non-faulty process. As p_k is faulty, there is a time after which it does no longer send ALIVE() messages. Consequently, $timer_j[k]$ expires, and, consequently, p_i resets this timer. Hence, $timer_j[k]$ expires an infinite number of times.

Each time $timer_j[k]$ expires, p_j broadcasts SUSPECT(k). As this is done by each non-faulty process, it follows that, after a finite time, the predicate $|suspect_i[k]| \geq (n - t)$ is true at every non-faulty process p_i, which accordingly increases $count_i[k]$. As the timer $timer_j[k]$ of each correct process p_j expires an infinite number of times, it follows that $count_i[k]$ increases forever. End of proof of claim C4.

Let p_i be any non-faulty process. Due to the $\lozenge t$-source assumption, there is at least one non-faulty process p_j that has t eventually timely output channels. It then follows from claim C2 that there is at least one entry of $count_i[j]$ that remains bounded. Moreover, due to claim C4, only entries associated with non-faulty processes can remain bounded. It follows from these observations, and claim C1, that after some finite time, a non-faulty process elects forever the same non-faulty leader. Finally, it follows from claim C3 that the same eventual leader is elected by the non-faulty processes.
$\qquad\qquad\qquad\qquad\qquad\qquad\qquad\qquad\qquad\qquad\qquad\qquad\qquad$ $\square_{Theorem\ 7.8}$

7.5.3   EVENTUAL LEADER IN THE SYSTEM MODEL $\mathcal{AS}_{n,t}[\lozenge MP]$

This section presents an algorithm that constructs a failure detector of the class Ω without relying on timers or physical time-related assumptions.

A query/response mechanism   The following query/response mechanism can be built in $\mathcal{AS}_{n,t}[\emptyset]$. Process p_i broadcasts a message QUERY_ALIVE() and waits for the corresponding RESPONSE() messages from $(n - t)$ processes (the maximum number of messages from distinct processes it can wait for without risking to be blocked forever). To simplify the presentation (and without loss of generality), it is assumed that a process receives always its own response. An example of such an exchange message pattern is described in Figure 7.14.

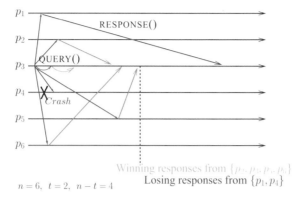

Figure 7.14: Winning vs losing responses

The first $(n - t)$ responses to a query that a process p_i receives are *winning* responses. The other responses are *losing*. As, after it has crashed, a process never answers a query, its (missing) responses are defined as being losing responses. In the example given in the figure, when considering p_3, the responses from p_2, p_3, p_5 and p_6 are winning responses, while the response from p_1 and p_4 are losing (the one from p_1 because it arrives late, and the one from p_4 because it is never sent).

The message pattern assumption $\diamond MP$ This assumption is as follows: there is a finite time τ, a non-faulty process q, and a set Q of $(t + 1)$ processes such that, after τ, each process p_j, with $j \in Q$, receives always a winning response from q to each of its queries (until p_j possibly crashes). (Time τ, process q and set Q need not be explicitly known by the processes.)

An example is given in Figure 7.15 where $n = 6$ and $t = 2$. We have $Q = \{1, 2, 4\}$, and $q = p_2$.

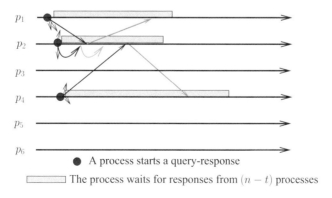

Figure 7.15: An example illustrating the assumption $\diamond MP$

The system model $\mathcal{AS}_{n,t}[\emptyset]$ enriched with $\Diamond MP$ is denoted $\mathcal{AS}_{n,t}[\Diamond MP]$. There is no timing constraint on message transfer delays in that model; they can increase forever. $\Diamond MP$ does not involve timers or physical time. It only states a delivery order on some messages.

Let us observe that the set Q can contain crashed processes. After a process p_j has crashed, it does no longer issue queries, and consequently, the predicate "each query issued after it has crashed receives a winning response from q" is satisfied. It follows that, if a set Q' of t processes crash, after they have crashed and the messages they sent have been received, all response messages are winning.

$\mathcal{AS}_{n,t}[\Diamond MP]$ vs $\mathcal{AS}_{n,t}[\Diamond t\text{-source}]$ These two behavioral assumptions cannot be compared, none of them is stronger than the other. Transit times are arbitrary in $\mathcal{AS}_{n,t}[\Diamond MP]$, while some channels are eventually timely in $\mathcal{AS}_{n,t}[\Diamond t\text{-source}]$. In the other direction, $\mathcal{AS}_{n,t}[\Diamond t\text{-source}]$ places no restriction on the order in which messages are received, while $\mathcal{AS}_{n,t}[\Diamond MP]$ does.

Electing an eventual leader in $\mathcal{AS}_{n,t}[\Diamond MP]$ An algorithm constructing a failure detector of the class Ω in $\mathcal{AS}_{n,t}[\Diamond MP]$ is described in Figure 7.16. The local variable r_i (initialized to 0) is used to identify the consecutive query/response exchange issued by p_i. Similarly to the previous algorithm, $count_i[j]$ counts the number of suspicions of p_j, as known by p_i. The set rec_from_i contains the identities of the processes from which p_i has received a response to its last query (its initial value is the set $\{1, \dots, n\}$).

---

init: $r_i \leftarrow 0$; $rec\_from_i \leftarrow \{1, \dots, n\}$; **for each** j **do** $count_i[j] \leftarrow 0$ **end for**.

repeat forever asynchronously
    $r_i \leftarrow r_i + 1$;
    for each $j \neq i$ **do** send QUERY_ALIVE$(r_i, count_i)$ to p_j **end for**;
    wait until (RESPONSE(r_i, rec_from) received from $(n - t)$ processes);
    let $prev\_rec\_from_i = \cup$ the rec_from sets previously received;
    for each $j \notin prev\_rec\_from_i$ **do** $count_i[j] \leftarrow count_i[j] + 1$ **end for**;
    let $rec_from_i = $ the set of processes from which p_i has previously received (RESPONSE$(r_i, -)$)
end repeat.

when QUERY_ALIVE$(r, count)$ **is received from** p_j:
    for each $k \in \{1, \dots, n\}$ **do** $count_i[k] \leftarrow \max(count_i[k], count[k])$ **end for**;
    send RESPONSE(r, rec_from_i) to p_j.

when $leader_i$ **is read by the upper layer**:
    let $(-, \ell) = \min(\{(count_i[x], x)\}_{1 \leq x \leq n})$;
    return (ℓ).

Figure 7.16: Building Ω in $\mathcal{AS}_{n,t}[\Diamond MP]$ (code for p_i)

The behavior of p_i is as follows.

- Process p_i executes an infinite sequence of asynchronous rounds. Any finite time can elapse between two consecutive rounds. Moreover, the notion of a round is purely local. During a round, p_i does the following.

- It first broadcasts QUERY_ALIVE(r_i, $count_i$), and waits for the $(n - t)$ winning responses. The response from p_x carries the value of rec_from_x. As indicated, this set contains the identities of the processes that sent winning responses to p_x's last query.

- Then, p_i suspects the processes p_j that do not appear in rec_from sets it has just received. Operationally, this suspicion is captured by an increase of $count_i[j]$.

- Finally, before proceeding to the next local round, p_i computes the new value of rec_from_i.

- When it receives a message QUERY_ALIVE(r, $count$) from a process p_j, p_i updates its array $count_i$ and sends by return the message RESPONSE(r, rec_from_i) to p_j. The sequence number r carried by the response message is related to the process that sent the QUERY_ALIVE(r, $-$) message (it is not related to r_i).

- Finally, when the upper layer application reads the variable $leader_i$, it obtains (as in the previous algorithm) the identity of the process that is currently the less suspected.

Theorem 7.9   *The algorithm described in Figure 7.16 builds an eventual leader failure detector in the system model $\mathcal{AS}_{n,t}[\Diamond MP]$, where $0 \leq t < n$.*

Proof   Given a run with failure pattern $F()$, let us consider the following sets of process identities (where PL stands for "potential leaders"):

$$PL = \{x \mid \exists i \in Correct(F) : count_i[x] \text{ is bounded}\},$$

$$\forall i \in Correct(F) : PL_i = \{x \mid count_i[x] \text{ is bounded}\}.$$

It follows from these definitions that $\forall i \in Correct(F) : PL_i \subseteq PL$.

Claim C1. $PL \neq \emptyset$.
Proof of claim C1. Due to MP, there is a time τ_0, a process p_i and a set Q of $(t + 1)$ processes such that, after τ_0, any process p_j in Q (until it possibly crashes) receives winning responses from p_i to each of its queries. Let us notice that Q includes at least one non-faulty process. Let $\tau \geq \tau_0$ be a time after which no more processes crash.

Let p_k be any non-faulty process. As, after it has issued a query, p_k waits for RESPONSE() messages from $(n - t)$ processes, and after τ, at most $(n - (t + 1))$ processes do not receive winning responses from p_i, it follows that there is a time $\tau_k \geq \tau$ after which i is always in $prev\_rec\_from_k$. Hence, after τ_k, p_k never executes $count_k[i] \leftarrow count_k[i] + 1$.

As this is true for any non-faulty process, there is a time $\geq \max(\{\tau_x\}_{x \in Correct(F)})$ after which, due to the permanent gossiping of the $count_x$ arrays between the non-faulty processes, we have forever $count_x[i] = count_y[i] = M_i$ (a constant value) for any pair of non-faulty processes p_x and p_y, which proves the claim. End of proof of claim C1.

Claim C2. $PL \subseteq Correct(F)$.

Proof of claim C2. We show the contrapositive, i.e., if p_x is a faulty process, each non-faulty process p_i is such that $count_i[x]$ increases forever. Thanks to the permanent gossiping of the $count_i$ arrays among the non-faulty processes, it is sufficient to show that there is a non-faulty p_i such that $count_i[x]$ increases forever if p_x is faulty.

Let τ be a time after which all the faulty processes have crashed and all their RESPONSE() messages have been received, p_i be a non-faulty process, and p_x a faulty process. We have the following:

1. Each query issued by p_i after τ generates a set rec_from_i such that $x \notin rec\_from_i$.
2. It follows that, after τ, the predicate $x \notin prev\_ref\_from_i$ is always true, and consequently, each query of p_i after τ entails the execution of the statement $count_i[x] \leftarrow count_i[x] + 1$. As p_i executes an infinite number of queries, $count_i[x]$ increases without bound. End of proof of claim C2.

Claim C3. $(i \in Correct(F)) \Rightarrow (PL_i = PL)$.

Proof of claim C3. Let p_i be a non-faulty process. Let us first observe that $PL = \cup_{x \in Correct(F)} PL_i$ (definition of PL). Hence, as already indicated, $PL_i \subseteq PL$. It follows that we have only to show that $PL \subseteq PL_i$. Moreover, due to claim C2, $PL_i \subseteq Correct(F)$.

Let $k \in PL$ (i.e., p_k is a non-faulty process such there is a non-faulty process p_j such that $count_j[k]$ is bounded). Let M_k be the greatest value taken by $count_j[k]$. We have to show that $count_i[k]$ is bounded. As, at any time, $count_j[k] \leq M_k$, it follows from the gossiping of the QUERY_ALIVE() messages exchanged between p_i and p_j, and the fact that M_k is a constant, that $count_i[k]$ is never greater than M_k, which proves the claim. End of proof of claim C3.

Claim C4. Let p_i and p_j be two non-faulty processes. If, after some time, $count_i[k]$ remains forever equal to some constant M_k, so does $count_j[k]$.

Proof of claim C4. This claim follows directly from the permanent exchange of QUERY_ALIVE() messages between p_i and p_j. End of proof of claim C4.

The proof of the theorem follows from claims C1, C2, and C3 which state that the non-faulty processes have the same set of potential leaders (PL); this set is not empty and includes only non-faulty processes. Moreover, the processes in PL are the only to be suspected a bounded number of times, and (claim C4) this number is eventually the same at each non-faulty process. It follows that the non-faulty processes eventually elect the one of them that is the less suspected. $\square_{Theorem\ 7.9}$

The case $t = 1$ In that case, $\lozenge MP$ can be reformulated as follows. There is a time after which there are two processes p_i and p_j such that the channels connecting them are never the slowest among the channels connecting any of these processes to any other process. (This ensures that the responses of p_j to p_i will always be winning, i.e., arrive among the $n - 1$ first responses). As we can see, this is a particularly weak assumption that allows solving consensus despite one process crash.

7.5.4   A HYBRID ALGORITHM: THE MODEL $\mathcal{AS}_{n,t}[\Diamond MP \vee \Diamond t\text{-}\mathbf{source}]$

Interestingly, the algorithms described in Figure 7.13 and Figure 7.16 can be combined to give an algorithm that builds a failure detector of the class Ω in a system model whose runs satisfy the $\Diamond t$-source assumption or the $\Diamond MP$ assumption, i.e., in the model $\mathcal{AS}_{n,t}[\Diamond MP \vee \Diamond t\text{-source}]$.

Let us rename $tsource\_count_i$, the local array used in Figure 7.13, and mp_count_i, the local array used in Figure 7.16. The hybrid algorithm is as follows. It is the union of both algorithms (each using its own local array $count_i$), where the processing associated with the reading of $leader_i$ is replaced by the following one:

> **when** $leader_i$ **is read by the upper layer**:
>   **for each** $x \in \{1, \ldots, n\}$ **do** $count_i[k] \leftarrow \min(mp\_count_i[x], tsource\_count_i[x])$ **end for**;
>   **let** $(-, \ell) = \min \big(\{(count_i[x], x)\}_{1 \leq x \leq n}\big)$;
>   return (ℓ).

Theorem 7.10   *The hybrid algorithm described previously builds an eventual leader failure detector in the system model $\mathcal{AS}_{n,t}[\Diamond MP, \Diamond t\text{-source}]$, where $0 \leq t < n$.*

Proof The proof follows from Theorem 7.8 and Theorem 7.9, plus the following observation.

Let p_i be a non-faulty process. If a process p_j crashes, both the local variables $tsource\_count_i[j]$ and $mp\_count_i[j]$ increase forever, from which we conclude that if at least one of these variables remains bounded, process p_j is non-faulty. $\qquad\qquad\square_{Theorem\ 7.10}$

The best of both worlds   This hybrid algorithm benefits from the best of both worlds, namely the world defined by the runs that satisfy the $\Diamond MP$ assumption, and the world defined by the runs that satisfy the $\Diamond t$-source assumption. As the hybrid algorithm is correct if any assumption is satisfied, it provides an increased overall assumption coverage.

7.5.5   WHEN THE MEMBERSHIP IS NOT INITIALLY KNOWN

System model   In this model, each process p_i has an (integer) identity, but it knows initially only its own identity. It knows neither the identity of the other processes nor the total number of processes. Moreover, the process identities are not necessarily consecutive integers. This defines a system in which the *membership* is not initially known. It is important to see that, if a process crashes before sending messages, no other process will ever know its identity. (Let us observe that it is not possible to build $\Diamond P$ in this type of system.)

Processes communicate by sending and receiving messages. The operation "broadcast()" allows a process p_i to send the same message to all the processes (like in Ethernet networks or IP-multicast).

The channels are unidirectional, and each pair of processes has a channel in each direction. The system has two types of channels, eventually, timely channels and lossy asynchronous channels.

Consequently, the broadcast operation is not reliable. Even if p_i never crashes, a message it broadcasts can be received by some processes and never received by other processes.

As for previous algorithms (and without loss of generality), it is assumed that local processing takes no time, only messages transfer takes times. Let $\mathcal{AS}\overline{M}_{n,t}[\emptyset]$ denote this type of system (the notation $\overline{M}$ is used to denote the initial lack of membership).

The behavioral assumption $\Diamond T\_Path$ A directed path connecting two non-faulty processes is *eventually timely*, if it is composed only of non-faulty processes and eventually timely channels.

Let $\Diamond T\_Path$ be the following assumption: There is a non-faulty process p such that, for each other non-faulty process q, there is an eventually timely path from p to q. A system in $\mathcal{AS}\overline{M}_{n,t}[\emptyset]$ that satisfies this assumption is denoted $\mathcal{AS}\overline{M}_{n,t}[\Diamond T\_Path]$.

```
init: allocate susp_nb_i[i]; susp_nb_i[i] ← 0;
      members_i ← {i}; contenders_i ← {i}.

repeat every β time units
      broadcast CANDIDATES(i, {(susp_nb_i[x], x)}_{x∈contenders_i})
      % All the messages CANDIDATES() broadcast here by p_i are different %
end repeat.

when CANDIDATES(k, view) with (k ≠ i) is received for the first time:
      broadcast CANDIDATES(k, view);
      if (k ∉ members_i)
         then allocate susp_nb_i[k], timer_i[k] and timeout_i[k];
              timeout_i[k] ← β; susp_nb_i[k] ← 0;
              members_i ← members_i ∪ {k}
      end if;
      set timer_i[k] to timeout_i[k];
      contenders_i ← contenders_i ∪ {k};
      susp_nb_i[k] ← max(susp_nb_i[k], sp_nb_k) where (sp_nb_k, k) ∈ view;
      if ((−, i) ∉ view) then susp_nb_i[i] ← susp_nb_i[i] + 1 end if.

when timer_i[k] expires:
      timeout_i[k] ← timeout_i[k] + 1;
      contenders_i ← contenders_i \ {k};
      broadcast CANDIDATES(i, {(susp_nb_i[x], x)}_{x∈contenders_i}).

when leader_i is read by the upper layer:
      let (−, ℓ) = min ({(susp_nb_i[x], x)}_{x∈contenders_i});
      return (ℓ).
```

Figure 7.17: Building Ω in $\mathcal{AS}\overline{M}_{n,t}[\Diamond T\_Path]$ (code for p_i)

Electing an eventual leader in $\mathcal{AS}\overline{M}_{n,t}[\Diamond T\_Path]$ An algorithm electing an eventual leader in the system model $\mathcal{AS}\overline{M}_{n,t}[\Diamond T\_Path]$ is described in Figure 7.17. Each process p_i manages the following local variables.

- $members_i$ is a set containing the identities of the processes that p_i is aware of. Initially, p_i knows only itself.

- $contenders_i$ is a set containing the identities of the processes that currently compete to become the final common leader, from p_i's local point of view. Hence, we always have $contenders_i \subseteq members_i$. Moreover, i belongs always to $contenders_i$. This is to force p_i to always compete to be leader, and consequently ensures that p_i has always a leader.

- $susp\_nb_i[k]$ is an integer local variable that is created when p_i discovers that process p_k belongs to the system. (The array notation is used to make the presentation easier.) This variable contains the greatest number of suspicions of p_k, as known by p_i.

- For each process p_k it is aware of (but itself), p_i manages a local timer $timer_i[k]$, and an associated timeout value $timeout_i[k]$. These allow p_i to monitor p_k when $k \in contenders_i$.

The aim is (as in previous algorithms) to elect the process that, among the current contenders, is the less suspected process. Hence, when p_i reads the local variable $leader_i$, that locally implements Ω, it returns the process identity ℓ such that $(-, \ell) = \min \left(\{(susp\_nb_i[x], x)\}_{x \in contenders_i} \right)$, where the minimum is defined with respect to lexicographical ordering.

Repeatedly, p_i broadcasts message CANDIDATES($i, \{(susp\_nb_i[x], x)\}_{x \in contenders_i}$) to inform the other processes on its current view of the leader competition. It is assumed that the consecutive messages CANDIDATES($i, -$) regularly broadcast by a process p_i are all different (this can be easily done by associating with each of them a pair made up of a sequence number and sender identity).

When it receives a new message CANDIDATES($k, view$), process p_i does the following. It first forwards this message to all. This forwarding is done to compensate the fact that channels from p_k to other processes might be lossy. Then, if p_i was not previously aware of p_k, it adds k to $members_i$, and allocates the associated local variables. It then sets $timer_i[k]$ to the current value of $timeout_i[k]$ in order to monitor p_k, adds k to $contenders_i$, and updates $susp\_nb_i[k]$ if needed (from the value it has received).

Then, p_i checks the predicate $(-, i) \notin view$. If it is true, we conclude that i was not in $contenders_k$ when p_k broadcast CANDIDATE($k, view$), which means that p_k was suspecting p_i or not aware of its existence. In that case, p_i increases its suspicion number $susp\_nb_i[i]$. Let us observe that only process p_i can increase this number (the other processes can only update their copies when they invoke the function max()).

Finally, when $timer_i[k]$ expires, p_i increases $timeout_i[k]$ (this is because the timer expiration could be due to a too small timeout value), suppresses k from $contenders_i$, and broadcasts its new view of the leadership competition.

Theorem 7.11   *The algorithm described in Figure 7.17 elects an eventual leader in $\mathcal{A}\overline{S\mathcal{M}}_{n,t}[\Diamond T\_Path]$, where $0 \leq t < n$.*

Proof Claim C1. Let p_i and p_j be a non-faulty process and a faulty process, respectively. There is a time after which $j \notin contenders_i$ is forever true.

Proof of claim C1. Let us first notice that, as p_j crashes, there is a finite time after which all the messages CANDIDATES$(j, -)$ whose broadcasts have been initiated by p_j have been received or are lost (these messages include the messages CANDIDATES$(j, -)$ forwarded by other processes; let us remember that a process p_k forwards such a message only once, when it receives it for the first time). There are two cases.

- If p_i never receives a message CANDIDATES$(j, -)$, it never includes j in $contenders_i$ and the claim follows.

- In the other case, let us consider the last message CANDIDATES$(j, -)$ that p_i receives. When, it receives it, p_i sets $timer_i[j]$ to the current value of $timeout_i[j]$. Then, as this message is the last message CANDIDATES$(j, -)$ received by p_i, $timer_i[j]$ necessarily expires, and p_i withdraws j from $contenders_i$, and (because it was the last message) never adds it thereafter. End of proof of claim C1.

Definition. Given a run with failure pattern $F()$, let $PL = \{x \mid (x \in Correct(F)) \wedge (\forall y \in Correct(F) : \text{there is an eventually timely path from } p_x \text{ to } p_y\}$. It follows from the behavioral assumption $\Diamond T\_Path$ that $PL \neq \emptyset$.

Definition. Let $B = \{i \mid (i \in Correct(F)) \wedge (susp\_nb_i[i] \text{ remains bounded})\}$.

Claim C2. $B \neq \emptyset$.
Proof of claim C2. Due to its very definition, $PL \neq \emptyset$. The proof consists in showing that $PL \subseteq B$. Let $i \in PL$. Due to the fact that p_i regularly broadcasts new messages CANDIDATES$(i, -)$, and these messages are forwarded along eventually timely paths from p_i to any non-faulty process p_j, there is a finite time after which $timeout_j[i]$ no longer increases and $timer_j[i]$ never expires. It follows that there is a finite time τ_j after which the local predicate $i \in contenders_j$ remains forever true. Consequently, all the messages CANDIDATES$(j, view)$ whose broadcast is initiated by p_j after τ_j are such that $(-, i) \in view_j$. As this is true for any non-faulty process p_j, it follows that there is a finite time τ after which each message CANDIDATES$(-, view)$ is such that $(-, i) \in view$. Finally as, after some time, all the messages broadcast by faulty processes have been received or are lost, it follows that eventually p_i no longer increases $susp\_nb_i[i]$. End of proof of claim C2.

Definition. Let M_i be the greatest value of $susp\_nb_i[i]$ if any, $+\infty$, otherwise.

Claim C3. $\forall j \in B$, there is a finite time after which, $\forall i \in Correct(F)$: j belongs forever to $contenders_i$ and $susp\_nb_i[j] = M_j$.
Proof of claim C3. Let $j \in B$ and $x \in PL$ (let us remember that we have $\emptyset \neq PL \subseteq B \subseteq$

$Correct(F)$). All times considered in this proof are after eventually timely paths have become timely and messages broadcast before they became timely have been received or are lost.

Let us first show that any process $p_x, x \in PL$, allocates a timer ($timer_x[j]$) to monitor p_j. If p_x never receives a message CANDIDATES($j, -$), we have forever $j \notin contenders_i$. It follows that the infinite number of messages CANDIDATES($x, view_x$) broadcast by p_x are such that $(-, j) \notin view_x$. As $x \in PL$, it follows that after the eventually timely channels have become timely, p_j receives a copy of each of these messages and each time increases $susp\_nb_j[j]$, and $susp\_nb_j[j]$ is consequently unbounded. Hence, if $susp\_nb_j[j]$ is bounded, p_x has received at least one CANDIDATES($j, view_j$) message and has consequently allocated a timer ($timer_x[j]$) associated with p_x.

As it is non-faulty, p_j regularly broadcasts messages CANDIDATES($j, view_j$) with $(M_j, j) \in view_j$. We claim that p_x has necessarily received such a message CANDIDATES($j, view_j$). This is because, if p_x does not receive such a message: (a) $timer_x[j]$ would expire, (b) p_x would consequently withdraw j from $contenders_x$ and repeatedly broadcasts CANDIDATES($x, view_x$) messages with $(-, j) \notin view_x$, (c) as $x \in PL$, after the eventually timely paths become timely, each non-faulty process would receive such CANDIDATES($x, view_x$) messages. Hence, p_j would increase $susp\_nb_j[j]$ to $M_j + 1$, contradicting the assumption that M_j is the greatest value ever taken by $susp\_nb_j[j]$.

Finally, as (a) p_x has received message CANDIDATES($j, view_j$) with $(M_j, j) \in view_j$, (b) p_x regularly broadcasts CANDIDATES($i, view_i$) messages with $(M_j, j) \in view_i$, (c) $x \in PL$, it follows that, after the path from p_x to p_i has become timely, every non-faulty process p_i receives this message and updates accordingly $contenders_i$ and $susp\_nb_i[j]$. End of proof of claim C3.

Definition. Let $M = \min(M_1, \cdots, M_n)$ (due to claim C2, M exists and is unknown but bounded).

Claim C4. $\forall \, i \in Correct(F)$, $\forall j \in Correct(F) \setminus B$, there is a finite time after which ($j \in contenders_i$) $\Rightarrow$ ($susp\_nb_i[j] > M$).

Proof of claim C4. Let τ be the time at which p_j updates $susp\_nb_j[j]$ to a value $m > M$, and $\tau' \geq \tau$ be a time from which no message CANDIDATES($j, -$) whose broadcast has been initiated by p_j before τ is present in the system. This means that, after τ', any message CANDIDATES($j, view$) is such that $(m, j) \in view$, with $m > M$. We consider two cases.

- If, after τ', p_i receives a message CANDIDATES($j, view$) it adds j to $contenders_i$ and, as $(m, j) \in view$, updates $susp\_nb_i[j]$ to m and we have $susp\_nb_i[j] > M$.
- If after τ', p_i never receives a message CANDIDATES($j, view$), eventually the predicate $j \notin contenders_i$ remains forever true. (this is because this predicate was already true at time τ', or becomes true when $timer_i[j]$ expires after τ'). End of proof of claim C4.

Let us first observe that it follows from the text of the algorithm that, at any time, a process p_i elects as leader the process it currently suspects the less among the processes in $contenders_i$ (the set of processes it currently perceives as competing to be leader; as we always have $i \in contenders_i$ this set is never empty).

Due to claim C1, there is a time after which $leader_i$ is always a non-faulty process. Due to claims C2 and C4, there is a time after which $leader_i$ is a process p_x such that $susp\_nb_x[x]$ is bounded. Finally, claim C3 shows that, for each $i \in Correct(F)$ and $j \in B$, there is a time after which we have $susp\_nb_i[j] = M_j$. Hence, there is a time after which all the non-faulty processes have forever the same leader that is a non-faulty process.

$\square_{Theorem\ 7.11}$

7.5.6   WHEN PROCESSES CRASH AND RECOVER (OR ENTER AND LEAVE)

System model   This section considers a system model in which the processes may crash and recover. More precisely, the processes can be partitioned into three sets.

- The set of *eventually up* processes. This set contains the processes that, after some finite time, remain alive forever (i.e., they no longer crash). These processes are also called *correct* processes.

- The set of *eventually down* processes. This set includes all the processes that eventually remain crashed forever. These processes can recover a finite number of times, after which they remain crashed forever.

- The set of *unstable* processes. This set includes the processes that crash and recover infinitely often.

The system parameter t denotes the maximum number of processes that are unstable or eventually down. We have $0 \leq t < n$.

As in previous models, processing times are considered as negligible with respect to message transfer delays (which means that they are assumed to be equal to 0). Moreover, each process has a local clock that can measure time intervals with a bounded drift (known by the processes). These clocks are not required to be synchronized. Each clock progresses forever. This means that the clock of a crashed process continues running. Said differently, a process is not assumed to have access to a stable memory, but its clock never crashes and is always increasing.

Let $\Diamond WT$ denote the following behavioral property on channels: For every correct process p_i, there is an eventually timely channel from p_i to every correct or unstable process p_j. The other channels can be asynchronous and lossy. Let us observe that the bound δ associated with the "timely channel" assumption may never be explicitly known by the processes.

Notation   The previous system model is denoted $\mathcal{ASCR}_{n,t}[\Diamond WT]$.

Let us observe that this model captures systems made up of a fixed number of processes that can enter and leave the system dynamically. A *leave* is similar to a crash where the clock of the process continues progressing. An *enter* is similar to a recovery (assuming the current value of the local clock of the entering process is as large as the clock value of the processes already in the system, which can be easily ensured by accessing a GPS-like system).

Eventual leader in $\mathcal{ASCR}_{n,t}[\Diamond WT]$ The property the eventual leader failure detector has to satisfy is modified as follows to take into account the crashes (leave) and recoveries (enter) of processes.

- There is a finite (but unknown) time after which (1) all the correct processes have the same correct leader p_ℓ, and (2) each unstable process either has no leader or has p_ℓ as leader.

Intuitively, this means that, when an unstable process recovers, it is possible that it has no leader (and it does know it) during a finite period. This is because it has to remain alive during a sufficiently long period in order to be informed on which is the current leader. A too early crash after recovering can prevent it to know which is the leader.

Electing a leader $\mathcal{ASCR}_{n,t}[\Diamond WT]$ The idea is to elect the correct process that has been continuously alive since the longest time period. To that end, the local clocks are used to associate a date with each process recovery (and process identities are used -if needed- to select a process among the processes that recovered with the same clock value). The algorithm is described in Figure 7.18.

To read its local clock, a process p_i invokes the operation $\mathsf{clock}_i()$. It also manages the following local variables.

- $leader_i$ contains the identity of the process that is p_i's current leader, or $\perp$ if p_i has no current leader.

- $timer_i$ is a local timer. When needed, it is set to the value contained in $timeout_i$, a local variable that is increased each time the timer expires.

- lr_date_i contains the local date of p_i's last recovery, while $min\_lr\_date_i$ contains the date of the last recovery of the process that p_i considers currently as leader (i.e., p_{leader_i}).

The algorithm elects the correct process p_ℓ whose timestamp (lr_date_ℓ, ℓ) is the smallest. The behavior of a process p_i is consequently the following one.

- When a process p_i starts the algorithm, and each time it recovers, it resets $leader_i$ to $\perp$, and sets $timeout_i$, lr_date_i and $min\_lr\_date_i$ to the current value of its clock. Then, it waits for $timeout_i$ time units. This is an observation period during which it can receive messages that update its context and provides it a current leader (see next item). (The initialization of $timeout_i$ to the current value of the local clock, combined with the fact that this clock always increases, prevents unstable processes from forever disturbing the leader election.)

  When this observation period terminates, p_i considers it is leader if $leader_i$ has not been updated. Otherwise, it sets $timer_i$ to the value of $timeout_i$ in order to monitor the process that it considers as its current leader.

  Finally, p_i enters an infinite loop in which it regularly (every β_i time units) does the following: if it currently considers itself as leader, it sends the message LEADER (lr_date_i, i) to every other process.

- When p_i receives LEADER (lr_date, j), it does the following. If (a) $lr\_date < min\_lr\_date_i$) or (b) $leader_i \neq \perp$ and $(lr\_date, j) \leq (min\_lr\_date_i, leader_i)$, p_i demotes its current leader and replaces it by p_j. If p_i has no leader and p_j is a better candidate than itself (i.e., $leader_i = \perp$ and $(lr\_date, j) < (min\_lr\_date_i, i)$), p_i considers p_j as its current leader.

```
when p_i starts or recovers:
    leader_i ← ⊥;
    timeout_i ← clock_i(); lr_date_i ← timeout_i; min_lr_date_i ← timeout_i;
    wait timeout_i time units;
    if (leader_i = ⊥) then leader_i ← i else set timer_i to timeout_i end if;
    repeat forever every β_i time units
        if (leader_i = i) then
            for each j ≠ i do send LEADER (lr_date_i, i) to p_j end for
        end if
    end repeat.

when LEADER (lr_date, j) is received:
    if   (lr_date < min_lr_date_i)
        ∨ ((lr_date = min_lr_date_i) ∧ (leader_i ≠ ⊥) ∧ (j ≤ leader_i))
        ∨ ((lr_date = min_lr_date_i) ∧ (leader_i = ⊥) ∧ (j < i))
        then leader_i ← j;
            min_lr_date_i ← lr_date;
            set timer_i to timeout_i
    end if.

when timer_i expires:
    timeout_i ← timeout_i + 1;
    leader_i ← i;
    min_lr_date_i ← lr_date_i.
```

Figure 7.18: Building Ω in $\mathcal{ASCR}_{n,t}[\Diamond WT]$ (code for p_i)

If p_j is considered as new leader, p_i updates accordingly $leader_i$ and $min\_lr\_date_i$, and sets $timer_i$ to the current value of $timeout_i$ in order to start a monitoring period with respect to p_j.

- When $timer_i$ expires, p_i suspects its current leader p_{leader_i} to have crashed. It consequently increases $timeout_i$ and considers itself as the new leader. As indicated in the first item, this entails the sending of LEADER (lr_date_i, i) messages.

Theorem 7.12   *The algorithm described in Figure 7.18 elects an eventual leader in $\mathcal{ASCR}_{n,t}[\Diamond WT]$, where $0 \leq t < n$. Moreover, the algorithm is communication efficient: after some finite time, only the leader sends messages.*

Proof Definitions.

- Let us remember that $Correct$ denotes the set of eventually up processes.
- Let τ_0 be a time instant such that:
    - The assumption on timely channels (WT) is satisfied. This means that the channel from any correct process to any other correct process or to any unstable process is timely.
    - Every eventually down process has crashed and no longer recovers.

- Every eventually up (correct) process p_i is alive and no longer crashes. This means that, after τ_0, lr_date_i no longer changes. Let lr_d_i denote that value.

- Every unstable process p_x has a clock value greater than the value lr_d_i of any correct process p_i (i.e., we always have $lr\_date_x > lr\_d_i$).

- Let τ_1 be a time instant such that all the messages sent before τ_0 have disappeared from the system. Let us observe that this includes all the messages sent by the eventually up processes before they recover for the last time, all the messages sent by the eventually down processes, and all the messages sent by every unstable process p_x with $lr\_date_x \leq lr\_d_i$, for any eventually up process p_i.

- Let $\tau > \max(\tau_0, \tau_1)$. All time instants considered in the rest of the proof are after τ.

- Let p_ℓ be the correct process such that $(lr\_d_\ell, \ell) = \min(\{(lr\_d_i, i)\}_{i \in Correct})$.

The proof consists in showing that (a) for any eventually up process p_i, the predicate $leader_i = \ell$ becomes and remains true forever, and (b) for any unstable process p_j, the predicate $leader_j \in \{\ell, \bot\}$ becomes and remains true forever.

Claim C1. There is a time after which (a) the predicate $leader_\ell = \ell$ is always true, and (b) every β_ℓ time units, p_ℓ sends LEADER (lr_d_ℓ, ℓ) to every other process.

Proof of claim C1. Let us first show that there is a time after which the predicate $leader_\ell = \ell$ is always true. It follows from the algorithm that the only way for p_ℓ to have $leader_\ell \neq \ell$ is to receive a message LEADER (lr_date_x, x) that satisfies the predicate controlling the **if** statement. But after τ, there are only messages from correct processes and those messages carry values such that $(lr\_d_\ell, \ell) < (lr\_d_x, x)$. It follows that, after τ, $leader_\ell$ is not updated when a message is received. We consequently have the following.

- If $leader_\ell = \ell$ at time τ, it never changes thereafter, which proves the claim.

- If $leader_\ell = y \neq \ell$ at time τ, as the timer is not reset when LEADER (lr_date_y, y) arrives, it follows that eventually $timer_\ell$ expires. When this occurs, p_ℓ sets $leader_\ell$ to ℓ, and from then on, $leader_\ell = \ell$ remains forever true.

Finally, the fact that there is a time after which p_ℓ sends LEADER (lr_d_ℓ, ℓ) every β_ℓ time units, follows directly from the first part of the claim and the text of the algorithm. End of proof of claim C1.

Claim C2. There is a finite time after which (a) for any correct process p_i, $leader_i = \ell$ is forever true, and (b) only p_ℓ sends messages.

Proof of claim C2. Item (a) follows from claim C1 for p_ℓ. Let p_i be any other correct process. Due to claim C1, there is a time after which p_ℓ sends periodically LEADER (lr_d_ℓ, ℓ) to every correct process p_i. Due to the definition of ℓ, we have $(lr\_d_\ell, \ell) \leq (min\_lr\_date_i, leader_i)$ each time p_i receives LEADER (lr_d_ℓ, ℓ). Hence, it sets $leader_i$ to ℓ, $min\_lr\_date_i$ to lr_d_ℓ and resets $timer_i$ to $timeout_i$ each time it receives such a message. Moreover, as we are after τ, the channel from p_ℓ to p_i is timely, which means that $timer_i$ can expire only a finite number of times. It follows that, after a finite time, p_i always receives the next message LEADER (lr_d_ℓ, ℓ) before the timer expires. When this occurs, the predicate $leader_i = \ell$ remains forever true.

The proof of item (b) follows directly from item (a) and the text of the algorithm: after $leader_i = \ell$ has become true forever, the predicate $leader_i = i$ is never satisfied and p_i no longer sends messages. End of proof of claim C2.

Claim C3. Let p_x be an unstable process. There is a finite time after which (a) p_x does not send messages, and (b) $leader_x \in \{\ell, \perp\}$.

Proof of claim C3. It follows from claim C1 and the text of the algorithm that there is a time after which p_ℓ sends periodically the message LEADER (lr_d_ℓ, ℓ) to any unstable process p_x. As, after τ, (a) the channel from p_ℓ to p_x is timely, (b) p_x waits lr_date_x time units when it recovers (lr_date_x is then equal to the current value of its clock that always increases), it follows that there is a finite time after which p_x always receives a message LEADER (lr_d_ℓ, ℓ) before the end of its waiting period. When this occurs, p_x sets $leader_x$ to ℓ. Moreover, as $timeout_x$ is set to the current value of the clock when p_x recovers (and the clock always increases), it follows that there is a time after which $timer_x$ will no longer expire, and, consequently, p_x will not send any more messages. Hence, eventually $leader_x$ cannot take a value different from ℓ and $\perp$. End of proof of claim C3.

The fact that the algorithm eventually elects a single correct process and is communication efficient follows from the claims C1, C2 and C3.

$\square$ *Theorem 7.12*

7.6   BIBLIOGRAPHIC NOTES

- The failure detector abstraction has been introduced and investigated by Chandra, Hadzilacos and Toueg [33, 34]. They have introduced (among others) the classes P, $\Diamond P$ and Ω.

  It is shown in [103] that every problem has a weakest failure detector.

  Surveys on failure detectors can be found in [85, 127, 148]. A survey on the implementation of Ω can be found in [147].

- Transformations from one failure detector class to another can be found in [13, 34, 41, 132]. It is shown in [73] that there is no one-shot agreement problem for which $\Diamond P$ would be the weakest failure detector class. Weakest failure detector classes for fundamental distributed computing problems are presented in [48].

- Direct proofs of the impossibility to build Ω in $\mathcal{AS}_{n,t}[\emptyset]$ can be found in [6, 129].

- A construction of a perfect failure detector in an asynchronous system with "very high priority" messages is described in [99]. This construction is due to Hermant and Le Lann.

- The notion of α-fair communication pattern and its use to build failure detectors are due to Beauquier and Kekkonen-Moneta [21].

- The theta model is due to Widder and Schmid [158]. (This model is more general that what has been presented here.) A construction of Ω in this model is described in [25].

A model called ABC that is weaker than theta but where similar results hold is presented in [151].

- The construction of a failure detector of the class $\diamond P$ in an eventually synchronous system is from Chandra an Toueg [34]. The monitoring of a process by another process is due to Chen, Toueg and Aguilera [38]. The lazy adaptive algorithm is due to Fetzer, Raynal and Tronel [66].

- An algorithm that provides processes with an on-the-fly estimation of which processes are alive is given in [138].

- The algorithm that eventually elects the non-faulty process with the smallest identity is due to Larrea, Fernández and Arévalo [115].

  The notion of "eventual t-source" and its use to build a failure detector of the class Ω are due to Aguilera, Delporte-Gallet, Fauconnier and Toueg [6].

  The notion of " winning responses based on a message exchange pattern" used to implement failure detectors is due to Mostéfaoui, Mourgaya and Raynal [128]. Its application to build Ω is from [129].

- Hybrid Ω algorithms have been investigated in several works. As an example, [137] combines the "eventual t-source" assumption and the "message pattern base on winning responses" assumption at the level of each pair of processes, a channel being eventually timely of eventually winning.

  Such hybrid algorithms allows us to benefit from the best of several worlds and consequently provides solutions with a better assumption coverage [130, 144].

- The Ω algorithm in asynchronous systems where a process initially knows only its identity is due to Jiménez, Arévalo and Fernández [104]. A communication-efficient algorithm for this type of systems with limited initial knowledge is presented in [63].

- The Ω algorithm for the crash/recovery model is due to Martín and Larrea [121]. This algorithm is well-suited to dynamic systems where processes can connect and disconnect.

- Lots of Ω algorithms with additional properties have been designed (e.g., [7, 45, 65, 102, 114, 119, 122, 137] to cite a few). Interestingly, the algorithm described in [65] has a generic structure from which several existing algorithms and new algorithms can be derived.

- People interested in the construction of a failure detector of the class Ω in asynchronous shared memory systems prone to process crashes should consult [64, 88].

Bibliography

[1] Afek Y., Attiya H., Fekete A.D., Fischer M., Lynch N., Mansour Y., Wang D. and Zuck L., Reliable Communication over Unreliable Channels. *Journal of the ACM*, 41(6):1267-1297, 1994. DOI: 10.1145/195613.195651 96

[2] Aguilera M.K., A Pleasant Stroll Through the Land of Infinitely Many Creatures. *ACM SIGACT News, Distributed Computing Column*, 35(2):36-59, 2004. DOI: 10.1145/992287.992298 38

[3] Aguilera M.K., Chen W. and Toueg S., Heartbeat: A Timeout-Free Failure Detector for Quiescent Reliable Communication. *Proc. 11th Int'l Workshop on Distributed Algorithms (WDAG'97)*, Springer-Verlag LNCS #1320, pp. 126-140, 1997. 96

[4] Aguilera M.K., Chen W. and Toueg S., Using the Heartbeat Failure Detector for Quiescent Reliable Communication and Consensus in Partitionable Networks. *Theoretical Computer Science (TCS)*, 220(1):3-30, 1999. 96

[5] Aguilera M.K., Chen W. and Toueg S., On Quiescent Reliable Communication. *SIAM Journal of Computing*, 29(6):2040-2073, 2000. DOI: 10.1137/S0097539798341296 96

[6] Aguilera M.K., Delporte-Gallet C., Fauconnier H. and Toueg S., Communication Efficient Leader Election and Consensus with Limited Link Synchrony. *23th ACM Symposium on Principles of Distributed Computing (PODC'04)*, ACM Press, pp. 328-337, 2004. DOI: 10.1145/1011767.1011816 230, 231

[7] Aguilera M.K., Delporte-Gallet C., Fauconnier H. and Toueg S., On Implementing Omega in Systems with Weak Reliability and Synchrony Assumptions. *Distributed Computing*, 21(4):285-314, 2008. DOI: 10.1007/s00446-008-0068-y 231

[8] Aguilera M.K., Englert K. and Gafni E., On Using Networks Attached Disks as Shared Memory. *Proc. 22th Int'l Symposium on Principles of Distributed Computing (PODC'03)*, ACM press, pp. 315-324, 2003. DOI: 10.1145/872035.872082 38

[9] Aguilera M.K., Keidar I., Malkhi D. and Shraer A., Dynamic Atomic Storage without Consensus. *Proc. 28th Int'l Symposium on Principles of Distributed Computing (PODC'09)*, ACM press, pp. 17-256, 2009. DOI: 10.1145/1582716.1582726 38

[10] Aguilera M.K. and Toueg S., Failure Detection and Randomization: a Hybrid Approach to Solve Consensus. *SIAM Journal of Computing*, 28(3):890-903, 1998. DOI: 10.1137/S0097539796312915 188

[11] Aguilera M.K. and Toueg S., A Simple Bi-valency Proof that t-Resilient Consensus Requires $t + 1$ rounds. *Information Processing Letters*, 71:155-158, 1999. 187

[12] Aguilera M.K., Toueg S. and Deianov B., Revising the Weakest Failure Detector for Uniform Reliable Broadcast. *Proc. 13th Int'l Symposium on Distributed Computing (DISC'99)*, Springer-Verlag LNCS #1693, pp. 19-33, 1999. 96

[13] Anceaume E., Fernández A., Mostéfaoui A., Neiger G. and Raynal M., Necessary and Sufficient Condition for Transforming Limited Accuracy Failure Detectors. *Journal of Computer and System Sciences*, 68:123-133, 2004. DOI: 10.1016/j.jcss.2003.08.003 230

[14] Attiya H., Efficient and Robust Sharing of Memory in Message-passing Systems. *Journal of Algorithms*, 34(1):109-127, 2000. DOI: 10.1006/jagm.1999.1025 38

[15] Attiya H., Bar-Noy A. and Dolev D., Sharing Memory Robustly in Message Passing Systems. *Journal of the ACM*, 42(1):121-132, 1995. 38

[16] Attiya H. and Welch J., Distributed Computing: Fundamentals, Simulations and Advanced Topics, (2d Edition), *Wiley-Interscience*, 414 pages, 2004. 38

[17] Baldoni R., Bonomi S., Kermarrec A.-M. and Raynal M., Implementing a Register in a Dynamic Distributed System. *Proc. 29th IEEE Int'l Conference on Distributed Computing Systems (ICDCS'09)*, IEEE Computer Press, pp. 639-647, 2009. DOI: 10.1109/ICDCS.2009.46 38

[18] Baldoni R., Cimmino S. and Marchetti C., A Classification of Total Order Specifications and its Application to Fixed Sequencer-based Implementations. *Journal of Parallel and Distributed Computing*, 66(1): 108-127, 2006. DOI: 10.1016/j.jpdc.2005.06.021 62

[19] Baldoni R., Mostefaoui A. and Raynal M., Causal Delivery of Messages with Real-Time Data in Unreliable Networks. *Real-Time Systems Journal*, 10(3):245-262, 1996. DOI: 10.1007/BF00383387 62

[20] Basu A., Charron-Bost B. and Toueg S., Simulating Reliable Links with Unreliable Links in the Presence of Process Crashes. *Proc. 10th Int'l Workshop on Distributed Algorithms (WDAG'96)*, Springer-Verlag LNCS #1151, pp. 105-122, 1996. DOI: 10.1007/3-540-61769-8_8 96

[21] Beauquier J. and Kekkonen-Moneta S., Fault-tolerance and Self-stabilization: Impossibility Results and Solutions Using Self-stabilizing Failure Detectors. *Int'l Journal of Systems Science*, 28(11):1177-1187, 1997. DOI: 10.1080/00207729708929476 230

[22] Ben-Or M., Another Advantage of Free Choice: Completely Asynchronous Agreement Protocols. *Proc. 2nd ACM Symposium on Principles of Distributed Computing(PODC'83)*, ACM Press, pp. 27-30, 1983. DOI: 10.1145/800221.806707 188

[23] Bernstein Ph.A., Hadzilacos V. and Goodman N., Concurrency Control and Recovery in Database Systems. *Addison Wesley Publishing Company*, 370 pages, 1987. 13, 132

[24] Bhatt V., Christman N. and Jayanti P., Extracting Quorum Failure Detectors. *Proc. 28th ACM Symposium on Principles of Distributed Computing (PODC'09)*, ACM Press, pp. 73-82, 2009. DOI: 10.1145/1582716.1582733 39

[25] Biely M. and Widder J., Optimal Message-driven Implementations of Omega with Mute Processes. *ACM Transactions on Autonomous and Adaptive Systems*, 4(1), article 4, 22 pages, 2009. DOI: 10.1145/1462187.1462191 230

[26] Birman K., Reliable Distributed Systems, Technologies, Web Services and Applications. *Springer*, 668 pages, 2005. 62

[27] Birman K., Hayden M., Özkasap Ö., Xiao Z., Budiu M. and Minsky H., Bimodal Multicast. *ACM Transactions on Computer Systems*, 17(2):41-88, 1999. DOI: 10.1145/312203.312207 62

[28] Birman K.P. and Joseph T.A., Reliable Communication in Presence of Failures. *ACM Transactions on Computer Systems*, 5(1):47-76, 1987. DOI: 10.1145/7351.7478 62

[29] Bonnet F. and Raynal M., The Price of Anonymity: Optimal Consensus despite Asynchrony, Crash and Anonymity. *Proc. 23th Int'l Symposium on Distributed Computing (DISC'09)*, Springer-Verlag LNCS #5805, pp. 341-355, 2009. DOI: 10.1007/978-3-642-04355-0_35 188

[30] Bonnet F. and Raynal M., A Simple Proof of the Necessity of the Failure Detector Σ to Implement a Register in Asynchronous Message Passing Systems. *Information Processing Letters*, 110(4):153-157, 2010. DOI: 10.1016/j.ipl.2009.11.011 39

[31] Bonnet F. and Raynal M., Early Consensus in Message-passing Systems Enriched with a Perfect Failure Detector and its Application in the Theta Model. *Proc. 8th European Dependable Computing Conference (EDCC'10)*, IEEE Computer Press, Valencia (Spain), April 28-30, 2010. 187

[32] Brasileiro F., Greve F., Mostéfaoui A. and Raynal M., Consensus in One Communication Step. *Proc. 6th Int'l Conference on Parallel Computing Technologies (PaCT'01)*, Springer Verlag LNCS #2127, pp. 42-50, 2001. DOI: 10.1007/3-540-44743-1_4 188

[33] Chandra T.D., Hadzilacos V. and Toueg S., The Weakest Failure Detector for Solving Consensus. *Journal of the ACM*, 43(4):685-722, 1996. DOI: 10.1145/234533.234549 188, 230

[34] Chandra T. and Toueg S., Unreliable Failure Detectors for Reliable Distributed Systems. *Journal of the ACM*, 43(2):225-267, 1996. DOI: 10.1145/226643.226647 38, 96, 132, 187, 230, 231

[35] Chandy K.M. and Misra J., How Processes Learn, *Distributed Computing* 1(1):40-52, 1986. DOI: 10.1007/BF01843569 63

[36] Chang J.-M. and Maxemchuck N.F., Reliable Broadcast Protocols. *ACM Transactions on Computer Systems*, 2(3):251-273, 1984. 62

[37] Charron-Bost B., Guerraoui R. and Schiper A., Synchronous System and Perfect Failure Detector: Solvability and Efficiency Issue. *Proc. Int'l Conference on Dependable Systems and Networks (DSN'00)*, IEEE Computer Press, pp. 523-532, 2000. DOI: 10.1109/ICDSN.2000.857585 188

[38] Chen W., Toueg S. and Aguilera M., On the Quality of Service of Failure Detectors. *IEEE Transactions on Computers*, 51(5):561-580, 2002. DOI: 10.1109/12.980014 231

[39] Chockler G. V. and Malkhi D., Active Disk Paxos with infinitely Many Processes. *Proc. 21th ACM Symposium on Principles of Distributed Computing (PODC'02)*, ACM Press, pp. 78-87, 2002. DOI: 10.1145/571825.571837 189

[40] Chockler G. V., Gilbert S., Gramoli V., Musial and Shvartsman A.A., Reconfigurable Dynamic Storage for Dynamic Networks. *Journal of Parallel and Distributed Systems*, 69(1):100-116, 2009. DOI: 10.1016/j.jpdc.2008.07.007 38, 39

[41] Chu F., Reducing Ω to $\Diamond W$. *Information Processing Letters*, 76(6):293-298, 1998. 230

[42] Cristian F., Aghili H., Strong R. and Dolev D., Atomic Broadcast: From Simple Message Diffusion to Byzantine Agreement. *Information and Computation*, 118(1): 158-179, 1995. DOI: 10.1006/inco.1995.1060 62

[43] Cristian C. and Fetzer Ch., The Timed Asynchronous Distributed System Model. *IEEE Transactions on Parallel and Distributed Systems*, 10(6):642-657, 1999. DOI: 10.1109/71.774912 189

[44] Defago X., Schiper A. and Urbàn P., Total Order Broadcast and Multicast Algorithms: Taxonomy and Survey. *ACM Computing Surveys*, 36(4):372-421, 2004. DOI: 10.1145/1041680.1041682 62

[45] Delporte-Gallet C., Devismes S. and Fauconnier H., Robust Stabilizing Leader Election. *Proc. 9th Int'l Symposium on Stabilization, Safety, and Security of Distributed Systems (SSS'07)*, Spinger-Verlag #4838, pp. 219-233, 2007. DOI: 10.1007/978-3-540-76627-8_18 231

[46] Delporte-Gallet C., Fauconnier H. and Guerraoui R., A Realistic Look at Failure Detectors, *Proc. Int'l Conference International on Dependable Systems and Networks (DSN'02)*, IEEE Computer Press, pp. 345-353, 2002. DOI: 10.1109/DSN.2002.1028919 96

[47] Delporte-Gallet C., Fauconnier H. and Guerraoui R., Shared memory *vs* Message Passing. To appear in *Journal of the ACM*, 2010 (*Tech Report* IC/2003/77, EPFL, Lausanne). 39, 96

[48] Delporte-Gallet C., Fauconnier H., Guerraoui R., Hadzilacos V., Kouznetsov P. and Toueg S., The Weakest Failure Detectors to Solve Certain Fundamental Problems in Distributed Computing. *Proc. 23th ACM Symposium on Principles of Distributed Computing (PODC'04)*, ACM Press, pp. 338-346, 2004. DOI: 10.1145/1011767.1011818 38, 39, 132, 188, 230

[49] Delporte-Gallet C., Fauconnier H., Hélary J.-M. and Raynal M., Early Stopping in Global Data Computation. *IEEE Transactions on Parallel and Distributed Systems*, 14(9):909-921, 2003. DOI: 10.1109/TPDS.2003.1233713 188

[50] Delporte-Gallet C., Fauconnier H. and Tielmann A., Fault-Tolerant Consensus in Unknown and Anonymous Networks. *Proc. 29th IEEE Int'l Conference on Distributed Computing Systems (ICDCS'09)*, IEEE Computer Society Press, pp. 368-375, 2009. DOI: 10.1109/ICDCS.2009.36 188

[51] Dolev D., Dwork C. and Stockmeyer L., On the Minimal Synchronism Needed for Distributed Consensus. *Journal of the ACM*, 34(1):77-97, 1987. DOI: 10.1145/7531.7533 189

[52] Dolev D., Reischuk R. and Strong R., Early Stopping in Byzantine Agreement. *Journal of the ACM*, 37(4):720-741, 1990. DOI: 10.1145/96559.96565 187

[53] Dolev S., Gilbert S., Lynch N.A., Shvartsman A.S., and Welch J., Geoquorum: Implementing Atomic Memory in Ad hoc Networks. *Proc. 17th Int'l Symposium on Distributed Computing (DISC'03)*, Springer-Verlag LNCS #2848, pp 306-320, 2003. 38

[54] Dutta P. and Guerraoui R., Fast Indulgent Consensus with Zero Degradation. *Proc. 4th European Dependable Computing Conference (EDCC'02)*, Springer Verlag, LNCS #2485, pp. 192-208, 2002. DOI: 10.1007/3-540-36080-8_18 188

[55] Dutta P., Guerraoui R., Levy R. and Chakraborty A., How fast Can a Distributed Atomic Read be? *Proc. 23th ACM Symposium on Principles of Distributed Computing (PODC'04)*, ACM Press, pp. 236-245, 2004. DOI: 10.1145/1011767.1011802 39

[56] Dwork C., Lynch N. and Stockmeyer L., Consensus in the Presence of Partial Synchrony. *Journal of the ACM*, 35(2), 288-323, 1988. DOI: 10.1145/42282.42283 189

[57] Dwork C. and Moses Y., Knowledge and common knowledge in a Byzantine environment: Crash failures. *Information and Computation*, 88(2):156-186, 1990. DOI: 10.1016/0890-5401(90)90014-9 187

[58] Englert B., Georgiou Ch., Musial P.M., Nicolaou N. and Shvartsman A.A., On the Efficiency of Atomic Multireader Multiwriter Distributed Memory. *Proc. 13th Int'l Conference on Principles of Distributed Computing (OPODIS'09)*, Springer-Verlag LNCS #5923, pp 240-253, 2009. 39

[59] Eugster P.Th., Guerraoui R., Handurukande S.B., Kouznetsov P. and Kermarrec A.-M., Lightweight Probabilistic Broadcast. *ACM Transactions on Computer Systems*, 21(4):341-374, 2003. DOI: 10.1145/945506.945507 62

[60] Ezilchelvan P., Mostéfaoui A. and Raynal M., Randomized Multivalued Consensus. *Proc. 4th Int'l IEEE Symposium on Object-Oriented Real-Time Distributed Computing (ISORC'01)*, IEEE Computer Press, pp. 195-200, 2001. DOI: 10.1109/ISORC.2001.922837 188

[61] Fagin R., Halpern, J.Y., Moses Y. and Vardi M., Reasoning about Knowledge, *MIT Press*, Cambridge (MA), 491 pages, 2003. 63

[62] Fekete A.D., Lynch N., Mansour Y. and Spinelli J., The Impossibility of Implementing Reliable Communication in Face of Crashes. *Journal of the ACM*, 40(5):1087-1107, 1993. DOI: 10.1145/174147.169676 96

[63] Fernández A., Jiménez E. and Raynal M., Eventual Leader Election with Weak Assumptions on Initial Knowledge, Communication Reliability, and Synchrony. *Proc. Int'l IEEE conference on Dependable Systems and Networks (DSN'06)*, IEEE Computer Society Press, pp. 166-175, 2006. DOI: 10.1109/DSN.2006.34 231

[64] Fernández A., Jiménez E., Raynal M. and Trédan G., A Timing Assumption and two *t*-Resilient Protocols for Implementing an Eventual Leader Service in Asynchronous Shared-memory Systems. *Algorithmica*, 56(4):550-576, 2010. DOI: 10.1007/s00453-008-9190-2 231

[65] Fernández A. and Raynal M., From an Intermittent Rotating Star to an Eventual Leader. *IEEE Transactions on Parallel and Distributed Systems*, to appear, 2010. (Preliminary version in *Proc. 11th Int'l Conference On Principles Of Distributed Systems (OPODIS'07)*, Springer-Verlag LNCS #4878, pp. 189-203, 2007.) DOI: 10.1109/TPDS.2009.163 231

[66] Fetzer C., Raynal M. and Tronel F., An Adaptive Failure Detection Protocol. *Proc. 8th IEEE Pacific Rim Int'l Symposium on Dependable Computing (PRDC'01)*, IEEE Computer Society Press, pp. 146-153, 2001. DOI: 10.1109/PRDC.2001.992691 231

[67] Fischer M.J. and Lynch N.A., A Lower Bound for the Time to Ensure Interactive Consistency. *Information Processing Letters*, 14:183-186, 1982. DOI: 10.1016/0020-0190(82)90033-3 187

[68] Fischer M.J., Lynch N.A. and Paterson M.S., Impossibility of Distributed Consensus with One Faulty Process. *Journal of the ACM*, 32(2):374-382, 1985. DOI: 10.1145/3149.214121 62, 132

[69] Fridzke U., Ingels Ph., Mostefaoui A. and Raynal M., Fault-Tolerant Consensus-Based Total Order Multicast. *IEEE Transactions on Parallel and Distributed Systems*, 12(2):147-157, 2001. DOI: 10.1109/71.910870 132

[70] Friedman R., Mostefaoui A., Rajsbaum S. and Raynal M., Distributed Agreement Problems and their Connection with Error-correcting Codes. *IEEE Transactions on Computers*, 56(7):865-875, 2007. 132

[71] Friedman R., Mostéfaoui A. and Raynal M., Asynchronous Bounded Lifetime Failure Detectors. *Information Processing Letters*, 94(2):85-91, 2005. DOI: 10.1016/j.ipl.2004.12.011 39

[72] Friedman R., A. Mostéfaoui A. and Raynal M., Simple and Efficient Oracle-Based Consensus Protocols for Asynchronous Byzantine Systems. *IEEE Transactions on Dependable and Secure Computing*, 2(1):46-56, 2005. DOI: 10.1109/TDSC.2005.13 188

[73] Friedman R., A. Mostéfaoui A. and Raynal M., On the Respective Power of $\Diamond\mathcal{P}$ and $\Diamond\mathcal{S}$ to Solve One-Shot Agreement Problems. *IEEE Transactions on Parallel and Distributed Systems*, 18(5):589-597, 2007. DOI: 10.1109/TPDS.2007.351708 230

[74] Friedman R., Raynal M., Travers C., Two Abstractions for Implementing Atomic Objects in Dynamic Systems. *Proc. 9th Int'l Conference on Principles of Distributed Systems (OPODIS'05)*, Springer-Verlag #3974, pp. 73-87, 2005. DOI: 10.1007/11795490_8 38

[75] Gafni E., Round-by-round Fault Detectors: Unifying Synchrony and Asynchrony. *Proc. 17th ACM Symposium on Principles of Distributed Computing (PODC'00)*, ACM Press, pp. 143-152, 1998. DOI: 10.1145/277697.277724 189

[76] Gafni E. and Lamport L., Disk Paxos. *Distributed Computing*, 16(1):1-20, 2003. DOI: 10.1007/s00446-002-0070-8 189

[77] Garcia-Molina H. and Spauster A.-M., Ordered and Reliable Multicast Communication. *ACM Transactions on Computer Systems*, 9(3):242-271, 1991. DOI: 10.1145/128738.128741 62

[78] Garey M.R. and Johnson D.S., *Computers and Intractability: a Guide to the Theory of NP-Completeness*. Freeman W.H. & Co, New York, 340 pages, 1979. 96

[79] Gifford D.K., Weighted Voting for Replicated Data. *Proc. 7th ACM Symposium on Operating System Principles (SOSP'79)*, ACM Press, pp. 150-172, 1979. DOI: 10.1145/800215.806583 38

[80] Gorender S., Macêdo R. and Raynal M., An Adaptive Programming Model for Fault-Tolerant Distributed Computing. *IEEE Transactions on Dependable and Secure Computing*, 4(1):18-31, 2007. DOI: 10.1109/TDSC.2007.3 189

[81] Gray J., Notes on Database Operating Systems: and Advanced Course. *Spinger Verlag*, LNCS #60, pp. 10-17, 1978. 132

[82] Guerraoui R., Revisiting the Relationship Between Non-Blocking Atomic Commitment and Consensus. *Proc. 9th Int'l Workshop on Distributed Algorithms (WDAG'95)*, Springer Verlag LNCS #972, pp. 87-100, 1995. DOI: 10.1007/BFb0022140 132

[83] Guerraoui R., Indulgent Algorithms. *Proc. 19th Annual ACM Symposium on Principles of Distributed Computing (PODC'00)*, ACM Press, pp. 289-297, 2000. DOI: 10.1145/343477.343630 188

[84] Guerraoui R., Non-blocking Atomic Commit in Asynchronous distributed Systems with Failure Detectors. *Distributed Computing*, 15(1):17-25, 2002. DOI: 10.1007/s446-002-8027-4 132

[85] Guerraoui R., Failure Detectors. *Encyclopedia of Algorithms*, Springer Verlag, pp. 304-308, 2008. DOI: 10.1007/978-0-387-30162-4_140 38, 230

[86] Guerraoui R. and Lynch N., A General Characterization of Indulgence. *ACM Transactions on Autonomous and Adaptive Systems*, 3(4), article 20, 19 pages, 2008. DOI: 10.1145/1452001.1452010 188

[87] Guerraoui R. and Raynal M., The Information Structure of Indulgent Consensus. *IEEE Transactions on Computers*, 53(4):453-466, 2004. DOI: 10.1109/TC.2004.1268403 188

[88] Guerraoui R. and Raynal M., A Leader Election Protocol for Eventually Synchronous Shared Memory Systems. *4th Int'l IEEE Workshop on Software Technologies for Future Embedded and Ubiquitous Systems (SEUS'06)*, IEEE Computer Press, pp. 75-80, 2006. DOI: 10.1109/SEUS-WCCIA.2006.6 231

[89] Guerraoui R. and Raynal M., The Alpha of Indulgent Consensus. *The Computer Journal*, 50(1):53-67, 2007. DOI: 10.1093/comjnl/bxl046 188, 189

[90] Guerraoui R. and Rodrigues L., Introduction to Reliable Distributed Programming. *Springer*, 299 pages, 2006. 62

[91] Guerraoui R. and Vukolić M., How fast Can a very Robust Read be? *Proc. 25th ACM Symposium on Principles of Distributed Computing (PODC'06)*, ACM Press, pp. 248-257, 2006. DOI: 10.1145/1146381.1146419 39

[92] Hadzilacos V., On the Relationship Between the Atomic Commitment and Consensus Problems. *Asilomar Workshop on Fault-Tolerant Distributed Computing*, Springer Verlag LNCS #448, pp. 201-208, 1990. DOI: 10.1007/BFb0042336 132

[93] Hadzilacos V. Toueg S., A Modular Approach to Fault-Tolerant Broadcasts and Related Problems. *Tech Report 94-1425*, 83 pages, Cornell University, Ithaca (USA), 1994. 62, 132

[94] Halpern J.Y. and Moses Y., Knowledge and Common Knowledge in a Distributed Environment; *Journal of the ACM*, 37(3):549-587, 1990. DOI: 10.1145/79147.79161 63

[95] Hélary J.-M., Hurfin M., Mostefaoui A., Raynal M. and Tronel F., Computing Global Functions in Asynchronous Distributed Systems with Perfect Failure Detectors. *IEEE Transactions on Parallel and Distributed Systems*, 11(9)897-909, 2000. DOI: 10.1109/71.879773 96

[96] Herlihy M., Wait-free Synchronization. *ACM Transactions on Programming Languages and Systems*, 13 (1):124-149, 1991. DOI: 10.1145/114005.102808 132, 133

[97] Herlihy M., Asynchronous Consensus Impossibility, *Encyclopedia of Algorithms*, Springer Verlag, pp. 71-73, 2008. DOI: 10.1007/978-0-387-30162-4_36 133

[98] Herlihy M.P. and Wing J.M, Linearizability: a Correctness Condition for Concurrent Objects. *ACM Transactions on Programming Languages and Systems*,12(3):463-492, 1990. DOI: 10.1145/78969.78972 12

[99] Hermant J.-F. and Le Lann G., Fast Asynchronous Uniform Consensus in Real-Time Distributed Systems. *IEEE Transactions on Computers*, 51(8):931-944, 2002. DOI: 10.1109/TC.2002.1024740 230

[100] Hopcroft J.E. and Ullman J.D. *Introduction to Automata Theory, Languages and Computation.* Addison Wesley, Reading (MA), 418 pages, 1979. 96

[101] Hurfin M., Mostéfaoui A. and Raynal M., A Versatile Family of Consensus Protocols Based on Chandra-Toueg's Unreliable Failure Detectors. *IEEE Transactions on Computers*, 51(4):395-408, 2002. DOI: 10.1109/12.995450 188

[102] Hutle M., Malkhi D., Schmid U. and Zhou L., Chasing the Weakest System Model for Implementing Ω and Consensus. *IEEE Transactions on Dependable and Secure Computing*, 6(4): 269-281, 2009. DOI: 10.1109/TDSC.2008.24 231

[103] Jayanti P. and Toueg S., Every Problem has a Weakest Failure Detector. *Proc. 27th ACM Symposium on Principles of Distributed Computing (PODC'08)*, ACM Press, pp. 75-84, 2008. DOI: 10.1145/1400751.1400763 38, 230

[104] Jiménez E., Arévalo S. and Fernández A., Implementing Unreliable Failure Detectors with Unknown Membership. *Information Processing Letters*, 100(2):60-63, 2006. DOI: 10.1016/j.ipl.2006.05.009 231

[105] Keidar I. and Rajsbaum S., A Simple Proof of the Uniform Consensus Synchronous Lower Bound. *Information Processing Letters*, 85:47-52, 2003. DOI: 10.1016/S0020-0190(02)00333-2 188

[106] Keidar I. and Shraer A., How to Choose a Timing Model. *IEEE Transactions on Parallel Distributed Systems*, 19(10):1367-1380, 2008. DOI: 10.1109/DSN.2007.55 189

[107] Lamport L., Time, Clocks, and the Ordering of Events in a Distributed System. *Communications of the ACM*, 21(7)-558-565, 1978. DOI: 10.1145/359545.359563 62, 132

[108] Lamport L., The Implementation of Reliable Distributed Multiprocess Systems. *Computer Networks*, 2:95-114, 1978. DOI: 10.1016/0376-5075(78)90045-4 132

[109] Lamport L., How to Make a Multiprocessor Computer that Correctly Executes Multiprocess Programs. *IEEE Transactions on Computers*, C28(9):690-691, 1979. DOI: 10.1109/TC.1979.1675439 13

[110] Lamport. L., On Interprocess Communication, Part 1: Basic formalism, Part II: Algorithms. *Distributed Computing*, 1(2):77-101,1986. DOI: 10.1007/BF01786227 12, 38

[111] Lamport L., Shostack R. and Pease M., The Byzantine Generals Problem. *ACM Transactions on Programming Languages and Systems*, 4(3)-382-401, 1982. DOI: 10.1145/357172.357176 132

[112] Lamport L., The Part-time Parliament. *ACM Transactions on Computer Systems*, 16(2):133-169, 1998. DOI: 10.1145/279227.279229 189

[113] Lamport L., Fast Paxos. *Distributed Computing*, 19(2):79-103, 2006. DOI: 10.1007/s00446-006-0005-x 189

[114] Larrea M., Fernández A. and Arévalo S., On the Implementation of Unreliable Failure Detectors in Partially Synchronous Systems. *IEEE Transactions on Computers*, 53(72):815-828, 2004. DOI: 10.1109/TC.2004.33 231

[115] Larrea M., Fernández A. and Arévalo S., Optimal Implementation of the Weakest Failure Detector for Solving Consensus. *Proc. 19th IEEE Symposium on Reliable Distributed Systems (SRDS'00)*, IEEE Computer Press, pp. 52-59, 2000. DOI: 10.1109/RELDI.2000.885392 231

[116] Loui M. and Abu-Amara H., Memory Requirements for agreement among Unreliable Asynchronous processes. *Advances in Computing Research*, 4:163-183, JAI Press Inc., 1987. 133

[117] Lynch N.A., Distributed Algorithms. *Morgan Kaufmann Pub.*, San Francisco (CA), 872 pages, 1996. 38, 96, 187

[118] Lynch N.A. and Shvartsman A.S., RAMBO: A Reconfigurable Atomic Memory Service for Dynamic Networks. *Proc. 16th Int'l Symposium on Distributed Computing (DISC'02)*, Springer-Verlag LNCS #2508, pp. 173-190, 2002. DOI: 10.1007/3-540-36108-1_12 38

[119] Malkhi D., Oprea F. and Zhou L., Ω Meets Paxos: Leader Election and Stability without Eventual Timely Links. *Proc. 19th Int'l Symposium on Distributed Computing (DISC'05)*, Springer Verlag LNCS #3724, pp. 199-213, 2005. 231

[120] Malkhi D. and Reiter M.K., Byzantine Quorum Systems. *Distributed Computing*, 11(4):203-213, 1998. DOI: 10.1007/s004460050050 39

[121] Martín C. and Larrea M., A Simple and Communication-efficient Omega Algorithm in the Crash-recovery Failure Model. *Information Processing Letters*, 110(3):83-87, 2010. DOI: 10.1016/j.ipl.2009.10.011 231

[122] Martín C., Larrea M. and Jiménez E., Implementing the Omega Failure Detector in the Crash-recovery Failure Model. *Journal of Computer and System Sciences*, 75(3):178-189, 2009. DOI: 10.1016/j.jcss.2008.10.002 231

[123] Misra J., Axioms for Memory Access in Asynchronous Hardware Systems. *ACM Transactions on Programming Languages and Systems*, 8(1):142-153, 1986. DOI: 10.1145/5001.5007 12

[124] Mizuno M., M. Neilsen M. and Raynal M., A General Method to Define Quorums. *Proc. 12th IEEE Int'l Conference on Distributed Computing Systems (ICDCS'92)*, IEEE Computer Press, pp. 657-664, 1992 DOI: 10.1109/ICDCS.1992.235110 38

[125] Moses Y., Dolev D. and Halpern J.Y., Cheating Husbands and other Stories: A Case Study of Knowledge, Action, and Communication, *Distributed Computing*, 1(3):167-176, 1986. DOI: 10.1007/BF01661170 63

[126] Moses Y. and Rajsbaum S., A Layered Analysis of Consensus. *SIAM Journal of Computing*, 31(4):989-1021, 1998. DOI: 10.1137/S0097539799364006 187

[127] Mostéfaoui A., Mourgaya E. and Raynal M., An Introduction to Oracles for Asynchronous Distributed Systems. *Future Generation Computer Systems*, 18(6):757-767, 2002. DOI: 10.1016/S0167-739X(02)00048-1 38, 230

[128] Mostéfaoui A., Mourgaya E., and Raynal M., Asynchronous Implementation of Failure Detectors. *Proc. Int'l IEEE Conference on Dependable Systems and Networks (DSN'03)*, IEEE Computer Society Press, pp. 351-360, 2003. DOI: 10.1109/DSN.2003.1209946 231

[129] Mostéfaoui A., Mourgaya E., Raynal M. and Travers C., A Time-free Assumption to Implement Eventual Leadership. *Parallel Processing letters*, 16(2):189-208, 2006. DOI: 10.1142/S0129626406002575 230, 231

[130] Mostéfaoui A., Powell D., and Raynal M., A Hybrid Approach for Building Eventually Accurate Failure Detectors. *Proc. 10th IEEE Int'l Pacific Rim Dependable Computing Symposium (PRDC'04)*, IEEE Computer Society Press, pp. 57-65, 2004. DOI: 10.1109/PRDC.2004.1276553 231

[131] Mostéfaoui A., Rajsbaum S. and Raynal M., Conditions on Input Vectors for Consensus Solvability in Asynchronous Distributed Systems. *Journal of the ACM*, 50(6):922-954, 2003. DOI: 10.1145/950620.950624 189

[132] Mostéfaoui A., Rajsbaum S., Raynal M. and Travers C.: From $\Diamond\mathcal{W}$ to Ω: a Simple Bounded Quiescent Reliable Broadcast-based Transformation. *Journal of Parallel and Distributed Computing*, 67(1) 125–129, 2007. DOI: 10.1016/j.jpdc.2006.06.002 230

[133] Mostéfaoui A., Rajsbaum S., Raynal M. and Travers C., The Combined Power of Conditions and Information on Failures to Solve Asynchronous Set Agreement. *SIAM Journal of Computing*, 38(4):1574-1601, 2008. DOI: 10.1137/050645580 188, 189

[134] Mostéfaoui A. and Raynal M., Solving Consensus Using Chandra-Toueg's Unreliable Failure Detectors: a General Quorum-Based Approach. *Proc. 13th Int'l Symposium on Distributed Computing (DISC'99)*, Springer-Verlag LNCS #1693, pp. 49-63, 1999. DOI: 10.1007/3-540-48169-9_4 188

[135] Mostéafoui A. and Raynal M., Low-Cost Consensus-Based Atomic Broadcast. *7th IEEE Pacific Rim Int'l Symposium on Dependable Computing (PRDC'2000)*, IEEE Computer Press, pp. 45-52, 2000. DOI: 10.1109/PRDC.2000.897283 132

[136] Mostéfaoui A. and Raynal M., Leader-Based Consensus. *Parallel Processing Letters*, 11(1):95-107, 2001. DOI: 10.1142/S0129626401000452 189

[137] Mostéfaoui A., Raynal M. and Travers C., Time-free and Timer-based Assumptions can be Combined to Get Eventual Leadership. *IEEE Transactions on Parallel and Distributed Systems*, 17(7):656-666, 2006. DOI: 10.1109/TPDS.2006.95 231

[138] Mostéfaoui A., Raynal M. and Trédan G., On the fly Estimation of the Processes that are Alive in an Asynchronous Message-passing System. *IEEE Transactions on Parallel and Distributed Systems*, 20(6):778-787, 2009. DOI: 10.1109/TPDS.2009.12 231

[139] Mostéfaoui A., Raynal M. and Tronel F., From Binary Consensus to Multivalued Consensus in Asynchronous Message-Passing Systems. *Information Processing Letters*, 73:207-213, 2000. DOI: 10.1016/S0020-0190(00)00027-2 188

[140] Mostéfaoui A., Raynal M. and Tronel F., The Best of Both Worlds: A Hybrid Approach to Solve Consensus. *Proc. Int'l Conference on Dependable Systems and Networks (DSN'00)*, IEEE Computer Society Press, pp. 513-522, 2000. DOI: 10.1109/ICDSN.2000.857584 188

[141] Papadimitriou C., The Theory of Database Concurrency Control. *Computer Science Press*, 239 pages, 1986. 13

[142] Peleg D. and Wool A., Crumbling Walls: a Class of Highly Availability Quorum Systems. *Proc. 14th Int'l Symposium on Principles of Distributed Computing (PODC'95)*, ACM press, pp. 120-129, 1995. DOI: 10.1145/224964.224978 38

[143] Peterson L.L., Bucholz N.C. and Schlichting R.D., Preserving and Using Context Information in Interprocess Communication. *ACM Transactions on Computer Systems*, 7(3):217-246, 1989. DOI: 10.1145/65000.65001 62

[144] Powell D., Failure Mode Assumptions and Assumption Coverage. *Proc. of the 22nd Int'l Symposium on Fault-Tolerant Computing (FTCS-22)*, IEEE Computer Society Press, pp.386-395, 1992. 188, 231

[145] Prakash R., Raynal M. and Singhal M., An adaptive Causal Ordering Algorithm Suited to Mobile Computing Environments. *Journal of Parallel and Distributed Computing*, 41(1):190-204, 1997. DOI: 10.1006/jpdc.1996.1300 62

[146] Rabin M., Randomized Byzantine Generals. *Proc. 24th IEEE Symposium on Foundations of Computer Science (FOCS'83)*, IEEE Computer Society Press, pp. 116-124, 1983. DOI: 10.1109/SFCS.1983.48 188

[147] Raynal M., Eventual Leader Service in Unreliable Asynchronous Systems: Why? How? *Proc. 6th IEEE International Symposium on Network Computing and Applications (NCA'07)*, IEEE Computer Society Press, pp. 11-21, Cambridge (MA), 2007. DOI: 10.1109/NCA.2007.19 230

[148] Raynal M., Failure Detectors for Asynchronous Distributed Systems: an Introduction. *Wiley Encyclopedia of Computer Science and Engineering*, Vol. 2, pp. 1181-1191, 2009 (ISBN 978-0-471-38393-2). 38, 230

[149] Raynal M., Schiper A. and Toueg S., The Causal Ordering Abstraction and a Simple Way to Implement *Information Processing Letters*, 39(6):343-350, 1991. DOI: 10.1016/0020-0190(91)90008-6 62

[150] Raynal M. and Singhal M., Mastering Agreement Problems in Distributed Systems. *IEEE Software*, 18(4):40-47, 2001. DOI: 10.1109/MS.2001.936216 132

[151] Robinson P. and Schmid U., The Asynchronous Bounded-Cycle Model. *Proc. 10th Int'l Symposium on Stabilization, Safety ansd Security of Distributed Systems (SSS'08)*, Springer-Verlag LNCS #, pp. 246-262, 2008. DOI: 10.1145/1400751.1400815 231

[152] Rodrigues L. and Raynal M., Atomic Broadcast in Asynchronous Crash-Recovery Distributed Systems and its Use in Quorum-Based Replication. *IEEE Transactions on Knowledge and Data Engineering*, 15(5):1206-1217. DOI: 10.1109/TKDE.2003.1232273 132

[153] Roy M., Bonnet F., Querzoni L., Bonomi S., Killijian M.O. and Powell D., Geo-Registers: an Abstraction for Spatial-Based Distributed Computing. *Proc. 12th Int'l Conference on Principles of Distributed Systems (OPODIS'08*, Springer Verlag LNCS #5401, pp. 534-537, 2008. DOI: 10.1007/978-3-540-92221-6_34 38

[154] Schneider F.B., Implementing Fault-Tolerant Services Using the State Machine Approach. *ACM Computing Surveys*, 22(4):299-319, 1990. DOI: 10.1145/98163.98167 62, 132

[155] Shao C., Pierce E. and Welch J.L., Multi-writer Consistency conditions for Shared Memory Objects. *Proc. 17th Int'l Symposium on Distributed Computing (DISC'03)*, Springer Verlag LNCS #2848, pp. 106-120, 2003. 12

[156] Skeen D., Nonblocking Commit Protocols. *Proc. ACM-SIGMOD Conference on Management of Data*, ACM Press, pp. 133-142, 1981. DOI: 10.1145/582318.582339 132

[157] Wang D.-W. and Zuck L.D., Tight Bounds for the Sequence Transmission Problem. *Proc. 8th ACM Symposium on Principles of Distributed Computing (PODC'89)*, ACM Press, pp. 73-83, Edmonton (Canada), 1989. DOI: 10.1145/72981.72986 96

[158] Widder J. and Schmid U., The Theta-Model: Achieving Synchrony Without Clocks. *Distributed Computing*. 22(1):29-47, 2009. DOI: 10.1007/s00446-009-0080-x 189, 230

[159] Wu W., Cao J., Raynal M. and Lin J., Using Asynchrony and Zero-degradation to Speed up Indulgent Consensus Protocols. *Journal of Parallel and Distributed Computing*. 68(7):984-996, 2008. DOI: 10.1016/j.jpdc.2008.02.007 188

[160] Wu W., Cao J., Raynal M. and Yang J., Design and Performance Evaluation of Efficient Consensus Protocols for Mobile Ad Hoc Networks. *IEEE Transactions on Computers*, 56(8):1055-1070, 2007. DOI: 10.1109/TC.2007.1053 188

[161] Zhang J. and Chen W., Bounded Cost Algorithms for Multivalued Consensus Using Binary Consensus Instances. *Information Processing Letters*, 109(17):1005-1009, 2009. DOI: 10.1016/j.ipl.2009.06.004

[162] Zhang J. and Chen W., Implementing Uniform Reliable Broadcast with Binary Consensus in Systems with Fair-lossy Links. *Information Processing Letters*, 110(1):13-19, 2009. DOI: 10.1016/j.ipl.2009.09.013 132

Author's Biography

MICHEL RAYNAL

Michel Raynal is a professor of computer science at the University of Rennes, France. His main research interests are the basic principles of distributed computing systems. Michel Raynal is the author of numerous papers on distributed algorithms and a world leading researcher in the domain of distributed computing. He has chaired the program committee of the major conferences on the topic, such as the IEEE Int'l Conference on Distributed Computing Systems (ICDCS), the Symposium on Distributed Computing (DISC), the Int'l Colloquium on Structural Information and Communication Complexity (SIROCCO), and the Int'l Conference on Principles of Distributed Systems (OPODIS). He has also served on the program committees of many international conferences, and he is the recipient of several "Best Paper" awards. Michel Raynal has been invited by many universities all over the world to give lectures on distributed computing.

Index

Printed in the United States
by Baker & Taylor Publisher Services